Collective Defense or Strategic Independence?

Collective Defense or Strategic Independence?

Alternative Strategies for the Future

Edited by

Ted Galen Carpenter
Cato Institute

Cato Institute, Washington, D.C.

Lexington Books
D.C. Heath and Company/Lexington, Massachusetts/Toronto

Library of Congress Cataloging-in-Publication Data

Collective defense or strategic independence? : alternative strategies for the future / edited by
  Ted Galen Carpenter.
    p. cm.
    Includes bibliographies and index.
    ISBN 0–669–20295–9 (alk. paper). ISBN 0–669–20448–X (pbk. : alk. paper)
    1. United States—National security. 2. National security. 3. World politics—1985–
  1995. I. Carpenter, Ted Galen.   II. Title:
    Title: Alternative strategies for the future.
    UA23.C595   1989
    355′.03—dc19   88–29411
                                                                                                                  CIP

Published simultaneously in Canada
Printed in the United States of America
Casebound International Standard Book Number: 0–669–20295–9
Paperbound International Standard Book Number: 0–669–20448–X
Library of Congress Catalog Card Number 88–29411

The paper used in this publication meets the minimum requirements of American National
Standard for Information Sciences—Permanence of Paper for Printed Library Materials, ANSI
Z39.48–1984. ∞™

89 90 91 92 8 7 6 5 4 3 2 1

Contents

Acknowledgments

This book is an outgrowth of a Cato Institute conference on U.S. global security commitments held in December 1987. The idea for the conference and the subsequent collection was nurtured at every stage by Edward H. Crane and William A. Niskanen. It is indicative of their innovative stewardship of the Cato Institute that they encourage critical inquiries into important foreign policy issues rather than regard the cold war status quo as sacrosanct.

Appreciation is also owed to my collaborators in this book, who gave a great deal of time and energy to their assignments, and to James Chace, Jonathan Kwitny, and Hodding Carter III, who provided helpful critiques of the various contributions. Jaime Welch-Donahue at Lexington Books recognized the importance of the collection and diligently kept the project on schedule. Richard J. Dennis deserves special thanks for his generous support of this effort to reassess the fundamental components of U.S. foreign policy.

Introduction

A power configuration that was virtually unique in world history developed from the war-shattered environment of the late 1940s. Overwhelming political, economic, and especially military power resided in but two nations, the United States and the Soviet Union. The latter country also seemed to possess an ambitious expansionist agenda with an uncertain geographic scope. As the Soviet Union consolidated its control of Eastern Europe, leaders in the United States and other noncommunist nations sought ways to counter the perceived threat.

The twin doctrines of containment and collective defense emerged as the guiding principles of U.S. foreign policy in that atmosphere of alarm and mutual suspicion. George F. Kennan, then an official at the Moscow embassy, articulated the elements of containment in his famous "long telegram" and subsequently in the seminal "X" article in *Foreign Affairs*. Contending that Soviet expansionism resulted from the melding of factors peculiar to Russian history with the dynamics of Leninist ideology, he presented an evocative image of the threat facing the West: "[The Soviet Union's] political action is a fluid stream which moves constantly, wherever it is permitted to move, toward a given goal. Its main concern is to make sure that it has filled every nook and cranny available to it in the basin of world power." The West's response, said Kennan, must be equally determined and comprehensive. He advocated "a long-term, patient but firm and vigilant containment . . . designed to confront the Russians with unalterable counterforce at every point where they show signs of encroaching upon the interests of a peaceful and stable world."[1]

The strategy of containment merged with an attachment to collective security that had become pervasive in the United States during and immediately following World War II. During the war, a majority of Americans concluded that the republic's traditional policy of detachment from conflicts outside the Western Hemisphere (typically and inaccurately termed "isolationism") was no longer viable. Influenced by an incessant propaganda barrage by the Roosevelt and Truman administrations, they conceded that "isolationism" had failed to keep the United States out of either world war and that a new policy based on collective security was required to maintain the peace.[2] U.S. officials and the public initially placed their hopes in the newly formed United Nations, assuming that the members of the "Grand Alliance" that had defeated the fascist powers would continue their cooperation in the postwar period and prevent the emergence of future aggressors. Their assumption proved naive. The Soviet Union and the Western powers had been linked by little more than their mutual fear and hatred of Nazi Germany, and when that factor was removed, the wartime alliance dissolved in mutual recrimination. The United Nations became an early and prominent casualty of the cold war.

Truman administration leaders then sought, with considerable success, to channel the American public's commitment to collective security into an endorsement of anti-Soviet collective defense measures. The Truman Doctrine, promulgated in March 1947, pledged the United States to assist friendly nations that faced either external aggression or threats from "armed minorities." Later that same year the United States helped create the Rio Pact, explicitly linking its security interests to those of its hemispheric neighbors and officially "mutualizing" the Monroe Doctrine. Even more dramatic was the creation in 1949 of the North Atlantic Treaty Organization (NATO). Approval of that treaty marked the end of the 150-year-old tradition of U.S. nonparticipation in European alliances. NATO also became the prototype for several other U.S.-sponsored multilateral security arrangements, including the Southeast Asia Treaty Organization (SEATO), the ANZUS (Australia–New Zealand–United States) alliance, and the Baghdad Pact. In addition to the multilateral commitments, the United States concluded bilateral treaties with South Korea, Nationalist China, and Pakistan in the 1950s.

Proponents of that globe-girdling network of security ties argued that the United States had no acceptable alternatives. Their reasoning was based on three crucial assumptions. First, they believed the Soviet Union to be an implacable adversary bent on unlimited expansionism and, ultimately, global domination. Second, they concluded that World War II had irrevocably disrupted the global balance of power, leaving the United States as the only nation capable of leading a free world coalition against Soviet aggression. Third, advocates of containment and collective defense insisted that the United States had the economic, political, and military strength to maintain this leadership role for however long it became necessary to thwart Soviet ambitions.

It is important to emphasize, however, that the architects of this cold war policy did not assume that the United States would have to bear the predominant portion of that burden indefinitely. Kennan, for example, was confident that containment would be needed for only ten or fifteen years.

Other leaders such as Dean Acheson, George Marshall, and Dwight D. Eisenhower seemed less sanguine about the longevity of the Soviet threat, but they too stressed that these burdens were not temporally open-ended. They looked forward to the time when the nations of Western Europe would recover from the devastation of World War II and would be able to assume primary responsibility for their own defense.[3] U.S. leaders were also confident that new pro-Western power centers capable of blunting Soviet expansionist probes would emerge in the Third World.

Their expectations have not been realized. The basic features of U.S. commitment to the doctrines of containment and collective defense remain largely intact despite the passage of four decades, and there has been a marked reluctance to reassess in any comprehensive manner the nation's approach to world affairs. Even the costly and divisive Korean and Vietnam interventions produced only sporadic and incomplete appraisals of overall cold war strategy. Today the United States remains obligated, both explicitly and implicitly, to defend a host of allies and clients. The financial cost of this undertaking has been staggering. Some estimates (see chapter 16 by Earl Ravenal) conclude that more than two-thirds of the U.S. defense budget goes for the protection of overseas allies. Prominent scholars such as Richard Rosecrance and Paul Kennedy now openly express concern that the United States may be jeopardizing its long-term economic health by maintaining such extensive commitments.[4]

There is an increasingly urgent need to reassess the nation's security strategy. The basic features of the existing policy were created to meet the perceived dangers of a global environment far different from today's. Three particularly important changes have taken place in the last forty years. At the dawn of the cold war, the United States had a nuclear monopoly, and it maintained a decisive strategic advantage over the Soviet Union well into the 1960s. The realization of American leaders that they could credibly threaten to use the U.S. arsenal to defend allies from attack gave birth to the doctrine of extended deterrence. But the Soviet Union has now achieved at least strategic nuclear parity with the United States. This development inevitably alters the calculus concerning the level of risk associated with linking the nuclear deterrent of the United States to the security of other nations. It also impinges directly on the credibility of extended deterrence. The Kremlin would be reasonably certain that the United States would use its nuclear weapons in response to an attack on its homeland, but Soviet leaders might be far more skeptical about U.S. willingness to risk devastation to defend third parties.

Economic changes have been nearly as dramatic as the shift in the strategic nuclear balance over the past four decades. The United States enjoyed unprecedented global economic preeminence in the late 1940s and for more than two decades after. At the end of World War II, the U.S.

economy accounted for an astounding 50 percent of the world's gross national product (GNP). Five years later, the total was still nearly 40 percent. Japan and the war-ravaged nations of Western Europe were minor factors in the global economy, and even the other political and military superpower offered only a feeble economic challenge.

The situation is dramatically different today; the economic leadership of the United States is under siege by a revitalized Japan, Western Europe, and several new competitors. The more competitive global economic environment raises serious questions about whether the United States can afford to continue subsidizing the defense of wealthy allies. The original expectation that the economic recovery of Japan and the nations of Western Europe would be matched by a greater willingness on their part to assume a larger portion of the West's defense obligations has not been realized. While the United States continues to spend nearly 7 percent of its GNP on defense, the NATO powers spend approximately 3.5 percent and Japan barely 1 percent.

Beyond considerations of equity, the expensive U.S. global security network poses other problems. Paul Kennedy observes perceptively that the United States faces the challenge of all previous great powers: "Whether, in the military/strategical realm, it can preserve a reasonable balance between the nation's perceived defense requirements and the means it possesses to maintain those commitments; and whether as an intimately related point, it can preserve the technological and economic bases of its power from relative erosion in the face of ever-shifting patterns of global production." He is pessimistic, concluding that "the United States now runs the risk, so familiar to historians of the rise and fall of previous Great Powers, of what might roughly be called 'imperial overstretch': that is to say, decision makers in Washington must face the awkward and enduring fact that the sum total of the United States' global interests and obligations is nowadays far larger than the country's power to defend them all simultaneously."[5]

The erosion of the nuclear and economic preeminence of the United States might be cause for unalloyed dismay were it not for another significant change that has occurred in the last four decades. The onset of the cold war was marked by a stark political, economic, and military bipolarity. In the immediate postwar period, it was reasonable to assume that only the United States stood in the path of Soviet expansionism. Although U.S. leaders may have seriously overestimated both the inclination and the capability of the Soviet Union to achieve global domination, that danger could not be dismissed. But the world of the late 1980s is already multipolar in the economic realm, and it is gradually becoming so in the political and military realms. The Sino-Soviet split in the 1960s destroyed any possibility of a monolithic communist threat, and a host of new or restored regional powers (Japan, West Germany, France, Britain, China, India, and others) now pose or are capable of posing daunting obstacles to any would-be global hegemonic state. That increasingly multipolar environment has created foreign policy options for the United States that were not available forty years ago.

The emergence of a plethora of Third World states has also created a vastly different geopolitical environment, posing both new problems and new opportunities for U.S. foreign policy. A proliferation of left-wing regimes and movements, many of which have displayed a pronounced pro-Soviet bias, is cause for some concern. At the same time, most Third World countries jealously guard their independence and have no inclination to become vassals of either superpower. The emphasis on at least official nonalignment and an unwillingness to become active participants in the cold war struggles is testimony to the strength of nationalism throughout the developing world. Such nationalism is not conducive to hegemonic aspirations on the part of external powers. The deterioration of Moscow's relations with onetime friendly countries—Egypt, Ghana, and Mozambique are the most prominent examples—demonstrates that reality with ample clarity.

Vastly changed global conditions underscore the need to reassess fundamental features of U.S. foreign policy. The last comprehensive discussion of foreign policy fundamentals occurred during the "Great Debate" of 1950–1951.[6] Even the aftermath of the Vietnam debacle did not produce the kind of searching reexamination that one might have expected. Instead U.S. foreign policy entered a period of drift and uncertainty, still wedded to the basic precepts of containment and collective defense but no longer confident that the American people were willing to make the requisite sacrifices.

Reassessment, of course, does not necessarily imply repudiation, as several of the chapters in this book attest. Eugene Rostow contends that there is no acceptable alternative to the current strategy. Moscow's goal of global domination remains undiminished in his judgment, and the United States must stay the course, defending its allies in order to preserve its own security. The continuing commitment to Japan and the NATO member countries is especially important since Soviet control of these increasingly wealthy regions could pose a mortal threat to the United States. Rostow concedes that many important changes have taken place since the onset of the cold war but concludes that those changes do not alter the need for a vigorous containment policy. Only the United States has the political, economic, and military might to lead an effective free world coalition.

As Rostow notes, NATO is the keystone of the U.S. global alliance system. Any meaningful appraisal of U.S. foreign policy must address the question of the republic's military relationship with the nations of Western Europe. Melvyn Krauss strongly disputes Rostow's contention that NATO is a wise commitment and an indispensable component of Western defense strategy. Quite the contrary, Krauss asserts that the U.S. nuclear guarantee to Europe and the U.S. troop presence on the Continent have given the United States "weak allies." U.S. willingness to assume a disproportionate share of NATO's burdens has enabled Western European governments to neglect their own conventional defenses in favor of welfare state expenditures and to pursue détente as a means of bribing the Soviet Union not to attack. In Krauss's view, the result is unsatisfactory for the United States: NATO consumes approximately $135 billion—some 45 percent—of the annual U.S. defense budget; the Alliance's overreliance on U.S. nuclear weapons to deter an attack on Western Europe makes the nuclear threshold dangerously low; and the European commitment to détente impels the allies to undercut any hard-line U.S. policies toward the Soviet Union.

Aaron Wildavsky shares Krauss's concern that the European nations have done too little for the common defense, but he contends that Alliance strategists have overestimated the danger of a Soviet attack on Western Europe. He insists that Moscow would hardly launch such an attack while leaving U.S. and Chinese military power intact. A Soviet military bid for global domination would present the opposite scenario: an initial assault to neutralize the United States followed by moves against secondary power centers such as Western Europe. That being the reality, U.S. leaders should encourage the Europeans to develop credible independent conventional and nuclear deterrents to complicate Moscow's task. A more substantive and assertive European role in the Alliance, Wildavsky contends, would not only give reality to the "two pillars" concept first articulated during the Kennedy years, but it would also clearly be in the security interests of the Western Europeans themselves. In the process, NATO would become a true partnership rather than a thinly disguised U.S. protectorate.

Christopher Layne proposes a far more ambitious alternative strategy for the United States. Layne argues that the advent of strategic nuclear parity between the United States and the Soviet Union has rendered the U.S. nuclear guarantee to the European allies unreliable. Rather than risk possible annihilation of the American homeland in defense of Western Europe, he urges Washington to launch a diplomatic offensive designed to secure a mutual superpower withdrawal from Central Europe. Such a strategy would appeal to an increasingly nervous European (especially West German) public opinion, place the Kremlin on the defensive, and, perhaps, heal the artificial division of Europe that has existed since the end of World War II. Disengagement, Layne emphasizes, would not be synonymous with abandonment of U.S. interest in the security of Western Europe. There would always be an element of "residual deterrence" since Soviet leaders could never be certain how the United States would respond to an attempt to dominate the Continent. At the same time, disengagement would restore U.S. control over its own destiny rather than make its involvement in a

European conflict virtually automatic, as is now the case with the doctrine of extended (or as Layne terms it) "suicidal" deterrence.

NATO may constitute the most important component of the U.S. global security network, but military arrangements with the Pacific Basin nations also represent a vital issue, the more so because commercial ties between the United States and those countries are becoming increasingly significant. Japan is now the principal overseas trading partner of the United States, but the Orient's economic giant is still heavily dependent on the United States for military protection. Edward Olsen insists that Japan can and should contribute far more to its own security and that of its East Asian neighbors. Olsen urges U.S. leaders to adopt a hard line toward Tokyo on the issue of burden sharing. Not only should a heightened military effort include substantial increases in the Japanese defense budget from the currently anemic level of 1 percent of GNP but also a willingness to assume greater responsibility for regional security and such operations as protecting the Persian Gulf oil routes. If Japan fails to be more cooperative on the matter of burden sharing, Olsen suggests that the United States reconsider its entire security arrangement with that country.

Stephen D. Goose proposes a reassessment of military ties to the other major U.S. ally in Northeast Asia, South Korea. Goose argues that South Korea's rapid economic progress in recent years has enabled it to create a credible independent deterrent to aggression from communist North Korea. Since Chinese or Soviet participation in any North Korean attack is exceedingly improbable, there is no legitimate need to continue the presence of nearly 44,000 U.S. forces on the peninsula. Indeed, Goose maintains, the presence of those troops only serves to involve the United States unnecessarily in the domestic politics of South Korea.

The scenario of a multipolar military environment in the Far East depends to a great extent on the emergence of China as a counter to Soviet power. This development has led to various informal arrangements between Washington and Beijing, including modest amounts of military aid to help modernize China's armed forces. But A. James Gregor contends that the United States may be overestimating the military capabilities of its de facto ally. Despite some improvements in its military, Gregor concludes, China is still no match for the powerful Soviet forces arrayed along its border. Moreover, Beijing has perceived that continuing military disparity and has moved to adopt a position equidistant from both superpowers. Because the United States cannot rely on China to counter Soviet power and there is no evidence that Moscow's expansionist aims in the Far East have diminished, Gregor believes that Washington should strengthen rather than downgrade security ties with the noncommunist states in the region.

Doug Bandow's essay on the ANZUS alliance reaches a rather different conclusion. He maintains that ANZUS is a relic of the "pactomania" that characterized U.S. policy in the 1950s. With New Zealand estranged from the other two members, as a result of the Lange government's ban on vessels or aircraft carrying nuclear weapons, ANZUS is now little more than a "rump" alliance—a de facto bilateral defense pact between Australia and the United States. U.S. security interests in the region are minimal, Bandow insists, and New Zealand, at least, does not fear a Soviet threat. If the rationale for the alliance no longer exists, it makes little sense for the United States to insist on maintaining the association. Washington should call for the dissolution of ANZUS—the least important U.S. alliance—thereby setting an important precedent for the reconsideration of other multilateral and bilateral pacts.

Paul Kattenburg shares Bandow's skepticism about the relevance of ANZUS, but he proposes a more far-reaching retrenchment of U.S. commitments in the Pacific Basin. He outlines a proposal for a mutual U.S.-Soviet disengagement not only from the southern Pacific but also from Southeast Asia and the Indian Ocean region. Negotiations between Moscow and Washington might well produce a zone of peace instead of creating new arenas for superpower confrontations, according to Kattenburg. He contrasts the marginal significance of those regions to U.S. security interests with the continuing importance of the Northwest Pacific, where a reexamination of commitments should be undertaken only with extreme caution.

Relations with the nations of the Third World have proved troublesome for U.S. policymakers since decolonization began after World War II. The United States has established formal and informal security ties with a variety of anti-Soviet regimes and has provided tangible support through economic and military assistance programs. But the underlying goal of Third World stability remains elusive. Washington's Third World "allies" are rarely more than protectorates, and many are governed by authoritarian regimes that retain only a precarious hold on power. The collapse of U.S. clients in South Vietnam, Iran, Nicaragua, and the Philippines underscores the problems associated with U.S. policy throughout the Third World.

The chapter by Peter Schraeder suggests that the United States has been on the wrong side of revolutionary change in the developing world, backing doomed reactionary governments. U.S. leaders, he contends, have mistakenly equated a left-wing political or economic orientation with subservience to Moscow. Attempts to stifle indigenous forces for change have earned the United States the needless enmity of suffering Third World populations. Schraeder urges U.S. policymakers to be more tolerant of ideological diversity in the Third World and to avoid making potentially dangerous political and military commitments to "friendly" authoritarian governments.

Although Washington has assisted anti-Soviet Third World governments throughout most of the cold war, the promulgation of the Reagan Doctrine has added a new dimension to U.S. policy. That doctrine pledges the United

States to assist various insurgent groups in their attempts to overthrow radical left-wing regimes. As David Isenberg points out in his chapter, the Reagan Doctrine's rhetoric has been more universally proclaimed than applied. During the Reagan years, the United States has actively assisted rebel movements in Afghanistan and Nicaragua (and to a much more modest extent in Angola), but it has provided only meager humanitarian assistance to Cambodian insurgents and has spurned appeals from rebels in Ethiopia and Mozambique. Isenberg contends that even this limited version of the Reagan Doctrine is an ill-considered approach to complex Third World affairs and that the more comprehensive version favored by some of the administration's conservative supporters would have the United States embark on quixotic ideological crusades that have little relevance to the nation's security interests.

A succession of U.S. leaders has criticized the preference of many Third World nations for an official policy of nonalignment. U.S. opposition to neutralism was most intense during John Foster Dulles's tenure as secretary of state, when it was viewed as akin to a pro-Soviet orientation, but subsequent policymakers have been only marginally more tolerant. Terry L. Deibel argues that U.S. hostility toward Third World neutralism is misplaced. In his view, nonalignment does not menace U.S. security interests, and Washington gains nothing by attempting to pressure reluctant Third World states into endorsing a global containment strategy directed against the Soviet Union.

Defining vital U.S. interests in the Third World is perhaps even more difficult than it is with respect to Europe and the Pacific Basin. In chapter 13, I examine that problem and suggest that U.S. policymakers have tended to confuse ideological and economic objectives with essential security concerns. I argue that U.S. defense obligations in the Third World must be limited geographically and functionally and that interventionist initiatives should be undertaken with great caution. I also warn against making rigid, formal military commitments to Third World countries in either bilateral or multilateral formats.

The wisdom of the U.S. containment policy is discussed in the final part of this book. Stephen M. Walt offers "two cheers" for containment, contending that it has generally served the republic well during the past four decades. NATO remains especially important to U.S. security, he maintains, and while Washington should insist that its European allies play a more responsible role in the collective defense effort, abandoning the Alliance would constitute a grave error. Indeed the main problem with containment in Walt's view is that it has been applied indiscriminantly to peripheral concerns in the Third World at the expense of more important U.S. commitments to Western Europe and Japan.

In contrast to Walt's qualified endorsement of the status quo, Alan

Tonelson argues that most advocates of containment have implemented a reflexive policy based upon an obsession with a vaguely defined Soviet threat. The adoption of a threat-based rather than an interest-based strategy has led the United States to strategic overcommitment, creating a variety of severe domestic strains. It has also unnecessarily limited Washington's freedom of action, frequently making U.S. policy hostage to the goals of allies and clients. Tonelson advocates a sober assessment of vital U.S. interests and the jettisoning of commitments unnecessary for the defense of those interests. The United States, he contends, can no longer afford to defend a laundry list of global obligations; it must learn to distinguish between needs and wants.

Earl Ravenal goes beyond Tonelson's call for a more selective defense strategy and advocates a policy of strategic disengagement. He contends that increasing domestic and international constraints render an interventionist foreign policy untenable. Politically and economically, the U.S. system will no longer pay the price of sustaining a global containment policy, as evidenced by the reaction to the Vietnam War. Ravenal also argues that an inexorable diffusion of power away from Moscow and Washington makes the international system impervious to control by either superpower. The United States must adjust to these changed conditions by adopting a new strategy based on self-reliance and avoidance of war while encouraging other nations to become more self-reliant. Ultimately, Ravenal insists, the United States will have to adopt a far more restricted definition of its vital interests. Those essential interests will be the sum of what the republic must defend to preserve its sovereignty and liberty and what it is capable of defending without jeopardizing either national solvency or domestic freedom.

The contributors to this book provide widely differing critiques of U.S. foreign policy. Some analysts generally defend the doctrine of collective defense, but even within that faction there is considerable divergence about specific features. Their suggestions range from calls for a more Eurocentric policy based on strategic considerations to advocacy of a truly universal approach to containment.

The critics of existing cold war policy are equally diverse in their prescriptions. Most of them stress the need to reduce the number of security commitments, and they appreciate the finite nature of U.S. economic and military resources. But the degree of appropriate retrenchment is a matter of considerable disagreement. Some propose a more selective version of containment, either pursued in conjunction with a limited roster of allies or in a largely unilateral fashion. Others spurn such modest reforms to advocate a new strategy based on the concept of U.S. strategic independence.[7] A policy of strategic independence incorporates two important principles: an unabashedly unilateralist approach to world affairs and a greatly restricted definition of the vital interests of the United States.

That such respected scholars can disagree so profoundly about the fundamental features of U.S. foreign policy underscores the seriousness of the embryonic public and professional debate on the republic's approach to world affairs in the coming decades. Policymakers should welcome the emergence of such a debate, not view it with alarm. The world of the late 1980s is vastly different from that which existed in the late 1940s when the principal components of U.S. policy were adopted. Although it would be a mistake to abandon effective policies merely because they are old, it would be an even greater error to cling to obsolete policies because of ossified thinking or misplaced nostalgia. There should be no sacrosanct assumptions, particularly with respect to a subject as vital as determining the optimal method of preserving the security and freedom of the American people.

In a broad sense, the choice facing Americans is whether the republic should continue its adherence to containment and collective defense or should move toward greater strategic independence and a more restrained definition of vital interests. The chapters in this book are offered in the hope that they will make significant contributions to that critical policy debate.

Notes

1. "X" [George F. Kennan], "The Sources of Soviet Conduct," *Foreign Affairs* 25 (July 1947): 566–82.

2. For a discussion of that repudiation of isolationism, see Robert A. Divine, *Second Chance: The Triumph of Internationalism in America during World War II* (New York: Atheneum, 1971).

3. Christopher Layne, "Atlanticism without NATO," *Foreign Policy* 67 (Summer 1987): 22–45; Ted Galen Carpenter, "United States' NATO Policy at the Crossroads: The 'Great Debate' of 1950–1951," *International History Review* 8, no. 3 (August 1986): 389–415.

4. Richard Rosecrance, *The Rise of the Trading State: Commerce and Conquest in the Modern World* (New York: Basic Books, 1986); Paul Kennedy, *The Rise and Fall of the Great Powers: Economic Change and Military Conflict from 1500 to 2000* (New York: Random House, 1987).

5. Kennedy, *Rise and Fall*, pp. 514–15.

6. Carpenter, "United States' NATO Policy," pp. 399–413.

7. For an early discussion of the concept of strategic independence, see Christopher Layne, "Ending the Alliance," *Journal of Contemporary Studies* 6 (Summer 1983): 5–31.

I
U.S. NATO Commitments

1

A Breakfast for Bonaparte:
There Is No Alternative Strategy

Eugene V. Rostow

F or more than forty years, the necessity to limit Soviet expansion has imposed immense costs on the United States and many other nations—costs measured in blood as well as in treasure. The American people and the other Western peoples are tired of the burden. In 1947, they were assured by the theorist of the Truman Doctrine, George Kennan, that ten or fifteen years of containment would mellow Soviet foreign policy, and then all would be well. Alas, there has been no mellowing. The pressures of Soviet expansion are worse than ever. It is altogether natural, therefore, that some Americans are restless and irritable. There are few open advocates of appeasement and surrender, but many are casting about for easier and cheaper ways to protect our independence than those we and our allies have developed since the time of Truman and Acheson.

My role here is that of the Commendatore in Don Giovanni, or Banquo's Ghost, or perhaps the little boy in Hans Christian Andersen's story—the little boy who pointed out that the emperor was naked. The question we are invited to address is "Collective Security or Strategic Independence? Alternative Strategies for the Future." Much as I sympathize with the mood of frustration that lies behind the question, my answer is that there are no alternative strategies for the future. We must pursue, reform, and improve the strategy of collective security we have been building for the last forty years or perish. Strategic independence for the United States is a chimera. Dean Rusk once remarked that no other country has less sovereignty than the United States. Like everything that wise and staunch man says, his comment confronts reality. The United States shares the fate of every other country in history. To recall the warning of the greatest of our diplomatic historians, Samuel Flagg Bemis, the United States must adapt its security policies to the changing patterns of the world balance of power or "sink amid the strife of nations."

It is conceivable that Mikhail Gorbachev has seen a blinding light over the domes of St. Basil's Cathedral and that his domestic policies of "openness"

An earlier version of this essay was published in the Spring 1988 issue of *Global Affairs*. Reprinted with permission.

and "restructuring" will lead to genuine peace between the Soviet Union and the other nations of the world. That is a consummation devoutly to be desired, and we should of course explore such possibilities and encourage their fruition. But there has been no sign as yet of change in Soviet foreign policy in any of the areas of current friction, in the arms control talks, or in Soviet propaganda. The Soviet Union has not even fully withdrawn from Afghanistan, to say anything of the Caribbean, the Western Hemisphere, or Eastern Europe. In the Middle East, Soviet policy is the worst it has been in twenty years, and there are disturbing reports of considerable Soviet support for the insurrection against Corazon Aquino in the Philippines. Gorbachev is more agile and ingenious than his predecessors. His tactics are dazzling, but Soviet goals are unchanged. In the nuclear arms control talks, Gorbachev is bidding with new boldness to neutralize Western Europe and achieve decisive superiority in nuclear weapons. A change will come some day, no doubt, but Western policy cannot rest on the assumption that it has already taken place. We should recall that in his day Khrushchev, like Gorbachev, aroused high hopes in the West. He denounced some of the crimes of Stalin and allowed Solzhenitsyn and other free spirits to be published. Then, however, he gave us the Cuban missile crisis. As Lyndon Johnson once said, "In dealing with the Russians, always have your right hand out and your left hand up."

The U.S. system of collective security is not perfect, of course. It needs to be modernized and supplemented by a policy of more active defense, going beyond its original function of pure containment. That is the thrust of the Reagan Doctrine. Since 1972, we have foolishly allowed the Soviet-U.S. nuclear balance to deteriorate, raising the specter of Western paralysis in the face of Soviet nuclear superiority. Clearly the nuclear balance must be restored and stabilized. This can be done easily by a U.S. buildup, by arms control agreements, or by a combination of the two, as the Soviets may prefer. Unless that step is taken, the United States will be unable to have a security policy at all, even for its own territory. In the future as in the past, moreover, the U.S. policy of collective security will be conducted erratically, sometimes spasmodically, with varying degrees of intelligence, foresight, skill, and luck. My point is different. Our policy of collective security cannot be replaced by a policy of hunkering down behind the Conestoga wagons or by one of global or regional unilateralism. Such proposals—and there are many of them—defy the geography and arithmetic of power. More particularly, they defy the inexorable logic of the nuclear weapon and other modern high-technology weapons.

Now, having stated my thesis, let me attempt to defend it.

U.S. National Security Interests

The first step in that effort is to define the national security interests of the United States.

The principal driving force behind the behavior of states in world politics is the set of impulses summed up as the balance of power. They represent the oldest, most familiar, and most important idea in the theory and practice of international relations. The instinct behind the concept is simplicity itself: never allow an adversary or potential adversary to become too strong if you can possibly help it. The corollary of the precept is equally simple: if you cannot help it, know your place, pull your forelock, and behave accordingly.

Over and over again in history, the emergence and rise to power of a predatory state has led those threatened by its ambition to regroup: to form alliances and other combinations, often with former enemies, in order to check and if necessary defeat the would-be conqueror. The last forty years vividly demonstrate that the conditioned reflexes of the balance of power concept are alive and well. Thucydides would have found the pattern of history since 1945 altogether familiar.

For reasons nearly beyond understanding, *balance of power* is a pejorative phrase in the American language. Our constitutional order at home is perhaps the supreme example of the balance of power principle at work. But we prefer to talk about foreign policy in a vocabulary dominated by the rhetoric of liberty and human rights. On the other hand, we have always conducted foreign affairs as committed practitioners of the balance of power. Although the thought was rarely articulated, we fought in both world wars in order to keep Germany from conquering Russia and therefore dominating the entire Eurasian landmass. We knew in our bones that a state that controlled such an enormous aggregation of power would be too strong to be resisted. And we have taken the lead in the formation and maintenance of the North Atlantic Treaty Organization (NATO) in order to prevent the Soviet Union from conquering Germany and Western Europe. The same kind of reasoning explains the Korean War, the war in Indochina, and the Shanghai Communiqué issued by China and the United States in 1972. In that communiqué, the two nations agreed on only one point, but the point was crucial: their opposition to any hegemonic power in Asia. Japan publicly declared its acceptance of the policy at a later date. The American people know without being told why we are helping China against Soviet pressure, just as they understood in 1941 why we made common cause with Stalin against Hitler.

No one has stated the maxim more colorfully than Jefferson, commenting on Napoleon's invasion of Russia in 1812:

> Surely none of us wish to see Bonaparte conquer Russia, and thus lay at his feet the whole continent of Europe. This done, England would be but a breakfast. . . . Put all Europe into his hands, and he might spare such a force to be sent in British ships, as I would as leave not have to encounter. . . . No. It cannot be to our interest that all Europe should be reduced to a single monarchy.[1]

For more than a century, the American people were screened from this fundamental truth, but the Americans of the Revolutionary period knew it well. Their minds were concentrated by the imminent prospect of disaster. Their leaders succeeded by skillfully exploiting the dynamics of the European balance of power in order to win the war and then to consolidate the peace and the early expansion of the nation. But in the period of relative peace between the end of the Napoleonic Wars and World War I, Americans had free security as the wards of the Concert of Europe, protected by the British fleet. After 1919, we refused to notice that the Concert of Europe had lost the capacity to manage the world balance of power. Indeed it took another war to make us realize that we could no longer rely on Britain and France to defend our security and that we had to take part in the process ourselves. Now, with the emergence of nuclear bipolarity, we have discovered that there is no escape from the necessity of American leadership in the quest for a balance of power and a reasonably stable system of world public order based on it.

What is implied by the concept of the balance of power for U.S. policy in the closing years of the twentieth century? The problem of achieving a balance of power today is exactly what it was in the world of Thucydides or the Roman emperors, or in the worlds of Philip II and Queen Elizabeth I, Louis XIV, Napoleon, or Germany in the first half of this century. But the task is different. The political universe is entirely different, the distribution of power is different, and the technology of war is different.

Following Mackinder's classic analysis,[2] the United States should be viewed as a small island off the coast of the vastly larger land area, population, and economic potential of the Eurasian landmass. The disproportion is even greater if one adds Africa and its resources to the scale, as one must. Any state that succeeded where Napoleon, the Kaiser, and Hitler failed—succeeded, that is, in controlling the whole of Europe and Russia—would automatically control China, Japan, the Middle East, and Africa. The relative power and potential power of Eurasia is far greater than it was in 1914. The Soviet Union, India, and Japan are modern, industrial countries, and China is moving toward that status with intelligence and determination. Jefferson's comment about Napoleon's breakfast is more compelling now than when it was made.

It follows that the United States does not have and cannot achieve the capacity to defend its security single-handed. Our population is a small and declining fraction of world population, and our gross national product is down to 22 percent of world production and still falling. Geographically, our posture would be hopeless without Great Britain, Japan, and the other island states as allies, as well as coastal states like France, Italy, Greece, Turkey, China, and Germany, at a minimum. Our security problem is like that of Great Britain during the four centuries between the two Queens

Elizabeth. Britain was always smaller and weaker than its principal adversaries, the predator state that sought the mastery of Europe in turn. But during that period, Britain skillfully deployed its diplomacy, its armed forces, and its money to prevent Spain, France, and Germany from becoming too strong.

In the political universe of the late twentieth century, we must do similarly: lead coalitions and alliances to counter and, if necessary, to defeat the Soviet bid for dominion. The NATO allies, Japan, and China in combination have more than enough power and potential power to prevent the Soviet Union from gaining control of Western Europe, and thus of China and Japan as well. To ensure the political independence and territorial integrity of those key countries has therefore been the first strategic goal of U.S. foreign policy since the end of World War II. For as far ahead as we can see, this will necessarily remain the case. For cognate reasons, the first strategic goal of the Soviet Union has been and remains to break the ties between the United States and its allies in the Atlantic and the Pacific basins so that it can add those territories to its empire and reduce the United States to impotence.

In the long run, the United States and China are the most dangerous obstacles to the Soviet strategy. At this stage of China's development, Soviet strategic planners could reasonably conclude that if they succeed in neutralizing the United States, Europe, China, and Japan would come to heel automatically. If the Soviet Union gains control of the 300 million people of Western Europe and of its skills, capital, productive capacity, and geographical position, China, Japan, and a great many other countries around the world would conclude that the balance of power had turned irreversibly against the United States. They would also conclude that the United States had lost its mind. As a consequence, they would make the best possible accommodation the Soviet Union would allow them, and the United States would be left helpless, isolated, and impotent, too weak to protect its territorial integrity and political independence but too strong to be ignored by the Soviet Union and allowed to remain neutral indefinitely.

Soviet hegemony in Asia would have precisely the same consequences for Europe and the United States. The Western-oriented nations would face the nightmare described by Thucydides in the debate between the general of an invading Athenian military force and the leaders of Melos, a Spartan colony that sought to remain neutral. The Melians pleaded for mercy in the name of justice. The Athenian replied:

> You know as well as we do that, when these matters are discussed by practical people, the standard of justice depends on the equality of power to compel and that in fact the strong do what they have the power to do and the weak accept what they have to accept.

We discovered soon after World War II that safeguarding the independence of the key states required us also to protect their approaches. The world is round, and nations can be surrounded and neutralized without being attacked head on. In the hands of the Soviet Union, South Korea and Taiwan would threaten both Japan and China; Europe can be outflanked from the north and from the Mediterranean, the United States from Central America and the Caribbean. For the United States and the rest of the West generally, access to critical raw materials is a matter of the highest urgency, and the list of such raw materials is getting longer. In fact, no area of the world can be excluded a priori from the purview of U.S. security concerns because nearly all could become significant in the context of Soviet programs of expansion.

While analysts differ, it is my view that Soviet strategy is one of America first. As I read the tea leaves, the Soviet Union has been and is moving in the first instance against the United States rather than against China. It is seeking to accomplish that end by separating Western Europe from the United States while building up flanking positions of strength in the Caribbean and Central America. This is the objective served by its conventional and nuclear forces, its Middle Eastern and African policy, and its arms control diplomacy. Above all, this hypothesis explains the Soviet enthusiasm for the zero-zero intermediate-range nuclear forces (INF) agreement, which it regards as a key weapon to denuclearize and neutralize Western Europe. The INF agreement would leave Europe, Japan, and China protected only by longer range American nuclear weapons. With the Soviet–American nuclear balance now favorable to the Soviet Union, the credibility of retaliation from the United States is diminished. The INF treaty will thus reduce the deterrent credibility of the U.S. nuclear force unless arms control agreements for long-range offensive weapons and defensive systems succeed in stabilizing the Soviet–American nuclear balance as a whole.

Position of the Global Unilateralists

The second step of my task is to address the arguments of those who say they fully understand the supreme national interest of the United States in keeping Western Europe, Japan, China and other key countries out of Soviet control but argue that the United States could safeguard that interest more cheaply and more surely by withdrawing its troops and fleets from Europe and other forward positions, abrogating the security arrangements made during the administrations of Truman and Eisenhower, and conducting all our actions from the United States. Some of this persuasion think U.S. treaty commitments should continue; all members of the group would end forward deployments. With or without treaties, they would have us protect our stake in the balance of power by judicious intervention as circumstances required. I shall call supporters of this position global unilateralists, for convenience.

The global unilateralists are the only group proposing alternative strategies worth discussing. The others ignore the problem of the balance of power altogether and imagine that the United States could be secure within its own territory, or in a hospitable Western Hemisphere, or in a world where it remained allied to Western Europe, or Western Europe plus Japan, and allowed the Soviet Union to dominate the rest. They are the Pied Pipers of the foreign policy debate, and their arguments do not merit attention.

The position of the global unilateralists suffers from four fatal weaknesses, in my view. First and primarily, it rests on an inadequate appreciation of the nuclear weapon in general, the mutation nuclear arms have brought about in world affairs, and the nature of Soviet nuclear policy. Second, it assumes that in the modern world the United States would have the luxury of waiting two or three years (or two or three months) before making up its mind that a war somewhere really did affect its security. Third, it ignores the immense geopolitical consequences of our worst postwar mistake: the failure to insist on the fulfillment of the Soviet promises at Yalta and Potsdam to allow free elections in Eastern Europe. And finally, it assumes that a policy of abrogating our security arrangements with Canada, Western Europe, Japan, China, Korea, the Philippines, Israel, Pakistan, Thailand, and a number of other countries would save us money and improve the character of our European allies and Japan, whom the global unilateralists excoriate mercilessly—and quite unjustly—as spongers and appeasers whose influence the Soviet leadership exploits to disarm and emasculate the United States.

I shall start with the unilateralists' fourth point. Emotionally if not analytically, it is the heart of their case.

Like everybody else, the global unilateralists are frustrated and enraged by the apparently endless character of the cold war. They discharge their feelings by blaming our friends and associates rather than ourselves and our enemies. It is safer thus, and less dangerous. Every alliance in history has suffered from this disease. Who can forget slogans of enemy propaganda in World War II that England would fight to the last Frenchman and America to the last Russian? The global unilateralists believe, as Angelo Codevilla put it recently, "that if our European and Japanese allies were put on notice that they would bear the primary and final responsibility for their own safety, they would be better able to help themselves and more disposed to help us. Without the psychological and financial burdens of present arrangements, we too would be better able to take care of ourselves and to help our allies in time of real need. This argument," Codevilla adds, "may be mistaken, but it deserves serious consideration."[3] I fully agree that the argument Codevilla summarizes deserves serious consideration. And I believe it is profoundly mistaken, as he suspects.

The central feature of every article the unilateralists write is the angry charge that the European NATO allies are not paying their fair share of the costs of our common defense. To make their point, those articles tell us that we spend a larger share of our GNP on defense than the allies do. Such charges prove nothing. We spend more than half our military budget on the pay of troops and pensions; our allies, most of whom have conscription, spend far less. Our military procurement is notoriously expensive, as compared to everyone else's. And we have the nuclear burden and the cost of defending our interests outside the area covered by the North Atlantic Treaty. It is far more significant that the bulk of the troops, planes, tanks, and even ships of the NATO forces is supplied by our allies, not by the United States. In most important categories, that fraction is well over 80 percent.

But waving the bloody shirt about burden sharing is not the most important weakness in the unilateralist case. The fatal flaw in global unilateralism is revealed in the vocabulary Codevilla uses. Two words run through Codevilla's sentences: *them* and *us*. He talks about the allies helping "themselves" and helping "us." Those two words are evidence of an unresolved contradiction that runs through the entire literature. The global unilateralists have not accepted the fact that for U.S. security policy since 1945, the distinction between "us" and "them" does not exist. When we defend key components of the world balance of power, we are not defending "them" but "ourselves." Part of the unilateralist mind is still in the nineteenth century, when the world political system was managed by the Concert of Europe and the United States for the most part could ignore the problem of its security. The sad fact is that the unilateralists give only lip-service to the proposition that the balance of power must be the first objective of U.S. foreign policy. None of them has really confronted the fact that the United States cannot achieve the goal alone.

It is revealing that the unilateralists never attack Canada for spending less of its national income for defense than the United States, although it would not be difficult for them to do so. The unilateralists know that we must defend Canada against the Soviet Union in order to defend the United States, however little Canada spends for its own forces. The strategic relationship of Western Europe, Japan, China, and the United States is exactly the same as our strategic relationship with Canada or Mexico. The burden-sharing argument of the unilateralists is not only wrong; it is irrelevant. Of course, fair burden sharing among the allies is to be encouraged but not by making threats we cannot afford to carry out.

The global unilateralists make another untenable charge against our European allies: that most of them are timid and parochial appeasers whose influence in U.S. affairs prevents us from pursuing a vigorous, effective policy of power politics all over the world. The absurdity of the charge underlines its importance. No one can seriously contend that the United States lacks a large and influential army of entirely native isolationists, illusionists, wishful thinkers, Soviet apologists, appeasers, and assorted doves. It is an insult to them and to the strong congressional groups that represent them to suggest that they are the puppets of the German foreign minister, the U.S. Foreign Service, or any other popular devils or bugaboos. The slogan "No more Vietnams" is made in America, and it is powerful political medicine. The American people have never achieved an agreed vocabulary for thinking about foreign affairs and are still talking and writing about national security policy in terms that would have made Theodore Roosevelt blush. But even so astute and experienced a student as Angelo Codevilla can say that "the U.S. Government, for NATO's sake, has again and again weakened itself militarily, pulled its punches in the Nicaraguas of this world, and, worst of all, confused its own policy making."[4] Europe should not be made the scapegoat for our own mistakes. Our errors in Nicaragua, Lebanon, and many other scenes of recent trouble have been serious and entirely our own.

The model Codevilla and the unilateralists have in mind for U.S. strategic policy is that of General de Gaulle, under whom France withdrew from NATO's integrated command while remaining a signatory of the North Atlantic Treaty. In that period and since, France has rebuilt its military forces, including a small modern nuclear force, and has pursued a vigorous and seemingly independent foreign policy.

De Gaulle's example confirms my view of the matter, however, not that of the global unilateralists. De Gaulle's policy was one of political theater, designed to help restore the national pride of France after defeat and occupation during World War II and the painful process of decolonization in Asia and Africa after the war. No one knew better than de Gaulle that his policy was not in any sense one of accepting "primary and final responsibility," for the safety of France. The primary and final responsibility for the security of France is borne both by France and by France's allies, emphatically including the United States and its nuclear arsenal. France can eat its Gaullist cake and have the protection of NATO as well because of its geographical position. It is to the west of Germany and the main bulk of the NATO integrated command. The excellent French troops in Germany work in harmony with those of France's allies. If the United States should ever be so misguided as to follow de Gaulle's example and withdraw from NATO's integrated command, its security position would not be comparable in any way to that of France today. A U.S. policy of Gaullism would automatically terminate our security arrangements with our European and

Asian allies. Then we would realize that the only superpower behind the United States is the Soviet Union.

"Ah," the unilateralists say, "you forget that France has its own nuclear force de frappe." France does indeed have a nuclear force de frappe, as does Britain. But the French and British nuclear forces, separately or together, cannot be regarded as a strategic deterrent in relation to the Soviet Union. A Soviet diplomat once commented that from the Soviet point of view, the French and British nuclear forces "are not worth a sand box exercise." In the military sense—and therefore in the political sense as well—that is unquestionably true. Without the full nuclear support of the United States, France and Britain cannot plausibly threaten the Soviet Union with a force that is and will inevitably remain minute in comparison with the Soviet nuclear arsenal. The Soviet Union is too far ahead and its building program has too much momentum to allow Britain and France to contemplate catching up. And if the United States withdrew from Europe, the Soviet Union would never allow France and Great Britain to undertake such an effort. The Soviet reaction would be even more violent and predictable if Germany or Japan sought to become nuclear.

The British and French nuclear forces have a well-understood function under circumstances of extreme tension if the United States should happen to have a weak and indecisive president: to start a war the United States would have to finish. It is not an idea we enjoy. But no American, looking back at our record since World War II, can dismiss the policy as irrational.

There is thus no way in which Japan, China, Western Europe, or any other country or group of countries can meet the challenge of "primary and final responsibility" for their own safety against the credible menace of a Soviet threat. The Gaullist metaphor of the global unilateralists rests on illusion about the nuclear dimension of the security problem. As Edward Luttwak remarks:

> The destructive power of thermonuclear weapons overshoots by far the culminating point of military utility. . . . It is no longer possible to slight the destructive consequences of any nuclear attack, as the consequences of anticipated cavalry incursions, sieges, or even conventional bombing raids could always be minimized in the past by animal optimism, and by the perceptual asymmetry between war gains vividly imagined and war losses dimly feared. It is the definitive, indeed measurable, character of nuclear destruction rather than the possible but uncertain magnitude of its scope that inhibits the resort to nuclear war. This quality of scientific predictability has altered the millennial terms of comparison between the worth of war aims and their cost. In the presence of nuclear weapons, the perceptual balance that was once achieved only in the midst of war, when its costs were experienced in the flesh, is now in effect before war begins. . . . Even powers amply supplied with nuclear weapons may yet fight

'conventionally' or employ only a few of the smallest weapons as gestures of token effect.[5]

Luttwak's analysis does not suggest that nuclear weapons are irrelevant to war or politics. While the risk of nuclear war, at least among the major industrial countries, is minimal, uncertainty persists. No one can say there is no risk of nuclear war, even between the major powers, since these weapons are controlled by human beings or their computers. For countries governed by irrational leaders, the probabilities are different. The fear of nuclear war, however remote, is and will remain a powerful political force.

Both the Soviet and U.S. nuclear arsenals exist therefore not primarily as military instruments to be used in war but as sources of political influence designed to deter. To deter what? It is generally assumed that Soviet and U.S. policies are the same in this respect, but they are not. There is a fundamental difference between the Soviet and U.S. concepts of deterrence. The United States builds its weapons in order to deter Soviet conventional or nuclear attacks or threats against the vital interests of the United States. The Soviet Union, on the other hand, regards its nuclear weapons as the ultimate sanction behind its program of expansion. The Soviet nuclear force is configured to deter any resistance to Soviet expansion and above all to persuade the United States to remain neutral in the event of Soviet threats or attacks against third countries and to back down in the face of threats against the United States itself. In short, the Soviet Union seeks to use its nuclear weapons as an instrument of aggression, while U.S. nuclear doctrine treats our forces as a defensive shield against aggression.

The global unilateralists hold that the threat of U.S. nuclear retaliation even against Soviet moves against our most vital interests has lost all credibility. They argue that the Soviet leaders "know" we would never use nuclear weapons and face a nuclear reply from the larger, more modern, and more sophisticated Soviet nuclear arsenal. Therefore they urge us to pull back from forward deployments and reduce our forces.

It is hard to imagine a more dramatic demonstration of the political effect of military power. It is breathtaking to find the global unilateralists, many of whom are intellectuals of impeccable anticommunist credentials, enthusiastically following the Soviet line, but that is what they are doing. They propose precisely the policy the Soviet Union has been trying for a generation to induce the West to adopt. We should recognize and accept the correlation of forces, the Soviets say, and duly pay tribute to our suzerain, like every other subject people in history. Their model of détente and peaceful coexistence is the relationship of Finland and the Soviet Union.

Such defeatism is premature. The threat of nuclear retaliation still restrains the Soviet Union. Soviet behavior, even in recent years, belies the unilateralist hypothesis. The Soviets are pursuing an enveloping strategy in the Third World precisely because they do not dare to threaten the great centers of Western power directly. The strength of the West is more than sufficient to maintain and fortify both our nuclear and our conventional strength, and that fact is clearly still a restraint on Soviet adventurism.

Henry Kissinger was quite right to say that "no great power commits suicide for an ally." No power, great or small, willingly commits suicide at all. So long as we retain a credible nuclear retaliatory capacity, the issue will not arise. And no U.S. president ought to be put into the position of having to choose between capitulation and the use of the nuclear weapon. That is why the Soviet-U.S. nuclear equation is so important.

If we allow the Soviet Union to achieve crushing nuclear superiority, of course, we shall have no choice but to accept defeat without war. Under such circumstances, the Soviet Union would be able decisively to exploit the political effects of what Luttwak calls the "perceptual balance" between the putative gains and costs of war.

This is one of the many reasons why the counsel of those who advocate pulling our troops and fleets out of forward positions in Europe and Asia is so dangerous. Their emphasis on the money to be saved by such a course raises serious question about whether they are global unilateralists in fact or old-fashioned isolationists in a new costume. Both our allies and our adversary know that under the circumstances of modern war, forces that would take months or years to assemble, train, mobilize, equip, and transport have no military significance, especially as a deterrent. If the unilateralists were serious about maintaining the balance of power, their policy would cost more money, not less. It would require more forces and more transport to deter the Soviet Union from Kansas and Texas than from forward bases in Europe, the Middle East, and Asia—and such methods are inherently less credible and reliable than the present system, for all its faults. Forward deployment is the only rational policy for a strategy of deterrence. Our formidable armored divisions are more useful either as a deterrent or as a fighting force in Germany than in the United States. Moreover, they cost less to maintain abroad than at home, because many facilities are supplied by our allies.

The zero-zero INF agreement between the Soviet Union and the United States, reinforced by the American performance at Reykjavik, has stirred powerful tides of anxiety, neutralism, and nationalism in Europe, China, and Japan. Against that background, a U.S. policy of withdrawal and demobilization would be perceived everywhere as one of retreat to isolation and neutrality. The U.S. nuclear guarantee would lose credibility; Western Europe, Japan, China, and many other countries would move toward neutrality, at a minimum, or toward Gaullism and militarism; and the United States would be truly isolated and at the mercy of events.

Even a hint or expectation of a U.S. withdrawal from forward positions in Europe, Asia, and the Middle East would have another consequence: it would necessarily trigger the rapid spread of nuclear weapons and the breakdown of the regime of the Non-Proliferation Treaty of 1967. The influence of that treaty has not been negligible. There are many fewer nuclear powers today than most observers thought likely twenty years ago, when the treaty was signed. And the treaty is supported by powerful political instincts throughout the world. Adopting the unilateralists' policy would release a political fire storm far more serious than the controversy over the reinterpretation of the Anti-Ballistic Missile Treaty. But if the United States reduced its forces abroad, many countries that now rely on the nuclear power of the United States would feel driven to become nuclear powers themselves. I know of no government and no responsible political party in any allied country that would favor such a development. In my experience, the feeling against nuclear proliferation is stronger in Germany and in Japan than in any other nations. The nuclearization of those two countries would arouse fears and passions among both the German and Japanese peoples and many others. The world political system would become far more volatile and unpredictable. And the Soviet Union would have a plausible excuse for attacking Germany and Japan under Article 107 of the United Nations Charter, which provides that nothing in the charter "shall invalidate or preclude action, in relation to any state" which during World War II had been any enemy "of any signatory of the Charter," taken or authorized as a result of that war by the government having responsibility for such action.

With a sublime indifference to history and political feeling, the global unilateralists are not only willing but eager to take this step, necessarily a central feature of their policy. That it would be imprudent is obvious. It would in fact be far worse than imprudent. Coupled with a zero-option INF treaty, standing alone, and a U.S. withdrawal of conventional forces from Europe and the Far East, it would risk global war under circumstances that could neither be predicted nor controlled.

There is no conceivable reason to run such a risk. The far-ranging American impulse to retreat, caused in larger part by the fear of nuclear war, has an ironic dimension. As an isolated "neutral" state, we would have to maintain at least as large a nuclear arsenal as we do now. The unstated assumption behind the arguments of the global unilateralists is that while we may not have enough nuclear weapons to protect Europe, China, or Japan, we surely have enough to protect our own territory. Their assumption is wrong. The retaliatory nuclear force required to keep the Soviet Union from attacking Western Europe, China, or Japan is mathematically the same as that required to prevent attacks on the United States itself. The force required for nuclear deterrence is determined by the nuclear forces of the Soviet Union, not by the particular target chosen for a Soviet attack. This is one of the most important lessons of the Cuban missile crisis of 1962.

Because we had full nuclear retaliatory capability then, the Soviet Union could not have opposed a U.S. invasion of Cuba and therefore withdrew its missiles in the face of U.S. preparations for an invasion. If the nuclear balance were unfavorable to the United States, could we oppose a Soviet landing in Florida?

The global unilateralists have one more arrow in their quiver: the Strategic Defense Initiative (SDI). They write as if SDI were a magic solution for all our ills. The problem of missile defenses is important and urgent, but missile defense systems are not and can never be an alternative strategy for protecting the security of the United States, for making offensive nuclear weapons obsolete, or for eliminating the need to maintain the balance of power. Even a perfect SDI astrodome could not make a policy of neutrality safe for the United States standing alone. And there are no present prospects for a perfect astrodome.

The Soviet Union has been testing and developing antimissile defenses since 1948. Its program has been carried forward steadily and on a large scale. The Soviet scientists and engineers have made impressive progress and are far ahead of the United States, which greatly reduced its efforts in the field after the ABM Treaty was ratified in 1972. Indeed the Soviet Union has recently modernized the ABM system around Moscow, the only functioning ballistic missile defense system in the world, and tested antisatellite weapons, laser weapons, and other defensive systems based on novel technologies. One of its major objectives in the SALT I negotiations in 1972 was to stop U.S. research and development in this field. All the portents indicate that a major Soviet goal in the current nuclear arms negotiations is to derail the U.S. and allied SDI effort, thus preserving the Soviet Union's virtual monopoly in defensive systems.

Missile defenses should be viewed as an integral part of the Soviet-U.S. nuclear equation. If both sides had equal offensive systems but one had a moderately effective system of defense against ballistic missiles, the side having defenses would have what amounts to a first-strike capacity. The other side would know it and would therefore yield without actually fighting. In the Cuban missile crisis of 1962, the Soviet leaders retreated because the overwhelming nuclear retaliatory capacity of the United States at the time made it impossible for them to threaten to use their nuclear weapons. Equally, and for the same reason, our nuclear power made it possible for us to invade Cuba effectively with conventional forces. When President Kennedy demonstrated his willingness to invade Cuba with conventional forces, the Soviets drew back.

The United States has no choice but to go forward with the SDI program. It cannot leave the field entirely to the Soviet Union, and it must act soon or fall so far behind as to be in a position of hopeless weakness. A reasonably effective SDI program should help restore the credibility of the

U.S. retaliatory deterrent against Soviet aggressive moves in third countries or against the territories or armed forces of the United States.

On the other hand, there can be no stability in the nuclear environment unless the Soviet Union and the United States reach agreement on all three phases of the nuclear equation: intermediate-range and intercontinental offensive weapons and defensive systems as well. With the advance of technology, the ABM Treaty is becoming obsolete. There can be no progress toward nuclear calm unless the Soviet Union accepts the principle of deterrence as the United States defines it and gives up its frantic drive for nuclear superiority. Even a nuclear agreement based on the U.S. view of deterrence would be worthless if it were regarded as a license for Soviet expansion accomplished by the aggressive use of conventional weapons, proxy wars, guerrillas, and subversion.

The strong regional combinations we have helped organize since 1947 to thwart the Soviet bid for mastery thus have a powerful internal coherence. There is no escape from their logic. Only the United States can frustrate the formidable nuclear arsenal of the Soviet Union, so the United States is an indispensable member of each combination. And only by maintaining its nuclear guarantee for its allies and other vital interests can the United States sustain the balance of power on which its own primitive safety depends.

Conclusion

The angry, passionate argument for a policy of global unilateralism thus vanishes upon examination, destroyed by its contradictions. It professes to be based on a full acceptance of the view that the most vital security interest of the United States is to keep Western Europe, Japan, China, Canada, South Korea, and certain other countries out of Soviet hands. But its advocates are willing to withdraw U.S. forces from forward bases and to demobilize them. Only by demobilizing those forces could we hope to save the $100 billion or more the unilateralists claim we spend in the defense of Europe and correspondingly large sums we spend on forward deployments elsewhere.

The argument that the economic troubles of the United States are caused by the level of our defense expenditures, especially in Europe, is without substance. Our military budget absorbs 5 or 6 percent of our GNP, a level far below wartime mobilization levels and comfortably within the capacity of our expanding economy. During the Eisenhower administration, for example, we spent about 9 percent of GNP. The Soviet Union is now spending nearly 20 percent of a smaller GNP, and that figure is rising toward 25 percent. The United States, like other advanced industrial countries, must adjust its output patterns in accordance with the principle of comparative advantage. The inefficiency of our adjustment process is not caused by military spending but by a low level of savings, poor business management, inadequate entrepreneurship, appalling performance by the government in the field of fiscal policy, and a deteriorating educational establishment. The policy proposals of the global unilateralists could make no contribution toward restoring the U.S. balance of payments and the international competitiveness of the U.S. economy in general.

Codevilla calls the unilateralists' withdrawal proposal a bet. It is a bet the United States cannot win. The unilateralists believe that if we undertake to withdraw from Europe and other forward bases, Europe, Japan, China, and other countries under our protection will replace U.S. conventional and nuclear forces with conventional and nuclear forces of their own, so that deterrence will be maintained at least at its present level and U.S. forces could be demobilized or used unilaterally in dealing with Third World hostilities. It would, of course, be easy for Europe or Japan to replace U.S. conventional forces, but there is no conceivable way in which either could replace the U.S. nuclear forces because the Soviet Union is so far ahead of Britain and France and is most unlikely to allow Britain and France, and especially West Germany and Japan, to become formidable nuclear powers if the United States withdrew its forces and signaled a retreat to neutrality. Without nuclear forces capable of offsetting and neutralizing the Soviet nuclear arsenal, neither our erstwhile allies nor the United States itself could use conventional forces against those of the Soviet Union. Under those circumstances, resistance being manifestly impossible, it would not occur.

If our allies fail to meet the challenge of duplicating the Soviet nuclear arsenal, the global unilateralists would have the United States wash its hands of their defense and allow them to be drawn into the Soviet sphere as unworthy partners who deserve the fate of Poland, Czechoslovakia, or Finland. This is the step the United States should never take. If the unilateralists really accepted the balance of power principle, they could never propose so dangerous a bet.

Nor do the global unilateralists explain why, even if their dreams came true, it would be preferable from the point of view of U.S. security to have the countries of the free world fragmented into a series of separate nuclear regional combinations rather than linked with each other in a more and more coordinated community based ultimately on U.S. nuclear power. It would seem obvious in the light of historical experience that since the United States would inevitably be drawn into the general convulsions of the world state system, as was the case during the Napoleonic Wars and both world wars, it would be infinitely better for us to participate fully and actively in the preliminary diplomacy of seeking to head off such convulsions rather than delegate the task entirely to our allies. It would seem equally apparent, at a time when country after country throughout the world is moving massively away from socialism toward capitalism, that it would make no sense to dissolve the pluralist Western community based on the power of the capitalist state system.

Both the world wars of this century could have been prevented by wise and vigorous diplomacy backed by adequate force. Those wars did catastrophic damage to the fabric of civilization. Beyond even the deaths and injuries of servicemen and civilians and the destruction of cities and towns, millions of refugees were forced to wander the earth; fascism and communism emerged from the ruins; and totalitarian government challenged the concept of social order governed by just law. This century has known barbarism without precedent in human history. Confronting the terrible risks of general war in a nuclear environment, the policy of the United States, its allies, and their associates in security arrangements around the world should be to improve and strengthen their programs of collective security, not dismantle them, thus precipitating a cycle of retreat before the menace of the Soviet nuclear arsenal. A policy of *sauve qui peut* and the devil take the hindmost can only result in general war or general surrender without war. In a nuclear environment, aggressive war itself must be the enemy.

The program of the global unilateralists is fueled by two emotions wise policy must overcome: anger and fear amounting to panic. The anger is an unworthy and unjustified rage against our friends. That feeling is in fact a displacement of the anger we feel against the Soviet Union, whose policy of expansion has cost us so much since 1945. It is dangerous to express such anger against the Soviet Union, so we discharge it against our allies. The fear is our reaction to the reality of the Soviet Union's growing advantage in nuclear weapons. The purpose of the Soviet arsenal is to persuade the United States to withdraw its forces from forward deployments and become neutral. That, in fact, is the policy the global unilateralists are recommending. It would be suicidal to accept the policy and unnecessary even to consider it. It is easily within our power to strengthen our own nuclear forces and the conventional forces of the Western alliances so as to make our policies of collective security as credible as they were before Vietnam and the other disastrous events of the 1970s. But unless we restore the Soviet-U.S. nuclear balance, we shall be unable to protect either the balance of power or the liberty of the United States itself.

Notes

1. Letter to Thomas Lieper, January 1, 1814, in Paul Leicester Ford, ed., *The Writings of Thomas Jefferson* (1898), 9: 445.

2. Halford Mackinder, *Democratic Ideals and Reality* (New York: H. Holt and Company, 1919).

3. Angelo Codevilla, "American Soldiers in Europe: Hostages to Fortune," *National Interest* (Summer 1987): 89, 92.

4. Ibid.

5. Edward Luttwak, *Strategy, the Logic of War and Peace* (Cambridge, Mass.: Belknap Press, 1987), pp. 60–61.

2

Let the Europeans Negotiate with Gorbachev

Melvyn Krauss

By offering to eliminate medium-range nuclear missiles from Europe, Soviet leader Mikhail Gorbachev has demonstrated consummate skill in exploiting current U.S. political weakness to Soviet advantage. He knows that the so-called zero option is extremely favorable to Soviet strategic interest because of the substantial Soviet advantage in Europe in conventional weapons, chemical weapons, and short-range nuclear missiles. Indeed, without auxiliary accords, the INF treaty will increase the ability of the Soviets to intimidate West European allies of the United States, lead to their further Finlandization, split Europe from the United States, and, ultimately, weaken U.S. resolve toward the Soviets as the United States moved to restore transatlantic unity with a weakened Europe.

The reason the Europeans are likely to respond to the U.S. missile withdrawal by increasing détente instead of their own military spending relates to the continued presence of U.S. troops in Europe. So long as these troops—the symbol of U.S. defense guarantees to Europe—remain, no European politician will be able to muster sufficient popular support for what necessarily will be a costly military buildup. Remove the troops, on the other hand, and the most formidable obstacle to European militarization will be removed as well. How can it be justified that forty years after World War II has ended, U.S. troops remain in Europe?

The original purpose of the troops, it must be remembered, was to pacify European anxieties and deter a potential aggressor until Europe got back on its feet again. According to former President Dwight D. Eisenhower, first supreme commander of allied forces in Europe, the U.S. troops were to remain in Europe for a limited time only. When the economies of the European allies recovered, it was envisaged that those troops would be brought home. "When I went back to Europe in 1951, to command the forces of NATO," wrote President Eisenhower in 1963, "the United States agreed to supply in the equivalent of six infantry divisions which were to be regarded as an emergency reinforcement of Europe while our hard-hit allies were rebuilding their economies and capabilities for supporting defense. Now, 12 years later, those forces somewhat reinforced, are still there."[1]

Today, some thirty-seven years after President Eisenhower took up his

NATO command, more than 340,000 U.S. troops remain in Europe despite the fact that aggregate European GNP now equals that of the United States. The present cost of these troops to the U.S. taxpayer is enormous. It is estimated that the U.S. government currently spends between $130 billion and $160 billion per year to support NATO.[2] If the United States were to withdraw from Europe, a significant portion of this money could be saved— and used for other purposes. For example, as a result of the savings derived from a U.S. troop withdrawal, taxes could be cut, or the federal budget deficit reduced, or an antimissile system such as SDI financed.

Such savings, of course, would be foolhardy if sufficient benefits from U.S. expenditures on NATO could be proved—that is, if the benefits could be shown to be greater than the costs. NATO supporters in the United States claim that the most significant benefit from the troop presence is that it has kept the peace in Europe for some forty years—a dubious argument that makes the elementary error of confusing correlation with cause and effect. True, there has been peace in Europe for forty years. And just as true, the U.S. troops have been in Western Europe for nearly that same period of time. But just because one event correlates with another in no way implies a causal relationship between the two.

For example, President Eisenhower wrote in 1963: "I believe the time has now come when we should start withdrawing some of the U.S. troops. . . . One American division in Europe can 'show the flag' as definitely as can several."[3] Do U.S. NATO defenders really mean to imply that had the United States followed the advice of this most preeminent NATO expert and removed five infantry divisions from Europe, war would have broken out?

NATO-philes also claim that the alliance has strengthened our European allies. The truth, however, is the opposite: by providing Europe with a defense guarantee (symbolized by the troops in Europe), the United States has robbed its allies of the incentive to defend themselves. In 1985, for example, the United States spent 6.9 percent of its GNP on defense, while non-U.S. NATO spent only 3.5 percent of its GNP. Table 2–1 lists defense expenditure as a proportion of gross domestic product for the various NATO countries.

That NATO would weaken Europe's own defenses was seen clearly by both President Eisenhower and French president Charles de Gaulle. Eisenhower wrote: "Unless we take deterrent action, the maintaining of permanent troop establishments abroad will continue to overburden our balance-of-payments problem and, most important, will discourage the development of the necessary military strength Western European countries should provide for themselves."[4] In October 1949, six months after the NATO treaty was signed, Charles de Gaulle said: "France must first count

Table 2–1
Total Defense Spending as Percentage of GDP, 1985

	Percentage of GDP	*Percentage of Highest Nation*	*Rank*
Belgium	3.0	42.6	10
Canada	2.2	31.1	13
Denmark	2.2	30.5	14
France	4.1	57.0	5
Federal Republic of Germany	3.2	44.9	7
Greece	7.1	100.0	1
Italy	2.7	38.0	12
Luxembourg	1.1	15.0	15
Netherlands	3.1	43.5	9
Norway	3.3	46.0	6
Portugal	3.1	44.1	8
Spain	2.9	39.9	11
Turkey	4.5	62.9	4
United Kingdom	5.2	72.5	3
United States	6.9	96.9	2
Japan	1.0	14.1	16
Non-U.S. NATO	3.5	49.1	
Non-U.S. NATO plus Japan	2.7	37.9	
Total NATO	5.5	76.4	
Total NATO plus Japan	4.7	65.9	

Source: Department of Defense, *Report on Allied Contributions to the Common Defense* (Washington, D.C.: Government Printing Office, April 1987), p. 72.

upon itself, independent of foreign aid" and NATO "takes away the initiative to build our national defense."[5]

It should come as no surprise, then, that of all our West European allies, France, which is the least dependent on the United States for its defense, is the least accommodationist toward the Soviet Union, while West Germany, which is the most dependent on the United States for its defense, is the most accommodationist.

Not only has NATO created weak allies when it is supposed to create strong ones, but to a large extent it is responsible for the world's living on the nuclear precipice. Feeling safe because of U.S. nuclear guarantees, the Europeans neglected to build up their conventional defenses as their economies recovered from the devastation of World War II. At the same time, the Soviet Union built up its conventional forces to the point where it enjoys a three-to-one edge in tanks, a five-to-one edge in infantry fighting vehicles, a five-to-one edge in artillery, better than parity in attack aircraft, a monopoly on automated tactical fire control, a one-and-a-half to one edge in manpower, a huge edge in chemical weapons, and a virtual monopoly in 50- to 500-mile range ballistic missiles.

Indeed, because the current balance of conventional forces so strongly favors the Soviet Union, if Moscow were to launch a conventional attack against Western Europe, according to the former NATO supreme commander, Bernard Rogers, NATO could fight for "days, not weeks" before facing the doomsday decision of surrender or launching a nuclear first strike. This is the problem of the so-called low nuclear threshold. The only way the nuclear threshold can be increased is for Europe to spend more on its conventional forces. But Europe has been unwilling to do this so long as the U.S. troops remain on European soil—that is, so long as the U.S. defense guarantee persists.

The low nuclear threshold puts the lie to the often-heard claim by NATO supporters that the U.S. troops in Europe provide the United States with "forward defense." The forward defense argument, beggar-my-neighbor in the extreme, is that in case of a Warsaw Pact conventional attack, it is better for the United States that the fighting take place on European rather than its own soil. Forward defense, however, is a myth. Because of the conventional imbalance, a prolonged conventional exchange is not very likely; conventional fighting could be expected to escalate rapidly to nuclear weapons. The sad truth is that because of NATO, the West has little, if any, conventional deterrent—as opposed to conventional defense—in Europe.

What deterrent is there, then, to prevent a Soviet invasion? The centerpiece of NATO, of course, has been the U.S. nuclear umbrella. But as the Soviet Union has approached, and perhaps surpassed, nuclear parity with the United States, the credibility of the U.S. nuclear guarantee has been called into question. Would the destruction of U.S. troops by invading Soviet forces serve as a trip wire to bring on U.S. nuclear strikes against Moscow? "Emphatically not," says Angelo Codevilla of the Hoover Institution. According to Codevilla, "the destruction of U.S. forces in Europe would break many hearts, but trip no wires."[6] Irving Kristol agrees: "The American nuclear umbrella today is 99 percent bluff."[7]

Thus, U.S. troops in Europe today promise the Europeans something the United States has no intention of delivering. But the troops do serve an important function as a political symbol: they give European politicians the excuse they are looking for to justify their unwillingness to cut into their welfare states and spend on defense. In the meanwhile, these leaders offer the Soviets economic and political favors, to give Moscow a vested interest in preserving the status quo in Europe.

Anti-Americanism

Not only have the U.S. troops in Europe created weak allies who are more likely to appease than confront an enemy, they have fanned the flames of anti-Americanism abroad, particularly in West Germany. Some West Germans view the U.S. troops as protectors, but others, still traumatized by Germany's defeat in World War II, see the troops as a continuing army of occupation. "The Americans did a great deal for Germany," writes French general Etienne Copel, "but that did not alter the fact that a lot of Germans perceive the American presence there as a kind of occupation. They have not forgotten they were defeated in 1945."[8]

General Copel's argument is given credence by noted psychoanalyst Bruno Bettelheim. According to Bettelheim, U.S. troops in Germany remind the Germans on a daily basis that they must now depend for their protection on the same forces that defeated them in World Wars I and II. Whatever the rational justification of their presence in the Federal Republic, on an emotional level many Germans see the U.S. troops as a continuing army of occupation that makes Germany an inferior partner in the Atlantic Alliance. Rather than make the Germans feel part of the Western team opposing Soviet imperialism, U.S. troops make them feel both disengaged and resentful.

If the U.S. troops in Europe serve U.S. interests so poorly, why is there such resistance in the United States to calls for their withdrawal? Perhaps because of the association in the American public's mind of troop withdrawal with isolation. But this association clearly is mistaken. Isolationists typically argue that the United States needs no allies. Yet advocates of U.S. troop withdrawal from Europe typically recognize that the United States needs strong allies and are concerned that NATO has made our allies weak. Ironically, pulling the troops out of Europe is not an isolationist argument; it is an internationalist one.

A more likely explanation of the resistance to withdrawal is simply that the Europeans are vehemently against it. The State Department, for example, typically seeks to please the U.S. allies even when such an attitude is less than appropriate. To justify their compliant posture, State Department officials argue that a U.S. troop withdrawal would split, or decouple, Europe from the United States, which, we are told, is precisely what the Soviets want. It is indeed amazing how many foreign policy experts subscribe to this view despite the fact there is so little evidence for it. The Soviets have made no concerted effort to get the U.S. troops out of Europe comparable, for example, to their effort to get the Pershing missiles out of Europe, or short-circuiting President Reagan's SDI. This should come as no surprise. The NATO link between the United States and Europe has worked very much to the Soviets' advantage.

Writes Angelo Codevilla, "No one who reads Communist literature can fail to notice that the Soviet Union's main message to its followers in Europe is *not* to 'decouple' the U.S. from NATO, but to use that coupling to Soviet advantage."[9] Adam B. Ulam of Harvard University agrees:

Although the Soviets want to encourage tensions between Western Europe and the United States, they may not want to see the United States withdraw or greatly reduce its land forces in Europe. Such a shock might make West European leaders decide they have no choice but to unite politically. Or it might cause West Germany to reconsider its decision not to acquire nuclear weapons. Moreover, the present uneasy state of U.S.-Western European relations provides certain benefits to the USSR. America's European allies usually act as a moderating influence on Washington's anti-Soviet attitudes and initiatives.[10]

Finally, resistance to U.S. troop withdrawal also comes from neoconservatives like Norman Podhoretz, editor of *Commentary* magazine, Midge Decter, Steven Munsen, and Alvin Bernstein who fear that Europe would collapse if the United States pulled its troops out—as if the only obstacle standing between Europe and total Finlandization is the political symbolism provided by U.S. troops. The implicit assumption of this argument is that Europe's values have deteriorated so badly that Europe could not or would not stand on its own feet and oppose the Soviets. The evidence, however, does not support this view: Europe's values appear as sound, or otherwise, today as do values in the United States. For example, the recent severe decline of the influence and popularity of the Communist party in several West European countries—France and Italy, in particular—is evidence that Western values have strengthened, not declined, in Europe. The defeat of domestic terrorists in Italy and West Germany through legal means is evidence that Western values of due process and democracy are alive and well in these countries. The British proved their values meant more to them than many had expected when, in 1982, they fought a war with Argentina to recover the Falkland Islands. By this action, the British showed they were willing to fight, and die, to keep the Falklands British. Would they dare do less for Britain itself?

Unlike presidents Eisenhower and de Gaulle, "*Commentary* conservatives" fail to appreciate the role incentives play in foreign affairs. NATO has given our allies a strong incentive to be weak, and they have responded accordingly. Change the incentives and European behavior surely will change with them.

In all their lamentations about failed U.S. resolve and the expansion of Soviet power, *Commentary* conservatives fall into the Soviet trap by their apparent willingness to concede substantial amounts of political influence within the Atlantic Alliance to forces that serve Soviet interests. The myth that Europe would collapse if the United States withdrew its troops is a powerful lever Europeans—and their spokesmen in the United States—use to shape U.S. foreign and military policy. The troops in Europe are the symbol that keeps NATO and the doctrine of allied unity alive—a doctrine the Soviets use to influence U.S. foreign policy to their advantage. If NATO did not exist, an important avenue of influence over U.S. policy would be closed to the Soviets.

Europeanizing the Missiles

Instead of agreeing to pull out the Pershing missiles, the Reagan administration should have left them in Europe, but under European control.[11] The West could have reaped at least three major advantages from this alternative strategy.

First, Europe would have been less likely than the United States to bargain away the Pershings. The Europeans know that once the Pershings go, to be secure they will have to make substantial investments in conventional arms. They, not the United States, will have to bear the costs of a conventional-arms buildup.

Second, the Europeans could have gotten a better deal for the missiles from the Soviets than the United States did. According to Adam Ulam, "The Soviet nightmare is that Western Europe will unite politically and rearm itself vigorously, thereby leaving the Soviet Union facing two superpowers instead of one." The Soviets would have been even more anxious—and thus willing to pay more in terms of concessions—to get rid of the Pershings and the cruise missiles if the Europeans rather than the Americans were at their controls.

Third, the INF episode underscores the point that transferring control of nuclear weapons to Europe would make the European allies stronger by undermining European neutralism and pacifism. Because the United States controls nuclear missiles located on European soil, profoundly affecting Europe's fate, Europeans have been made to feel less like players and more like spectators to the East-West struggle. Neutralism feeds off such feelings of disengagement. Peter Bender, a West German political commentator and neutralist, traces the growth of German neutralism to "the feeling that our country has become the training ground for a battle with which the Germans themselves have less and less to do."[12]

Moreover, Europe's inability to control the nuclear weapons on its soil has led to an unnecessary hostility toward nuclear weapons in general and the U.S. weapons in particular. This has proved a rallying point for Europe's peace movement. The message is clear: if the United States wishes to give the Europeans the incentive to behave as responsible allies, they must be given responsibility, particularly over the trade-off between nuclear and conventional weapons in their own countries.

The need to give the Europeans greater voice in the disposition of U.S. nuclear weapons located on their soil has been noted by formidable foreign policy experts. For example, writing in *Time* magazine in April 1984, Henry

Kissinger argued that "Europe should take over those arms-control negotiations that deal with weapons stationed on European soil."[13] (The INF negotiations were conducted by Americans.) His plan is for a negotiating team headed by a European chairman, with an American deputy and a mixed, though predominantly European, delegation.

The strength of the Kissinger plan is that, with Europeans bargaining with the Soviets, it would be less likely that the nuclear missiles would be traded away. And, clearly, tensions within the Alliance would be diminished. Its major weakness is that it would leave the United States in control of the missiles that remained in Europe. Thus the serious problems of European disengagement, neutralism, and pacifism, which are associated with the location of foreign nuclear weapons on European soil, would remain, though perhaps in somewhat diminished form.

Skeptics may wonder, though, whether the United States can give nuclear weapons to West Germany. This is an extremely important question since a substantial number of the missiles in Europe are located in West Germany.

Forty years after the end of World War II, West Germany's period of rehabilitation has come to a close. The United States cannot force this view on the Europeans, of course, but it can signal to them that the United States is now ready to treat Germany as an equal member of the alliance by offering it the missiles. Even former French president Giscard d'Estaing recognizes that Germany is a "target without a shield." He writes: "We cannot let Germany remain in this posture for long or its support for the Western Alliance will be destroyed."[14]

The late, and distinguished, French philosopher Raymond Aron agreed. He wrote in 1966:

> If the possession of nuclear arms has all of the value which General de Gaulle attributes to it, why should the Germans accept indefinitely to remain an inferior nation and to be deprived of them? . . . France is in the process of adopting, with regard to the Federal Republic, the attitude which the United States and Great Britain adopted with regard to France ten years ago (in 1956). We are condemning the Federal Republic to a permanent discrimination.[15]

Europeans may or may not accept the American lead in this matter; that is for them, not the United States, to decide. The United States should transfer control of nuclear weapons to the nation-states in which the weapons are located. If the Europeans want an alternative arrangement, the United States should stand ready to accommodate them. For example, the Europeans may opt for a regional approach and choose to revive the moribund Western European Union (WEU) as an alternative to control by nation-states. The

WEU consists of Britain, West Germany, France, Italy, and the Benelux countries. Unlike the European Economic Community, the WEU excludes "soft" allies like Denmark and Greece and is totally separate from NATO. Alternatively, Germany could make a separate arrangement with France or a joint one with France and Britain.

Can a European Defense Work?

Given the widespread feeling, both in and outside the Federal Republic, that a nuclear Germany would be premature, a U.S.-European decision to place the Pershings under European control undoubtedly would have led to some form of European regional arrangement to accommodate the missiles. Indeed the decoupling implied by the INF treaty has surprised many experts by encouraging increased military cooperation among the European powers. According to a story in the *Wall Street Journal*, for example, "Common security fears following the Reagan-Gorbachev meeting in Iceland have prompted West Germany, Britain and France into an unprecedented agreement to coordinate their nuclear-arms-control policies. . . . Under the coordination efforts, Bonn, London and Paris aim to speak with one voice in arms control discussions with the superpowers."[16]

The *New York Times* reports that Prime Minister Margaret Thatcher has moved closer to her European partners as a result of Reykjavik: "President Reagan's ability to manage foreign affairs and the durability of American commitments—especially conspicuous in the aftermath of the Iceland summit meeting—appears to have much to do with the urge to find an enhanced role for Britain in Europe. . . . A common fear that Washington might be tempted to negotiate away their deterrents leaves Britain and France, Western Europe's two nuclear-armed nations, with a sense of common interests on national security."[17]

A concrete step to increase military cooperation in Europe following upon the zero-option proposal has been the formation of a joint brigade of French and German troops announced by the French and German defense ministers in July 1987. The 3,000-man brigade is to be headed by a French officer and kept outside NATO's integrated military command. Both Manfred Worner, West Germany's defense minister, and his French counterpart, André Giraud, said the new joint brigade would be an effective military force in the defense of Western Europe. "It will have an essential mission that we still have to define," Worner said. "In the event of a crisis, it will fight alongside the other European and Atlantic forces, but it won't be part of NATO's integrated command."[18] Although the French-German brigade had been in the works for some time, it is doubtful that it would have been approved by political leaders in the two countries had it not been for European fears of U.S. withdrawal from Europe's defense.

"There is more and more worry in France the closer we get to the total de-nuclearization of Europe," says former French foreign minister Jean François-Poncet. "Then maybe the U.S. troops will go, too." Indeed, the *Wall Street Journal* reports that "European fears have brought new urgency to the renewal of peaceful Franco-German ties that began in earnest a decade ago. Experts on both sides of the border say that relations between Paris and Bonn now are the best they have been since the war and that European cooperation, on defense and other matters, is no longer just a dream. This time, with the two nations united by their common security fears, rapprochement should last."[19]

But will it? Although there can be no doubt that the INF treaty has brought the European powers into closer military cooperation with one another, it is not at all clear that such cooperation can be sustained so long as U.S. troops remain in Europe, for the troops will tend to comfort the Europeans when, to create an autonomous defense entity, the Europeans need to be provoked.

Zbigniew Brzezinski, President Carter's national security adviser, understands this point and argues that U.S. troops in Europe constitute a serious obstacle to the emergence of the autonomous European defense entity he favors. "Europe must be prodded if it is to move in the direction of increased military cooperation," says Brzezinski.

> Left as it is, Europe's cultural hedonism and political complacency will ensure that not much is done. Even the modest 1978 NATO commitment to a three percent per annum increase in defense expenditures was not honored by most European states. America should, therefore, initiate a longer-term process to alter the nature of its military presence in Europe gradually, while making it clear to the Europeans that the change is not an act of anger or a threat . . . but rather the product of a deliberate strategy designed to promote Europe's unity and its historic restoration.[20]

Brzezinski is undoubtedly correct that without the catalyst of a U.S. troop pullout, European military cooperation is likely to remain but another entry on the long list of European "cooperative efforts" that fail to materialize. The reality of Europe, after all, is division, not unity. The European peoples are divided by different cultures, different languages, different religions, and different economic interests. Moreover, historical antagonisms have separated one country from the other. Only the ignorant would deny the dissonance and discord that has existed among the Europeans in the past and undoubtedly will continue to exist in the future as well.

Can it be said, then, that the nations of Europe are so hopelessly divided that they cannot make common cause with one another under any circumstances? Of course not. Those who preach the lessons of history should remember that mutual distrust between France and Great Britain did not prevent the two nations from joining forces to defeat the kaiser in World War I and Hitler in World War II. Nor did mutual national antagonism prevent the Germans and Russians from joining forces to defeat Napoleon, and so on. By themselves, national differences and traditional antagonisms are bad predictors of how disparate and desperate nations will behave in any given situation. If history does have a message, it is that despite differences and antagonisms, the European nations can come together when there is a common interest to do so. The coalescing force in European politics most often has been the existence of a common enemy.

Since the Soviets are the common enemy today, the question arises as to why the European countries remain disunited. The answer is that Europe's gross defense dependence on the United States has voided the common danger that, in the absence of a U.S. defense commitment to Europe, could unite the European nations in common cause against the Soviets. Unwisely, the United States has pacified Europe to outside threats and thus removed the potentially congealing element from European politics. Should that pacification be discontinued, however, the political unification feared by the Kremlin could come about.

It is true that the argument that Europe's severe defense dependence on the United States is responsible for European political disarray is exactly the opposite of what the defenders of the status quo in NATO believe. Their position is that U.S. troops in Europe have pulled the Europeans together, not pushed them apart. Secretary of State Dean Rusk, for example, said in 1967 that the "presence of our forces in Europe under NATO has also contributed to the development of intra-European cooperation. . . . Without the visible assurance of a sizable American contingent, old frictions may revive and Europe could become unstable once more."[21] In 1984 the idea of the United States as pacifying Europe's internal tensions and antagonisms was resurrected by West German journalist Josef Joffe, who argues for the continued presence of U.S. troops in Europe on the grounds that "the postwar West European system has not only been stable, but ultra-stable. While some hundred wars and civil wars have battered the rest of the world, Western Europe has remained a solitary island of peace. . . . NATO's detractors ignore the central role America has played in pacifying a state system that almost consumed itself in two world wars."[22]

At the time Joffe published his article, "Europe's American Pacifier," extolling "cooperation between ancient regimes as having become routine within the expanding framework of the European Community," this same community was coming within a hairbreadth of total collapse because of a vicious squabble over contributions to the EEC budget and farm subsidies.

Here is what European "cooperation" looked like in the spring of 1984 when Joffe wrote. After the Athens summit of December 1983 failed to resolve British complaints that it was paying more than its fair share to Common Market budgets, Prime Minister Andreas Papandreou of Greece, chairman of the meeting, said the heads of government could not agree on anything despite six months of preparatory work. "We were not able to reach a unanimous position on a single issue."[23] President Mitterand predicted that "Europe will become nothing more than an 'unfinished construction site' " if the dispute continued.[24] He also spoke of the possibility of a "two-speed Europe" or a "Europe with variable geometry," expressions that have come to mean accepting a division between those Common Market countries that want to move toward more political cooperation and those—like Britain and Denmark—that have considerable reservations about increasing the community's powers. Here, then, was the Common Market on the verge of breaking up, and Joffe whistles in the dark about today's Europe being "ultrastable" simply because the European countries have not yet gone to war with one another.

Europe's New Militarism

Besides creating a certain amount of increased European military cooperation, the Reykjavik summit, and the subsequent zero-option INF treaty, also have given rise to the beginnings of what may be called a new militarism in Europe—one characterized by the sentiment that if the United States is no longer willing to defend Europe, the European members of NATO will have to defend themselves. The *Economist* of London writes:

> Europe's left is generally reluctant to spend more on soldiers, because it wants to spend more on health and schools. It is the conservative half of European politics that is likelier to raise defense spending; but Europe's conservatives saw no reason to do so while they reckoned they could take America's contribution for granted. Their inertia has now been jolted. In the Euromissile deal between America and Russia, many of these conservatives see evidence that the Americans are washing their hands of Europe. In 1987, the ritual talk about improving Europe's defense performance has suddenly taken on a new reality. Nervous European fingers may now be readier to open up European wallets."[25]

Nervous Europeans also may be looking at nuclear weapons with a new sense of reality as a result of the INF treaty. It was only a short time ago that there was a great deal of fashionable talk in Europe—and not only from the extreme left—about the desirability of a world free of nuclear weapons. Reykjavik and the INF accord have put an end to such antinuclear fantasies—

and in the process delivered a weighty blow to Europe's "peace movement." In Britain, for example, Margaret Thatcher won an unprecedented third term in office, in large part because the Labour party wanted to make Britain nuclear free.

Thatcher's impressive election victory is particularly interesting in that it provides evidence as to which political groups are likely to benefit, and which suffer, as a result of a U.S. withdrawal from the defense of Western Europe. Most political commentators in Britain agree that the party that was most pro-defense in Britain—the Conservative party—gained as a result of zero option, while the antidefense Labour party lost. Since a continued decoupling of the United States from Europe seems likely, European parties across the political spectrum can be expected to become less hostile to defense spending than hitherto has been the case. Indeed, for the first time in decades, there would appear to be votes in Europe for greater defense spending.

The impending withdrawal of U.S. intermediate range missiles from Europe also has had the beneficial effect of concentrating European attention on the adverse conventional arms balance in Europe. So long as the Pershings remained, the implications of this imbalance were not considered serious by the Europeans. But with the Pershings gone, the imbalance is more intimidating than ever.

Accordingly Europe now wants to link nuclear arms control to agreements on conventional forces. But the only way the Soviets are likely to reduce their conventional force strength in Europe is for the Europeans to give them the proper incentive, by demonstrating their own willingness to increase their conventional strength. And this is unlikely so long as U.S. troops, the symbol of U.S. defense guarantees, remain in Europe. Thus, while the Pershing pullout has made defense spending politically respectable in Europe, without the added incentive of a U.S. troop withdrawal, it is inconceivable the Europeans would be willing to spend the necessary sums of money to rectify the present adverse conventional imbalance. The zero option therefore is certain to lead to increased European economic and political favors to the Soviets—that is, to increased détente—which is presumably why Mikhail Gorbachev showed interest in the offer in the first place.

On the other hand, the Europeans would not feel the need to intensify détente because of increased intimidation had the United States placed the intermediate-range missiles under European control rather than agreeing to withdraw them.

To summarize, the INF treaty provides evidence that decoupling the United States from Europe's defense can move Europe into a more militaristic posture than hitherto has been the case. It has made nuclear weapons respectable in certain European countries, focused attention on the adverse conventional arms imbalance in Europe, and demonstrated to European politicians that there are votes in being pro-defense. These are all positive developments. But because the form of decoupling implied by zero option is suboptimal, its net result could harm Western security. Instead of withdrawing missiles and leaving the troops, as the Reagan administration did with the INF treaty, the United States should withdraw the troops and place the remaining missiles under European control.

Notes

1. Dwight D. Eisenhower, "Let's Be Honest with Ourselves," *Saturday Evening Post*, October 26, 1963.

2. See Melvyn Krauss, *How NATO Weakens the West* (New York: Simon and Schuster, 1986), chap. 2.

3. Eisenhower, "Let's Be Honest."

4. Ibid.

5. Quoted in C.L. Sulzberger, "Foreign Affairs: Poker as Played in Paris," *New York Times*, February 23, 1966.

6. Angelo Codevilla, "American Soldiers in Europe: Hostages to Fortune," *National Interest*, no. 8 (Summer 1987).

7. Irving Kristol, "What's Wrong with NATO?" *New York Times Magazine*, September 25, 1983.

8. Etienne Copel, "Foreign Media," FBIS, December 3, 1984.

9. Codevilla, "American Soldiers."

10. Adam Ulam, "Western Europe Key Area for Soviet Power Dreams," *Pittsburgh Press*, November 3, 1983.

11. This section is based on Melvyn Krauss, "Let Europe Negotiate with Gorbachev," *Wall Street Journal*, March 9, 1987.

12. Quoted in Scott Sullivan, "The Decline of Europe," *Newsweek*, April 9, 1984, p. 44.

13. Henry Kissinger, "A Plan to Reshape NATO," *Time*, April 5, 1984.

14. Quoted in Dick Parker, "Giscard: Soviets Won't Allow W. German Nukes," *Atlanta Journal*, December 11, 1984.

15. Raymond Aron, "Anarchical Order of Power," *Daedalus* 95, no. 2 (Spring 1966): 491.

16. Peter Gumbel, Thomas F. O'Boyle, and Robert Keately, "Three European Nations to Coordinate Arms Control in an Unprecedented Move," *Wall Street Journal*, November 5, 1986.

17. Joseph Lelyveld, "Thatcher is Quietly Moving Closer to European Partners," *New York Times*, December 6, 1986.

18. Paul Lewis, "French-German Force Outside NATO Is Planned," *New York Times*, July 18, 1987.

19. Thomas F. O'Boyle and Philip Revzin, "Nuclear-Missile Talks Lend a New Urgency to Paris—Bonn Amity," *Wall Street Journal*, June 12, 1987.

20. Zbigniew Brzezinski, "The Future of Yalta," *Foreign Affairs* 63, no. 2 (Winter 1984–1985).

21. Quoted in Josef Joffe, "Europe's American Pacifier," *Foreign Policy* 54 (Spring 1984).

22. Ibid.

23. Quoted in Paul Lewis, "Common Market Showdown Today," *New York Times,* March 19, 1984.

24. Ibid.

25. "Europe's Braver Colours," *Economist,* July 11, 1987.

3
Growing Together Apart: Restoring Mutuality to the Atlantic Alliance through Pluripolarity

Aaron Wildavsky

F rom the beginning, the main focus of NATO and the Western Alliance has been deterrence of attack on the European democracies. The United States, acting behind its nuclear shield, has been assumed to be safe. All that remained to be determined, therefore, was how it and Europe could best jointly contribute to Europe's defense. Since the United States was assumed to be invulnerable and the Soviet Union insatiable, but neither could attack the other for fear of retaliation, the superpowers would have to limit their struggle for dominance to areas outside their territories. Just as the Soviet Union strove to include Eastern Europe within its heartland, so an attack there would be treated as an assault upon the Soviet empire itself, the United States would, by extending nuclear deterrence to Western Europe, treat it as part of its homeland where an invasion would automatically result in a nuclear response. While much thought and not a little angst has been devoted to coping with the many anomalies this commitment has generated, from European free riders to U.S. decoupling, no one, so far as I know, has questioned the basic premises: U.S. invulnerability, European vulnerability, primary Soviet interest in attacking or controlling Europe rather than the United States. I propose to challenge these assumptions, putting in their place quite the opposite understandings— secondary Soviet interest in attacking Europe, primary Soviet interest in eliminating the only force that can resist it, the United States, hence U.S. vulnerability—and to draw from these considerations a strategy of mutual support.

If the likelihood of a Soviet attack on Western Europe is far lower than a first strike on the United States, contrary to the common wisdom, neither European nor American views of their alliance are justified. Since a Soviet attack on Europe would alert the United States without disarming it, the Soviet Union is far more likely to attack its primary rather than its secondary opponent. From this change of sequence—America first—comes another: Europe can best defend itself by first helping to defend the United States. By helping to preserve an independent nuclear deterrent in Europe, moreover, the United States helps defend itself. In this as in other ways I will discuss, mutuality can be restored to the Alliance.

Growing Apart Together

The Western Alliance is threatened from many directions, not the least of which is its origins in a unilateral guarantee by the United States to Europe. So long as the main threat is perceived to be a Soviet main force attack on Europe, the United States is necessarily cast in the role of the benefactor. Its troops in Europe are held hostage to Soviet forces, and its people and cities expose themselves to nuclear devastation by the promise to retaliate with nuclear weapons against an invasion. Yet suicide, even in defense of allies, is unpalatable. As the nuclear capability of the Soviet Union grows, moreover, American desire for a more substantial European conventional force takes on an ominous tone. Perhaps the United States wishes to confine a conflict to Europe. This fear of an overwarm embrace squeezing the life out of the loved one is met by European efforts to play balance of power politics. The pipeline project and other economic deals seek Soviet support through barely hidden subsidies. Allies turn into neutral arbiters, still dependent yet independent. Jealousy results. Conflict between West and East remains, but the focus shifts to internal differences among allies.

The price of independence is doing more, but Europeans are seen by Americans as doing less and wanting more in the way of guarantees. The United States is tempted to make European support in a matter outside that continent a litmus test of the Alliance, only to discover that it cannot get the support while it still wants the Alliance. Whether one is referring to Central America or the Middle East, support either is withheld or slow in coming. What the United States wants the Alliance for grows dimmer as internal differences become more visible. Each component of the Alliance accuses the other of that horrendous sin of decoupling, as if it were equivalent to adultery. Since neither the United States nor Europe institutes proceedings for divorce, the status quo becomes a marriage of convenience in which the partners remain legally connected but socially distant. They grow apart together.

If Europeans believe that any war, conventional or nuclear, would be suicidal for them, they are ever more reluctant to build up their forces. If war is unthinkable, why prepare? If all alternatives lead to Armageddon, they might as well seek to deter by a U.S. commitment to first use while wishing no use at all. This ambivalence, the protector as potential destroyer, accounts for the popularity of NATO as U.S. deterrence and the unpopularity of NATO as a war fighter. Armaments are supported to avoid their use. In this conception, the Alliance, far from being extended outside Europe, exists to permit a gradual accommodation to the Eastern bloc within Europe.

To the degree that the United States views European defense as a drain on its resources, without recompense in third or peripheral areas, Soviet ability to gain economic advantages from Western Europe appears as a betrayal, a transfer, in effect, of U.S. resources to its adversary through its allies.[1] Since the United States cannot now guarantee the defense, let alone the preservation, of Europe, it is not in a position to make effective demands for greater European efforts, which, in any event, may prove insufficient. Or so it seems in the long history of our lover's quarrels.

America First, or Why a Nuclear Attack on the United States Is Far More Likely Than a Soviet Conventional or Nuclear Thrust into Western Europe

While I am not sure that nuclear weapons have ended war in the pursuit of political aims, as some claim, I am more confident that they have ended the threat of all-out attack on secondary targets while leaving one's own country to be attacked by the other superpower.

Why should the Soviet Union leave itself vulnerable to its main opponent by attacking a subsidiary one? A nuclear attack on Western Europe would destroy whatever the Soviets might hope to gain; nothing would be left to take over. There is always the possibility, in addition, that the United States, fearing it is next or acting reflexively under treaty obligations, would respond with a nuclear strike. Alternatively, the French or the British might retaliate with their nuclear forces. A broad conventional attack on Western Europe might fail on its own terms, thereby destabilizing the Soviet empire. The Soviet Union might be gravely damaged while the United States remained unhurt.

Even if a Soviet conventional attack succeeded in the conquest of Western Europe, it would be a failure in the long run, for at the very least, the United States would arm itself to the hilt. In a genuine nuclear arms race, with few domestic divisions in the United States to limit its extent, the Soviet Union would be left behind. It would have gained a victory in Europe at the cost of increasing its inferiority in relation to the United States, the only other nation able to challenge its supremacy. Having shown its hand in an unmistakable way, moreover, the Soviet Union would feel vulnerable to a preemptive U.S. attack, so it would contemplate preempting the preemptor, greatly increasing nuclear instability. This would be a bad bargain. Such a self-defeating strategy—lose if they lose, lose if they win—is extremely unlikely to appeal to the leaders of the Soviet Union.

The instant the Soviet Union invaded Western Europe, moreover, the People's Republic of China (PRC) would conclude that it was next and consequently would make every sacrifice to mobilize its conventional and nuclear forces. Long fearful of the Chinese, the Soviets would then conclude it was safer to take them out before they could attack. Immediately the Soviet leadership would face what it has promised itself to avoid: a two-front war. The only way to avoid such a war is not to start it.

The principle that emerges from these considerations is stark: it is not worthwhile for the Soviet Union to launch a major attack on the members of the Western Alliance unless it attacks the United States first, and, if it does so successfully, attacking Europe is unnecessary.

By its very existence, whether it wishes to or not, therefore, the United States is and must remain the shield of the West. The United States threatens the vital principle of Soviet rule: no independent centers of power. So long as there is a global alternative, the Soviet system cannot fully consolidate its rule either inside or outside. Isolationism is not an option for the United States because it is the Soviet target of choice.

European worries about decoupling—being left in the lurch by the United States so as to invite a Soviet attack—are misplaced because it does not make sense for the Soviet Union to attack Europe first. The Soviets have been accused of many things, but planning their own destruction is not among them.

From its inception, NATO has been sustained by the myth of a Soviet conventional, main force attack. This myth may have a certain substance. The Atlantic community does share deeply held values; its members are reassured by knowing that the others are around; the Soviet Union would like to neutralize the Western community of nations, even to siphon off a portion of their resources for its own use. But all this, important as it is, is not the same as justifying the disproportionate attention devoted to a Soviet conventional attack on Western Europe as the first and, for the most part, the only concern of the Alliance.[2]

Worse still, the unexamined premise of Western defense mythology is that the United States has achieved deterrence of a Soviet first strike so that it can concentrate on blunting the expected conventional attack against Europe. The moment this premise is challenged—the balance of terror being not robust but, as Albert Wohlstetter had it, "delicate"—the whole house of cards collapses.[3] And not only from the American side.

Uncertainty Cannot Be Certain: Deterrence May Fail to Deter

America first may be America never. The arguments of those who believe the nuclear balance is stable—uncertainty over success, coupled with fear of reprisal, guarantees against a premeditated Soviet first strike—may turn out to be correct. Then again, they may not.

Proponents of stable deterrence believe one thing—nuclear weapons have transformed war because neither superpower can afford to chance it in view of the immensely destructive outcome—more than statesmen should believe anything. If they are mistaken, guarding against the worst that can happen is prudent. How to do so without simultaneously increasing the likelihood of war is the problem.

No one, no matter how often they repeat their mantra—uncertainty guarantees against nuclear attack—can be sure either that there will be no surprise attack or that the nuclear bluff will not get out of control. Indeed the residual uncertainty that is the keystone of stable deterrence should tell us that no certainty can emerge by multiplying uncertainties. Like relativists, whose position involves denial of their own truth value, the argument from uncertainty is self-defeating: if we are uncertain about a surprise attack, we cannot be certain about deterrence.

The implications of this reversal of causality for NATO mythology—the United States, not Europe, is the target—are profound. In the orthodox NATO version, the United States is supposed to endanger the survival of its people in order to roll back a Soviet conventional attack on Western Europe. This is incredible, as de Gaulle knew from the start, and everyone knows it now.[4] But that is not all that is incredible. The NATO nations do not in fact want the United States to defend them in this way, for they rightly feel their survival is at stake. They may fantasize about the missiles of the polar powers bypassing Europe, but they know better and fear worse. Slews of opinion polls show that both the general public and elites value nuclear weapons for deterrence, not for war fighting. While Europeans insist on coupling to ward off an attack, once a nuclear attack occurs, they would immediately tell the United States that they do not wish to be defended in this deadly way. The recent, anxious, official German concern over battlefield nuclear weapons, on the grounds they can be used only within national boundaries, leaves no doubt about how they would feel about risking more destructive encounters.

All that is required to sustain NATO mythology is for the Soviet Union to attack lesser powers that cannot harm it so as to encourage the superpower that can harm it to attack the Soviet Union. Nonsense. Instead of this Eurocentered strategy, which is hopeless, I propose a U.S.-centered strategy, which is hopeful.

Toward an Independent and Survivable European Deterrent

Defense of the United States is part and parcel of the defense of Western Europe. It follows that if Europeans wish to retain their liberties and their independence, their most important action is to strengthen the beginnings of a survivable nuclear deterrent in Britain and France. Whether or not this (on the U.S. side) is part of a NATO deterrent, it should (on the European side) be an independent deterrent so that even if the Soviet Union might conceivably calculate overwhelming the United States, the uncertainties of the aggressor would be compounded by having to take France and Britain or some other European retaliatory force into account. Add to these a Japanese and/or a Chinese survivable deterrent, and the prospect of a Soviet nuclear strike will be reduced to as low a level as one can imagine outside a transformation of the Soviet regime.

For those who believe that any uncertainty is sufficient to deter, additional independent nuclear deterrents are not only redundant but dangerous in that they increase the danger of accident. But for those who believe that nothing is certain, especially uncertainty, and that the Soviet leadership might be tempted to reverse their fortunes at one blow, just as they did with collectivization, industrialization, farming the Virgin lands, and installing missiles in Cuba, multiple, independent deterrents are a more certain safeguard. Faced with problems of immense scale in the past, the leaders of the Soviet Union have several times sought to overcome them by swift and radical action. Even (or especially) if deep cuts in heavy long-range missiles are negotiated between the superpowers, Europeans and Asians should be encouraged to maintain independent deterrents, for that will in fact increase mutual security.

This European force or forces would have the advantage of being perceived as independent. Yet by themselves, European forces would be insufficient to launch a successful attack. They would therefore be less provocative than if these weapons were under U.S. control. Of course, it could be claimed that by prearrangement the United States might attack the Soviet Union first, the Europeans following on with their own missiles against a weakened Soviet Union. But rational political leaders will give little credence to such an improbable scenario.

A European deterrent would add elements of mutuality to the relationship with the United States within NATO. The twin pillars concept was much discussed during President Kennedy's time, but it was not believable. Instead of the United States's always importuning its allies about doing their share, they would be known to be helping defend the United States. What could be more mutual than helping oneself by helping others?

The problem of the declining credibility of the U.S. nuclear guarantee should be addressed by a more survivable European nuclear force. This capability should also accommodate the desire of many Europeans for less dependence on U.S. policy while augmenting the effectiveness of deterrence.

Since the inception of the Alliance, the United States has hoped for a greater European effort that would relieve its budget pressures. At the same time, nonetheless, the United States has believed that it has the right to have the dominant voice in common issues due to its strength and contribution. This combination of greater contribution and lesser influence explains U.S. ambivalence toward European unity, which could have increased Europe's contribution but also its influence. Europeans, for their part, have felt they should have a stronger voice in determining their security policies. They still expect, however, that the United States will protect them.[5]

Both parties should change these incompatible sets of expectations. The United States should expect less voice in exchange for greater European help. Once they prove more forcefully their willingness to defend themselves by helping to defend the United States, Europeans will enjoy a larger role in making defense decisions. The outcome would thus be more European self-reliance and less U.S. influence in European affairs.

The small size of the French and the British nuclear forces should not write them off as effective deterrents. The crucial factor that determines deterrent capacity is not the number of warheads and their destructive power but the balance of interests at stake. The party whose interests are paramount will be seen as more resolute, and thus its threat to raise the risk to a given level will be more credible. "Since the state defending the status-quo usually values the issue or territory at stake more than its opponent does," Robert Jervis writes, "the defender will have the advantage in most conflicts."[6]

Although its nuclear forces thus far have been serving only a national role, France may be able to extend its deterrence to West Germany. Such extended deterrence will be especially credible due to the geographical proximity to Germany, which makes a threat to the latter also a menace to the former's security. Hence a French commitment could have more credibility than a U.S. nuclear guarantee because Soviet control of Germany would be much more threatening to France than to faraway America.

Cuts in U.S. forces in Europe would probably not lead to Finlandization. This scenario assumes that, facing an external threat, states are likely to bandwagon rather than to balance, that is, to join the strongest state and not to combine against it. The expectation of balance of power theory, by contrast, is that most states will balance rather than bandwagon in order to preserve their autonomy. Because the threatened states are affluent, socially cohesive, organizationally competent, and politically viable, as the Europeans obviously are, balancing is likely to be the norm.[7]

The Three Europes

The number of ground forces (including air support) the United States should keep on the Continent depends on the kind of Europe to which it is relating. Europe I has its own independent and survivable deterrent, thereby markedly contributing to U.S. security. It also has its own strategic defense, making it capable of limiting damage from a weak attack and thereby helping defend U.S. troops as well as its own people. A Europe that is actively engaged in its own defense, as well as contributing to that of the United States, deserves support.

Europe II, by contrast, seeks neither an independent and survivable deterrent nor strategic defense, but it does substantially increase its conventional defense. This Europe may reduce its reliance on the early use of nuclear arms to stem a Soviet advance in a conflict initially limited to conventional weapons. Europeans can indeed raise the nuclear threshold by increasing their conventional force levels to the point where they will provide an acceptable balance against those of the Warsaw Pact. By modestly raising the level of defense spending, increasing defense cooperation, and using their reserve military manpower, Europeans could maintain balance with the Soviet Union even if most U.S. forces were withdrawn.

A Europe III does none of the above; it provides neither a survivable and independent deterrent nor European strategic defense nor strengthened conventional forces. The result would be dissolution of NATO. On one side, the United States will conclude that it cannot make the ultimate sacrifice for a Europe that cannot help its own people or its ally.[8] On the other side, the inadequacy of European defense in the context of a growing belief that war is worse than any alternative will lead (indeed, in my judgment, is leading) to de facto dissolution. Why maintain an alliance that subjects one's people to the ultimate horror? Worse still, doing something but not enough tempts attack, a belated realization that one should respond, and thus a process of escalation in which all may be enveloped.

Holding the Western Alliance Together

The West now is somewhere between Europe I and one-half and I and three-quarters. The French and British deterrents are nearly survivable, independent, and large enough to matter. The 1987 British election was fought (and partly won) over retention and modernization of nuclear forces. France remains committed to modernization. NATO plus French ground forces are not far—perhaps 10 percent—from being adequate. Not bad, certainly not a cause for despair; just good enough, in fact, to keep Europe and the United States dissatisfied without either party's being sufficiently motivated to break up an arrangement that has worked well enough for four decades.

The focus of interallied relationships should move from whether the United States should withdraw troops from Europe to the strengthening of an independent and survivable European deterrent. The creation of a pluripolar nuclear world, together with a nearer-to-zero reduction of long-range missiles, say to a few hundred, should be the dual priorities of U.S. foreign policy. The possession of a deterrent capability outside the United States would substantially increase its security by protecting it against the only external threat to its existence, a Soviet first strike. A withdrawal from Europe, even if total, does not provide this protection.

Withdrawing troops from Europe could reduce U.S. defense expenditures, or it could allow these resources to be deployed elsewhere. Since a major reason for concern about third areas, such as the Persian Gulf, is their connection to Europe, it does not make much sense to abandon the center for the periphery. If by U.S. security one means only a nuclear attack on (or an invasion of) its territory, then no other place in the world, including Central America and Europe, possibly Canada and Mexico, may be deemed vital.

Even an isolationist United States, however, would not be safe. On the contrary, it would become more fearful. While it would be less likely to be drawn into nuclear war by defending others, it would be more likely, being alone, to be or to feel more vulnerable. There is also the historical experience of Britain in World Wars I and II and the United States in Korea where these nations thought in the abstract they would not but (in the heat of the event) actually did intervene. Each situation has its own dangers. Only if the quarrel between the United States and the Soviet Union had its basis in a contest over third areas would isolation improve U.S. security. If the quarrel is, as I believe, based on Soviet inability to tolerate a potential rival, isolation will succeed only in bringing the evil day closer.

A pluripolar nuclear world would increase U.S. security. By focusing its policy on areas of convergence with its allies—nuclear deterrence and strategic defense—rather than areas of divergence—how little conventional force can the partners get away with—the prospects of our Alliance's enduring may improve.

The Western Alliance may flounder. It could split because of an inability to agree to disagree about policies in non-European areas. For example, the United States could insist on support in Central America. Worse, Soviet preponderance may grow so that the certainty of Western destruction looms, leading to a collapse of will without a shot (or only a few shots) being fired. I give no guarantees. I do say that altering the Alliance under conditions in which the defense of each is seen to be the defense of the other might hold it together into the next century.

Ameliorating the Nuclear Dilemma

The nuclear dilemma knows no solution, but it may be ameliorated. One well-advertised way is for both Europe and the United States to do considerably more so that at every step in the level of violence, there is a response short of an intercontinental nuclear exchange. Neither Europe nor the United States now appears ready to devote the necessary resources. Evidence consists of the continuing decline of defense as a proportion of GNP and of total spending. Another step is a combination of Europe I and II, devoting marginally more resources to both conventional and nuclear defense. The United States benefits because nuclear and conventional deterrence has been strengthened. Europeans benefit both because U.S. defense is part of their own and because the United States can and does make a graded commitment, fighting fire with fire, not with nuclear weapons. The dilemma is there—conventional wars may become more likely by being decoupled from nuclear wars—but it becomes more tolerable.

Pluripolarity is not abandonment; that could happen only if the joint interest of Western Europe and the United States in deterring Soviet attack were to disappear. Acting independently but in parallel would better secure our joint objectives. Since the Soviet Union must attack the United States first, Europe best defends itself by helping to defend the United States. Since a conventional or nuclear attack on Europe would be the most severe threat to the United States short of an attack on its own soil, the United States has every reason to deter that possibility by maintaining its own deterrent. And since Europe would be contributing to U.S. defense, the Western Alliance would not only be stronger but be publicly recognized as stronger. Instead of growing apart together, Europe and the United States would be growing together apart.

Notes

1. See Melvyn Krauss, *How NATO Weakens the West* (New York: Simon & Schuster, 1986).

2. See "Discriminate Deterrence," Report of the Commission on Integrated Long-Term Strategy, Fred Iklé and Albert Wohlstetter, co-chairmen (Washington, D.C.: Government Printing Office, January 1988). "If deterrence really depended on mutual vulnerability," Iklé, Wohlstetter et al. argue, "then NATO's foundation idea—that an attack on one is an attack on all—would be overboard. In the long run, the doctrine could not even deter selective attacks on the United States. It would be seen as a bluff, and the bluff would be called. The criticism above is scarcely original. Extreme versions of the doctrine of mutual vulnerability as a guarantor of 'stability' have been assailed for their contradictions ever since they first surfaced. Yet such views have, incredibly, retained an extraordinary hold over political and military elites in the West, especially in Europe" (p. 35).

3. Albert Wohlstetter, "The Delicate Balance of Terror," *Foreign Affairs* 37, no. 2 (January 1959): 209–34.

4. See Henry Kissinger, *The Troubled Partnership* (Garden City, N.Y.: Double-day, 1965).

5. Ibid.; Robert E. Osgood, *Alliances and American Foreign Policy* (Baltimore: Johns Hopkins Press, 1968).

6. Robert Jervis, "Why Nuclear Superiority Doesn't Matter," *Political Science Quarterly* 94, no. 4 (Winter 1979–1980): 628.

7. See Stephen M. Walt, "Alliance Formation and the Balance of World Power," *International Security* 9, no. 4 (Spring 1985): 3–43; Kenneth Waltz, *Theory of International Politics* (Reading, Mass.: Addison-Wesley, 1979).

8. A recent study concludes that "NATO staff and European defense establishment pessimism regarding NATO's conventional capabilities has been an important barrier to a greater conventional emphasis in NATO strategy. The European side considered reliance on nuclear first use and escalation as crucial to compensate for NATO's 'conventional inferiority.' Because the Europeans and NATO staffs believed that the requirements for a robust conventional posture were much higher than estimated by OSD [U.S. Office of the Secretary of Defense], their cost estimates for such a capability were equally higher. Significant improvements were considered beyond reach, and marginal increases were seen to make little major difference.

"The pessimistic threat assessments therefore were the cause of a dilemma. European governments either faced public opposition to NATO policies because of its emphasis on the nuclear element or they feared public opposition to their defense policies if the budgets were greatly increased. . . . Whereas Washington favored conventional requirements aimed at building a conventional posture able to halt any but a major (all-out) conventional attack by the Pact, Europeans planned for a less ambitious posture with greater nuclear emphasis." Jorg Baldauf, "How Big Is the Threat to Europe: Transatlantic Debates over the Balance of Forces," RAND Corporation Report P-7372 (Santa Monica, Calif.: RAND, October 1987), p. 39.

4
Europe between the Superpowers: New Trends in East-West Relations

Christopher Layne

Τ he political order that evolved after World War II has proved quite resilient. In a sense, its durability is quite remarkable because, as John Lewis Gaddis has observed, it is a structure "which nobody designed or even thought could last for very long, which was based not on the dictates of morality and justice but rather upon the arbitrary and strikingly artificial division of the world into spheres of influence, and which incorporated within it some of the most bitter and persistent antagonisms short of war in modern history."[1]

Europe is the paradigm example of the postwar system's stability. What Hajo Holborn called the "political collapse of Europe"—in reality the collapse of Europe's traditional balance of power in 1945—created a power vacuum that the two victorious superpowers filled. The ensuing division of the Continent reflected the distribution of power between them. Given the geopolitical realities of 1945, the partition was probably unavoidable. Notwithstanding its undeniable costs, the Yalta settlement has not been all bad: Europe has been at peace for more than forty years, and if Yalta excluded Western influence from Eastern Europe, it also excluded Soviet influence from Western Europe. The U.S. commitment to Europe's defense provided a shield behind which Western Europe's political and economic recovery occurred. Moreover, the postwar settlement seemingly provided a permanent solution to the German question that had bedeviled Europe since 1871, and the superpowers' presence has pacified Europe by suppressing the historic national rivalries that have beset its states.[2] Although it has imposed significant burdens on the superpowers and severe constraints on the Europeans, the postwar system has lasted, it is suggested, because all concerned recognize that there are no feasible alternatives to the present geopolitical structure.[3]

Today, however, the permanence of the post-1945 settlement is very much in doubt, and present trends suggest that the postwar era of world history is drawing to a close. Both superpowers are strained by their imperial burdens in Europe, and there is reason to question whether either can much longer afford to sustain its European commitment at present levels. At the same time, the Europeans have been increasingly dissatisfied with the ossified structures of the postwar status quo, and in both halves of the artificially divided continent, they chafe under the hegemony of their respective superpower patrons. This discontent is reflected in the concept of Mitteleuropa, a belief that Central Europeans on both sides of the Elbe are linked by history, culture, and destiny and must overcome the "bloc logic" to achieve Europe's reunification.

The forces of change are at work in Europe, and pluralist trends are fueling the continuing erosion of the Western Alliance and the growing unrest in Eastern Europe (where glasnost's uncertain effects and economic difficulties could lead to new disturbances). As William Hyland has observed, "Both superpowers occupy declining positions in Europe as their respective allies grow in autonomy and strength."[4] Left unmanaged, the political and historical forces driving European events could threaten both superpowers' interests and, indeed, the peace between them. Washington and Moscow therefore have a common interest in a managed, orderly transition from the postwar system to a new postalliance security arrangement in Europe.

Although a few Atlanticist pollyannas maintain otherwise, it is clear that NATO is in disarray. The transatlantic discord is both a cause and a consequence of the fluidity of the European situation. Although many factors contribute to this malaise, the core of the problem is NATO's nuclear dilemma. By exposing the inconsistencies of the Alliance's military strategy, the Reagan "shocks"—Reykjavik and the double-zero INF treaty—have underscored the wide divergence in the politico-strategic interests of its two most important members, the United States and the Federal Republic of Germany. These differences have surfaced at the worst possible time because Moscow is showing particular skill at identifying and exploiting the Alliance's fissures. Indeed, with his domestic program of openness and revitalization and his subtle and appealing Westpolitik, Mikhail Gorbachev bids fair to transform Europe's diplomatic landscape. The diplomatic "struggle for mastery in Europe" has been renewed. It is to this challenge that Washington must respond.

Weakening of Extended Deterrence

Because of its military and economic power, the Federal Republic of Germany (FRG) is the Western Alliance's European linchpin. Since the 1950s NATO has defended West Germany from Soviet attack and integrated the FRG into the Atlantic security and economic systems. The U.S. strategic nuclear guarantee to West Germany—extended deterrence—is the underlying foundation of the U.S.-FRG relationship, and much of NATO's recent history consists of U.S. attempts to reassure Bonn that it will risk nuclear war in West Germany's defense.

Since the early 1950s U.S. strategic doctrine has been embodied in several linguistic formulations (massive retaliation, graduated deterrence, and flexible response), but its central premise has remained constant: the United States will respond to a Soviet attack (conventional and/or nuclear) on West Germany by using tactical, intermediate, and, if necessary, strategic nuclear weapons. Because NATO historically has eschewed building a convincing conventional defense capability, in the event of war the United States almost certainly would be compelled to have recourse to the early and first use of nuclear weapons, thereby initiating a process that would lead from the use of tactical nuclear weapons in Europe to a central nuclear exchange between the superpowers. This probable sequence of events may deter the outbreak of war in Europe, but if extended deterrence fails, the U.S. homeland would be exposed to Soviet nuclear attack.

The inner contradictions of extended deterrence have long been recognized.[5] From the early 1950s through the mid-1970s, strategic analysts perceived that the U.S.-Soviet strategic nuclear parity would compromise fatally the credibility of the U.S. strategic nuclear guarantee to West Germany. At the time, this was only a contingent future possibility. During the 1980s, however, extended deterrence has been the subject of renewed, intensive discussion because superpower strategic nuclear parity is a reality and its implications too important to ignore.

Today the U.S. nuclear commitment to Europe is incredible in both senses of the term because it depends on the believability of a threat that rational American decision makers could not (and should not) carry out. As French president Charles de Gaulle realized early on, once the Soviet Union attained strategic nuclear parity with the United States, the United States would not expose its cities to nuclear destruction for the sake of Western Europe's defense.

Washington has responded in two somewhat contradictory ways to the erosion of extended deterrence's credibility. One is by attempting to move away from reliance on nuclear weapons and giving a greater emphasis to conventional capabilities. Thus flexible response is a strategy that aims to raise the nuclear threshold—the point at which NATO would use nuclear weapons. Stronger nonnuclear forces enable the Alliance to counter a Soviet conventional attack without using nuclear weapons during a conflict's early stages. The other U.S. approach is to bolster extended deterrence by adopting new doctrines and deploying new nuclear systems in Europe. In practice— notwithstanding the Alliance's official declaratory policy—NATO strategic policy has followed the latter course, and the Alliance remains wedded to a strategy strongly biased in favor of nuclear weapons.

Western Europe's governments and traditional security elites prefer a deterrent strategy with a low nuclear threshold to a credible conventional defense posture because they fear, as Western German chancellor Helmut

Kohl (and others) said after the October 1986 Reykjavik summit, that removing the U.S. nuclear umbrella would "make Europe safe for conventional war" by weakening the credibility of extended deterrence.

Because of West Germany's geographic exposure, any European war, conventional or nuclear, would be disastrous to it. Bonn's overriding concern is war avoidance, an objective achieved through a NATO strategy that makes U.S. use of nuclear weapons in a conflict as nearly automatic as possible. As Egon Bahr, one of the Social Democratic Party (SPD's) leading security policy analysts, argues: "Europe does not want to allow America freedom to decide when to put its own existence on the line, but rather wants to link the United States indissolubly, in an almost automatic manner with Europe's own destiny."[6]

In 1982, four leading West German defense analysts underlined that for Bonn, war avoidance depends on keeping the U.S. nuclear umbrella in place.[7] The tight and indissoluble coupling of U.S. strategic nuclear forces to Europe's defense, they argue, binds the fate of the United States to Europe's and thus presents Moscow with the risk that even a conventional attack on NATO would lead inexorably to an all-out nuclear war between the superpowers. This realization, the West German analysts argue, deters war in Europe. Without the U.S. nuclear guarantee, they believe, Germany alone would bear the destruction of conventional war—a war that would involve no "existential risk" for either Soviet or U.S. territory.

Because few believe Washington would cold-bloodedly initiate nuclear warfare, NATO's military structure is designed to ensure that the United States will do reflexively what it will not do deliberately. U.S. strategists see flexible response as a strategy that allows for carefully controlled escalation through three levels of conflict: conventional, theater nuclear, and strategic. They view it as essentially a war-fighting strategy; thus the use of tactical and intermediate-range nuclear weapons is seen as an intervening step between conventional conflict in Europe and a strategic nuclear exchange between the two superpowers.

The West Germans, however, are interested in deterrence, not war fighting, and for them there is nothing flexible about flexible response. As Paul Bracken observes, theater and intermediate-range nuclear weapons in Europe are a means of ensuring that any European war would automatically become a nuclear conflict; these weapons are not a means to gain battlefield advantage.[8] Bracken explains that these weapons are the key to NATO's real strategy: one of "suicidal deterrence," not flexible response:

> In the face of the suicidal consequences of a war in Europe, it is easy to see why a rational political leader would never take steps leading to devastation. What is needed instead of a rational procedure for going to war is a posture

that is so complex that war could be triggered in any one of a number of different ways without rational control.[9]

NATO's nuclear strategy serves this objective perfectly. In wartime, eight NATO nations (not including France) would control nuclear weapons, and no centralized organization exists to exercise command and control over these weapons. Whereas strategic forces are assigned to functionally specialized organizations (a fact that underscores nuclear weapons' distinctive character-istics), tactical nuclear weapons are embedded in the structure of conventional military units where they are likely to be regarded as just another weapon once the shooting starts. Notwithstanding the public statements of the Alliance's political and military officials to the contrary, they probably will not be the ones to decide whether to use tactical nuclear weapons.

In peacetime, NATO's tactical nuclear weapons are kept at a relatively small number of storage facilities. Because of their vulnerability to attack, in a crisis these weapons would have to be dispersed to their assigned units. Because of the short reaction times imposed by the geographically confined nature of the possible European battlefield—and the inevitable confusion and disruption of communications that would occur during combat—the authority to use these weapons would, in reality, be predelegated to battlefield commanders if these weapons are dispersed with the intention of actually using them.[10]

In the late 1970s, West German strategists found themselves in a quandary. Although firmly wedded to the concept of suicidal deterrence, they became concerned about the consequences if deterrence should somehow fail. After all, most of NATO's tactical nuclear arsenal consists of short-range weapons that can only be used on German soil (East and West). This possibility was unpalatable, and such a strategy became increasingly difficult to defend politically. Moreover, given strategic parity, a strategy resting on the use of tactical weapons created strong incentives for the United States to attempt to confine any use of nuclear weapons to Europe—a fact that reinforced preexisting German fears. West Germans have always wanted to couple U.S. strategic forces to their defense because—if war should ever come—they prefer a nuclear conflict be fought over their heads, not on their territory. Strategic parity negated the utility of tactical nuclear weapons as a coupling device.

The 1979 decision to deploy Pershing II and cruise missile INFs was intended to recouple U.S. strategic nuclear forces to West Germany's defense. In most key respects, the INFs possessed all the bad attributes of tactical nuclear weapons; unlike tactical nuclear weapons, however, they could reach targets in the Soviet Union and thus trigger Soviet retaliation at the United States itself. Thus, for West German strategists, the INFs would have reestablished the credibility of suicidal deterrence by restoring the risk that a Soviet conventional attack on West Germany would inexorably lead to an all-out nuclear war involving both superpowers' homelands. Of course, this is not the justification for the deployments advanced by many U.S. leaders. Henry Kissinger has argued that the INFs would have given Washington the option of a "less cataclysmic response" to a Soviet attack on Western Europe:

> The INF made it difficult for the Soviets to threaten America's allies with a nuclear or conventional attack confined to Europe because the Kremlin would have to calculate that either might trigger the American missiles. And even a 90% successful attack on the missiles in Europe would leave tens of missiles (and scores of warheads) capable of damaging Soviet territory while the United States strategic forces remained intact. But to attack the United States simultaneously would mean general war. Thus, the INF closed a gap in deterrence; it "coupled" the defense of Europe with that of the United States and the defense of Germany with the defense of Europe.[11]

Such arguments are, at best, indicative of sloppy thinking and, at worst, outright sophistry. They rest on the dubious assumption that Moscow would react differently to an attack on the Soviet Union by West German–based Pershing IIs than it would to an attack by North Dakota–based Minuteman missiles. In fact, as Assistant Secretary of State Richard Burt admitted in a moment of ill-advised candor, the INFs would increase the risk of a nuclear apocalypse, not lower it. "The Soviet Union," he said, "would most likely respond to an attack on its homeland by U.S. systems in Europe with an attack on the United States. Thus, the emplacement of long-range U.S. cruise and ballistic missiles in Europe makes escalation of any nuclear war to involve an intercontinental exchange more likely, not less."[12]

For nearly a decade, a growing number of U.S. foreign policy experts have suggested that extended deterrence is no longer a viable strategy because it would be catastrophic for the United States to honor its nuclear pledge to Western Europe. As Henry Kissinger (presumably the same Henry Kissinger quoted above) said in Brussels in September 1979, "Don't you Europeans keep asking us to multiply assurances we cannot possibly mean and that if we do mean we should not want to execute, and which if we do execute would destroy our civilization?"[13] Former defense secretary Robert S. McNamara has written that he advised presidents John F. Kennedy and Lyndon B. Johnson that they should not under any circumstances initiate the use of nuclear weapons.[14] The problem with NATO strategy was succinctly stated by McNamara and three colleagues: "Deterrence can[not] safely be based forever on a doctrine that looks like either a bluff or a suicide pact."[15] It seems apparent that concern about extended deterrence has now reached official Washington. Collectively, President Ronald Reagan's

Reykjavik offer to scrap all ballistic missiles, the double-zero INF treaty, and the SDI are an implicit acknowledgment that U.S. leaders are deeply troubled about the implications of extended deterrence for U.S. safety.

The INF treaty and the events leading up to it have sparked a debate about NATO strategy. Because, as former defense secretary James Schlesinger recently wrote, U.S. nuclear weapons are the "glue" that holds NATO together, this debate will affect the Alliance's cohesion.[16] But NATO's erosion should not come as a surprise. Coral Bell noted nearly a quarter of a century ago:

> The root cause of the decline in the cohesiveness of NATO is not to be looked for in the quarrels of its members among themselves, but in the fact that, as the invulnerability of America is reduced, the real *raison d'etre* of the alliance, its convincingness as a deterrent to attack becomes less.[17]

Implications of the Weakening of Extended Deterrence

The weakening of extended deterrence has profound implications for West Germany and for relations between Bonn and Washington. Geography and political constraints on military strategy make the FRG nearly indefensible militarily. West Germany is NATO's most militarily exposed and important European member; because it lacks its own nuclear weapons, it must rely on the United States to protect it against the Soviet Union's superior conventional forces.

At the same time, however, Bonn's relations with the Western Alliance have always been ambivalent because of West Germany's commitment to Ostpolitik and Deutschlandpolitik—its outreach to East Germany and Eastern Europe. West Germany cannot be indifferent to the fate of the 17 million Germans in the German Democratic Republic. Reunification may be a distant goal, but by chipping away at the barriers separating Germans on one side of the wall from those on the other, Bonn helps to ameliorate East Germans' living conditions while simultaneously perpetuating a shared national consciousness. The fulfillment of Bonn's short- and long-term interests depends critically on the prevailing climate of superpower relations. Bonn's overriding commitment is to relax political tensions in Europe and avoid any moves that could heighten the East-West confrontation. In recent years under both former Social Democratic chancellor Helmut Schmidt and Christian Democratic chancellor Helmut Kohl, Bonn has made clear that it will not subordinate Ostpolitik/Deutschlandpolitik to the requirements of Alliance cohesion.

Bonn is vulnerable to Soviet carrot-and-stick policies that link progress in intra-German relations to West German political, security, and economic concessions. Moreover, Bonn's decreasing confidence in the strategic reliability of the United States is a strong incentive to seek a political accommodation with Moscow that will resolve its security dilemma and preserve its interests in closer links with the other Germany.

In a classic illustration of the historical maxim that political actions often have unintended consequences, NATO's decision to deploy the INFs exposed the deep fissures in U.S.-West German relations and catapulted the German question—the eventual unification of East and West Germany—back onto the East-West political agenda.[18] The INFs were supposed to recouple the United States to West Germany by serving as a visible symbol of Washington's determination to honor its nuclear pledge to Bonn. But rather than reaffirming the basic identity of their interests, the deployments and their aftermath dramatized the politico-military differences that separate the United States and West Germany.

On the West German left, the INFs raised fears that the United States might actually use nuclear weapons in Europe's defense and that the Pershing IIs would enable the United States to fight a limited war confined to East and West German soil. (American officials found this reaction to the INFs ironic and aggravating; after all, the missiles' ability to reach the Soviet Union ensured that a European war would involve the United States at the outset and thus could not be waged as a regional conflict confined to the Continent.) The left feared also that the superpower rivalry in the Third World could drag Europe into a nuclear war. Because extended deterrence placed responsibility for Germany's security in U.S. hands, the INF deployments fanned a widespread feeling that Germans were caught in the middle of a conflict that affected their fate but over which they exercised no control. Moreover, the German question became linked to antinuclear sentiment. Left-wing opposition to the INFs rested on a revival of German national consciousness; the "peace" movement's relative success was attributable to its ability to portray itself as a nationalist, not a pacifist, phenomenon. The West German left believed the INF deployments increased superpower tensions at Germany's expense. Germany's division was seen as both a cause and a consequence of the East-West confrontation in Europe. According to the West German left, if political tensions in Europe were reduced, the two blocs would dissolve, and the impediments to German unity would disappear. As an essay in a leading peace movement tract, *German Unity Is Sure to Come*, stated: "If the German peace movement wants success, it must take as its starting point the golden rule that the division of Germany plays a significant role in the growing military confrontation in Europe."[19]

Like the noble duke of York (who marched his men to the top of the hill and then marched them down again), NATO, having expended much of its reserve political capital to deploy the INFs, has now reversed course and reluctantly embraced Washington's decision to remove them (along with short-range U.S. missiles) as part of the double-zero arms pact. What their deployment did for the German question on the West German left, their departure has done for it on the West German right. On the right, the overriding fear is that Washington will not use nuclear weapons in West Germany's defense. Correctly concluding that the INF treaty is a tacit admission that Washington is having second thoughts about the wisdom of its nuclear link to Europe, conservative members of the Christian Democratic Party have reacted with bitterness. Alfred Dregger, the party's Bundestag floor leader, has accused the United States of "betraying" German interests and "abandoning" the Federal Republic. In a position paper, Dregger's colleague, Bernhard Friedmann, argued that because the United States inevitably is going to withdraw from Europe in the near future, Bonn should seek Soviet support for a united, neutral German state.[20] Reviewing the twists and turns of the INF affair, the *Economist* recently noted: "Last time round, the missile row fed the familiar anti-Americanism of the left. The danger this time is that it will create a new anti-Americanism on the right, which could make a fearful mixture when stirred up with the left-wing sort."[21]

Although the INF episode has been proclaimed by some as a victory for the Western Alliance, another such victory will undo NATO completely. In fact, the deployment decision has been a political disaster that shattered the postwar security consensus in Germany (and perhaps in the United States too). Within the SPD, Helmut Schmidt's Atlanticist followers have been driven to cover. The party's likely future chancellor candidate, Saarland premier Oskar Lafontaine, has stated that the Federal Republic should withdraw from NATO's integrated command, and Andreas von Bulow, another key SPD official, in 1985 circulated a paper calling for the withdrawal of U.S. troops from West Germany coupled with Bonn's shift to a neutralist foreign policy. The SPD has called for a security partnership between Western Europe and the Warsaw Pact and endorses a nuclear-free zone in Central Europe.[22]

The SPD's neutralist drift reflects changing public attitudes. National War College professor Stephen F. Szabo has observed that West Germans under forty are "more distant from America and more skeptical of American intentions and policies" and "will remain independent in [their] foreign policy orientation and more distant from both superpowers."[23] They are less committed to NATO and favor the dissolution of the superpower blocs in Europe. At the same time, public opinion polls continue to show—as they have throughout the postwar period—that the vast majority of West Germans want the two Germanies united in a single neutral state.

Some observers profess to see these survey results as insignificant because the neutrality-for-reunification option is only hypothetical. Nevertheless, this option is theoretical only because Moscow has not yet offered Bonn a realistic choice. Whether the Soviets will make such an offer remains conjectural, but they certainly are well positioned to take advantage of the nascent left-right coalition favoring West German national neutralism. Because of the tension between Bonn's interests in the East and its allegiance to the West, the Kremlin knows it has a German card, and it is again hinting that it might play it.

Gorbachev probably is not serious about playing the German card—now. But as recent events demonstrate, it is a useful and potent weapon in Moscow's diplomatic arsenal. Regardless of whether the Kremlin elects to play the card, its very existence is a double source of instability. By flashing the German card without playing it, the Kremlin pulls Bonn eastward and causes West Germany to slide into a de facto neutrality, notwithstanding its NATO membership, thereby sharpening the strains between the United States and West Germany. And if the Soviets decide in the future that the time is ripe for embarking on the reunification gambit, they could bring about NATO's sudden collapse. Notwithstanding the virtually unchallenged official Washington conventional wisdom (which holds the Soviets will never allow German reunification on any terms), it is never wise to base one's strategy on the assumption that one's adversary is not smart enough to make an obvious winning move. This is doubly true when the opponent is a nation famous for producing chess grandmasters and is led by a man who already has dazzled the diplomatic world with his intellectual suppleness, innovativeness, and flair for the unexpected.

Moscow's dangling of the German card must be seen in the broader context of its Westpolitik, which has skillfully targeted the Western Alliance's weak points. Hardly a month passes without some superficially attractive arms control proposal emanating from Moscow, or an appeal to the West Europeans to assert their own interests independently of Washington, or even hints that both superpowers should "weigh anchor" and leave Europe. Unbelievably, the Soviet Union—which believes it has a deep stake in preserving the postwar status quo—has been able to present itself as a force for peace and constructive change while simultaneously successfully depicting Washington—which has no interest in preserving the Yalta system intact—as the chief obstacle to the stabilization of East-West relations in Europe. Throughout Western Europe and especially in West Germany, the United States is on the defensive. As an article in *Die Welt* recently observed, there are obvious dangers in this state of affairs:

> Both the German domestic debate and the Euro-American debate show how
> the Russians can make military, political and psychological gains by

disarmament proposals involving partial U.S. withdrawals from Europe. What is lacking is the grand design, the offer that can't be refused.

If Mr. Gorbachev establishes a link of any substance between military disengagement and political solutions for continental Europe—a link the Americans at present fail to establish—progress . . . might be made.

It certainly would be in Germany. . . . It alone could be enough to make the national debate in Germany come to a head over the country's elected representatives.[24]

Indeed, even without actually offering reunification, Moscow could shake NATO to its core. What would happen, for example, if Gorbachev offered to take down the Berlin Wall in exchange for Bonn's agreement to a Central European nuclear-free zone and/or the withdrawal of all foreign troops from the two Germanies? The summer 1988 rumors of a unilateral Soviet troop withdrawal from Hungary demonstrated that the possibility of dramatic gestures by Gorbachev cannot be discounted.

Regaining the Initiative

The United States is in danger of losing a game it should win and cannot afford to lose. Its predicament is due less to the Soviets' deftness than it is to its own lack of imagination and flexibility, resulting from Washington's reflexive attachment to the crumbling structures of the postwar system. Instead of waiting to see what Gorbachev will do next, the United States should preempt Moscow and regain the political and psychological initiative by linking superpower military disengagement with a political solution to Europe's division. It should propose the following package: (1) an interim solution to the German question—short of reunification—that guarantees unhampered travel between the two Germanies; (2) removal of both superpowers' military forces and nuclear weapons from Central Europe (the two Germanies, Poland, Czechoslovakia, and Hungary); (3) asymmetrical demobilization of the superpowers' conventional forces withdrawn from Central Europe; and (4) a pledge that neither Washington nor Moscow will be the first to reintroduce its forces into Central Europe.

The immediate objectives of this plan are to negate Moscow's German card, put the United States on the right side of West German (and Western European) opinion, and pressure the Soviets in Eastern Europe. Such a proposal recognizes the obvious: because the credibility of extended deterrence cannot be restored, NATO's cohesion is fatally compromised. Thus it is necessary to seek a political solution to West Germany's security dilemma. Disengagement would neutralize Moscow's conventional superiority after the U.S. nuclear umbrella is lifted because it would put the Soviet army back where it belongs—in the Soviet Union. (Disengagement would also have the salutary effect of bringing the U.S. Army back home where it belongs and allowing the United States to reduce its ground forces to a size commensurate with its status as a maritime, not a continental, power.)

By championing a settlement based on ameliorating the German question and superpower disengagement, the United States will put the Soviet Union on the defensive. Such an initiative will have widespread popular appeal in Germany, unlike current U.S. policies, which have resonance only among a narrow (and shrinking) spectrum of politically conservative West Germans. Moreover, Western Europe is far better placed than Eastern Europe to adjust to disengagement. When the United States departs Europe, it will leave behind a group of democratic, socially cohesive, economically dynamic countries. And disengagement is the logical culmination of U.S. postwar policy. As Kennan wrote in 1958, the purpose of cultivating the Western Alliance's strength was to put the West in a position to negotiate an end to Europe's partition. Having helped to rebuild Europe with the Marshall Plan, the United States now should seek to reunify the Continent.[25]

A post-Yalta package will enable the United States to take advantage of the Eastern bloc's fault lines. When the Soviets retire from Eastern Europe, they will leave behind economically stagnant, socially fragmented states with governments of dubious popular legitimacy. Because of the potential spillover effects of the simmering discontent inside the Eastern bloc, both superpowers have a stake in finding a way to reconcile Soviet security concerns with Eastern Europe's desire for internal reforms and political autonomy. In November 1987, Gorbachev himself acknowledged Moscow's problems in holding the Warsaw Pact together when he conceded that the Kremlin is being compelled to accept (within limits) the deepening pluralist trends in Eastern Europe. "We have satisfied ourselves," Gorbachev said, "that unity does not mean identity and uniformity."[26] The goal of disengagement, therefore, would not be to induce states to leave Moscow's security orbit but rather to persuade the Soviets to accept Eastern Europe's Finlandization. Disengagement is one way to test the sincerity of Moscow's new thinking and its commitment to glasnost.

No one can say for certain whether Moscow will talk seriously about a post-Yalta settlement, but there are strong objective reasons for the Kremlin to deal along these lines. Disengagement would allow Moscow to make the substantial reductions in defense spending that are necessary if economic modernization is to succeed. Many experts, including analysts in Eastern Europe, believe Gorbachev's overriding foreign policy goal at the moment is to lessen the arms burden on the Soviet Union.[27]

There is another strong reason for the Soviets to be interested in disengagement as a solution. When the United States leaves Europe or substantially reduces its European presence (as it inevitably must), the

Atlantic Alliance will most probably be replaced by a European defense community based on Franco-German collaboration. Indeed, since the beginning of the 1980s, Bonn and Paris have drawn perceptibly closer as both have recognized the ultimate certainty of U.S. withdrawal. (The French have also been motivated by a desire to stem Bonn's eastward drift in search of reunification.) However, as French statesmen such as former president Valery Giscard D'Estaing and premier Jacques Chirac have acknowledged, in a post-Alliance world, a viable Franco-German military axis would necessitate some type of nuclear role for West Germany.[28] For many Europeans, especially for the Soviets, this is an unsettling prospect. A July 22, 1987, *Izvestia* commentary by Soviet foreign policy analyst Yuri Kovalenko underscored Moscow's deep misgivings about the political, military, and nuclear implications of Franco-German strategic cooperation. Moscow's fear of a nuclear Germany should be a strong incentive for it to agree to a post-Yalta arrangement. The fewer troops the Soviets have and the farther away from Germany they are, the less need there will be—if any—for the Germans to have nuclear weapons. And unless it agrees to disengage, Moscow will face another problem as well. With the United States out of Europe, a more cohesive Western Europe would exert a strong pull on the Eastern bloc countries and make it more difficult for the Kremlin to maintain the Warsaw Pact's solidarity.

From the Soviet viewpoint, a neutral reunified Germany should be a more attractive prospect than a purposeful Western Europe led by a Franco-German condominium. Moreover, in a post-Yalta system, Eastern Europe's newly pluralistic states would still look to Moscow for insurance against a resurgence of German revanchism. This would be a cheaper and less risky way for the Kremlin to protect its regional strategic interests than its current policy of keeping Eastern Europe in line through coercion. Finally, the Kremlin could reap the full benefits of Soviet-German economic cooperation and thus give a much-needed boost to its own modernization efforts.

Gorbachev's "new thinking" may be nothing more than propaganda. On the other hand, generational change in the Kremlin may offer opportunities for diplomatic movement that have not existed since the early 1950s. Either way, the time has come to put the Soviet Union's intentions and sincerity to the test and force Moscow to fish or cut bait.

Regardless of Moscow's reaction, however, the United States has its own good reasons to press for disengagement, and Washington should not allow Moscow to define the international diplomatic agenda. By advocating disengagement, the United States would deny Moscow the political leverage it gains from U.S.–West European differences on arms control and nuclear strategy, a leverage that may not produce short-run breakthroughs (vide the INF deployments) but does have a cumulative long-term corrosive effect. In contrast to arms control, which deals with the symptoms, not the causes, of the superpower rivalry, disengagement offers the real prospect of reducing the political tensions that could lead to war. Far more than any foreseeably attainable nuclear arms accord, disengagement would radically reduce the chances of nuclear war in Europe, and it would resolve the conventional imbalance there. Unlike the conventional arms control proposals now being mooted, disengagement would not get bogged down in discussions about proper units of account, definitions of "offensive" versus "defensive" weapons, and the problem of reducing forces that are asymmetrical both quantitatively and qualitatively. By advocating a post-Yalta package, Washington would stop Gorbachev's present diplomatic momentum and regain the confidence of European public opinion. Unlike the technical minutae of arms control, the pristine simplicity of disengagement could easily be grasped by European publics, strengthening the U.S. position politically and morally. If the Soviets stubbornly cling to their East European position while the United States is declaring its willingness to withdraw from Western Europe, reasonable people will have no doubt as to which superpower has embraced Europe's aspirations and which is blocking them.

The obvious objection to disengagement is that geographical asymmetry would give the Soviets a major edge over the United States if they broke the agreement and moved back into Europe. This argument is superficially plausible, but the search for militarily flawless arrangements is always the enemy of diplomacy. On the other hand, disengagement would be much easier to verify than an arms control agreement and more costly politically to violate. The Soviets would know that provocative actions on their part could spur vigorous West European rearmament efforts and cause West Europeans to cut off trade, technology transfers, and credits to the Soviet Union and Eastern Europe. It is thought that this is one of the main reasons that Moscow refrained from invading Poland in 1980–1981.

The Soviets would have strong incentives to behave reasonably in Europe during and after U.S. withdrawal. By explicitly linking its own defense, arms control, and Third World policies to Soviet conduct in Europe, Washington can reinforce those incentives. Moscow's behavior in post-Alliance Europe would become the litmus test of the Soviet-U.S. relationship.

Washington should use the arms control process as a lever to induce the Soviets to agree to mutual superpower disengagement from Central Europe. The United States should not throw away this leverage by rushing headlong into a strategic arms control agreement with the Soviet Union. Although it is not widely understood, strategic nuclear force reductions (START) and SDI are intimately linked to European security because the force posture needed to extend deterrence to protect Europe is far different from that needed to deter a direct attack on the United States itself. Direct deterrence is easy as long as the U.S. maintains secure second-strike retaliatory forces capable of inflicting unacceptable damage on the Soviet Union even after absorbing a Soviet first strike. SDI is not critical to the credibility of direct deterrence.

Extended deterrence is a far more complex proposition, however, because it requires that Washington be prepared to initiate nuclear warfare across the spectrum of conflict. That is, in a war, the United States must be the first to use strategic as well as tactical nuclear weapons. A credible extended deterrence strategy requires that it have counterforce–first strike weapons (like the MX and Trident D-5) and an effective strategic defense system. In the event of war in Europe, U.S. strategic forces would be used in a counterforce role; by their destroying Soviet missiles in their silos, Moscow's ability to hit back would be seriously reduced. The strategic defense of the United States would be effective against the Soviet Union's weakened retaliatory forces, and U.S. population centers would thus be largely protected. Extended deterrence would be undermined by deep cuts in strategic nuclear forces and restrictions on SDI.

By the same token it is clear that if the United States did not have to extend deterrence to cover Western Europe, its strategic requirements would be much different, and it could be much more forthcoming on strategic force reductions and restrictions on SDI. Washington could make such concessions, however, only if Moscow agreed to measures that strengthened Western Europe's security. That is why there is an obvious linkage between deep cuts in strategic nuclear forces and SDI limitations, on the one hand, and disengagement, on the other. U.S. negotiators should make this linkage explicit and insist on a package deal.

Why would the Soviets strike such a bargain at a time when they have justifiable reasons to think a unilateral U.S. pullout from Europe is on the horizon? After all, if they wait, the Soviets can hope to see NATO dissolve without any political concessions on their part. There is, however, an important reason that it would still be in the Kremlin's interest to reach an agreement with Washington.

Even if the United States should, in the next ten to fifteen years, sever its formal military ties to NATO and withdraw from Western Europe, it still would retain a strong interest in European security matters. If it maintained the strategic nuclear force configuration appropriate to an extended deterrent strategy and deployed SDI, Western Europe still would benefit from the residual deterrent effect of U.S. power. Deterrence can be effective even without the explicit understandings and visible symbols of a formal alliance. This was demonstrated in the late 1960s when Washington used its deterrent threat to dissuade Moscow from launching a preemptive war against China, a nation with which the United States at that time did not even have official diplomatic relations.

For the United States, however, there would be a critical difference between residual deterrence in a post-Alliance world and NATO's present strategy of "suicidal" extended deterrence. Today the United States does not control its own fate. At West European insistence, the Alliance's strategy and force structures have been designed to ensure that the United States is locked in to using nuclear weapons in Western Europe's defense in a virtually automatic fashion. Under residual deterrence, however, the United States would retain responsibility for the decision to use nuclear weapons. U.S. nuclear forces would not be tightly and indissolubly coupled to any other nation's defense and—after deliberately balancing the U.S. interests at stake against the risk of nuclear intervention—Washington would have the freedom to choose whether, when, and in what manner its nuclear forces would be employed.

There are risks in raising the post-Yalta issues related to mutual superpower disengagement, but there is even a greater risk in pretending that history ended in 1945 and attempting to preserve the postwar order that now is visibly collapsing. Neither the United States nor Europe has an interest in maintaining the status quo. As long as Soviet and U.S. forces confront each other along the Elbe, divided Germany remains the most dangerous theater of the superpower rivalry (and the United States must bear the nuclear risks and economic costs of its NATO commitment). As long as this superpower standoff continues, Europe will remain partitioned, and the hopes of the increasingly restive East Europeans for political and economic freedom and Europe's restoration as a single cultural entity will be foreclosed.

A New Negotiating Strategy

As the postwar era draws to a close, U.S. foreign policy will confront both danger and opportunity. Washington's ability to deal realistically with the Soviet Union will determine whether the United States will be able to manage successfully the transition to a post-Alliance world. It is vital that Americans break free of their paradoxical tendency to see the Soviet Union (in Walter Lippmann's words) "as both a cadaver and a worldwide menace."

This viewpoint, which portrays a malevolent Soviet Union determined to break the power of the United States and simultaneously so internally unstable as to be on the verge of possible collapse, distorts U.S. policy by making its primary goal the alteration of the Soviet Union's domestic political system. Although this view is normally associated with the neoconservative right, it is shared by many Democrats as well. Senator Bill Bradley (D–New Jersey) has said:

> A society governed by a centralized, one-party state that insists on dictatorial control is inherently unstable. History teaches that instability and great

military power are a dangerous combination. That is why Soviet power has been such a problem for the rest of the world.[29]

Bradley has proposed that any Western economic assistance for Gorbachev's reform efforts be tied to domestic reform of the Soviet Union.

The Reagan administration's Soviet policy also is a prisoner of the cadaver-menace paradox. Reagan has stated his belief that the Soviet regime will collapse from its own weaknesses and end up on the "ash heap of history." Yet in his 1986 State of the Union address, he spoke darkly of the "Soviet drive for domination" of the world. At the same time, the administration's neoconservative backers, who believe that the United States cannot be secure until Soviet communism is eliminated, have resuscitated the chimerical hope that the Soviet regime is so fragile that the sustained application of U.S. political, military, and economic power will trigger its collapse.

"Reform" of the Soviet system—its displacement by a new, presumably less threatening form of government—is what neoconservatives want, and like former Reagan adviser Richard Pipes, they believe it will come about "only under duress caused either by humiliations abroad or upheavals at home." To cause the latter, they advocate denying Moscow trade, credits, and technology access—and using the U.S. defense buildup—in an attempt to drive the Kremlin to the brink of economic collapse. To bring about the former, neoconservatives have formulated the Reagan Doctrine, which holds, as Irving Kristol has said, that the United States can undermine the Kremlin's domestic legitimacy and bring about the "internal transformation" of the Soviet regime by inflicting a series of "small defeats" on the Soviets in the Third World.[30]

It should be obvious by now that, after seventy years of trying, the United States lacks the leverage to compel a transformation of the Soviet system. Moscow may make tactical concessions when it suits its purposes to do so, but it never will make fundamental concessions that would jeopardize the Communist party's political authority. American liberals and conservatives alike badly overestimate Soviet weaknesses. Although, for example, the Soviets confront a deepening economic crisis, they do not face impending economic collapse. Similarly, the Soviet Union is far more stable politically than is often assumed. The Kremlin has managed multiple leadership successions over seven decades and can count on the support of the vast majority of the Soviet people. Whatever the difficulties of the Soviet state, its ability to survive for the foreseeable future is not in doubt.

The liberals' approach to inducing change in the Soviet Union is ineffectual. Even if domestic considerations did not get in the way, the United States does not have enough carrots to tempt Moscow into major concessions on its internal policies. And, at best, the neoconservatives' Soviet policy of beating Moscow with sticks is futile. The Kremlin will do whatever is necessary to keep pace militarily with the United States. If the United States will not provide the Soviets with credits and technology, Western Europe and Japan will. And, finally, no series of setbacks in the Third World will lead to a Soviet collapse. Small defeats affecting peripheral interests do not cause the demise of great powers.

At worst, the neoconservatives' policy is fraught with risk. Inflicting a big defeat on the Kremlin—in Eastern Europe, for example—might shake its domestic legitimacy, but it also would likely provoke a direct confrontation that could be disastrous for both superpowers. And even if the United States could somehow push the Soviet Union to the edge of political and/or economic collapse, it would be foolhardy to do so. Like a similarly desperate Austria-Hungary in 1914, the normally cautious Kremlin might be impelled to undertake reckless acts in the belief it had nothing to lose.

Instead of trying to change the Soviet Union's internal behavior, U.S. policy should attempt to identify common areas of interest where both superpowers could benefit from diplomatic agreements. That Washington and Moscow have some overlapping interests does not mean (as some today believe) that the cold war is over. Conflict and cooperation are not mutually exclusive. Because they are part of a continuum of political behavior, the superpower competition will continue, although the severity of the tensions thereby engendered can be alleviated. By the same token, it is foolish to argue that because the United States and the Soviet Union are rivals, negotiation is impossible. Walter Lippmann wrote, "The history of diplomacy is the history of relations among rival powers, which did not enjoy political intimacy. . . . Nevertheless there have been political settlements. . . . For a diplomat to think that rival and unfriendly powers cannot be brought to a settlement is to forget what diplomacy is all about."[31]

The Soviet Union has never been as strong as we have feared or as weak as we have hoped. But both our hopes and our fears have caused us to defer serious negotiations with Moscow that could ameliorate the underlying political causes of the superpower rivalry. Negotiations have always been put on hold until the United States attains a position of strength. That goal—and the negotiations that would follow—remains elusive because, no matter how strong the United States is, it always believes it is not strong enough. Today, however, the United States is in a position of strength relative to the Soviet Union. It is time to test the waters and see if the Gorbachev era offers new diplomatic opportunities in Soviet-U.S. relations. Europe is the place to begin.

Notes

1. John Lewis Gaddis, *The Long Peace* (New York: Oxford University Press, 1987), p. 216.

2. On the U.S. role in this respect, see Josef Joffe, "Europe's American Pacifier," *Foreign Policy* (Spring 1984).

3. See, for example, A.W. DePorte, *Europe between the Superpowers: The Enduring Balance* (New Haven: Yale University Press, 1979), p. 180.

4. William G. Hyland, "The United States and the USSR: Rebuilding Relations," in Arnold L. Horelick, ed., *U.S.-Soviet Relations: The Next Phase*, (Ithaca, N.Y.: Cornell University Press, 1986).

5. See Lawrence Freedman, "NATO Myths," *Foreign Policy* (Winter 1981–1982).

6. Egon Bahr, "Peace: A State of Emergency," in Rudolf Steinke and Michael Vale, eds., *Germany Debates Defense: The NATO Alliance at the Crossroads* (Armonk, N.Y.: M.E. Sharpe, 1983), p. 146.

7. Karl Kaiser, Georg Leber, Alois Mertes, and Franz Joseph Schulze, "A German Response to NATO First Use," *Foreign Affairs* (Summer 1982).

8. Paul Bracken, *The Command and Control of Nuclear Forces* (New Haven: Yale University Press, 1984), pp. 163–64.

9. Ibid.

10. See ibid., chap. 5.

11. Henry A. Kissinger, "Missiles: A Zero Option Is No Choice," *Los Angeles Times*, April 5, 1987.

12. Michael R. Gordon, "Pushing the Pershing," *National Journal*, August 20, 1983, p. 1745.

13. Paul Lewis, "U.S. Pledge to NATO to Use Nuclear Arms Criticized by Kissinger," *New York Times*, September 2, 1979, p. A7.

14. Robert S. McNamara, "The Military Role of Nuclear Weapons," *Foreign Affairs* (Fall 1983): 79.

15. Hedrick Smith, "Four Former Officials Urge West to Drop First Strike Plan," *New York Times*, April 8, 1982, p. 1.

16. James Schlesinger, "Reykjavik and Revelations: A Turn of the Tide?" *Foreign Affairs: America and the World 1986*, p. 430.

17. Coral Bell, *Negotiation from Strength* (New York: Alfred A. Knopf, 1963), p. 192.

18. For an extended analysis of the link between the INF deployments and the revival of German nationalism, see Christopher Layne, "Toward German Reunification?" *Journal of Contemporary Studies* (Fall 1984).

19. John Vinocur, "Rally in Bonn during Reagan's Visit Focal Point of Antinuclear Campaign," *New York Times*, June 3, 1982, p. 8.

20. James M. Markham, "Angst in Bonn: Debate over the Missiles," *New York Times*, February 10, 1988, p. 8.

21. "Achtung Angst!" *Economist*, May 23, 1987, p. 11.

22. On the SPD's current views on security issues and East-West relations, see Horst Ehmke, "A Second Phase of Detente," *World Policy* (Summary 1987), and Oskar Lafontaine, "European Security Policy" (Washington, D.C.: Friedrich Ebert Stiftung, 1987).

23. Stephen F. Szabo, ed., *The Successor Generation: International Perspectives of Postwar Europeans* (London: Butterworth, 1983), p. 71.

24. Herbert Kremp, "Soviet Proposal on German Reunification Fires Imaginations and Illusions," *Die Welt*, May 15, 1987 (reprinted in *German Tribune*, May 31, 1987, p. 3).

25. George F. Kennan, "A Chance to Withdraw Our Troops in Europe," *Harper's* (February 1958).

26. Philip Taubman, "Soviet Won't Push Policy on Allies, Gorbachev Says," *New York Times*, November 5, 1987, p. 1.

27. Henry Kamm, "Yeltsin's Fall Reminds a Hungarian of the Past," *New York Times*, November 18, 1987, p. 8.

28. "Plea for German Role in Nuclear Defence," *Manchester Guardian* (*Le Monde* English section), October 30, 1983, p. 11; Dick Parker, "Giscard: Soviets Won't Allow West German Nukes," *Atlanta Journal*, December 11, 1984, p. 29.

29. A.M. Rosenthal, "The Bradley Doctrine," *New York Times*, October 27, 1987, p. A37.

30. Robert Pear, "Push the Russians, Intellectuals Say," *New York Times*, November 25, 1985, p. 9.

31. Quoted in Ronald Steel, *Walter Lippmann and the American Century* (Boston: Little, Brown, 1980), p. 445.

II
U.S. Security Ties in the Pacific Basin

5

U.S.-Japan Security Relations after Nakasone: The Case for a Strategic Fairness Doctrine

Edward A. Olsen

Security relations between the United States and Japan were shielded from deserved criticism during the Nakasone-Reagan years. For much of the Reagan era, U.S.-Japan ties have been buffered by the upbeat atmospherics of the "Ron-Yasu" relationship. That positive public relations facade was worn thin by abrasive tensions arising from Japan's tremendous advantage over the United States in bilateral trade, but the buffer proved more durable in security affairs. By the end of Nakasone Yasuhiro's years (1982–1987) as prime minister, most Americans heaped praise on him for his efforts in reducing trade frictions and his accomplishments in resolving many defense frictions. While Nakasone clearly deserves some kudos on trade issues, the level of praise accorded him on defense issues is excessive. He neither tried to do, nor achieved, as much as he is given credit for on the security front.[1] Nakasone was, however, excellent at public relations. He was an outstanding front man for Japan.

Former prime minister Tanaka Kakuei is reported to have denigrated Nakasone as "a first class geisha for entertaining foreigners."[2] That put-down of what Tanaka saw as his surrogate prime minister from the hybrid "Tanakasone" faction of the ruling Liberal Democratic party obviously did a disservice to Nakasone because he was much more than a political geisha. Nakasone had some sound ideas, and he was a charismatic leader who enjoyed remarkable popular support. Moreover, as Tanaka's health ebbed, Nakasone long ago stopped being merely his surrogate and became a boss in his own right. Nonetheless, the geisha metaphor is an apt one because Nakasone was most skilled at presenting to foreigners a pleasant veneer: saying what they wanted to hear, gesturing in a stereotyped manner, whispering sweet nothings in their ears, and seeming to offer something that cannot actually be provided because that service is not within the purview of the political geisha. Conversely, the ill-informed foreigner expects to receive services from the geisha that are never forthcoming yet walks away from the encounter feeling vaguely satisfied at having been pampered and sweet-talked. Those are precisely the interactions Nakasone deftly performed for Japan as prime minister. U.S. officials often were satisfied customers. The problem today is that Nakasone's successor is a terrible geisha, lacking the necessary talents and incapable of going through the motions believably.

Three men were in the running to succeed Nakasone: Takeshita Noboru, Miyazawa Kiichi, and Abe Shintaro. Although Takeshita emerged victorious, in the larger sense it did not matter who replaced Nakasone because none of them could have fulfilled his geisha role. With Nakasone out of office, Japan is again represented by a more orthodox, and lackluster, prime minister. As the others take their turns as prime minister, we can expect still more of the same. None is as capable of selling a flawed policy product to the United States. The Nakasone-Takeshita shift, and the bland lineup of probable successors, has tremendous implications for U.S.-Japan relations.

Tokyo is no longer represented by a Japanese version of a conservative great communicator. Unlike Nakasone, neither Takeshita nor those waiting in the wings subscribe to a personal vision of U.S.-Japan cooperation in security and economic affairs that approximates prevailing U.S. perceptions of such cooperation. Consequently the public relations buffer has been sharply reduced. Japan's actual policies on trade and defense, which did not change greatly for the better under Nakasone, are not likely to change rapidly for the better or worse under his successor(s) either. Those policies have their own momentum, driven by Tokyo's ability to balance Japan's domestic priorities against U.S. pressures for change in Japanese policies. They are also effectively established and guided by the Japanese bureaucracy. However, the ways in which those policies are presented by Japan to the United States are likely to suffer in the hands of more pedestrian prime ministers. Consequently overinflated American expectations created during the Ron-Yasu years are due to be deflated severely by the new political era in Japan. U.S. reactions to less adept presentations of Japan's positions are likely to be characterized by feelings of being let down. Although that feeling of disappointment is mainly perceptual, because little will actually change in a Japanese government run by cautious bureaucrats, that will not make disillusioned U.S. reactions any less serious.

In the largest sense, U.S. officials have, with the help of well-meaning people in Japan and the United States, set themselves up for this relapse. Instead of being candid about how little was being done by Tokyo to improve Japan's trade and security policy during the Nakasone years, they chose to accept exaggerated Japanese claims and rest their hopes on Nakasone's pleasing rhetoric. Now that his leadership and rhetoric are gone, they must face more typical prime ministers whose explanations of what Japan is doing, and plans to do, fall flatter than Nakasone's. The era of artificial good feelings is over. The United States now has to confront the real Japan that has been obscured by Nakasone's happy talk for years. Japan still is a reluctantly cooperative trade partner and an ally that refuses to engage in truly collective security.

Notwithstanding the reassuring (and generally accurate) statements of President Reagan, Ambassador Mike Mansfield, and other senior U.S. officials about the importance of U.S.-Japan relations, the United States's frustrations with Japan's self-centered trade and security attitudes have not been resolved by the de facto moratorium of the Ron-Yasu era. There is no comparable political bond to take its place. Equally important, the value of such public relations gestures has declined dramatically. We are unlikely to see anything similar evolve between subsequent leaders of U.S. and Japanese administrations. Now that the moratorium is over, U.S. and Japanese frustrations shall be more evident. The reemergence of these frustrations was facilitated by heightened attention in 1987–1988 to Japan's trade and defense policies, which was caused by a persistent U.S. trade deficit, highly damaging publicity surrounding Toshiba's involvement in COCOM-violating sales to the Soviet Union, and Japan's odd-man-out position among Western allies cooperating in the Persian Gulf. The trade frictions so evident in 1987–1988 became entangled in 1988 U.S. presidential politics. Almost all the presidential contenders in the Democratic party and some of them in the Republican party targeted Japan-related trade issues in the early stages of their 1988 primary campaigns. Fortunately for the future of U.S.-Japan ties, those specifically Japan-focused issues did not become important in the campaign; foreign policy issues seldom are. Regardless who becomes the next president, however, the United States will be compelled to address more squarely than it has the Japanese challenges on the trade, technological, financial, and security fronts. They are firmly ensconced on the national agenda.

Many American specialists in Japanese affairs, along with their Japanese counterparts, recoil in horror from that prospect. They do not want Japan-related problems raised in the heat of a political campaign and certainly do not appreciate the juxtaposition of bilateral trade and security issues that has occurred. One cannot overstate their reluctance to see these two areas linked overtly, or by implication, and put on Washington's agenda. It is easy to understand why Japanese hold this position. If I were a Japanese analyst, I would seek to buttress it too, so long as I could be confident that Americans would tolerate its inequities. However, U.S. acquiescence in this arrangement is a serious mistake. While many in the United States focus on the complicated and ambiguous controversies generated by Japan's allegedly unfair trade practices, few Americans understand the patently inequitable U.S.-Japan defense relationship, which subsidizes Japan's economic advantage. There are clear linkages between the two sectors that should be stressed by Washington to obtain the best possible arrangements from Tokyo. Instead of avoiding these linkages, the United States ought to emphasize them as the basis for fairness in both mutual security and trade.

To Washington, Japan is the only Asian country with economic and technological power, and political and military potential, capable of being a regional equal of the United States. Japan could become another superpower; in economic terms it already is. None of that can safely be jeopardized by the United States's making Japan vulnerable to setbacks, intimidation, or co-option by the Soviet Union. However, U.S. interests in preventing those possibilities do not equate with an interest in perpetuating the status quo. It is not necessary for the United States to remain a perennial benefactor of Japan, protecting it from common threats. Japan can, and should, do much more in its own defense.

Japan has the potential to relieve the United States of part of the heavy strategic burdens it has borne in Asia since 1945, partly on Tokyo's behalf. Although temporarily assuaged by Prime Minister Nakasone's forthcoming attitude, increasing numbers of Americans are irritated by Japan's failure to bear its own defense burdens. This is less evident on the mass level, where polls suggest average Americans are unaware of the unequal, one-way-street nature of the not very "mutual" security treaty between the United States and Japan. Popular opinion polls tend to accept the view that the U.S.-Japan alliance is as mutually supportive as NATO. In this light, Japan is often seen as a reliable ally. However, numerous members of Congress, the business elite, and specialists in strategic and Asian affairs are fully aware of the blatantly unequal nature of the U.S.-Japan security relationship. American irritation with Japan's self-centered security policies is most acute at the elite societal level. Were the growing popular animosity now directed at Japan's trade practices to spread to its security ties with the United States, American-Japanese rancor would surely mount.

In *US-Japan Strategic Reciprocity*, I took existing elite concerns about inequities in bilateral security ties further and argued that Japan also should step up its contribution to regional security.[3] It is important that the United States put teeth into its past assertions that U.S.-Japan relations are the cornerstone of regional interdependency, internationalism, and mutual interests. A "golden rule" that should inform U.S.-Japan defense relations, and by which the United States would do no more for Japan than Japan is willing to do for the United States, ought also to become the operative control for overall U.S.-Asian relations, especially in Northeast Asia, a strategically sensitive area.

Too much of what Japan has done defensively was motivated by a desire to appease American desires and deflect U.S. pressures, while not arousing domestic opposition to Tokyo's responses. There is little emphasis on coping militarily with the Soviet Union. That is a poor basis for policymaking, and Americans should not encourage such Japanese behavior. Tokyo should recognize that it is in Japan's interest to provide security reciprocity with the United States because that type of relationship would best ensure Japan's ability to cope with the Soviet Union. It also would be its best guarantee that Americans will not be so frustrated with Japanese economic and strategic selfishness that bilateral relations would be damaged. Ultimately such damage could lead to a rupture in U.S. strategic ties with Japan and laggard NATO countries of the sort advocated by Christopher Layne.[4]

Tokyo and Washington know Japan is not a free rider, but neither does it pay a full fare. I tried to explain that difference to a Japanese audience by coining the expression *chiipu raida* ("cheap rider").[5] Japan's annual defense expenditures are sizable in absolute amounts—about $26 billion in recent years. Tokyo also contributes greatly to the cost of keeping U.S. forces in Japan. Moreover, Japan is a major supplier of invaluable high-technology components in various weapons systems that are essential to the defense of the entire West. No one should discount any of these assets. They pale, however, in comparison to what Japan could—and should—do on its own, and the West's, behalf. Japan's defense contributions remain decidedly minimalist, parsimonious, and inordinately cautious. Japan is indeed getting a cheap ride. It benefits from an international security system predicated on collective security but refuses to pay its fair share of the costs or bear a fair share of the risks.

The U.S.-Japan defense burden-sharing issue is frustrating to many Americans, who consider it virtually insoluble in the short run. On the contrary, the free or cheap rider issue is eminently soluble if both sides treat each other with respect and seek to share burdens by sharing power and decision making. The United States cannot mandate Japan's future strategy any more than Japan can shirk its responsibilities indefinitely. Neither should the United States subsidize a prosperous ally's economy, providing funds for Japan's defense so that Tokyo does not need to spend from its own resources on Japan's defense and can allocate them to economic purposes. These amount to an opportunity cost for Japan, increasing its ability to compete with the United States.

Some critics allege that this is a false comparison because U.S. deficit financing means that no one today actually is paying for U.S. defenses.[6] Although that argument has some apparent logic, it is misleading in the no-free-lunch sense. Clearly future Americans will bear the heaviest burdens if huge budget deficits are not remedied. Present U.S., and allied, security is being mortgaged to the future. Those Americans may look back to the 1980s and understand why they are paying for past U.S. security but will likely question why they should be stuck with the costs of former spendthrift allies who used unspent monies to challenge the United States economically. How might they, in the twenty-first century, feel about having to pay for Japan's twentieth-century security, which allowed the Japanese to take a leading role in global economic affairs that shaped Americans' status in life well before they were born? Contemporary U.S. policy of going further into debt, borrowing from allies to provide for the security of the same allies when they choose not to defend themselves fully or pay for their own defense, is odd, to say the least. If many Americans now doubt the wisdom of these perverse arrangements, one can readily imagine how future generations, who will be saddled with that debt, probably will feel about them.

A compromise that sees Japan doing its fair share for regional security is necessary for smooth relations. There is an urgent need to redress this inequity lest it complicate burgeoning economic frictions that threaten a trade war. These are not discrete issues that can be treated in isolation. When the American people and their representatives in Washington fully grasp the relationships between the U.S.-Japan trade deficit and the strategic subsidy the United States provides for Japan, U.S.-Japan tensions will rise. Both sides of the equation need to be brought into balance. Arm-twisting linkages would be counterproductive. Instead the emphasis should be on developing a common appreciation of the joint interests we all share in keeping each other's economies and defense networks viable. Some may think such an approach naive, but it is likely to be persuasive to the Japanese who appreciate such linkages. Most pointedly, all U.S. allies, including Japan, require the United States to remain capable of reinforcing the security of allies. To do this, the United States must retain a viable economy with a strong and broad defense industrial base within its own borders.

Allies who persist in chipping away at that U.S. base pose a collective challenge to the bedrock of common security interests. The allies that most acutely confront an armed threat, and are extremely sensitive to the ability of the United States to rescue them (South Korea and West Germany), seem to appreciate the U.S. need to maintain a strong defense industrial base. They want such a base for themselves and show some empathy for the United States's need to retain a strong and resilient economy, not unduly controlled by foreign economic interests, for national security reasons.

On the other hand, allies that do not sense a palpable threat, imminent or on the horizon, do not show much sympathy with U.S. desires to maintain a resilient economy capable of being the foundation of greater Western security. Despite a somewhat improved sense of strategic realism in recent years, Japan is the prime example of an unsympathetic ally. It remains essentially unconcerned about the threat of external aggression. Tokyo's threat perceptions are highly abstract and not really in sync with Washington's. Actually, compared to what is widely considered by the Japanese to be a remote possibility of Soviet military aggression against Japan, the Japanese often see the pressures from the United States on trade and burden sharing as a more tangible threat, prompting Tokyo to pursue its "appeasement" policies regarding U.S. pressures without being sufficiently motivated by the

Soviet threat. Consequently Japan is not well disposed to listening to what it considers parochial U.S. security-based arguments for greater fairness in economic and defense relations. To remedy this situation and explain its case to all allies not sufficiently sympathetic to U.S. needs, there is a clear need for a U.S. strategic doctrine that encompasses fairness in trade and defense.

Such prospective burden sharing should not be seen as a panacea automatically rectifying U.S.-Japan trade problems or necessarily saving the United States money for Asian defenses. Japan, militarily weak or strong, will likely remain a competitive economic partner. As a strong ally with a strong economy, Japan can undertake tasks that permit the United States to spend its defense dollars more efficiently. Such a Japanese role, however, might not guarantee overall savings because dollars not expended by the United States in Japan's defense may well be allocated to other defense priorities. It would, however, ensure crucial improvements in the superpower balance in Asia, serving Japanese as well as U.S. interests.

Americans need to understand the nature of Japan's stake in the Pacific, the Indian Ocean, and adjacent countries. Throughout the region, the United States is committed in varying degrees to defend countries whose security benefits Japan as much as the United States, and often more. In neighboring Korea, the United States expends major resources and faces great risks to defend the Republic of Korea against North Korea. Although this is in the United States's interests, too, in certain respects it is overwhelmingly beneficial to Japan. The United States is a de facto surrogate for Japan in Korea, doing what the Japanese do not want to do (and what South Koreans are not ready to accept from Japan) in defense of Japanese security interests on the Korean peninsula. In many ways the Korean demilitarized zone is Japan's front line. In nearby China, the United States, in pursuit of what Washington considers converging U.S. and Japanese interests versus the Soviet Union, has shaped an alignment of U.S.-PRC security interests that benefit the United States and Japan equally. But it is the United States that takes the lead in these matters, not Japan. In Southeast Asia, the United States projects its armed power from Philippine bases for the benefit of regional freedom of the seas. Though this is valuable to the United States and all its friends and allies in the area that rely extensively on the oceans for trade, the country benefiting the most is, again, Japan. Going east or west in the Pacific, the United States bears the brunt of the responsibility for protecting freedom of the seas near the Panama Canal and in the Persian Gulf, two more areas strategically crucial to Japan's economic security.

In all of these cases and several lesser ones, the United States is in the front lines while Japan remains far behind in relative safety, taking advantage of U.S. strategic largesse. Except for Panama, where the United States exerts a unique presence, these are examples of the United States doing more than its share and Japan doing far less than a fair share. Japan contributes very little to Korean security, except for allowing the United States the privilege of access to bases in Japan so that Americans might defend militarily interests that Japan refuses to accept. Similarly in China and Southeast Asia, Japan is reluctant to accept a fair share of the responsibility and risks in defense of its strategic interests. While one can sympathize with Japanese, and other Asian, reluctance to avoid Japanese reinvolvement militarily in the region less than half a century after Pearl Harbor, where is it written that Americans must perennially pay an onerous price for having won World War II? Are we to be stuck with these security responsibilities and risks forever? Most egregious, perhaps, was the situation in the Persian Gulf where the United States speedily provided naval assistance to friendly oil-producing states so that the flow of oil to the West would not be impeded by the Iran-Iraq War. U.S. complaints about lack of help from the Western European and Japanese recipients of nearly all those Middle Eastern oil exports motivated several NATO allies to dispatch naval vessels to help maintain freedom of the seas. In stark contrast, Japan, with much wringing of hands, fell back upon its no-war constitutional inhibitions and popular domestic opposition to its getting involved in collective security. This was but the most glaring example of Japan's sanctimoniously evading responsibility for defending its own interests and relying on the United States to pull its chestnuts out of the fire. This is grossly unfair when one remembers that Japan's interests in the region's security are comparable to those of the United States and often are greater.

Considering Japan's great indigenous stake in Asian-Pacific security, Americans should not be more willing than the Japanese to maintain regional strategic well-being. The United States has a right to expect Japan to behave in a militarily responsible manner and act to prompt such behavior. The United States should not accept all the responsibilities from which it and Japan receive approximately equal benefits. In some parts of the world, Americans may still echo President Kennedy's inaugural remarks about paying any price and bearing any burden, but these words ring hollow in Northeast Asia, where both U.S. allies (South Korea is the other) can pay a full share of the price and bear a full share of the burden for our mutual security. If a moderate French politician can ask, "Do you think 320 million Europeans can continue forever to ask 240 million Americans to defend us against 280 million Soviets?" surely the Asian version of such a query would be far more portentous.[7] Americans have a right to expect the Japanese to ask such questions too and to help devise answers more appropriate to circumstances that are far different from those prevailing when Washington committed the United States to Japan's security in the 1950s.

Moreover, the United States has good reasons to seek strategic integration with Japan as a major partner and a regional equal in an asymmetrical global strategic system because of what Japan, alone in Asia, can do for U.S. security. Japanese advanced technology probably will become an even more integral portion of the strategic hardware and software systems that enable the United States to survive in the nuclear age. Although the United States long has relied on dual-use Japanese technology, in June 1985 the first formal request for transfer of Japanese military high technology was made under the terms of a 1983 agreement. In cooperative circumstances, this may flourish and dramatically underscore Ambassador Mansfield's frequently repeated admonition that U.S.-Japan ties are the most important bilateral relationships of the United States. The possibilities of Japanese participation in SDI and other high-tech defense research are extremely encouraging and would intensify bilateral interdependency.

On a regional level, Japan could offer the United States much to ease financial burden sharing. Until the major revaluation of the yen versus the dollar in the mid-1980s, Japan's defense budget and the amount it reimbursed the United States to maintain its forces in Japan in recent years totaled about $12 billion annually, about twice the amount North and South Korea combined (countries with a radically different military image than Japan's) spend on defense. Because of the greatly increased value of the yen coupled with small actual increases, Japan now appears to be spending close to $26 billion per year, but such a figure is somewhat artificial and illusory because the actual amount of yen involved in yearly expenditures has not changed nearly as much as the dollar-denominated figures suggest. The much-vaunted surpassing by the Nakasone government in 1987 of Japan's self-imposed 1 percent of GNP defense spending limit was largely symbolic. Defense expenditures went from a tiny fraction under 1 percent to an equally tiny fraction over it. Though Japan's percentage of yearly defense budget increases often exceeds that of other U.S. allies, there is no sign that cracking that barrier means Japan will move quickly to match the proportions of GNP spent on defense by other Western powers. It stands in dramatic contrast to neighboring South Korea's 6 percent of GNP spent on defense. Furthermore, most of those Japanese funds are not ordinarily spent abroad, so their actual purchasing power has not increased appreciably. In sharp contrast, the United States spends over $40 billion per year on Asian defense. And U.S. dollars spent in the Japanese security environment today buy markedly less than in prerevaluation days. U.S. bases in Japan, albeit partially underwritten by Tokyo, still cost the United States a great deal to maintain in a high-cost environment. Were Japan to expend a portion of its GNP equivalent to the 6 to 7 percent share spent by the United States, it would have available an additional $60 billion to $72 billion in prerevaluation terms or a contemporary (but artificial) figure of about $125 billion to $150 billion. That is more than double the defense expenditures of all other Asian states combined. Japan clearly could become once more a major military power, perhaps a nuclear power, if it decides to do so.

No one expects Japan to spend close to that amount in the near future. This is especially true if the United States continues to spend so much on Japan's security that Tokyo lacks any incentive to expand seriously its responsibilities or expenditures. Yet with an increase to half the U.S. percentage spent on defense, Japan could readily meet all its current and future needs and pay for about half of what the United States spends on the Asia-Pacific region, largely to protect Japanese interests. If this happens (and it should), it must not be seen by China, the Republic of Korea, or other Asian states as an attempt by the United States to make Japan a U.S. proxy or surrogate, for the reverse is true. The United States has acted on Japan's behalf for four decades. It is time for a change. A new, improved security scheme for Northeast Asia is long overdue. Washington should explain its effort to get Tokyo to share burdens throughout Asia, which are more properly Japanese, in terms of a reduction in its acting as a proxy for Japan, which should shoulder its own burdens. Japan can do much more in defense of its security in the Asia-Pacific region and in more distant areas of concern such as the Persian Gulf. Despite the legitimacy of U.S. intentions to stop being a surrogate for Japan, some Japanese and other Asians will interpret any such move as an effort by the United States to dump its responsibilities on the Japanese and force Japan into a level of cooperation it does not want. These perceptions should not be ignored—they are hot political issues in Japanese domestic politics—but they must not be permitted to obstruct what is necessary for the United States to meet the changing needs of its national interests.

Those interests have not changed in any important way. They revolve around minimizing negative Soviet influence in Asia politically, militarily, and economically and maximizing U.S. participation in a Western-oriented, progressive, and prosperous region. Once the United States bore the brunt of the responsibility for bolstering the region's security. Now U.S. allies can provide their fair share. If Japan does nothing overtly for regional security, the United States's willingness to pursue improvement in the status quo could be seriously jeopardized by the most radical neoisolationist elements in U.S. society that periodically threaten important alliances. In that regard, one must put what should be considered prudent neoisolationists, such as Layne and Melvyn Krauss, into a different light.[8] They do not "threaten" alliances but seek to instill into U.S. allies a greater sense of responsibility for shared security concerns. Their goals and means are admirable. The real "threat" comes from leftist critics of U.S. involvement in global security whose versions of neoisolationism would not replace troubled alliances with anything better. Those alliances can, and should, be made more equitable without jettisoning them. If that proves impossible, however, those alliances may be replaced by a system that links loose or soft alignments among friendly states. As they seek to defend their national security in a manner that would allow major areas of overlap, they could produce a significant level of separately autonomous yet coordinated security. Such a soft alignment system could produce a credible alternative to formal collective security networks if the latter cannot be made to work properly.

Although many specifics of what Japan might do to help itself and the United States build a more viable collective security system could be offered, exposing them at this stage would be premature and counterproductive because the point of involving Japan further is not to order Tokyo to follow an agenda devised by Washington. Instead Japan should consult with the United States to negotiate an appropriate role commensurate with its abilities and potential. Out of those negotiations a joint U.S.-Japan security policy should emerge, predicated on a doctrine of strategic fairness. If Tokyo is unwilling to cooperate on such terms, which would strengthen the desirability of close U.S.-Japan security ties, the United States ought to rethink seriously the prevailing wisdom of retaining its present security ties with Japan. Without serious restructuring that would make them truly fair to both partners, those ties should be considered outmoded.

It is not too soon to contemplate such improved measures. They will take time to negotiate and implement. The efforts in 1988 of ex–prime minister Nakasone to develop a Peace Strategy Research Institute suggest the Japanese are starting to get serious about their thinking about Japan's strategy.[9] There is a major strategic thinking gap between Americans and Japanese that urgently needs to be bridged and, ultimately, narrowed. Nakasone's proposed institute, and other comparable institutions in Japan, are capable of taking the lead there to match American initiatives for a fundamental dialogue. Rapid movement toward such an agenda would help defuse the trade problems plaguing U.S. ties with its ally and preempt damaging spillover from trade disputes into security issues.

Japan may never be willing to do as much as Americans might like, but it is clear that it is capable of doing much more to defend itself. The current pressures on it to become defensively self-reliant are inadequate. Furthermore, this approach allows Japan to drag its feet in pursuit of limited objectives. Japan should expand its objectives and do something concrete, beyond economic measures, to help the United States and other allies with regional security. Japan's renowned comprehensive security doctrine, which stresses the economic and political components of augmenting stability as crucial ways to preserve security and minimize the need for armed defensive measures, is an admirable concept. Unfortunately the Japanese use that doctrine as a rationale for contributing minimally to armed security while emphasizing its unarmed (economic and political) contributions to global peace and security. This approach leaves the United States responsible for military security. If Washington allows the situation to persist, Japan will be able to play a benign role in international affairs while the United States plays the "heavy." It is an unfair division of labor, responsibility, and risk that should not be perpetuated.

The comprehensive security doctrine should not be ignored or undercut, but neither should it be accepted as a pretext for Japan to avoid the most difficult portion of the major powers' responsibility for security. Perhaps the best way for the United States to approach the creation of a joint strategic agenda with Japan would be to base it on the principles of comprehensive security but insist that those principles be applied equitably to both parties. The United States should assume relatively larger responsibilities for economic and political stability, and Japan should expand its responsibilities for armed defense of common or overlapping interests. By postulating a larger regional defense agenda involving Japan, Washington and Tokyo should be able to motivate Japan to achieve self-defense and use that ability as the basis for a larger role in the region. By setting greatly expanded goals, even the accomplishment of something short of the ostensible new target will yield more than the United States is likely to achieve by pussyfooting around with cautiously limited goals.

There is no guarantee that Japan will respond in ways that are scripted in Washington. Nonetheless, joint burden sharing is likely to be most effective if it is accomplished through joint decision making, not imposition of decisions on an unwilling Japan. Lest fear of Japanese erraticism prevent meaningful efforts at regional security cooperation, U.S. planners should familiarize themselves with the pragmatic, sound thinking of some contemporary Japanese leaders and not be misled by false images of revived militarism. Clearly the Japanese are as trustworthy as the United States' European allies or their Asian neighbors.

There is, however, one area where Japan differs greatly from other U.S. allies. None of them poses a truly serious challenge to the United States as a global economic leader; Japan does. There is something terribly wrong with a strategic relationship in which one economic giant does so much more than the other economic giant. Japan's attitude is reminiscent of selfish individuals who say, "What's mine is mine; what's yours let's negotiate." Such self-centered behavior is intolerable and should be rejected by Americans. Although there may be other ways of getting Japan to treat the United States more fairly, one promising venue is to try to build a new consensus between the two nations based on a strategic fairness doctrine. Although neither the United States nor Japan (nor any other ally) is likely to be rid of the nation-state concept or national sovereignty any time soon, we all would do well to incorporate our national interests within the Western transnational geopolitical and economic entity that really constitutes the superpower led by Washington. Many Europeans and Asians wish they had the right to vote for U.S. presidents since the U.S. leaders' decisions may determine the fate of the entire West. Those unattainable desires amount to recognition that the United States, alone, does not equate to the superpower that confronts the Soviet Union and its associated states.

If the United States and its allies are an interdependent economic and political gestalt, within which the allies occupy an increasingly large proportion of the entity, should not that whole be considered the true superpower? The United States alone is not the sort of unilateralist superpower it once was. One of the overriding motives of the post–World War II reconstruction period was to rebuild the Western world into a cohesive unit. This has largely been accomplished in economic terms. As important, Japan now occupies an enormous place in that Western transnational structure. In this context, the United States has every right to call upon its allies and trade partners that enjoy roughly equal benefits to share the costs, responsibilities, burdens, and decision-making powers in the defense of the redefined superpower's interests. If the United States cannot convince Japan or the European allies that they should share this involvement fairly, Americans ought to reexamine the validity of everything the United States now does for its allies.

The world faces some difficult decisions about long-term tendencies toward interdependent globalism versus divisive regionalism that threaten to disrupt the interdependent relationships binding the extended West together throughout the postwar era. Should Western allies choose not to participate on a more equal footing commensurate with their levels of prosperity, they will jeopardize the enthusiasm of the American people for U.S. commitments to a variety of alliances. If alliances cannot be made more equitable, perhaps Americans ought to reconsider the advice of the less radical U.S. neoisolationists who advocate a gradual distancing of the United States from uncooperative allies. This is the sort of message that needs to be conveyed to Tokyo's leaders so that the United States and Japan can work with a similar sense of urgency on joint problems. If Tokyo and Washington are able to accept each other as full-fledged partners, the U.S.-Japan partnership stands an excellent chance of fulfilling its great potential. The disruptive alternatives to such cooperation are unpleasant to contemplate and should motivate Americans and Japanese to work more harmoniously in the future.

Notes

1. For an insightful Japanese analysis of these developments, see Kataoka Tetsuya, "Japan's Defense Non-Buildup: What Went Wrong?" (Washington, D.C.: Asia-Pacific Community Forum Monograph Series, Washington Institute, 1985).

2. *Far Eastern Economic Review*, August 27, 1987, p. 35.

3. Edward A. Olsen, *US-Japan Strategic Reciprocity* (Stanford: Hoover Institution Press, 1985).

4. Christopher Layne, "The Real Conservative Agenda," *Foreign Policy* (Winter 1985–1986): 73–93.

5. I devised the substitute term *cheap rider* for a Japanese journal; see my "Chiipu raida e no fuman," *Chuo Koron* (December 1985): 50–53.

6. See especially Chalmers Johnson, "Reflections on the Dilemma of Japanese Defense," *Asian Survey* (May 1986): 561–62.

7. Jean-Pierre Bechter, secretary of the French Parliament's National Defense Committee, quoted in *Washington Post* (weekly), July 27, 1987, p. 17.

8. Melvyn B. Krauss, *How NATO Weakens the West* (New York: Simon & Schuster, 1986), and "It's Time for U.S. Troops to Leave Korea," *Christian Science Monitor*, August 24, 1987, p. 13.

9. *Far Eastern Economic Review*, January 21, 1988, p. 24.

6

U.S. Forces in Korea: Assessing a Reduction

Stephen D. Goose

The December 1987 presidential election and the April 1988 National Assembly elections in South Korea have generated a great deal of optimism about the prospects for democracy in that nation. Similarly, the 1988 Summer Olympics are being enthusiastically heralded as the formal emergence of South Korea as an important member of the international community. The Republic of Korea (ROK) has one of the world's fastest-growing economies and has made impressive improvements in its military production and combat capabilities. Indeed, as Admiral Ronald Hays, commander in chief of the U.S. Pacific Command, told Congress in early 1988, "The Republic of Korea has grown militarily, economically, and politically from one of the poorest nations among the underdeveloped, to a thriving industrialized nation, on the threshold of world power status."[1]

There has been conspicuously little discussion, however, about what these developments might mean for what is perhaps the dominant feature of South Korea's existence during the past four decades: the massive U.S. military presence. Yet new realities—particularly the transcendent political, economic, and military changes in South Korea—demand a reexamination of the U.S.-ROK security relationship. This has been acknowledged by U.S. and Korean leaders. The Joint Communiqué of the Nineteenth Annual U.S.-ROK Security Consultative Meeting in May 1987 stated: "Both sides agree it is necessary to begin planning now to accommodate changes in the relationship and that, as the relationship matures, particular attention should be paid to the growing capabilities of the Republic of Korea."[2] In his testimony, Admiral Hays said, "Growing ROK nationalism and military capabilities, the question of U.S. military presence in Korea, and regional roles of military forces stationed in Korea, need careful review."[3] Thus far acknowledgment has not translated into action.

In many respects, the U.S. military presence in South Korea reflects a policy stuck in the 1950s. Military ties have not kept up with other changes in U.S.-Korean relations resulting from Korea's rapid modernization. The time has come to reconsider the rationales for the U.S. presence, the nature of the U.S. commitment, and the appropriateness of the current size and composition of U.S. forces in Korea.

Circumstances are more propitious than ever before to begin the process of carefully planning and implementing a phased reduction in U.S. military forces in South Korea. As South Korea comes of age politically, economically, and militarily, it is increasingly obvious that the U.S. military presence is a relic of the past and increasingly unnecessary. The time is ripe for a demilitarization of U.S. policy toward South Korea and for taking the first steps in an inevitable U.S. withdrawal—not a massive, hasty abandonment of the ROK but a laying of the groundwork for a thoughtfully considered, gradually implemented reduction in the U.S. force level.

This view is not shared by most officials in Washington and Seoul. In the spring of 1987, Assistant Secretary of State for East Asia and the Pacific Gaston Sigur responded in this way to a congressman's question: "If you mean to suggest that we reduce our troop presence in Korea, I believe strongly that this is an especially inopportune time for such a move. The Republic of Korea is presently going through one of the most crucial periods in its history. The country is struggling to achieve its first peaceful transfer of power while preparing to host the Olympic Games. Both events, for different reasons, could provide motives for North Korea to attack. A U.S. troop reduction now would send a very dangerous signal."[4]

Sigur is correct that this is a sensitive time, but U.S and Korean leaders have been saying for decades that the timing is bad. While the coming of the Olympics has understandably led to a certain nervousness and heightened military vigilance on the part of the ROK, the new, democratically elected government should, in the near future, be better able than any previous ROK regime to pursue a relaxation of tensions on the peninsula. This first truly civilian government should be more willing and able to deal with Pyongyang because its legitimacy is not tied to military confrontation with the North. For its part, the North can no longer use the political unpopularity of the ROK government to justify its hostility or to avoid direct negotiations. Moreover, the government of President Roh Tae Woo will in all likelihood ask for some change in the U.S. military presence, especially with regard to the command structure and, perhaps, nuclear weapons. As Korean democracy and independence grow stronger, the large U.S. presence, and the control exercised by the United States over Korean military forces, may increasingly be perceived by South Koreans as symbols of dependency and U.S. collusion with past military dictatorships.

For a number of years, many analysts have been stating that, given current trends—particularly regarding the ROK's ever-growing advantages in population, GNP, and technologically advanced industrial base—any North Korean military advantage will soon be gone. During the past year, Korean leaders have stated that they expect to have sufficient military strength to offset the North, and thus permit withdrawal of U.S. forces, by the mid-1990s. Some, including me, believe that South Korea has already reached the stage of sufficient deterrent strength.[5] But even if one accepts a mid-1990s timetable, it would be prudent to begin making concrete plans for a reduction in U.S. force levels, starting with those forces that contribute the least to South Korea's defense.

U.S. Forces in Korea

The level of involvement and integration of U.S. and foreign military forces is higher in Korea than anywhere else with the exception of a few NATO nations. This is evident in the large number of U.S. troops in Korea (more than in any other foreign nation except West Germany and Japan), the stationing of U.S. nuclear weapons, the combined command structure, the extensive joint training and planning for war, the prepositioning of war supplies on the peninsula, the 1954 Mutual Defense Treaty, and many other factors.

The United States has maintained combat troops and support units in South Korea since 1950. One of three U.S. Army divisions was withdrawn in 1954 and another in 1971, leaving roughly 40,000 U.S. military personnel. The frequently cited 40,000 figure is now actually low. General Robert Sennewald, former commander of U.S. forces in Korea, noted in 1984 that the United States had made "modest increases" in the number of ground troops in Korea since 1981 and would continue to do so, adding "a total of 2,000 to 2,500 soldiers."[6] According to quarterly Department of Defense fact sheets, the number of U.S. troops has not been as small as 40,000 since the end of 1983, averaging closer to 43,000 in recent years. During the March 1988 "Team Spirit" military exercise, the number swelled to 48,000.[7]

Of the forty U.S. military installations in Korea, the most notable are the army bases at Camp Casey and Yongsan and the air force bases at Osan, Kunsan, Suwon, and Taegu. The majority of U.S. forces are members of the 8th U.S. Army, the major element of which is the 2d Infantry Division. West Germany is the only other foreign country in which a full U.S. Army division is stationed. The 2d Infantry Division joins thirteen South Korean Army divisions to form the Combined ROK/U.S. Field Army. It is mostly deployed between Seoul and the demilitarized zone (DMZ) separating North and South Korea, in such a way that U.S. combat involvement in any Korean war would be automatic. U.S. air power in Korea is organized under the U.S. 7th Air Force, headquartered at Osan, and includes nearly 100 high-performance aircraft, most notably F-16 and F-4 fighter aircraft, A-10 "tank-buster" aircraft, OV-10 counterinsurgency planes, and U-2 reconnaissance planes.

Nuclear Weapons

Outside of Western Europe, South Korea is the only foreign country where the U.S. government has openly acknowledged that it stations nuclear weapons. In the mid-1970s, it was generally believed that the United States kept over 600 nuclear weapons in the ROK. Since then, however, the United States has withdrawn warheads for Honest John and Nike-Hercules missiles, as well as other systems. One reliable estimate puts the number of nuclear weapons currently in South Korea at 151: 60 aircraft bombs, 40 8-inch artillery shells, 30 155 mm artillery shells, and 21 atomic demolition munitions (ADMs, or land mines).[8]

There has been speculation that the United States will deploy the W-79 8-inch artillery shell, commonly known as the neutron bomb, in South Korea. Neutron bombs produce radiation as their primary lethal effect, rather than blast and heat, and are believed to be particularly effective against massive concentrations of tanks and armor, such as would be encountered in a war in Korea. The W-79 was originally intended for deployment in Europe, but various European governments refused permission. The stationing of a U.S. Lance surface-to-surface missile battery in Korea in the spring of 1987 has fueled speculation since it is a compatible system.

Command Structure

Technically, U.S. and Korean forces are still under the command of the United Nations Command in Korea. But the commander of the U.N. forces is always the commander of U.S. Forces, Korea. Thus exists the unique situation of a sovereign nation's armed forces being headed by a foreign commander. Today it is widely recognized that the U.N. presence is a legal figleaf to cover what has long been a U.S.-ROK arrangement. While several other nations contribute token military personnel, the United States is the only foreign nation that maintains combat troops in South Korea.

In recognition of the fact that the United States and South Korea are solely responsible for the defense of the ROK and to permit greater involvement of the ROK in war planning, the Combined Forces Command (CFC) was formed in 1978. The CFC, the only combined U.S.-Allied command outside NATO, is the war-fighting headquarters; its purpose is to "integrate ROK and U.S. forces into a cohesive organization capable of fighting coalition warfare" and to achieve an "integration of tactics and doctrine with an emphasis on interoperability and complimentarity."[9] The ranking officer of the CFC is the commander of U.S. Forces, Korea.

Costs

The cost of stationing U.S. troops in Korea is approximately $3 billion per year. The South Korean government contributes about $1.8 billion of that amount—$287 million directly and $1.5 billion indirectly. The major indirect contribution is rent-free use of real estate.[10]

U.S. officials maintain that "the relative cost to the United States of our military presence in Korea is among the lowest of all foreign countries where we have stationed troops."[11] But some in Congress, particularly those whose constituents have been hurt by Korean exports, believe that the United States is subsidizing the Korean economy through the presence of troops and that Korea could and should be paying much more. Faced with congressional pressures on the burden-sharing issue, the Reagan administration has pressed Korea to increase its direct contribution by $60 million to $120 million.[12]

The $3 billion total is somewhat misleading in that it includes only costs of stationing troops in Korea. It does not take into account equipment costs, costs for reinforcement, or a variety of other items. It is not reflective of the overall cost of U.S. preparations for fighting in Korea or the U.S. military commitment to Korea. One analyst put the total cost of U.S. forces for fighting in Asia at $47 billion for fiscal year 1985, of which the lion's share would be for Korea and Northeast Asia.[13]

Deepening Military Ties

Far from preparing for the day when the United States will lessen its military role on the peninsula and turn over more of Korean military responsibilities to the Koreans, U.S. military involvement is expanding, and U.S.-ROK military ties are deepening. The Nineteenth and Twentieth U.S.-ROK Security Consultative Meetings (held in May 1987 and June 1988, respectively) gave clear indications of this. The Joint Communiqué from the 1987 meeting called for the establishment of a hot line between U.S. and Korean defense ministers, creation of a committee to review interoperability, and a Memorandum of Understanding (MOU) on expanded cooperation of U.S. and Korean defense industries. It also announced the signing of an agreement to modernize the war reserve munitions stockpile. At the 1988 meeting, the MOU was formally signed, as was a Mutual Logistics Support Agreement.

That the United States has no plans to leave Korea soon is also indicated by the continued upgrading of weaponry for U.S. forces and by expanded U.S. military construction. In late 1985, the commander of U.S. Forces, Korea, stated that the 8th Army would receive some 135 new weapons systems over the next few years and would replace old, temporary structures with "modern, semi-permanent facilities."[14] The United States spent close to $1 billion on military construction in Korea during 1982–1986, and the ROK spent more than an additional $300 million on construction for U.S. forces during that time.[15]

North-South Military Balance

Any examination of the impact of a reduction in U.S. forces in South Korea should begin with an assessment of the military balance between the ROK and the DPRK (Democratic People's Republic of Korea). The threat from the North has been the primary justification for the continued stationing of U.S. troops, just as successive military dictatorships in South Korea have used the threat to justify large and increasing military budgets and continued military domination of national politics.

Common wisdom holds that there is no military balance between North and South Korea. While government officials from the United States and ROK have stated for many years that their combined forces are more than a match for North Korea, they continue to talk about the overwhelming military advantage of the North over the South by itself. Talk of a massive, aggressive North Korean military buildup has been constant during the past two decades. In testifying to Congress in 1986, Deputy Assistant Secretary of Defense James Kelly said, "The ROK has been unable to match the massive North Korean military buildup which began in 1970 and continues to this day. The North Korean military now poses as great a threat to the ROK as at any time since the Korean War."[16] Similar words are heard every year.

A litany of statistics is repeatedly recited: North Korea has 40 percent more military manpower; North Korea spends over 20 percent of its GNP on the military compared to the South's 6 percent; North Korea has a three-to-one advantage in tanks, artillery, and aircraft and a four-to-one advantage in ships. The implication is always that without U.S. troops and weapons, including nuclear weapons, North Korea could and would attack and overrun South Korea.

Although those statistics can be supported in one way or another, they are almost always misleading and often meaningless. Numbers alone reveal little about military capabilities. North Korea's quantitative advantages are offset by many other factors that favor the South. First and foremost is the superior quality of South Korea's weaponry and equipment, which in most cases is newer, more powerful, and more reliable. The qualitative edge of the ROK is probably the most important aspect to consider when comparing the militaries of North and South Korea. It is perhaps most pronounced, and most important, with respect to air power. While large in number, the DPRK air force is mostly antiquated hand-me-downs and castoffs from the PRC and the Soviet Union. Most analysts agree that superior air power would be the decisive edge in an ROK victory over the North because the ROK, with U.S. assistance, would quickly establish air superiority and then turn tremendous firepower against North Korean ground troops and supply routes. Major General James Smotherton, ex-commander of U.S. Air Forces in Korea, said in 1986, "If the North committed its air forces on the first day of battle, I think we'd win the war pretty quickly, in a few days."[17] Recent deliveries of Soviet MiG-23 aircraft, and even the possible delivery of MiG-29s recently reported, will make little difference.

Other factors of extreme importance in the South's favor in case of attack are geography, terrain, and defensive posture. The ROK would be fighting from highly fortified defensive positions on its own territory. The much-talked-about North Korean tank advantage largely disappears when one considers the terrain the tanks would have to traverse. There are only three north-south attack routes, all heavily defended with extensive in-place fortifications, which would channel DPRK forces, making them vulnerable to the vast array of ROK antitank weapons. In the event of a long war, South Korea has the advantage of larger numbers of reserves and paramilitary forces, as well as a population twice the size of North Korea's and an economy (GNP) four times larger.

Other intangible factors will also work in the ROK's favor, notably its superior experience, training, and leadership. Most experts agree that these factors would be a big plus for the ROK, though North Korea is thought to rate highly in the latter two areas. There is also a strong belief in the West that South Korea would benefit from superior fighting doctrine and tactics. In particular, military analysts point to the development of a new war-fighting strategy, "Deep Attack" or "AirLand Battle," which calls for active offense deep in enemy territory, using new high-technology weaponry. Developed primarily for the European theater, it is also being implemented in Korea.

South Korea has made tremendous strides toward improving its military capabilities in the 1980s. In addition to taking delivery from the United States of such powerful, sophisticated systems as F-16 aircraft, 155 mm self-propelled howitzers, and Improved-HAWK antiaircraft missiles, the ROK has developed an impressive defense production base capable of manufacturing more than three-quarters of its military needs. South Korea has even produced its own indigenously designed and manufactured main battle tank, the Tank 88, essentially a smaller version of the United States's best tank, the M-1. North Korea's military production capabilities, while impressive given the generally backward state of its industrial capacity, lag far behind that of the South.

In part because of U.S. fiscal constraints but also because of South Korea's economic and military advances, the United States terminated its military aid program to the ROK in 1986 except for a small training program. Cash sales of U.S. weapons, of course, continue. Assistant Secretary of Defense Richard Armitage told Congress in 1987, "The Republic of Korea has made great strides toward self-reliance in defense. Last year we 'graduated' the ROK from the Foreign Military Sales Credit program, as its extraordinary record of economic growth has transformed South Korea into a nation capable of assuming most of the cost of its own defense."[18]

A December 1985 study by the RAND Corporation, prepared at the request of the U.S. Department of Defense and the ROK Ministry of National Defense, reached these conclusions:

"South Korea's economic and technological advantages over North Korea are substantial."

"The South's economic preponderance over the North is growing rapidly."

"South Korea's economic and technological development affords major opportunities for it to realize significant advantages in the long-term military competition with the North."

"South Korea can plausibly aspire to an increasing degree of military self-reliance."

"South Korea's economic, technological and military capabilities can be expected to grow substantially relative to those of North Korea during the next decade. The resulting balance should increasingly and predominantly favor the South."[19]

The last point was recently reiterated by retired Brigadier General John Bahnsen, chief of staff of the Combined ROK/U.S. Field Army from 1982 to 1984: "Strategically, the war-fighting balance between North and South Korea shifts more in favor of our Korean friends each day."[20]

The authoritative International Institute for Strategic Studies in London made this judgment several years ago: "The opposing forces on the Korean peninsula are roughly equivalent. Neither is capable of a successful major offensive against the other without significant foreign assistance."[21]

In sum, South Korean forces are strong enough to deter and if necessary defeat a North Korean invasion force, although U.S. air and, to a lesser extent, naval reinforcements could play an important role. In the near future, even that assistance may not be necessary. The trends are strongly in South Korea's favor, and the military balance should increasingly favor the ROK.

U.S. Force Reductions

The implication of this assessment of the military balance on the peninsula is clear: given the basic equivalence of ROK and DPRK forces, large numbers of U.S. troops, particularly ground forces, are not militarily necessary. This essential truth led the Carter administration to advocate a troop withdrawal in 1977.

Professor Edward Olsen, coordinator of Asian studies at the U.S. Naval Postgraduate School, wrote in early 1985, "Clearly it is not popular today to suggest that Carter was right about the troop reduction idea, but I will say so in a modified way. The Carter administration's ideas were valid as far as they went." Olsen argued Japan could and should play a larger role: "It is time that the Carter troop proposal be taken off the shelf. . . . A workable formula between South Korean manpower and Japanese and U.S. subsidies for equipment and support would be both feasible and reasonable."[22]

A number of objections were raised to the Carter withdrawal plan. An examination of them will show that changing circumstances have further eroded whatever validity those arguments had at the time. The main objection was that the North's strength was so overwhelming that without the U.S. presence, a successful DPRK invasion was not only possible but likely. That conclusion was hotly debated at the time; however, there is little debate whether South Korea's military strength relative to North Korea's has been growing steadily throughout the 1980s, and there is a consensus that it will continue to do so at an ever-increasing rate in the foreseeable future.

A second major objection was the so-called ripple effect, that is, fear of loss of confidence in the U.S. commitment by other allies. The Reagan administration has often claimed that it has restored confidence in the U.S. commitment and willingness to act around the globe. Perhaps more to the point, many nations today are not concerned about U.S. troops as a symbol of the U.S. commitment. Indeed, a number of countries are threatening or trying to reduce or do away altogether with the U.S. military presence; Spain, Turkey, Greece, and the Philippines are notable examples.

Almost everyone would agree that U.S. forces should be removed from Korea at some time. No self-respecting Korean would tolerate an indefinite presence, certainly not at current levels. The question then becomes when force reductions might be appropriate, which in turn hinges on when the South will have sufficient military strength to permit reductions. While this chapter concludes that time is now, others at least concede that it is coming soon.

Among Korea watchers, predictions of the South's matching the North militarily within the next—take your pick—three, five, or ten years have become an annual occurrence. A congressional delegation that visited South Korea in August 1983 reported that Korean leaders predicted that by 1986 the ROK would reach military parity with North Korea.[23] In 1985 General William Livsey, then commander of U.S. Forces, Korea, said, "I believe that, by the early 1990s, all comparisons between South and North Korea, including the military, will favor the ROK."[24]

Prior to the December 1987 election, several of Korea's top officials made their own predictions. In early October 1987, according to *Korea Newsreview*, President Chun predicted, "In several years, the country will thus achieve a sufficient fighting and retaliatory capability not only to promptly beat back any form of enemy invasion in a one-on-one war with the Communist North, but also to deal the North a crushing blow to punish it." He noted that ROK firepower and mobility are "incomparably greater" than in the past due to the development of Korea's defense industry.[25] That same month Defense Minister Chung Ho-yong said that by the mid-1990s, South Korea would achieve the 70 percent of North Korea's military power necessary to defend itself without the United States.[26] Both during his campaign and after his election, President Roh Tae Woo has indicated that the South Korean military will reach the point of adequate self-reliance in the "early 1990s."[27]

Korea's leaders clearly do not believe that U.S. forces will be needed in the near future. The shifting military balance, as well as recent nonmilitary developments, make the planning and implementation of a reduction in U.S. forces now both feasible and desirable.

Planning a Phased Reduction

U.S. force reductions will have to be done gradually and carefully, making sure to inform American and, especially, Korean citizens, as well as allied and hostile governments, what is being done and why. U.S. reductions should be part of a bargaining process with North Korea, an effort to lessen military tensions and reduce force levels on both sides. A preconditional, gradual reduction, with intermediate steps and stages, with a high level of education, makes a great deal of sense militarily, politically, and economically.

Only a general outline of a U.S. force reduction plan will be presented here. The place to start is with the removal of all U.S. nuclear weapons from the peninsula. With a civilian government firmly in place, a second step is to turn control of Korean forces over to the ROK. Then elements of the 2d Infantry Division can be systematically withdrawn over a period of years. Finally, when they are clearly no longer needed, U.S. Air Force units can depart. Still left behind would be the less controversial but militarily important U.S. air defense, intelligence, and support units.

Removing Nuclear Weapons

U.S. nuclear weapons in Korea have always been justified as the ultimate deterrent to a North Korean attack, just as nuclear weapons in Europe have been deemed necessary to prevent a Soviet attack. However, the situations are not analogous. There are no nuclear weapons in North Korea, a point not disputed by anyone. Thus there is no need for U.S. nuclear weapons as a deterrent against nuclear attack by the DPRK. As for U.S. nuclear weapons as a deterrent against a conventional attack, ROK conventional military strength is sufficient to deter, and if necessary defeat, a North Korean invasion. Even if one does not accept the assessment of basic equivalence of conventional military strength, it becomes a question of weighing the advantages and disadvantages of any additional deterrent value that nuclear weapons may bring.

It is possible that North Korea may not be deterred by U.S. nuclear weapons in any event. The DPRK leadership may believe that the likelihood that the United States will ever use its nuclear weapons against a nonnuclear nation again is very low. It is doubtful the American public would support such a use, and world opinion would certainly be strongly against it. The United States did not use nuclear weapons from 1950 to 1953, though it suffered serious military defeats and had a monopoly on nuclear arms at the time.

On the other hand, the chances of their use in a war on the peninsula are greater now than during the Korean War because the nuclear weapons are already actually deployed inside the country. Indeed, some have argued, including House Armed Services chairman Les Aspin (D–Wisconsin), that "battlefield" nuclear weapons, such as those in Korea, are the most dangerous type of nuclear weapon.[28] Because they are located at or near the front lines, there is great incentive to use them or lose them. Others have pointed out that the incentive to use nuclear weapons will be greater in Korea than in Europe because, in addition to fear of losing them, there will be post-Vietnam pressures to keep any Asian war short and decisive. Moreover, U.S. policymakers seem sanguine that a nuclear war in Korea would not escalate to a global scale, and the risks are certainly less than in Europe where any use of nuclear weapons is virtually guaranteed to culminate in global catastrophe. But the attitude regarding escalation in Korea is troubling because it makes it easier to contemplate using the weapons.

Congressman Aspin argues that the United States should be moving away from battlefield nuclear weapons not only because they are dangerous but also because they are unnecessary. Modern technology has produced missiles that can be fired from hundreds and even thousands of miles away with accuracy approaching that of artillery guns only dozens of miles away. Moreover, the United States could rapidly deliver a wide variety of nuclear weapons on Korea from aircraft carriers and ships in the region should it deem this step essential to save the ROK.

The reality, however, is that the use of nuclear weapons in Korea would likely result in the destruction, not the saving, of the nation. These tactical nuclear weapons, many of which have greater destructive power than the bombs dropped on Hiroshima, would mutilate and kill untold numbers of Koreans and Americans, as well as cause immeasurable destruction of property. Fallout would endanger all Koreans, plus Japanese, Chinese, Soviets, and perhaps the innocent peoples of other nations. The use of nuclear weapons might even create the kind of widespread chaos that could lead to a North Korean victory.

Use of nuclear weapons in Korea would have broader ramifications. Letting the nuclear genie out of the bottle again could legitimize nuclear warfare elsewhere, particularly the notion of first use of nuclear weapons, and could encourage other nations to pursue nuclear weapons development, making a shambles of U.S. nonproliferation policy.

U.S. nuclear weapons in Korea have no military utility, are of questionable deterrent value, and bring with them the potential for disaster in many different ways. Removal of those weapons would go a long way toward increasing safety and security and reducing tensions on the peninsula.

As democracy grows in South Korea and the opposition movement gains a stronger voice in national politics, it is likely that the strict prohibition on discussion of U.S. nuclear weapons in the media will be relaxed. That, in turn, could lead to antinuclear sentiment on a widespread basis throughout the country, increased anti-Americanism, and possibly a demand for withdrawal of the weapons. The United States would be wise to remove them now before a problem develops.

Restoring Korean Control

General Richard Stilwell, former commander of U.S. Forces, Korea, reportedly once called the command arrangement in Korea the most remarkable concession of sovereignty in the entire world. It is clearly a relic of the past. The South Koreans are a proud and independent people with a strong, highly organized armed force. The absurdity of a U.S. general with 43,000 troops commanding more than 600,000 South Korean troops is increasingly evident. Indeed, prior to his election, Roh told *Washington Post* reporters, "Eventually the command structure will be changed. . . . It is natural for any sovereign country to exercise operational control over its own military forces."[29]

The democratic elections in December 1987 and April 1988 have put added strength into the two main arguments advanced for returning command of Korean forces to the ROK: the U.S. command is an affront to Korean independence and sovereignty, and that command has long been seen by many as bolstering successive dictatorial military governments and condoning human rights abuses by Korean forces.

Turning over command would be a sign of confidence in the new, democratically elected, civilian government, a recognition of South Korea's growing international stature, and a distancing of the United States from its perceived past practice of supporting military rule. If necessary in order to make a smooth transition, an interim step could put a Korean in charge of the ground force component of the CFC.

Withdrawing the 2d Division

Like nuclear weapons, U.S. ground forces in Korea, particularly the 2d Infantry Division, make little military sense and are unnecessary. Perhaps the most persuasive proponent of a withdrawal of the 2d Infantry Division is retired Army Brigadier General John Bahnsen, who from 1982 to 1984 was chief of staff of the ROK/U.S. Combined Field Army, which includes the 2d Infantry Division. In 1985, while still on active duty, General Bahnsen wrote: "The wisdom of maintaining any U.S. infantry in a country so rich in manpower is purely political. And with 40 million people in South Korea opposing 20 million in the North, even the political wisdom of supporting the current design of the 2nd Infantry Division is wearing thin. . . . The 2nd Infantry Division . . . is a political solution without any basis in war-fighting requirements."[30] In May 1988, he argued:

> Militarily, South Korea's strength is in ground forces, where a large standing Army is backed by over 4 million reservists, available in 24 hours. Against this massive ground force, the US commitment of a single infantry division is absurd. . . . Against this strategic backdrop, the American Second Infantry Division . . . is militarily insignificant. . . . If the purpose is to spill American blood early to insure US involvement in any war on the Korean peninsula, then there are many easier ways to do that. We should support Korea against any aggression, but with infantry divisions only as a last resort. . . . [The 2d Infantry Division is] not appropriate to meet the valid strategic requirement for air and sea power to complement ROK ground forces. Stated reasons to keep the Second Infantry Division in Korea are badly outdated and ignore the enormous progress made by the ROK in the past several decades.[31]

The RAND study cited above reached the same conclusions:

> U.S. ground forces in Korea derive their principal value as a symbol rather than as a combat force. The direct military contributions of these forces could be provided from an enhancement of South Korea's own corresponding ground force capabilities. . . . There is no inherent reason why the two allies could not maintain or even increase that symbol at a lower level of U.S. ground forces in Korea—perhaps by expansion of U.S. air units and a firmer reiteration of U.S. declaratory policy.[32]

In justifying the U.S. presence in Korea, Assistant Secretary of Defense Armitage told Congress in 1987 that the ROK "is still critically dependent on the U.S. for air, naval, logistic support, warning, and command, control and communications."[33] Notably missing from that list is a mission for the 2d Infantry Division.

The combat capability that the 18,000 personnel in the 2d Infantry Division add to South Korea's 540,000 army personnel (twenty-one divisions) is not important. It is probably true that the physical presence of some U.S. ground forces in South Korea helps to deter the North from attacking. Their presence not only reinforces the strength of the U.S. commitment to the defense of the ROK but also—by virtue of their forward location—creates a trip wire effect, ensuring U.S. involvement in conflict. However, it should be obvious that a trip wire function could be performed by a much smaller number of troops than 43,000—a battalion or less, perhaps even the 200 soldiers guarding the Joint Security Area at Panmunjom on the DMZ.

There is reason to question the wisdom of having trip wire forces at all. It may strengthen deterrence but at too high a price. It is not at all evident that the American public would support U.S. involvement in another Korean war. Automaticity of immediate and massive combat involvement may not be desirable. It might be more prudent to adopt a posture that would allow U.S. policymakers time to reflect on the circumstances at hand and on the necessity of extensive U.S. participation, to judge the attitude of Congress and the American public, and to determine whether the ROK needs more than just logistical and materiel support or just air and naval support.

U.S. ground forces are in Korea primarily for a political purpose: to demonstrate the depth of the U.S. commitment to South Korea. It would be much safer, and less costly, to demonstrate that commitment in a different fashion. The U.S. combat contribution to Korea's defense should focus on air and technical support away from the front lines in the manpower-rich ROK.

Promoting Détente

Although the current atmosphere is poisoned by the aftermath of North Korea's latest bombing atrocity, an important part of any master plan for the reduction of U.S. forces should be efforts to promote détente (ROK-DPRK and U.S.-DPRK) and pursue arms control measures on the peninsula. There have been some positive developments in this regard in recent years: the North's flood disaster relief aid to the South, ROK-DPRK talks on reopening economic relations and on family reunification, and the now-suspended U.S. diplomats' "social" contacts with North Koreans. Other encouraging proposals have been made but not acted on. South Korea has proposed a meeting of foreign ministers; North Korea has proposed that both sides reduce overall troop levels to 100,000 within five years. President Roh has committed himself to improved relations with North Korea.

Some other measures could lead to a lessening of tensions, thereby creating a proper climate in which to carry out a U.S. withdrawal: North-South exchange programs (scientific, educational, cultural, and otherwise); confidence-building measures along the DMZ (such as a hot line, removal of military facilities, and notification and dispatch of observers to military exercises); scaling back the annual U.S.-ROK Team Spirit military exercise; softening of U.S. trade restrictions with the DPRK, especially for food and medicine; and more contacts between U.S. and DPRK officials.

Beyond the DPRK Threat

Aside from the primary argument that a withdrawal is not wise because of the North's military strength, there are a variety of other reasons why the United States desires to keep its forces in Korea. A few have some validity; for example, Korea is an excellent, highly realistic training ground for U.S. troops. Others do not; for example, some have pointed to the parochial vested interests of the U.S. military as a motivating factor; top officers want to keep high-level billets and promotion possibilities open. None overrides the compelling reasons for reducing the U.S. military presence.

As the military balance shifts to the ROK, increasing emphasis is being put on the argument that the U.S. military presence in South Korea is considered essential to remaining a viable Pacific military power. Heretofore it has generally been accepted that U.S. forces in Korea were dedicated to operations on the peninsula only. Now U.S. military planners are viewing South Korea as an important location from which to fight the Soviet Union. Some contend that it would be inappropriate to reduce U.S. forces in Korea because of increased Soviet military strength in the region. The Soviet Union, especially its navy, has undeniably expanded its military power and reach in the Pacific in the past decade. But so have the United States and its allies.

In his annual assessment of the U.S.-Soviet military balance in the region, Admiral Hays told Congress in 1987, "In a security sense, we are in good shape in the Pacific. . . . The region is a maritime theater and our ability to prevail at sea is the cornerstone of our Pacific strategy. . . . I believe that if we engaged the Soviets in the Pacific in conventional warfare that we would prevail without resorting to nuclear weapons."[34] In 1988 he noted, "A simple statistical comparison of conventional capabilities in the Pacific area of operations would not be encouraging. The Soviets outnumber us in all areas except major naval combatants, where we are roughly equal. But numbers are not the only means of comparison. Our technological edge, higher level of training, tactical initiative and innovation, . . . geographical advantages, and the exceptional quality of our people in uniform, give us enough adequate advantage to overcome the conventional numerical deficiency."[35] The same could be said of the North Korea–South Korea military balance.

Improved Relations

The United States has paid a high price for its military presence in Korea, and not just the financial cost. It has also paid a political price: association with repressive ROK military regimes at the expense of democratic principles. This has been a major contributing factor in the surge in anti-Americanism in Korea during the past several years. Among those who are forcing democratic changes in Korea, there is widespread resentment of the U.S. role in perpetuating the military dictatorship. U.S. forces were viewed as saviors in the 1950s, but for increasing numbers of South Koreans, they are now unwelcome.

A U.S. troop reduction properly executed would lead to improved U.S. relations with the Korean people and would strengthen the establishment of democracy in South Korea. If accompanied by an end to U.S. operational control over ROK forces, a U.S. troop reduction would be viewed as an expression of respect for the Korean people. South Korea would no longer have to endure charges from other states about being a U.S. puppet. South Korean national independence and integrity would no longer be compromised in either the military or political realms. The military elements that have dominated U.S.-Korean relations would be deemphasized.

Because of the extreme hostility of the DPRK to the presence of U.S. forces, a U.S. troop reduction could result in reduced North-South tensions. The risk of war, given North Korea's unpredictability, might be slightly greater, but the chances for conclusion of a meaningful peace treaty would be increased immeasurably.

Conclusion

A U.S. troop reduction would promote democracy, demilitarize U.S.-Korean relations, recognize South Korean independence and capabilities, lessen tensions on the peninsula, and reduce the danger of nuclear war. A reduction would have to be done carefully and gradually. It would have to be planned jointly and cooperatively. There could be no repeat of President Carter's mistakes of inadequate prior consultation with Korea, other allies, or Congress.

The plan outlined here—removal of nuclear weapons, turning operational control over to the ROK, withdrawal of the 2d Infantry Division and eventually air force units, while leaving behind intelligence and support units (assuming the ROK does not object)—consists of militarily feasible steps toward the desirable goals of a militarily self-reliant South Korea, a Korean peninsula with no nuclear weapons or foreign combat troops, and a reduced, more rational, less costly U.S. military presence in Northeast Asia.

Notes

1. U.S. House, Appropriations Committee (HAC), 100th Congress, 2nd sess. Department of Defense (DOD) Appropriations for 1989, pt. 2, p. 133.

2. Joint Communiqué of the 19th Annual U.S.-R.O.K. Security Consultative Meeting, May 7, 1987, p. 3.

3. HAC, 100th Congress, 2nd sess. DOD, Appropriations for 1989, pt. 2, p. 134.

4. HAC, 100th Congress, 1st sess. Foreign Assistance and Related Programs Appropriations for 1988, pt. 4, p. 99.

5. For a detailed analysis of the North Korea–South Korea military balance, see Stephen Goose, "The Military Situation on the Korean Peninsula," in *Two Koreas–One Future?* ed. John Sullivan and Roberta Foss (Lanham, Md. and London, England: University Press of America and American Friends Service Committee, 1987), pp. 55–94.

6. *Asian Defense Journal* (September 1984): 144; *Jane's Defence Weekly*, July 28, 1984, p. 94.

7. Department of Defense, *Fact Sheet: Military Strength—Worldwide, As of March 31, 1988* (June 10, 1988), p. 4.

8. William Arkin and Richard Fieldhouse, *Nuclear Battlefields* (Cambridge, Mass.: Ballinger, 1985), pp. 120, 121, 231.

9. Statement by General Robert Sennewald before the House Armed Services Committee, March 8, 1983, p. 7.

10. For recent estimates attributed to U.S. officials, see *Washington Post*, May 12, 1988, *Dallas Morning News*, April 10, 1988, and *Korea Newsreview*, May 14, 1988, p. 7. For Korean contributions, see also HAC, 100th Congress, 1st sess. Military Construction Appropriations for 1988, pt. 5, p. 349; HAC, DOD Appropriations for 1987, pt. 1, p. 138; Brigadier General Robert Pointer, Jr., and Major Howard Nichols, "Host Nation Support the Korean Way," *Army Logistician* (September–October 1984): 23–24.

11. HAC, Foreign Assistance Appropriations for 1988, pt. 4, p. 98.

12. *Korea Newsreview*, June 11, 1988, p. 4; *Washington Post*, April 25, May 12, 1988.

13. Earl Ravenal, *Defining Defense: The 1985 Military Budget* (Washington, D.C.: Cato Institute, 1984), p. 16.

14. *Army* (October 1985): 149.

15. HAC, 100th Congress, 1st sess. Military Construction Appropriations for 1988, pt. 5, p. 385.

16. Deputy Assistant Secretary of Defense James Kelly, Statement before the House Appropriations Subcommittee on Foreign Operations, March 12, 1986, p. 6.

17. *Air Force* (October 1986): 87.

18. HAC, 100th Congress, 1st sess. Military Construction Appropriations for 1988, pt. 5, pp. 347–48.

19. Charles Wolf, Donald Henry, K.C. Yeh, James Hayes, John Schank, and Richard Sneider, Report R-3305/1-NA "The Changing Balance: South and North Korean Capabilities for Long-Term Military Competition" (Santa Monica, Calif.: RAND, December 1985), pp. v–vii.

20. *Armed Forces Journal International* (May 1988): 62.

21. International Institute for Strategic Studies, *The Military Balance, 1985–86* (London: IISS, 1984), p. 118.

22. Edward A. Olsen, "Security in Northeast Asia," *Naval War College Review* (January–February 1985): 19–21.

23. *DMS Intelligence Report,* September 19, 1983, p. 1.

24. *Army* (October 1985): 134.

25. *Korea Newsreview,* October 3, 1987, p. 5.

26. Ibid., October 17, 1987, p. 6.

27. *Washington Post,* February 29, 1988; *Dallas Morning News,* April 10, 1988; *Korea Newsreview,* October 24, 1987, p. 7.

28. *Washington Post,* April 27, 1987.

29. Ibid., September 15, 1987.

30. *Armed Forces Journal International* (November 1985): 82, 86, 88.

31. Ibid. (May 1988).

32. Wolf et al., "Changing Balance," pp. vi, vii.

33. HAC, 100th Congress, 1st sess. Military Construction Appropriations for 1988, pt. 5, p. 348.

34. HAC, 100th Congress, 1st sess. DOD Appropriations for 1988, pt. 4, pp. 1145–46.

35. HAC, 100th Congress, 2nd sess. DOD Appropriations for 1989, pt. 2, p. 139.

7

The People's Republic of China and U.S. Security Policy in East Asia

A. James Gregor

E ver since the first overt efforts at rapprochement between the PRC and the United States, the implications of that rapprochement in terms of policy have remained unclear. At one point, it was anticipated that the association of the PRC and the United States would compel the Soviets to pursue a more "conservative, détente oriented strategy" in East Asia.[1] The United States would no longer find its resources taxed by a containment policy that conceived both the Soviet Union and the PRC the proper objects of constraint. With rapprochement, the PRC, along with all its real and fancied attributes, could be transferred to the asset column of the anti-Soviet consortium, significantly changing the global distribution of military, political, and economic potential. Rapprochement was understood to have eased Washington's regional and international defense burdens.[2]

In some intuitive sense, all this seemed obvious enough.[3] Allied with the Soviet Union, the large land army of the PRC not only threatened U.S. interests but the security and integrity of Beijing's littoral and insular neighbors as well. Rapprochement with Washington was understood to have dissipated those threats and redirected Beijing's military potential against the burgeoning Soviet forces in Northeast Asia.

In the first euphoria that attended rapprochement, there were those who anticipated a rapid improvement of the PRC's armed forces until they might serve as a military counterweight to Soviet capabilities. The assumption was that the industrialized democracies would provide the Communist Chinese military with capabilities that would offset the growing Soviet forces in East Asia, releasing U.S. military assets for the defense of Washington's interests elsewhere in the world. For its part, Beijing apparently anticipated that such transfers of weapon systems and technology would rapidly modernize its forces until they could counter any Soviet initiatives launched against the PRC along the Sino-Soviet border.

Background

As Sino-Soviet hostility escalated after the tensions that developed in the 1960s, the leadership in Beijing found itself without a credible security policy. The armed clashes that broke out along the Sino-Soviet border in 1969 clearly revealed the deficiencies that afflicted the People's Liberation Army (PLA). Along the Amur and Ussuri rivers in the East and at the Dzungarian Gate in the West in Central Asia, Communist Chinese forces were badly mauled by Soviet armored forces, supported by artillery and rotary-winged gunships.[4]

The savaging of Communist Chinese units along the border apparently precipitated an aggressive reassessment of security policy in Beijing. The Soviet Union, the once-heralded "eternal ally" of Mao Zedong, was identified as the principal enemy of the PRC, and the industrial democracies, particularly the United States, began to be considered candidates for a Beijing-sponsored anti-Soviet united front. Throughout the 1970s, the authorities in Beijing made overtures to Washington and Tokyo to enter into some kind of security relationship with the PRC that might serve as a deterrent to Soviet initiatives in East Asia.[5] As late as December 1978, then, the vice-minister of defense of the PRC, Su Yu, was reported to have argued that Communist China could not defend itself against the Soviet Union in the event of hostilities and would have to "cultivate friendly relations with such advanced countries as the United States and Japan" in order to put together a credible deterrent.[6]

Between 1969 and 1979 several factors seem to have become increasingly evident to the leadership in Beijing. The armed forces of the PRC were inadequate to the defense of the community. Since the conflict on the Korean peninsula, the Communist Chinese leadership had been forced to acknowledge that the transportation infrastructure of the PRC was far too thin to support a major conflict on the nation's borders. In the Korean War hundreds of thousands of Communist Chinese troops had been sacrificed to the firepower of U.N. forces because of the obsolescence of PLA equipment and the inability of general service forces to provide adequate supplies to the combat troops. Years later Zhou Enlai was to assert that given the magnitude of those losses, it probably had been a mistake for Communist China to have become involved in the conflict.[7]

In the years between the Korean War and the armed clashes with Soviet elements along the border, the PLA could do little to solve the problems that had proved so costly on the Korean battlefield. Little could be done to solve the logistical problems that afflicted the armed forces of the PRC. By the end of the 1970s, the ground forces of the PRC remained composed essentially of foot-mobile infantry, armed with outdated weapons, supported by towed artillery, without effective air cover, and typified by impaired resupply and repair capabilities. It was apparent that the leadership of the PRC sought some policy that could provide protection for the nation's immediate interests. In early 1977, a media article produced by the PLA general staff called for rapid military modernization in order to prepare for a "surprise attack and a big, early nuclear war."

During the 1970s, in the course of what was apparently acrimonious and tortuous dispute, the Communist Chinese leadership had attempted to put together the components of a national security policy. Rapid military modernization was to be attempted, with the support of the advanced industrial democracies. At the same time, a policy was to be pursued that would unite all the anti-Soviet forces in the effort to preclude attack on Communist Chinese territory.[8]

All of this appears to have foundered. First, it early became evident that the industrialized democracies would not be able to supply the requisite weapon systems and their support adjuncts in sufficient abundance, and with sufficient dispatch, to ensure the survival of the PRC on the occasion of a determined Soviet attack. Second, even if the industrialized democracies could supply the weapon systems and their attendant adjuncts, it was clear that the PRC did not have the foreign exchange resources to pay for them, nor could such high-technology items be absorbed even if paid for. Moreover, the PLA could not easily absorb modern weapon systems because of a serious domestic scarcity of skilled personnel.[9]

Until the beginning of 1979, however, some factions among the leadership in Beijing were still not convinced of the full magnitude of the PLA's deficiencies. Even Su Yu, prepared to acknowledge the PLA's inability to defend the homeland from military attack by the Soviet Union, continued to maintain that, should it prove necessary, the armed forces of the PRC would bring the "little clowns in Vietnam" to their knees within a week.[10]

Unhappily, the performance of the Communist Chinese military in the course of their invasion of Vietnam left a great deal to be desired. Not only did the PLA take heavy casualties in the fighting, but there were serious equipment failures. Many of their weapon systems proved inferior in the face of Vietnamese resistance. And there had been intolerable delays in keeping troops at the front supplied, though they had not advanced far from the Chinese border. The PLA suffered about 65,000 casualties and lost about 420 battle tanks in the brief conflict.[11]

The attack against Vietnam did not result in the withdrawal of Vietnamese troops from Kampuchea, one of the principal motives for the invasion, nor did the PLA succeed in destroying any of the Vietnamese main force divisions. Most of the defenders encountered by the PLA were members of the militia—the local forces. For all that, the Chinese forces apparently were unable to pacify the border regions occupied by the PLA.

The conflict in Vietnam seems to have resolved some of the doubts that had afflicted the leadership in Beijing. It seems to have become indisputable that "the PLA [was] incapable of fighting a modern war"[12] The decision to undertake the "punitive" incursion into Vietnam came under severe criticism.

Chen Yun, one of the leaders of a major post-Maoist faction, is reported to have delivered a scathing indictment of the entire adventure. It seemed evident that the effort had failed in large part because the transportation and communications infrastructure of Communist China could not support the troops in the field. Much of the military equipment in PLA inventory proved inferior to that deployed by the Vietnamese. Chinese armor proved particularly vulnerable to Vietnamese antitank fire, and a fear of disabling losses in the air kept Communist Chinese aircraft out of the combat zone. PLA troops were forced to take strong points employing the same human wave tactics that had cost them such grievous casualties in the Korean conflict.[13]

With the evidence of the Vietnamese conflict at hand, it was apparent that the armed forces of the PRC would be at a suicidal disadvantage in any frontal conflict with the vastly superior forces of the Soviet Union. By the end of March 1979, the leaders of the PRC seem to have been compelled to reassess their alternatives and attempt a reformulation of policy that would protect the nation's most vital interests.

The New Policy

As an apparent aftermath of the Vietnamese episode, the leaders in Beijing seem to have settled on a new security policy. Less than a month after the armed incursion into Vietnam, Beijing signaled Moscow that it was prepared to enter into negotiations "to settle . . . outstanding issues . . . and improve bilateral relations."[14] On April 3, 1979, shortly after the end of the conflict in Vietnam, the Foreign Ministry of the PRC notified the Soviet embassy in Beijing that while there would be no renewal of the 1950 treaty of friendship between the two nations, it was prepared to enter into formal negotiations to reduce the measure of hostility that had arisen between them.

Almost immediately a number of Chinese officials who at one time had been condemned for recommending an effort to improve relations between the PRC and the Soviet Union were rehabilitated. Two days after the PRC proposed negotiations with Moscow to improve relations, the late Wang Jiaxiang, Beijing's first ambassador to Moscow, was exonerated for having advocated a moderation of hostilities between the PRC and the Soviet Union during the mid-1960s.

At the end of the subsequent summer, former Communist party general secretary Zhang Wentian, who had been charged with collusion with Moscow, was accorded a belated memorial service. In November, Yang Xianzhen, former director of the Communist party school system, was exonerated of the charge of trying to heal the rift between China and the "revisionists" of Moscow.[15]

During that same time there was an appreciable reduction in the frequency with which the Chinese referred to the Soviets as "revisionists" and "social imperialists." Although the process of accommodation was interrupted by the Soviet invasion of Afghanistan in 1979, there was a sustained effort on the part of the authorities in Beijing to reduce the level of hostility between the PRC and the Soviet Union.[16]

In March 1982, a Chinese gymnastics teams made its appearance at games held in the Soviet capital, and in October Deputy Foreign Minister Leonid Ilyichev, a major Soviet expert on the PRC, led a high-level diplomatic mission to Beijing for more than two weeks of exploratory discussions calculated to upgrade bilateral relations. In November of that year, the Chinese ambassador to Moscow attended the celebrations of the Bolshevik Revolution in Red Square. The Standing Committee of the PRC National People's Congress and the PRC State Council sent "warm greetings" to the Supreme Soviet Presidium and the Soviet Council of Ministers, proclaiming that "the Chinese side is sincerely striving to eliminate all obstacles hindering the normalization of Sino-Soviet relations and to direct the relations between the two countries onto a path of sound development."[17] Between 1977, when Deng Xiaoping announced that any effort at Sino-Soviet rapprochement was hopeless, and 1982, there had been a large change in the foreign policy agenda of the PRC. At the Twelfth Communist party Congress in 1982, Deng Xiaoping announced a policy of carefully crafted independence. The PRC no longer sought a united front against Soviet "social imperialism." Prudence recommended a reduction in hostility along its long border with the Soviet Union. There had been three or four years of vacillation, but by 1982 it was clear that a new policy orientation would direct Communist China's foreign and security policies for the immediate and perhaps foreseeable future. Efforts to forge security ties with the industrialized democracies gave way to appeals for capital funds through concessional loans, joint venture enterprise, and markets for light industrial and agricultural exports. Regional stability was to be sought through a moderation of hostility with both Moscow and Hanoi—with diplomatic normalization of relations and a restoration of party-to-party contact between the PRC and the Soviet Union a distinct possibility.[18]

The Durability of Policy

So many changes have overtaken the foreign and security policies of the PRC since the death of Mao Zedong in 1976 that it is hazardous to venture judgments concerning the durability of any particular policy. So many factors intersect in the formulation and durability of Communist Chinese policy that it is very difficult to anticipate the future.

With respect to security concerns, however, there are some constants, absent in the case of domestic economic policy and foreign exchange strategies, that suggest a considerable measure of continuity. The first is that the properties that characterize the PRC's military capabilities are resistant to rapid change. Any substantial upgrading of its armed forces would be costly and require a considerable lead time. By the late 1970s it had become reasonably clear that Beijing lacked the disposable income to underwrite the hardware and weapon systems procurement necessary to render the PLA a modern fighting force. Moreover, for the foreseeable future, the road, rail, and communications infrastructure of the PRC could not be improved sufficiently to support the requirements of modern warfare. Finally, the seriously impaired economic system inherited from the chaos of the final years of Maoist rule requires massive infusions of capital if it is to be rehabilitated and refurbished, allowing little in the way of resources that could be invested in rapid modernization of the armed forces.

Given the hard realities of their circumstances, it appears that by the early 1980s, the authorities in Beijing decided that military modernization would have to be their lowest priority in terms of budgetary allocation. After the end of the 1970s there appears to have been a real and relative decline in allocations made to the PRC military[19] with a corresponding reduction in the overall size of the PLA. Over a million members of the armed forces were either transferred to civilian tasks or demobilized in an undertaking that has been publicly characterized as an effort to produce a leaner and more capable military. Needless to say, the manpower reduction was also expected to achieve significant cost reductions.

If all the proposed reductions are effected, by 1989 the PLA will number 3 million men under arms. The PLA includes all Communist Chinese arms and services—strategic, ground, naval, and air defense components—and would still remain the largest military organization in the world. It would deploy the world's largest infantry force, the world's third largest air and naval forces, and perhaps the world's third largest nuclear strategic capability.[20] Whatever their size, however, these forces are equipped with largely obsolescent weapon systems and led by an officer corps that remains poorly trained and, in large measure, by general staff officers who are superannuated.[21]

Given these realities, Beijing's current security policy of maintaining its "independence" and seeking accommodation with its Soviet neighbor is recommended by every rational calculation.[22] Not only do the armed forces of the PLA face overwhelming Soviet forces on their extended border, but the Soviets have continued to improve their geostrategic position since the late 1970s with the occupation of Afghanistan and access to air and naval facilities to the south of the PRC in the Socialist Republic of Vietnam. Not only do Soviet forces in East Asia enjoy quantitative and qualitative advantages in critical weapon systems, they occupy important support and staging areas to the north, west, and south of the PRC.[23]

Since the mid-1960s, the Soviet Union has not only strengthened its war-fighting ability in East Asia but has gained access to out-of-area bases, storage facilities, and staging areas in South and Southeast Asia. In the immediate past, moreover, Moscow has succeeded in reactivating its military relationship with the Communist regime in Pyongyang and has negotiated overflight rights through North Korean airspace for its military aircraft, as well as calling rights for its naval vessels at the North Korean ports of Wonsan and Nampo, directly across from Communist China's most heavily industrialized regions.[24]

The fact is that in the last two decades there has been a dramatic strengthening of Soviet military capabilities in East Asia—to the disadvantage of not only the PRC but the United States and its allies as well.[25] Initially that change was characterized by the increased deployment of mechanized troops along the Sino-Soviet border, bringing the number of divisions east of the Urals to forty motorized rifle divisions, seven or eight armored divisions, and two airborne divisions. Today these forces are supported by the most advanced interceptor, air combat, ground support, and strike aircraft in Soviet frontal aviation.

In the past, it was often a decade before the most advanced weapon systems in Soviet inventory reached its forces in the Far East. Recently, however, the most advanced Soviet main battle tanks, the T-72s and T-80s, have made their appearance in the Soviet Far East and Pacific theaters of operations at about the same time they entered into inventory among the Warsaw Pact armies. Similarly, the Tu-22M Backfire bomber, as well as the MiG-27 Flogger, the MiG-25 Foxbat, the MiG-29 Fulcrum, and the Su-25 Frogfoot, have all been deployed in East Asia at almost the same time they appeared in Europe. These assets provide overwhelming superiority to anything available to the PRC forces across the border and also threaten the most advanced weapons systems available to the United States and its allies in the West Pacific.[26]

In that regard, it is significant that of all the Soviet combat forces deployed in East Asia, that which has undergone the most dramatic development has been the Soviet navy.[27] In East Asia, the Soviet Union has nothing to fear from the Communist Chinese navy, which remains essentially a coastal defense force.

It has become evident that the Soviet naval buildup in Asia is directed against the United States and its allies. The Soviets have built what was once a negligible force into the largest of Soviet fleets—a well-balanced, multimission-capable, blue-water force displacing about 1.78 million tons and composed of over 85 major surface combat vessels, 2 aircraft carriers, 12 missile cruisers, 25 destroyers, and 41 frigates—all missile capable. These are supplemented by a fleet of about 140 submarines, about 70 of them nuclear powered. Once confined to the coastal waters of the Soviet maritime provinces, the Soviet Pacific fleet now operates everywhere in Asian waters, with air support provided by an organic complement of both land-based and shipborne naval aviation.

To that formidable force, the Soviet military has now added the capabilities of its land-based intermediate- and short-range missile systems. The 5,000-kilometer range SS-20s, deployed in East Asia, threaten all of the continental, littoral, and insular nations of the region as far south as the Philippines. The command, control, and communication adjuncts necessary to the effective employment of these Soviet weapon systems have been hardened against nuclear blast effects and are serviced by a better logistical and intelligence network that has been emplaced in the Soviet Far East and Pacific military theaters of operation.

About one-third of the entire Soviet strategic nuclear capability now is deployed in East Asia, with a major reserve of submarine-borne nuclear strike potential located in the Sea of Okhotsk to the north of the Japanese home islands. In effect, over the last two decades the quality and quantity of Soviet forces in the Far East have been dramatically improved. For the first time in modern history, "the Soviets have projected their military power in the far East beyond their historic sphere of influence and have thereby enhanced their capability to challenge any nation or combination of nations in this region."[28]

Given present Soviet capabilities, the reluctance of the PRC to challenge the Soviet Union in East Asia is perfectly comprehensible. For all intents and purposes, the PRC armed forces are incapable of defending the nation against a determined Soviet assault.[29] Equally evident is the fact that the PRC could expect very little from the industrialized democracies once a Soviet attack had been launched. The industrialized democracies would be unable to resupply and rehabilitate PRC forces devastated by Soviet attack.[30]

Given these circumstances, there appear to be few options open to the leadership in Beijing. There is no quick fix for PRC military inferiority relative to the Soviet Union. For the foreseeable future, it is impossible to upgrade Communist Chinese forces or their combat effectiveness either through the domestic production of suitably advanced weapon systems or the construction of an adequate transportation and communications infrastructure. At least until the end of the century, the PRC will remain exposed to the real possibility of Soviet aggression in which Moscow has every reason to believe that it could prevail.[31] As long as that attack involved only conventional forces and limited objectives (the creation of a demilitarized buffer between the Soviet Union and the PRC), Beijing could expect little significant assistance from the industrialized democracies. Finally, it has become evident that the principal security concern of the Soviet military command since the early 1980s has not been the foot-mobile infantry of the PRC but the armed forces of the confederational alliance in East Asia led by the United States.

Beijing's response to these considerations has been to seek out some kind of accommodation with the Soviet Union in order to reduce the possibilities of Soviet aggression. A corresponding distance from any suggestion of security ties with the industrialized democracies—in order not to provoke the leadership in Moscow—also recommends itself.[32] At the same time, it is in the interest of the PRC to retain (and expand to the extent that it is serviceable) economic relations with the advanced industrial powers in order to augment and rationalize its retrograde productive system.

Implications

In general, most Americans have failed to appreciate the vast changes that have taken place in East Asia over the past two decades in terms of Soviet capabilities and corresponding Soviet opportunities. Certainly there was an acknowledgment of the importance of the Soviet aggression in Afghanistan, an undertaking that brought Soviet combat forces within effective range of the critical Persian Gulf region. There was also an acknowledgment of the significance of Mikhail Gorbachev's July 1986 Vladivostok speech, which signaled an intended Soviet economic, diplomatic, and security offensive throughout the entire East.

Nonetheless, all this really has not captured the American imagination. Sophisticated Soviet naval exercises off the coasts of Korea, Japan, Okinawa, the Philippines, and as far east as Hawaii have not engaged the interest of most Americans. The increasingly regular appearance of Soviet military aircraft over the South China Sea and along the air corridor from North Korea to Vietnam has provoked very limited response by the United States. The regular overtures made by the Soviet Union for fishing rights among the nations of the South Pacific—and the associated appeal for onshore calling privileges and servicing—have prompted limited response outside of specialist circles.

At a time when the Soviet Union in East Asia has undertaken some of the most important initiatives of its most recent history, most Americans have been preoccupied with events in Central America and the Middle East. However important those events might be, developments in East Asia have far-reaching implications for the future of Americans, as well as for more than one-quarter of all of humanity. The United States and its noncommunist allies in East Asia today face a formidable challenge to collective interests. Not only has the Soviet Union strengthened its force capabilities throughout all of Asia, but the hope that the PRC might provide a counterweight to those capabilities has shown itself to be illusory. The United States and its noncommunist allies in East Asia must put together a credible deterrent against Soviet initiatives in the region without any direct or collateral support from the PRC.[33] For the foreseeable future, unless the PRC came under direct attack, the United States and its allies could expect the PRC to remain scrupulously neutral regarding the Soviet Union.[34]

None of this as yet has engaged the concern of the average American. That is unfortunate, for a serious consideration of U.S. security policy in East Asia has important implications for its formal and informal defense partners along the entire archipelagic chain that stretches from Hokkaido to the Philippines–and involves the interests of littoral allies on the Korean peninsula and the land bridge in Southeast Asia.

U.S. security policy in East Asia necessarily is one of deterrence. The logic of deterrence requires that a defense environment be created in which the risks run would be so many and the costs incurred so great that any aggression would be too dangerous or expensive to undertake.

In East Asia the outlines of such a policy are evident. Any conflict between the United States and the Soviet Union would involve Soviet forces deployed in Asia. In Asia, the United States is required to attempt to confine Soviet forces, to the fullest extent possible, to the Seas of Japan and Okhotsk behind the archipelagic barrier created by the islands of Japan.[35] To demonstrate a credible capacity to do that requires the active involvement of the Self Defense Forces of Japan. More than that, it would require U.S. access to extensive base facilities, prepositioned supplies, and early warning systems in the Japanese home islands. It would require the armed forces of Japan to undertake the mining of the narrow choke points at the Soya, Tsugaru, and Tsushima straits through which Soviet combat forces would have to pass if they were to gain access to the open Pacific. Japanese aircraft would have to serve as first contact interceptors in the effort to thwart Soviet air strikes against high-value U.S. and Japanese ground and naval targets throughout the region. Japanese Ground Self Defense Forces would have to defend the Soya Strait against Soviet amphibious assault, and Japanese Maritime Self Defense Forces would have to undertake antisubmarine warfare missions in the effort to maintain the integrity of some length of the critical sea lines of communication that stretch from the South China Sea to ports in Korea and the home islands of Japan.

Japan, in effect, would be the linchpin of a defense system calculated to deter any Soviet military misadventure in Northeast Asia. For its part, the Republic of Korea would play a similar role in closing the Korean Straits to Soviet ship passage.[36] The Republic of Korea, like Japan, not only is required to provide substantial supplements to the armed forces of the United States stationed in Northeast Asia, it must ensure those forces adequate basing facilities, staging areas, intelligence, and supplies.

Without the active participation of Japan and South Korea, in effect, a deterrent defense of East Asia would be impossible. That, if for no other reason, makes the peace, prosperity, and political stability of both Japan and the Republic of Korea of critical concern to the United States.

It is in just such a context that the PRC can play a passive role in regional deterrence policy. However the Communist Chinese accommodate the Soviet Union, there will be sufficient suspicion remaining from the long years of Sino-Soviet hostility to prompt the Soviet military leadership to maintain a substantial force along the Chinese border in order to ensure Beijing's neutrality in the event of general conflict.

To profit from the passive involvement of the PRC in the defense of East Asia does not require any cultivation of Beijing by Washington. For the foreseeable future, the Communist Chinese can neither increase nor diminish their contribution to a regional defense. They cannot increase military pressure on the Soviet Union without incurring intolerable risks given the overwhelming Soviet advantages along the Sino-Soviet border. Conversely, they can do remarkably little to diminish their role simply because the Soviet Union has every reason to remain suspicious of Communist Chinese intentions given the recent history of the region.

Beyond all that, a credible deterrent against Soviet misadventure in East Asia requires that the United States and its allies have the capabilities adequate to defend the full length of the essential sea lines of communication vital to the viability and defense needs of the import-dependent economies of South Korea and Japan. At the same time, an effective deterrent policy involves the ability to deny the Soviet Union the use of those same sea passages in time of conflict. Those sea-lanes are important to the Soviet Union because existing Soviet logistical capabilities in East Asia are insufficient to supply Moscow's forces in the Pacific theater of military operations in the event of high-tempo conflict. Some of the Soviet Union's most important combat forces in East Asia are located on the Kamchatka peninsula and in the chain of Soviet bases around the Sea of Okhotsk. In times of crisis, those forces can only be supplied effectively over the ship routes from the south. For the United States and its regional allies, maintaining a credible capacity to interdict those routes has become important as a critical element in the prevailing policy of deterrence. To make a claim of such sea-denial capabilities credible requires basing facilities open to U.S. naval and air units along the major routes from the Indonesian narrows through the Bashi Channel and the Taiwan Strait.[37]

It is to the south of Japan that the conditions essential to the attainment and maintenance of effective sea-denial capability have become increasingly difficult for the United States to sustain. Access to adequate naval and air facilities in the region has become increasingly precarious for U.S. forces. In the late 1970s, with the withdrawal of diplomatic recognition from the

Republic of China on Taiwan, the armed forces of the United States lost access to facilities that had been useful to U.S. combat operations in Southeast Asia during the conflict in Vietnam. Almost immediately political crisis settled down over the Philippines, and, as a consequence, the availability of facilities in the archipelago has become increasingly problematic.[38]

At the same time, the situation along the major waterways of East Asia has become increasingly complicated. The Soviet Union has acquired calling, aircraft servicing, ship repair, storage, and personnel billeting rights at Cam Ranh Bay and Danang in Vietnam. Thirty Soviet naval vessels now use the facilities at Cam Ranh Bay with regularity, and Soviet reconnaissance and fighter aircraft use airfields in the vicinity. Thus, as the apparent availability of facilities has diminished for U.S. forces in East Asia, the Soviet Union has increased its out-of-area access to generous facilities in Southeast Asia along the major trading routes to the northeast. It has long since become clear to Moscow that ship passages along the East Asian coast are not only essential to the maintenance of the combat readiness of Soviet forces in the Far East provinces, but potential control of those waterways by the Soviet Union could significantly influence political judgment in Tokyo and Seoul and create problems for Washington. Both Japan and South Korea are necessarily sensitive to any threat to freedom of passage along the major ship routes in East Asia. Should the Soviet Union create a credible capability to interdict the sea-lanes of East Asia, the entire U.S. security posture in the region could be seriously impaired.

For at least these reasons, U.S. defense analysts have monitored developments in the Philippines with so much attention. The loss of the facilities in the Philippines would significantly undermine U.S. capabilities in the South China Sea and jeopardize sea control effectiveness along the shipping routes in the area. Should political developments in the Philippines compel the United States to abandon its facilities at Subic Bay and Clark Field, the security environment in East Asia could become increasingly inauspicious.

There are few alternatives available to the U.S. military in Southeast Asia that might be an adequate substitute for the Philippine bases other than Taiwan and the territories under the control of Taipei.[39] The island of Taiwan sits astride the critical waterways that pass through the Bashi Channel and the Taiwan Strait, the major sea routes traversed by the oil tankers and bulk carriers that supply Japan and South Korea. Those same routes are also the most direct sea-lanes available to the Soviets to supply their bases in the Far East and Pacific military theaters. Soviet vessels from Eastern Europe and the Middle East pass through both the Bashi Channel and the Taiwan Strait en route to termini in Vladivostok, Sakhalin Island, and the Kamchatka Peninsula.[40]

Given the potential role of Taiwan as an alternative to facilities in the

Philippines, the United States has every reason to continue to cultivate security relations, however informal, with the Nationalist Chinese. Whatever difficulties with Beijing might be entailed in continuing those relations, Washington has every calculated reason to sustain them. Beijing can do little either to increase or diminish its passive role in the anti-Soviet defense of East Asia. Taiwan, on the other hand, offers the anti-Soviet alliance access to critically important base facilities along sea and air corridors that are central to the defense of the entire region.

Conclusions

It has become evident that Washington can expect little more from Beijing than it has already received in terms of security benefits.[41] The presence of the PRC complicates Soviet defense strategy in East Asia, and the PRC will continue to complicate that strategy whatever Beijing's relationship with the United States or the Soviet Union. However affable Beijing's relationship with Moscow, the Soviet Union will have to maintain a sufficient force along the Sino-Soviet border to ensure Communist Chinese neutrality in any general conflict. The Soviet Union has far too much at stake in its Far Eastern provinces to accord the region anything less than a defense capability adequate to meet any contingency. The history of Sino-Soviet conflict is too recent and too bitter to imagine any major drawdown of Soviet forces— whatever the nature of diplomatic relations between the two communist powers.[42]

Washington can continue to expect this kind of passive security advantage in its relationship with the PRC. It is really not within the power of Beijing to increase or diminish significantly that advantage. Even if Beijing were to pursue security ties with the Soviet Union (a very unlikely prospect), simple prudence would require that the Soviet military command nonetheless maintain a force along the joint border that would ensure security.

Other than that, it is clear that Beijing would not actively assist the United States in any general conflict with the Soviet Union.[43] All Beijing's immediate and long-term interests would counsel against such a course. Moscow can only be fully cognizant of that fact.

The United States remains obligated to put together a credible policy of deterrence for East Asia with only passive Communist Chinese support. The noncommunist littoral states of East Asia will be required to provide the active support that will render U.S. war-fighting and sea-denial capabilities credible. Bases in Japan and the Philippines contribute to those capabilities and that credibility. Bases in the Philippine archipelago provide the staging areas and the resupply facilities that serve as major deterrents to Soviet actions along sea routes through the Indian Ocean and the South China Sea.

But developments in the Philippines threaten the continued U.S. presence in the region. Only the real possibility that U.S. forces could be rapidly relocated in close proximity can offset the threat to the integrity of current U.S. security policy. The availability of naval and air facilities within the territories controlled by the authorities in Taipei provides that requisite alternative. At least for this reason the continued U.S. relationship with the Republic of China on Taiwan is of significance to the peace and security of East Asia and the balance of power in the world.

The current security policy being pursued by the PRC is a function of a responsible assessment by the authorities in Beijing. Given the prevailing circumstances, military modernization in the PRC has been reduced to a secondary concern. The necessary consequence has been an overt effort by Communist China's leadership to reduce the potential for hostility between Beijing and Moscow. At the same time, that policy and its entailments render security cooperation between the United States, Japan, South Korea, and the Republic of China on Taiwan of increasing importance to any credible security policy in East Asia. The current policies of the PRC have succeeded in making more intense collaboration between the noncommunist littoral and insular nations of the region critical to the security and prosperity of the international community and the containment of the Soviet Union in East Asia.

Notes

1. Given the limitations of space, the argument presented here is stenographic. Only the major outline is presented. Most of the notes suggest where the point made in the text is dealt with more extensively. In this instance, see Justin Galen, "U.S.'s Toughest Message to the USSR," *Armed Forces International* (February 1979). *Justin Galen* is a pseudonym for an unidentified senior Department of Defense analyst.

2. See the discussion in Robert G. Sutter, *The China Quandary: Domestic Determinants of U.S. China Policy, 1972–1982* (Boulder, Colo.: Westview, 1983), pp. 110–13, 19–20, 73, 85, 118–21, 123.

3. See Robert S. Ross, "China's Strategic Role in Asia," in James W. Morely, ed., *The Pacific Basin: New Challenges for the United States* (New York: Academy of Political Science, 1986), p. 116.

4. See Gerald Segal, *Defending China* (New York: Oxford University Press, 1985), chap. 10; Harry Gelman, *The Soviet Far East Buildup and Soviet Risk-Taking against China* (Santa Monica: RAND, August 1982), pp. 31–36; John W. Garver, *China's Decision for Rapprochement with the United States, 1968–1971* (Boulder, Colo.: Westview, 1982), pp. 63–71.

5. See the account in Michael Yahuda, *China's Foreign Policy after Mao: Towards the End of Isolationism* (New York: St. Martin's, 1983), pp. 196–212. The

polemical but informative account of Pauly Parakal, *Peking's Betrayal of Asia* (New Delhi: Sterling, 1976) is useful.

6. Quoted in "Su Yu Reveals the Probability of War with Russia," *Inside China Mainland* (Taipei) (March 1979): 1–2.

7. Quoted in William V. Kennedy, "The Defense of China's Homeland," in Ray Bonds, ed., *The Chinese War Machine* (New York: Crescent, 1979), p. 102.

8. This is the more-or-less standard version. See A. Doak Barnett, *China and the Major Powers in East Asia* (Washington, D.C.: Brookings, 1977), pp. 227–30. Consult the alternative interpretation presented by Greg O'Leary, *The Shaping of Chinese Foreign Policy* (New York: St. Martin's, 1980), chap. 4. For details on the military modernization program, see David L. Shambaugh, "China's Defense Industries: Indigenous and Foreign Procurement," in Paul H.B. Godwin, ed., *The Chinese Defense Establishment: Continuity and Change in the 1980's* (Boulder, Colo.: Westview, 1983).

9. See Lawrence Freedman, "Economic and Technological Factors in the Sino-Soviet Dispute," in Douglas T. Stuart and William T. Tow, eds., *China, the Soviet Union, and the West* (Boulder, Colo.: Westview, 1982), pp. 73–86; Leslie H. Gelb, "U.S. Defense Policy, Technology Transfers, and Asian Security," in Richard H. Solomon, ed., *Asian Security in the 1980s: Problems and Policies for a Time of Transition* (Cambridge, Mass.: Oelgeschlager, Gunn & Hain, 1980), pp. 264–68; Sydney James, "Military Industry," and Karen Berney, "Aspects of Modernization," in Gerald Segal and William T. Tow, eds., *Chinese Defense Policy* (Urbana: University of Illinois, 1984), pp. 117–48.

10. "Su Yu Reveals the Probability of War," p. 2.

11. See King C. Chen, *China's War against Vietnam, 1979: A Military Analysis* (Baltimore: University of Maryland School of Law, 1983).

12. Ibid., p. 29.

13. See Segal, *Defending China*, chap. 12; James B. Linder and A. James Gregor, "The Communist Chinese Air Force in the 'Punitive' War against Vietnam," *Air University Review* 32, no. 6 (September–October 1981): 67–77.

14. Chi Su, "China and the Soviet Union: 'Principled, Salutary, and Tempered' Management of Conflict," in Samuel S. Kim, ed., *China and the World: Chinese Foreign Policy in the Post-Mao Era* (Boulder, Colo.: Westview, 1984), p. 135.

15. This process of reevaluation of the Soviet Union was already underway in 1978. See Gilbert Rozman, *The Chinese Debate about Soviet Socialism, 1978–1985* (Princeton: Princeton University Press, 1987). Of special interest is Carol Lee Harin, "Competing 'Policy Packages' in Post-Mao China," *Asian Survey* 24, no. 5 (May 1984): 503–4.

16. Hammond Rolph, "China's Changing World View," in Segal and Tow, *Chinese Defense Policy*, p. 168.

17. *Foreign Broadcast Information Service, PRC International Affairs (Soviet Union)*, November 8, 1982, p. C1.

18. See the discussion in Michael Oksenberg, "China's Confident Nationalism," in *America and the World 1986* (New York: Foreign Affairs, 1987), pp. 501–23.

19. Ibid., p. 507.

20. Estimates of the PRC's military order of battle are available in the annual account, *Military Balance,* published by the Institute of Strategic Studies in London.

21. See the discussion in Kenneth Hunt, "Sino-Soviet Theater Force Comparisons," in Stuart and Tow, *China, the Soviet Union, and the West,* pp. 103–14; Harlan Jencks, "Ground Forces," Bill Sweetman, "Air Forces," and Bruce Swanson, "Naval Forces," in Segal and Tow, *Chinese Defense Policy,* pp. 53–97; and Leo Yueh-yun Liu, "Military Modernization and Strategic Defense in the PRC in the 1980s," in King-yuh Chang, ed., *Perspectives on Development in Mainland China* (Boulder, Colo.: Westview, 1985), pp. 137–49.

22. See the more ample discussion in A. James Gregor, *Arming the Dragon: U.S. Security Ties with the People's Republic of China* (Washington, D.C.: Ethics and Public Policy Center, 1988).

23. See the discussion in David Armstrong, "The Soviet Union," in Segal and Tow, *Chinese Defense Policy,* pp. 180–95.

24. See James W. Nance, "Strategic Importance of North Korean Ports to the Soviet Union," and John Koehler, Jr., "Some Strategic Implications of New Soviet Military Technology Assistance to North Korea," in *Strategic Implications of the Soviet-North Korean Alliance* (New York: International Security Council, April 1987), pp. 45–62.

25. See A. James Gregor and Maria Hsia Chang, *The Iron Triangle: A U.S. Security Policy for Northeast Asia* (Stanford: Hoover Institution, 1984), chaps. 2, 8.

26. See Young Whan Kihl and Lawrence E. Grinter, "New Security Realities in the Asian Pacific: Perspectives, Purpose, and Approach," in Young Whan Kihl and Lawrence E. Grinter, eds., *Asian-Pacific Security: Emerging Challenges and Responses* (Boulder, Colo.: Lynne Rienner, 1986), pp. 1–15.

27. See *Soviet Naval Developments* (Annapolis, Md.: Nautical and Aviation Publishing, 1984), sec. 1.

28. For an account of the regional order of battle, see *Soviet Military Power* (Washington, D.C.: Department of Defense, 1986), chap. 1.

29. *Soviet Naval Developments,* p. 77; Hisatomo Matsukane, "The Strategic Significance of the Soviet-Vietnamese Alliance and Japan's Position," in *The Soviet-Vietnamese Alliance and the Security of Southeast Asia* (New York: International Security Council, November 1986), pp. 132–35.

30. See William C. Green and David S. Yost, "Soviet Military Options Regarding China," in Stuart and Tow, *China, the Soviet Union, and the West,* pp. 135–44; Kennedy, "Perceived Threat," pp. 168–81; Noel Gayler, "Security Implications of the Soviet Military Presence in Asia," in Solomon, *Asian Security,* p. 59. Remarkably little has changed since the publication of Drew Middleton, *The Duel of the Giants: China and Russia in Asia* (New York: Scribner's, 1978); Harrison E. Salisbury, *War between Russia and China* (New York: Norton, 1969).

31. See the discussion in William L. Scully, "The Military Dimension: Sino-American Relations," in Frederick Tse-shyang Chen, ed., *China Policy and National Security* (Dobbs Ferry, N.Y.: Transnational, 1984), pp. 31–43.

32. See the discussion in Jonathan D. Pollack, "China and the Global Strategic

Balance," in Harry Harding, ed., *China's Foreign Relations in the 1980s* (New Haven: Yale University Press 1984), pp. 158–76.

33. See, for example, Stephen P. Gibert, "Northeast Asia in American Security Policy," in William T. Tow and William R. Feeney, eds., *U.S. Foreign Policy and Asian-Pacific Security: A Transregional Approach* (Boulder, Colo.: Westview, 1982), p. 86.

34. See the more extended discussion in Gregor, *Arming the Dragon*.

35. See the discussion in Chang and Gregor, *Iron Triangle*, chap. 2; Hideaki Kase, "South Korea's Pivotal Role in Japan's Defense," in Richard B. Foster, James E. Dornan, Jr., and William M. Carpenter, eds., *Strategy and Security in Northeast Asia* (New York: Crane, Russak, 1979), pp. 145–53.

36. Hiroshi Kimura, "The Soviet Military Buildup: Its Impact on Japan and Its Aims," in Richard H. Solomon and Masataka Kosaka, eds., *The Soviet Far East Military Buildup; Nuclear Dilemmas and Asian Security* (Dover, Mass.: Auburn House, 1986), pp. 106–22; Worth H. Bagley, "U.S. Military Power in the Pacific: Problems and Prospects," and Norman Polmar, "Naval Aspects of Security in Northeast Asia," in *National Security in Northeast Asia*, International Security Council Conference, April 13–15, 1986 (New York: Causa International, 1986), pp. 77–98.

37. Byung Kyu Kang, "Defense of the Sea Lanes in Asia," and Osamu Kouzaki, "Japan's Contribution to Security in the South China Area," in *The Philippines and Security of the South China Sea Region*, International Security Council Conference, August 12–14, 1986 (New York: Causa International, November 1986), pp. 45–61.

38. See Virgilio Aganon and A. James Gregor, *The Philippine Bases: U.S. Security at Risk* (Washington, D.C.: University Press of America, 1987); Carolina G. Hernandez, "The Military Facilities in the Philippines: Some Implications for Regional and National Security," in *The Philippines and Security*, pp. 33–43; John M. Collins, *U.S.-Soviet Military Balance, 1980–1985* (New York: Pergamon-Brassey's, 1985), pp. 139–44.

39. Tun Hwa Ko, "Studies on Using Bases in Taiwan as Backup for the U.S. Military Bases in Philippines," in *The Philippines and Security*, pp. 75–81.

40. See the interesting discussion in Mohamed Noordin Sopiee, *The Russian Threat: Between Alarm and Complacency* (Kuala Lumpur: Institute of Strategic and International Studies, 1985), and Su-cheng Tan, *The Expansion of Soviet Seapower and the Security of Asia* (Taipei: Asia and the World Forum, April 1977).

41. See Todd R. Starbuck, *China and the Great Power Balance* (Carlisle Barracks, Pa.: Strategic Studies Institute, U.S. Army War College, August 18, 1983).

42. See Banning N. Garrett and Bonnie S. Glaser, *War and Peace: The Views from Moscow and Beijing* (Berkeley: Institute of International Studies, 1984), pp. 84, 108–30.

43. Ibid., p. 84.

8

ANZUS: A Case of Strategic Obsolescence

Doug Bandow

In the aftermath of World War II, the United States created a network of regional alliances to restrain the Soviet Union. The North Atlantic Treaty Organization (NATO), created in 1949, was the cornerstone of the U.S. policy of containment, but it was not alone. In fact, U.S. officials appeared to treat alliances as an end in themselves rather than a means to some fundamental policy goal. Over an eleven-year period, the United States initiated eight other agreements: the Rio Pact with twenty-two Latin American countries in 1947; mutual defense treaties with Japan and the Philippines in 1951; the Australia–New Zealand–United States (ANZUS) accord in 1951, a mutual defense treaty with Korea in 1953; the Southeast Asia Treaty Organization (SEATO) with Australia, Britain, France, New Zealand, Pakistan, the Philippines, and Thailand, in 1954; the Baghdad Pact (METO), with Britain, Iran, Iraq, Pakistan, and Turkey, in 1957; and the Central Treaty Organization (CENTO), which succeeded METO without Iraq, in 1959.

This treaty system, involving forty-seven different nations, looked impressive on paper, but many of the agreements proved to be of little practical value. METO disintegrated shortly after its creation. SEATO and CENTO were brain-dead for years before being formally dissolved in 1977 and 1979, respectively. The Rio Pact remains in force but is no longer taken seriously; Cuba is formally a member, and the United States tilted against treaty signatory Argentina in its ill-fated war with Great Britain over the Falkland/Malvinas Islands. And in 1984 ANZUS went on the critical list when New Zealand refused to allow U.S. ships to use its port facilities unless the United States certified that the vessels did not carry nuclear weapons. The Reagan administration subsequently repudiated its defense commitment to New Zealand, turning the agreement into, at most, a bilateral treaty with Australia.

The collapse of yet another U.S. security guarantee is cause for celebration, not alarm, however. ANZUS, like so many of this nation's other postwar military commitments, had become obsolete, a relic of another age. Australia and New Zealand face no serious threats to their security, and those nations, though they provide useful bases as part of the U.S. globalist strategy, are not vital to U.S. security. In short, New Zealand's attempt to separate itself from any U.S.–Soviet nuclear conflict and its slow slide toward neutralism merely highlighted the increasing divergence of interests among the three treaty members. Instead of pressuring New Zealand to reverse its stand, the United States should now accept strategic as well as political realities and dissolve ANZUS.

History of ANZUS

Unlike NATO and most of the other defense guarantees forged by the United States at the end of World War II, ANZUS was directed less at containing the Soviet Union, which had no military presence in the South Pacific, than at preventing a repetition of the past war—that is, Japanese aggression. Since Japan had been defeated and disarmed and was eventually to become an important member of the Western Alliance, the agreement was actually outmoded the day it was signed. Only as the Soviet Union expanded its navy did ANZUS gain any claim to being relevant militarily.[1]

Another objective of Australia and New Zealand, however, was more political: to direct Washington's attention toward the South Pacific. Otherwise, these nations feared, the United States, with so many defense guarantees elsewhere on the globe, would ignore the Pacific. Writes New Zealand opposition leader J.K. McLay, "The Australian and New Zealand leaders of that time wanted the United States to have a treaty commitment in our part of the world as well."[2] In short, the symbolic role of ANZUS was believed to be at least as important as its security function.

The treaty commits its parties "to maintain and develop their individual and collective capacity to resist armed attack." They are to consult if any member "is threatened in the Pacific" and to "act to meet the common danger." Although the parties assume that the United States would intervene militarily, the ANZUS pact does not explicitly refer to the use of military force, as does the NATO accord, for instance. Observes Joseph Camilleri, a professor at Australia's La Trobe University, "The cumulative impact of several ambiguities, including the geographical area covered by the Treaty, the absence of any explicit reference to armed force, and the stress on constitutional processes, has prompted several critics to question whether, in the event of an armed attack on Australia—the United States would be committed under ANZUS to pursue any particular course of action."[3]

The treaty's lack of purpose and its signatories lack of commitment was evidenced by the lackadaisical attitude of the United States toward the alliance. ANZUS facilitated the flow of information and opinions but little more. And if Australia and New Zealand initially looked to the United States as the guarantor of their security once their traditional protector, Great Britain, ceded its global role after World War II, in recent years they too have increasingly treated the pact less seriously. New Zealand prime minister David Lange, for instance, contends that ANZUS is more an affirmation of common interests than a serious military alliance: "A South Pacific NATO was not, and is not, needed. The contrast is absolute between Europe, a landmass divided ideologically and physically into antagonistic blocs," and the South Pacific.[4] Similarly, a controversial Australian defense report concluded that the "possibilities for calls of assistance under ANZUS" were "remote."[5]

Ironically, as the other nations were downgrading their reliance on ANZUS, the Reagan administration began treating it as a linchpin of its anti-Soviet strategy. The treaty, argued Paul Wolfowitz, assistant secretary of state for East Asian and Pacific affairs, in June 1984, "has been one of the critical factors supporting" the stability of the Pacific. He went so far as to warn that "the health of the ANZUS is vital to the global Western alliance."[6]

Yet less than a month after Wolfowitz made his speech, the Labour party came to power in New Zealand, having promised to bar any nuclear-powered or armed vessels from visiting that country. Prime Minister Lange, newly installed, reaffirmed New Zealand's support for ANZUS but warned that U.S. warships would not be welcome unless Washington guaranteed that they were nonnuclear. U.S. officials unsuccessfully tried to resolve the issue through negotiations and in February 1985 used the U.S.S. *Buchanan,* a conventionally powered destroyer, to test the ban. The Lange government requested a U.S. assurance that the vessel was not carrying nuclear weapons, the Reagan administration refused on principle, and New Zealand barred the ship from docking.

In the ensuing political imbroglio, ANZUS quickly became a dead letter.[7] The United States canceled joint military exercises, restricted the flow of intelligence information, and in June 1986 formally suspended its pledge to defend New Zealand.[8] There was even a congressional initiative, supported by some administration officials, to impose economic sanctions, such as the elimination of trade preferences and the increased use of agricultural subsidies for competing U.S. crops and prohibition of some New Zealand imports, against the South Pacific nation, as if New Zealand, by effectively leaving the alliance, had become an enemy.

While the U.S. position was not unreasonable—confirming which vessels do and do not possess nuclear weapons could provide useful intelligence to the Soviets and create convenient targets for terrorists—New Zealand credibly argued that nothing in the treaty required reliance on nuclear-powered or armed vessels. New Zealand's belief that it could maintain an alliance relationship with the United States while distancing itself from its nuclear arsenal may be naive, of course. But New Zealand's port restrictions do not explicitly violate the treaty's terms since that nation has been expanding its conventional force, which arguably fulfills the signatories' duty to "maintain and develop their individual and collective capacity to resist armed attack." Moreover, the treaty was signed at a time when nuclear weapons were not normally carried on ships. For this reason, Ramesh Thakur, a senior lecturer at New Zealand's University of Otago, contends that "the U.S. is more clearly—and intentionally—in breach of" the ANZUS treaty "than New Zealand."[9]

The Reagan administration's greatest fear apparently was not that New Zealand's rejection of nuclear weapons would threaten U.S. security but that U.S. acquiescence to Wellington's stance would encourage other, more important U.S. allies to attempt similarly to make themselves nuclear free. In effect, it was feared that New Zealand would act as a psychological domino, emboldening Denmark, Norway, Spain, and Canada, which ban nuclear weapons on their soil but allow visits by U.S. navy warships, and Japan and West Germany, which host influential peace movements, to reject U.S. nuclear forces. (In fact, in early 1988 Denmark precipitated a crisis in NATO when its parliament proposed to apply the nuclear prohibition to visiting warships.) The sharpness of the administration's attack on Wellington's policy was therefore an attempt to quarantine the New Zealand "disease." Observed State Department spokesman Bernard Kalb: "Some Western countries have anti-nuclear and other movements which seek to diminish defense cooperation among the allied states. We would hope that our response to New Zealand would signal that the course these movements advocate would not be cost-free in terms of security relationships with the United States."[10]

Although New Zealand has not chosen to withdraw from ANZUS, leaving the alliance formally alive, the country has been expelled as a member in everything but name. And while Australia has reaffirmed its commitment to the South Pacific defense arrangement, its government faces many of the same antinuclear and neutralist pressures that caused New Zealand's leftward lurch. For instance, Australia supports making the South Pacific a nuclear-free zone. Moreover, an influential faction of the ruling Labour party supports New Zealand's action. In fact, under pressure from the left, the government of Prime Minister Robert Hawke reversed itself and barred the use of its military facilities to monitor tests of the MX missile; it also has forbidden Washington from using joint U.S.-Australian communications facilities to help develop the SDI. And there is some popular support for closing all U.S. bases in Australia. In short, the future of even an ANZUS without the NZ is in serious doubt.

The Military Threat

The disintegration of ANZUS as a workable military alliance reflects the divergent perceptions and goals of its members. The U.S. government, especially during the early years of the Reagan presidency, has tended to view everything, including its relations with South Pacific nations, through an East-West prism. The United States therefore considers ANZUS to be one part of a global network intended to contain Soviet expansionism, even excluding any Soviet influence from the region, if possible. Australia and New Zealand, in contrast, are less concerned about the global U.S.-Soviet struggle and more interested in regional issues. They see few likely threats to their security and believe that any aggression against the two nations would likely be conventional and would therefore warrant only a conventional response.

Is ANZUS necessary to guarantee the security of the South Pacific? New Zealand is bounded by Australia to the northeast, Antarctica to the south, and a wide expanse of water and scattered islands in other directions. The Soviet Union, with only a limited ability to project military power and having achieved little diplomatic success in the region, remains at best an unlikely, theoretical threat. Argues Ramesh Thakur, "With an enemy like the USSR, many New Zealanders wonder if they need friends at all."[11] Even in the event of a superpower confrontation, New Zealand is unlikely to be the scene of combat unless its links to the United States turn it into a target. It should come as no surprise, then, that members of parliament like Helen Clark argue that "there are no threats to New Zealand's security. The only nation that has sufficient military projection to invade us is the United States, so we're not that worried."[12]

Australia is less isolated geographically and places more emphasis on ANZUS, but it too appears to face little military danger. Write defense analysts Amitav Acharya and Daniel Mulhall, "Australia is protected from invasion by formidable air and sea barriers, while high living standards and a democratic political system make the country an unlikely candidate for domestic instability."[13] Canberra's relations with Indonesia have been tense at times, but the latter nation is no military giant and war seems highly unlikely. Vietnam has a large army, but most of its troops are tied down in Cambodia and along its border with China; nor does Vietnam possess the navy and air force necessary to invade a distant continent. China and Japan are strengthening their armed forces, but neither is able to attack Australia or has an incentive to do so.

For this reason Australian defense officials believe that only the United States and the Soviet Union have sufficient military forces to threaten Australia and that "only the United States [has] sufficient aircraft carriers to provide an adequate degree of air superiority for a successful invasion of Australia."[14] A major 1986 review of Australia's defense needs pointed to potential lower-level dangers, such as incursions into Australian airspace and coastal waters and sabotage activities, but an alliance with the United States is not necessary to counter such threats.

U.S. interests in the South Pacific are far more diffuse than those of either Australia or New Zealand. The security of those island nations—as well as their neighbors throughout the region—is not vital to the survival of the United States. The United States has economic and cultural interests in the South Pacific, including trade with Australia and New Zealand and fishing activities in neighboring waters, and ANZUS promotes some important political ties, but these interests do not seem compelling enough to go to war.[15] Perhaps the most important value of Australia and New Zealand to the United States is in enhancing the interventionist capabilities of the United States. Port facilities in both nations increase the flexibility of the U.S. Navy, and joint exercises help train U.S. forces for action in the South Pacific. Moreover, the Australian bases in particular provide an important link in the international command, control, and communications network of the United States. The two South Pacific countries also gather intelligence and exert a generally pro-U.S. influence throughout the region, though they could continue doing so without a formal military alliance.

Supporters of ANZUS have made much of the Soviet Union's military buildup in the Pacific in recent years, particularly its use of Vietnam's Cam Ranh Bay.[16] The Soviet Union has also made some diplomatic inroads in the region, signing a fishing treaty with Kiribati, for instance, and establishing diplomatic relations with Vanuatu, both South Pacific island states.[17] Nevertheless, the Soviet advances appear more threatening than they actually are because U.S. influence throughout the Pacific has been predominant for so long. Washington developed unrealistic expectations about the future balance of power because of its past hegemony. "A complete denial of a Soviet presence in the region is not feasible or probably even desirable," observes Congressman Ben Blaz (Republican–Guam). "We have political and economic relations with the Soviet Union, as do our closest allies. Why shouldn't the South Pacific?"[18]

Militarily, the Soviet buildup has helped spur the U.S. naval construction program, with the goal of creating the much-ballyhooed 600-ship navy; many of those vessels are destined for the Pacific. The U.S. Navy still holds a numerical advantage, and many Soviet vessels are believed to be in disrepair and their crews poorly trained. The United States has far greater base access; Japan and South Korea could hinder if not block Soviet egress from its ports in Vladivostok and Petropavlovsk while U.S. forces are well positioned to blockade or destroy Cam Ranh Bay in the event of war.[19] Concluded the

Washington-based Center for Defense Information in 1985, "The Soviet Union will not be able to challenge the West for control of the open ocean in the foreseeable future."[20]

In any case, Soviet sea power is concentrated in the West and North Pacific, away from Australia and New Zealand, leaving the Soviet threat to those nations a remote one. Paul Dibb, formerly the deputy director of Australia's Joint Intelligence Organization, studied Soviet capabilities, concluding that "a Soviet invasion of Australia itself, even if it used Cam Ranh Bay as an intermediate staging base to provide the attacking force with effective air cover and to keep its shipping operational, would involve a very difficult military operation. . . . The USSR would not only need to be capable of achieving local air superiority but it would also need to overcome considerable logistic problems. . . . It would be unrealistic to imagine that the USSR would attempt such a futile mission."[21] An invasion of New Zealand would be even more difficult.

Thus, some analysts, such as Masashi Nishihara, of Japan's Yokosuka Defense Academy, believe that the Soviet military buildup is intended more to increase that country's prestige and influence in peacetime than to prepare for war. Moreover, hawkish New Zealand opposition leader J.K. McLay acknowledges that "the Soviets have not yet managed to turn their military advance into a significant political and economic presence in the region."[22]

In fact, the entire Pacific is a uniquely inhospitable region for the Soviet Union. Its relations with the PRC and Japan, the latter which has surpassed the Soviet Union as the second-ranking economic power in the world, are cool at best. Other than Vietnam, Moscow has no allies in the region. The South Pacific island states are largely conservative and traditional; Congressman Blaz argues that "the Pacific Way is diametrically opposed to everything communist doctrine and practice stand for."[23]

In this environment Australia and New Zealand seem capable of protecting their own interests. Australia has a 70,000-man military, with a 30,000-man reserve. It has added six new submarines in recent years, modernized its guided missile destroyers, and introduced antimine ships, as well as built a western port in Perth allowing officials to manage a two-ocean navy. It is upgrading its fighter force and army equipment. Finally, Canberra has been steadily increasing military spending, though budget stringency has held the most recent increases below original projections.[24] New Zealand's military, although substantially smaller, is also a capable force, which is being expanded; the Lange government pushed through an unprecedented 18 percent increase for the 1985–1986 budget year. And New Zealand, like its larger neighbor, has contributed troops to both world wars, Korea, and Vietnam, as well as several smaller conflicts.

Toward a New Regional Security Vision

With New Zealand's de facto withdrawal from ANZUS and the growing potential for Australia's estrangement for similar reasons in the near future, the United States should recognize the reality of the alliance's moribund military status and take the lead in formally dismantling ANZUS. At the same time, it should increase its economic and cultural ties, particularly by eliminating barriers to imports and subsidies for agricultural goods that have adversely affected both Australia and New Zealand. Similarly, the United States should encourage increased private trade with and investment in other South Pacific states.

Moreover, it should maintain informal military links, such as the sharing of intelligence information, with Australia and New Zealand. The absence of a treaty committing the United States to go to war does not bar cooperation that serves the best interests of all countries involved.[25] In the same way, terminating ANZUS need not impair U.S. use of foreign facilities that improve its monitoring and communications capabilities.

Washington needs to stop browbeating nations like New Zealand over their decisions to diverge from U.S. policy. The vision of a nuclear-free South Pacific may be naive since the Soviets eschew sentimentality when it comes to fighting wars, but Wellington's stance threatens the security of New Zealand, not the United States. New Zealand and similar states should be left, like consenting adults, free to make their own mistakes. Otherwise, writes Melvyn Krauss of the Hoover Institution, we both "humiliate ourselves by foisting our protection upon" them and strengthen "anti-American, neutralist and pacifist groups in these countries."[26]

At the same time, the United States should encourage Australia and New Zealand to continue to play a moderating and stabilizing role in the South Pacific. Not surprisingly, Australia and New Zealand have long cooperated themselves, even before the advent of ANZUS. They reached their first agreement to share military information in 1933 and have remained close partners ever since.[27] In fact, Australia responded to the cutoff of U.S. military ties by expanding its bilateral links to New Zealand, going so far as to create a separate intelligence bureau to pass along information generated in Canberra.[28]

Both nations also have good relations with other countries throughout the region and have provided economic and technical assistance to many of them. New Zealand once administered the Cook Islands, Nuie, and Western Samoa and has educated more than half of the South Pacific island leaders. Australia and New Zealand have forged important military links with their neighbors as well. Australia helped train Papua New Guinea's armed forces, developed a multipurpose patrol boat, and deployed an Orion surveillance aircraft for the South Pacific islands. It bases a number of aircraft and an army company in Malaysia and plans on conducting regular exercises with Thailand's armed forces. New Zealand maintains a troop battalion in Singapore.

The United States should promote even wider security ties among the important regional powers. Japan, for instance has the capability to play a much larger political and military role in the Pacific, but the memories of World War II continue to haunt many of its neighbors, even Australia and New Zealand, which were never occupied by Japan. Washington could work to help smooth relations among them. Australia, New Zealand, and the other South Pacific island states would be more secure if they forged a cooperative relationship with such emerging economic powerhouses as Japan and the Republic of Korea.

Moreover, the United States should negotiate with the Soviet Union to reduce tensions and the potential for military confrontation in the region. The Soviets have indicated that some sort of trade-off between Cam Ranh Bay and U.S. bases in Subic Bay and Clark Field in the Philippines might be possible. Since Washington may encounter serious difficulty maintaining those facilities in the face of increasing Filipino nationalism, such a deal might be a good one. In any case, the United States, with its dominant economic, political, and military position, holds the trump cards in any discussions with the Soviets.

Conclusion

The world today is a very different place than it was in 1945, yet U.S. "strategy is tied to fading facts, to relations that are changing," writes columnist Flora Lewis.[29] Washington was none too happy about dismantling such antiquated alliance relics as CENTO. A decade later Reagan administration spokesmen warned of the collapse of collective security with New Zealand's effective departure from ANZUS. But just as those earlier treaties lost their reason for being, ANZUS, a pact that has been in search of a purpose since it was signed, was not serving an important security role for any of its members even before New Zealand implemented its no-nuclear policy in 1984.

Therefore, the United States, observes foreign policy analyst Ted Galen Carpenter, "should promote the demise of ANZUS with a maximum of grace."[30] Rather than coercing friendly nations to abide by the terms of an irrelevant pact, Washington should simply withdraw from it. The termination of the formal alliance does not mean an end to military cooperation or economic involvement in the region; in fact, the United States could play an even more important role by attempting to foster improved relations between

Australia and New Zealand and Japan, which is capable of taking on far greater responsibility for the security of the Pacific.

The United States should drop its implicit commitment to go to war to protect Australia and New Zealand even should the latter decide to return to full ANZUS membership. For too long the United States has been subsidizing the defense of industrialized democracies that do not perceive the same threats that this nation does and are capable of handling any dangers that do exist. U.S. defense guarantees to the European states, Japan, and South Korea may be more expensive, but its military ties to Australia and New Zealand are more easily disposed of. It is time to dismantle ANZUS.

Notes

1. For a discussion of the "desperate search for new enemies whether real or imagined," see Ramesh Thakur, *In Defense of New Zealand: Foreign Policy Choices in the Nuclear Age* (Boulder, Colo.: Westview, 1986), pp. 215–18.

2. J.K. McLay, "Perceptions from the Pacific Basin of the Atlantic Community and the Interrelationship of the Two Regions," *Atlantic Community Quarterly* 5, no. 4 (Winter 1985–1986): 336.

3. Joseph Camilleri, *The Australia, New Zealand, U.S. Alliance: Regional Security in the Nuclear Age* (Boulder, Colo.: Westview, 1987), p. 8.

4. David Lange, "New Zealand's Security Policy," *Foreign Affairs* (Summer 1985): 1013.

5. *Report to the Minister of Defense by Mr. Paul Dibb, Review of Australia's Defense Capabilities* (Canberra: Australian Government Publications Service, March 1986), p. 5.

6. Paul Wolfowitz, "The ANZUS Relationship: Alliance Management," *Department of State Bulletin* (September 1984): 62.

7. For a concise summary of the Reagan administration's recriminations and retaliation against New Zealand, see Ted Galen Carpenter, "Pursuing a Strategic Divorce: The U.S. and the ANZUS Alliance," Cato Institute Policy Analysis No. 67, February 27, 1986, pp. 3–4.

8. "We part as friends but we part company as far as the alliance is concerned," said Secretary of State George Shultz. Don Oberdorfer, "U.S. Withdraws New Zealand's ANZUS Shield," *Washington Post*, June 28, 1986, p. A1. The United States did not try to oust New Zealand formally from the alliance because the treaty has no provision for expelling a signatory.

9. Thakur, *In Defense*, p. 194. See also Stuart McMillan, *Neither Confirm Nor Deny: The Nuclear Ships Dispute between New Zealand and the United States* (New York:Praeger, 1987), pp. 52–54.

10. "U.S. Plans Action to Answer Rebuff by New Zealand," *New York Times*, February 6, 1985.

11. Thakur, *In Defense*, p. 194.

12. Tom Breen, "ANZUS Bickering No longer Joking Matter to Lange," *Washington Times*, September 3, 1985, p. D4.

13. Amitav Acharya and Daniel Mulhall, "Australia's Defense Strategy in Transition," *International Defense Review* 20, no. 7 (1987): 827.

14. *Report of the Joint Committee on Foreign Affairs and Defense, Threats to Australia's Security—Their Nature and Probability* (Canberra: Australian Government Publications Service, 1981), p. 32.

15. Noteworthy is the fact that when Dean Acheson detailed the U.S. defense perimeter in January 1950, he excluded the South Pacific as well as the Asian mainland. It took the Korean War, in which the United States intervened more out of outrage over communist aggression than concern for U.S. security, to remove that line. See Thakur, *In Defense*, p. 45.

16. See, e.g., Richard Fisher, Jr., "Blocking Soviet Gains in Asia with a Reinvigorated Reagan Doctrine," Heritage Foundation (Asian Studies Center), Backgrounder No. 76, March 25, 1988.

17. Some analysts have also expressed concern that Libya, which has established diplomatic relations with Vanuatu and aided independence movements in New Caledonia and elsewhere, may be acting as a Soviet proxy. Colin Rubenstein, "The USSR and Its Proxies in a Volatile South Pacific," Heritage Foundation Lecture No. 161, March 8, 1988.

18. Ben Blaz, "Returning to Paradise: Combating the Soviet Threat to the South Pacific," Heritage Foundation Lecture No. 67, August 13, 1986, p. 4.

19. "The Soviet Union," argues Kusuma Snitwongse, director of Thailand's Institute of Security and International Studies at Chulalongkorn University, "would find little value in Cam Ranh Bay outside peacetime conditions." William Branigan, "Soviet Military Operations Seen Increasing in the Pacific," *Washington Post*, August 1, 1986, p. A24. In fact, the nations in Southeast Asia see China as a greater threat than the Soviet Union.

20. Quoted in Clyde Halberman, "Challenge in the Pacific," *New York Times Magazine*, September 7, 1986, p. 105. Similarly, one U.S. official told *Time* magazine that the Soviet buildup in the Pacific is "not something to be alarmist about." Jill Smolowe et al., "Pacific Overtures," *Time*, November 17, 1986, p. 59. For a discussion of potential Soviet difficulties in undertaking military action against Australia or New Zealand, see Camilleri, *Australia, New Zealand, U.S. Alliance*, pp. 70–72, and Thakur, *In Defense*, pp. 77–81.

21. Paul Dibb, "Soviet Strategy towards Australia, New Zealand and Oceania," Strategic and Defense Studies Center (Canberra), Working Paper No. 90, 1984, p. 9.

22. McLay, "Perceptions," p. 335.

23. Blaz, "Returning to Paradise," p. 4. Journalist Peter Samuel is less sanguine, citing changes in French New Caledonia and Vanuatu, for instance. Peter Samuel, "Dibb Defense Doctrine in Australia," *Atlantic Community Quarterly* 25, no. 1 (Spring 1987): 42–43.

24. See generally Peter Samuel, "Australian Turnaround: Out with Isolationism,"

Wall Street Journal, April 6, 1987, p. 29; Acharya and Mulhall, "Australia's Defense Strategy," pp. 827–33.

25. Washington's decision to sever all military ties with New Zealand has, not surprisingly, harmed that nation's ability to fulfill its regional defense responsibilities by leaving Wellington "with the problem of being almost completely cut off from one of its primary sources of defense doctrines, technical information, etc., upon which its three services have slowly become modeled over the past 30 years." Thomas-Durell Young, "New Zealand Defense Policy under Labor," *Naval War College Review* 39, no. 3 (May–June 1986): 27. See also McMillan, *Neither Confirm Nor Deny,* pp. 100–1.

26. Melvyn Krauss, "If the New Zealand Syndrome Spreads," *New York Times,* February 17, 1985, p. E19.

27. See, e.g., Thakur, *In Defense,* pp. 54–56.

28. Peter Costigan, "Australia, N. Zealand Boost Ties," *Washington Post,* April 6, 1985, p. A10.

29. Flora Lewis, "Needed: Pacific Strategy," *New York Times,* May 8, 1988, p. 29.

30. Carpenter, "Pursuing a Strategic Divorce," p. 13.

9
New Strategies for U.S. Security Interests in Southeast Asia, the Indian Ocean, and the South Pacific Region

Paul M. Kattenburg

Forty Years of U.S. Containment and Intervention

Some forty-two years ago, after its victorious war against the Japanese in the Pacific, the United States stood all powerful and virtually unchallenged in the Pacific–Indian Ocean zone. The salience of the United States, extending itself over this entire vast area from bases in occupied Northeast Asia (Japan, Korea, Okinawa) and in the reconquered and soon to be independent Philippines, was to become even more obvious during the ensuing decade, with the departure of the colonial powers from Southeast Asia and the Southwest Pacific.

From 1945 to about 1957, the metropolitan powers were gradually and sometimes grudgingly forced to abandon first India, Burma, and Ceylon (Sri Lanka); then Indonesia; then Indochina, which turned into Laos, Cambodia, and divided Vietnam, by 1954; and finally Malaya, Singapore, and the North Borneo territories, which became Malaysia and Singapore in the late 1950s. The United States, in turn, voluntarily ceded independence to the Republic of the Philippines in July 1946, concluding with it an agreement on the retention of military bases (MBA) in 1947 and a Mutual Security Treaty (MST) in 1951.

Eventually Britain, Australia, and New Zealand also relinquished their hold over South Pacific territories such as Papua New Guinea, Western Samoa, the Admiralties, Solomon and Cook islands, Vanuatu, Kiribati, Fiji, and a host of others, many of which acquired full independence and U.N. membership. Exceptions were the French possessions in the Pacific, most populous of which is New Caledonia, which are still French held.

During this entire vast process of change, the United States, operating largely from the bases mentioned above and additionally from rear-echelon positions in Guam, Hawaii, and the U.S. West Coast, loomed as the all-powerful actor in the region and the principal protector of its security and independence. As U.S. reach extended over the region, as well as progressively over the Indian Ocean after about the mid-1960s, the perception of U.S. interests seemed similarly to expand. In reality, however, U.S. interests in this vast oceanic realm of seas, archipelagoes, islands, and peninsulas were always more perceived than objective, more imagined than real. On the Southeast Asian peninsula proper, for example, the United States came to realize during its tragic Vietnam experience (1961–1975) that it had vastly overestimated the stakes for which it had originally involved itself so deeply.

Today the geopolitical environment appears vastly different from the situation that existed at the end of World War II. A cacophony of independent voices expresses the region's hopes and aspirations, some of them partially homogenized in regional associations like ASEAN. Except for France in the Pacific, the European powers have all departed the region, and the United States, though still present and in many respects powerful and regarded as the most dependable protector of the region's security and independence, is by no means as powerful as it was in the 1950s and 1960s. Most important, another actor has appeared in the region, one quite capable of competing for influence virtually everywhere and on nearly equal terms.

Since the end of the Vietnam War in 1975, the Soviet Union has begun seriously to project power and influence in Southeast Asia and the South Pacific. Moscow's influence in the Indochina peninsula, giving it access to a naval base originally developed by the United States at Cam Ranh Bay and, in a more limited way, to an air base at Danang, both on the coast of the South China Sea, has dramatically modified the balance of power at the southwestern end of the Pacific. The Soviets have also deployed vast numbers of ships and some aircraft in the Indian Ocean and compete directly for influence with the United States in the Persian Gulf and in South and Southwest Asia. While Washington lost a traditional position in Iran (and has not yet positively acquired equivalent status in either Iraq or the gulf states), the Soviets have attempted to gain a foothold in Afghanistan. Perhaps even more indicative of the rivalry, while the United States maintains a controversial diplomacy of influence seeking in Pakistan, the Soviet Union counterbalances this with gradually mounting influence in India.

The Soviet Union thus looms as a significant force throughout the region. The net, and certainly at least to some extent the sad, result of forty years of U.S. containment and interventionism, including eight murderous years of warfare in Indochina, has undeniably been to end forever the monopoly of U.S. power in that vast realm and to replace it by a duopoly in which the Soviet Union and the United States are uneasy coinhabitants.

Southeast Asia

Despite the considerable degrees of truculence that U.S. policy during the Reagan years has exhibited in Southeast Asia, the United States is neither very strong in that region nor likely to do much to demonstrate a continued capacity to affect its future, with the possible (but by no means certain) exception of the Philippines. This is above all the case because of the very weak domestic U.S. base of support for any renewed involvement in that part of the world.

Thus gestures such as strong U.S. rhetoric in support of ASEAN, symbolic backing of so-called freedom forces against Vietnam in Cambodia, or the alleged buildup of a U.S. munitions stockpile in Thailand, destined to reassure the Thais of support in the event of external aggression, may loom important in the region itself, but they are quite insignificant within the U.S. domestic context and are devoid of resonance with the American public or Congress. While Washington regularly reassures Bangkok of its intent to defend Thailand should that become necessary, there is no formal commitment obligating the United States to do so beyond the somewhat dubious Rusk-Thanat executive agreement of 1962, and it is doubtful that Congress would in fact in any foreseeable context support renewed U.S. military action on the Southeast Asian mainland. That is the reality behind the rather noble but largely empty rhetoric.

Developments in Southeast Asia in a quite different and perhaps unexpected direction are, however, a distinct possibility, which should be taken into account when we think of devising realistic new strategies in the region. First, U.S. relations with Indochina may well gradually thaw as the total futility of present policy emerges, as the pressure for rapprochement by at least some of ASEAN's key members (Indonesia and Malaysia) increases, and as the Vietnamese take appropriate steps to resolve key bilateral problems such as the MIA issue. A second possible development fraught with potentially serious consequences is that sentiment within ASEAN may soon lead to the proclamation of a nuclear weapons–free zone in Southeast Asia. A third possibility is that the leading countries of the region, and ASEAN as their association, will shortly be seriously and directly confronted with the question of internal Philippine security as the situation there slips into gradual chaos and the insurgency grows, probably regardless of the character of the central government in Manila. Finally, as doubts about the staying power of both superpowers grow throughout the area, the idea of a zone of peace, freedom, and neutrality (ZOPFAN) in Southeast Asia may well gain a second wind, with some efforts made to implement it regardless of the wishes of the United States or the Soviet Union.

If U.S. power is likely to wane in the region as a whole, what of its status in the Philippines? Are the Philippines still dependent enough on U.S. aid and advice, if not as strongly as heretofore on U.S. bases and military support, to retain the relationship with the United States, and will Washington reciprocate by striving on a sustained basis to keep the republic strong and secure? It seems likely that the U.S. position in the Philippines will become increasingly precarious as turmoil and insurgency wax there in the face of formidable problems to which probably no one, either in the United States or the Philippines, has any answers. The worsening situation could in a fairly short time span lead U.S. officials to consider once again the available options for military basing outside the Philippines. New alternative bases to Subic Bay Naval Base and Clark Air Base would most likely be found farther back in the Central and East Pacific, although both North Borneo and Singapore-Malaysia offer possibilities (Australia less so) if ASEAN became more willing to multilateralize the military installations used for its security and defense.

Even if the Philippine bases can be maintained on relatively reasonable terms after what will no doubt be difficult and onerous negotiations beginning in 1988 and probably running into 1991 or beyond, there is every reason to doubt that the United States could continue permanently to exercise from these bases the kind of symbolic presence and influence that have been their main raison d'être in the past. As I have described in greater detail elsewhere, the Philippine bases and the symbolic projection of a U.S. presence in East Asia are inextricably bound up with the maintenance of a special relationship between the United States and the Philippines in which the latter enjoys a wholly privileged position in U.S. world policy considerations.[1] While a surprising amount of special consideration for the Philippines did in fact animate Washington immediately after the anti-Marcos coup that brought Corazon Aquino to power in early 1986, that special aura is now gradually dissipating and, I believe, is unlikely to be sustainable permanently.

It should be clearly understood that the Philippine bases themselves have never been absolutely required to implement military plans envisaging the forward development of U.S. forces onto the mainland of Southeast Asia. (Those bases played only an ancillary role in the U.S. war in Vietnam.) Nor are they essential for U.S. protection of Australia or New Zealand, which would have to be assured by deployments from Hawaii, Guam, and the Central Pacific. Moreover, by far the greatest concentration of U.S. military power in the Pacific, and of U.S. interests in the Pacific Basin as a whole, relates to the defense of Northeast Asia, from which the Philippine bases are relatively far distant (as they are from Australia and New Zealand; it is a twelve-hour flight over three times zones from Manila to Sidney). Removal of these bases would deprive the United States of ancillary capabilities regarding the defense of Northeast Asia and the North Pacific Basin, as well eliminating logistical support capabilities to assist the PRC in the unlikely event of a Sino-Soviet conflict. But such removal would not otherwise fundamentally affect major U.S. interests in the world other than forward deployment in the Indian Ocean.

The ship repair base at Subic Bay is essential, however, if forward deployment in the Indian Ocean is to be carried out at anything like reasonable cost. The question then becomes, Is forward deployment in the Indian Ocean significant to the United States? Is so-called back-door entry into the Persian Gulf and Middle East a manageable proposition for a distant superpower, which would then be forced to rely for sustenance of its lifelines on bases situated thousands of miles eastward in the Pacific? What, in fact, is wrong with simple front-door entrance into Southwest Asia (via the Mediterranean and the Near East) if the region is truly important to worldwide U.S. interests?

How strong, in contrast to the United States, is the Soviet Union in Southeast Asia? Even assuming that the United States is effectively out of mainland Southeast Asia does not automatically make the Soviet Union very strong there, although it is certainly competitive in the region. A political, economic, and diplomatic presence in Vietnam, Laos, and Cambodia as the paramount external power, along with a lesser but consequential diplomatic profile in the rest of Southeast Asia, gives the Soviet Union weight, particularly when combined with its new military assets at Cam Ranh and Danang.

But this military presence, currently used mainly for symbolic purposes and for intelligence-gathering and reconnaissance activities in the South China Sea, has not yet significantly strengthened the Soviet Union's power projection capability. It is curious that the Soviet Union can derive so much apparent psychological benefit from a military presence that is really quite limited compared to that of the United States.

It seems clear to me that the major purpose of the Soviet presence in Southeast Asia is psychological and diplomatic. The Soviets hope to establish something that, for the right price and at the right moment, they will be able to barter or bargain away. They are not at Cam Ranh, or elsewhere in this oceanic zone, to prepare to fight a major war or to dominate the region politically. Instead it appears that they have established a military presence that can be eventually bargained away for concessions elsewhere that are more important to them.

That this is the major Soviet intent is demonstrated by Gorbachev's shrewd and effective initiative in his July 1986 Vladivostok speech in which he implicitly offered to bargain away Moscow's Indochina bases for U.S. withdrawal from the Philippines.[2] The same general message was also conveyed during the visit to Australia, New Zealand, and mainland Southeast Asia by Soviet foreign minister Shevardnadze in early March 1987, and Gorbachev finally made that offer explicit in the summer of 1988. No one in Southeast Asia has illusions that the Soviets have become the dominant player in the region or that they pose even a serious threat. The failure of the Soviets to make certain moves may be as significant a portent of their real intent as their positive steps. For example, there has been no known effort to build a naval base or any other kind of facility or installation at

Kampong Som (formerly Sihanoukville) in Cambodia, which would give the Soviets a direct and measurably advantageous window on the Gulf of Thailand, nor have there been significant moves to augment or militarize the existing diplomatic and economic Soviet civilian presence in Cambodia. It is true that the Soviets have expanded the original U.S. facilities at Cam Ranh Bay, but these were possibly inadequate for the distance patrolling activities that the Soviets contemplated, as contrasted with the limited coastal and land-logistical uses the United States made of the naval base during the Vietnam War.

On balance there can be little doubt that something new has become a reality in Southeast Asia: the Soviets are there and unless bought out are there to stay. The United States is therefore effectively matched in its extended superpower role by a prudent and careful but nonetheless capable rival, playing virtually the same role. Perhaps in Southeast Asia and even in the adjoining ocean areas, the time is coming to get both superpowers out.

Indian Ocean

Once in a while it is proper to pause and ask questions such as: "Why on earth is the U.S. Navy so heavily deployed in the Indian Ocean?" What is Washington seeking to achieve by means of power displays in that region other than the maintenance of the U.S. Navy's own chain of naval stations, bases, and interests? Why should naval operations, the validity of which ought to be confronted in Defense Department budget making and in congressional budget-slicing battles, become synonymous with the national interest?

One might argue, although the evidence is by no means clear-cut, that the United States has some direct, significant interests to maintain in the general region of the Persian Gulf. U.S. policy has in fact been based in the main on rather poor rationales ever since the oil embargo of the early 1970s. Washington then cemented a de facto alliance with, and informal commitment to, Saudi Arabia and the gulf states, presumably in return for a steady flow of oil at relatively reasonable, although historically high, prices. Since that time, the importance of Persian Gulf oil on world markets has greatly decreased, but older patterns of thought persist, and most interested parties seem to assume continuing Japanese and Western dependence on it.

Actually no country in Europe is now wholly dependent on gulf oil, though it is useful as a redundant source, and the gulf fields contain the world's largest known proved reserves. Even Japan finds or can find other accessible sources for oil (Indonesia, China, and even the Soviet Union), though it remains more dependent on Persian Gulf sources than any other major state. The question remains, moreover, why the United States should pull Japanese chestnuts out of the fire in the Persian Gulf, such as is now being done under the policy of flagging and then protecting foreign tankers by use of the forward deployed U.S. 7th (Pacific) Fleet.

It is pertinent to remember that for at least half of the post–World War II period (1945–1965), the United States was conspicuously absent from the Indian Ocean and the Persian Gulf, confining its interests and presence to the so-called northern tier of Southwest Asian states: Turkey, Iran, and Pakistan. Only in the mid-1960s did the U.S. Navy become enamored of the idea of forward deployment in the Indian Ocean, forcing U.S. diplomacy to obtain access to the British island of Diego Garcia in order to build a permanent base in that remote place. From that time, an extended actor role in the Indian Ocean seems to have become vital, though no great interest had existed before.

The explanation for the extended U.S. presence in the Indian Ocean region, including the Persian Gulf, is thus essentially twofold. The first factor involves the endless and sometimes mindless exertions of the U.S. Navy to be present everywhere and to seek access to every spot where the Soviet Union might at some future time be confronted, either directly or indirectly—or where U.S. naval presence might oblige the Soviets to draw down forces from other, more crucial places, thus weakening the overall Soviet posture in the central strategic balance.[3] (This goal of the navy, now termed the maritime strategy, became particularly prominent under Secretary John Lehman, but it has never been properly established as a major policy goal in a national debate or been officially adopted by Congress as a mainstay of U.S. strategy.) The second factor is the perceived presence of major U.S. interests in the Arabian Peninsula and Persian Gulf, related in imaginative Pentagon planning to the defense of Israel in the interminable Arab-Israeli conflict and, more important, to the unimpaired flow of oil from the Persian Gulf states. Neither rationale is very compelling.

South Pacific

Although basic U.S. hegemony is not yet seriously threatened anywhere in the South Pacific, the tide of events there may be slowly turning, as it is in Southeast Asia. There has never been a burning disposition on the part of the United States to engage itself deeply in the vast and distant realms of the South Pacific, despite U.S. possession dating back to the past century of areas like Guam and Eastern Samoa and the extensive and expansive U.S. presence throughout the region during and after World War II.

U.S. officials generally lack basic knowledge of the South Pacific and its diverse and variegated racial, ethnolinguistic, and cultural streams and strains. Comparing the United States with France, for example, is not necessarily flattering to the former in this regard. To France, its presence in the South Pacific, which dates back at least two centuries, has great symbolic meaning and a mystical quality related to French literature and mythology, as well as to history (the names La Perouse, Pierre Loti, and Gauguin are significant in France). Sadly, France has felt it necessary in this half-century to mar its presence by apparently endless nuclear testing from bases in beautiful Polynesia. (When confronted with the frequent displeasure of Pacific Islanders or of Australians and New Zealanders, the French respond with the basically irrelevant comment that Mururoa Atoll is farther from Sydney than Paris is from either the U.S. nuclear test site in Nevada or the Soviet nuclear site in western Siberia.)

America's lack of knowledge matches the minimal nature of its interests in the region. Even Washington's diplomatic representation is lacking. Embassies at Port Moresby and Suva in effect cover the whole span of the islands, despite the existence of so many independent states, with the embassies at Canberra and Wellington also keeping an eye on the situation. However, recent Soviet deployments and demonstrations of interest in the South Pacific, in particular the signing of a now-lapsed fishing agreement with Kiribati and the potential conclusion of other such agreements elsewhere, have apparently sent shudders of fear through Washington conservative circles, where one hears talk of Soviet-sponsored Libyan terrorism and of a "Red Orchestra" at work to undermine democracy in the South Pacific.[4]

U.S. interest in these independent ministates has consequently increased slightly since 1986. National Security Council missions have been sent out to inspect the islands; the Commander in Chief, Pacific traveled from Hawaii to tour several parts of the region; and General Vernon Walters, U.S. ambassador to the United Nations, conducted a rather mysterious mission of inspection in the spring of 1987. Secretary of State George Shultz even visited Apia, capital of Western Samoa, following a South Pacific Forum meeting there in early June 1987.

What is agitating the ministates and even the larger independent countries of the South Pacific (Australia, Fiji, and New Zealand) most is the persistent French nuclear testing going on in Polynesia. It was that problem that led directly to the signing by some fifteen countries in 1986 of the Treaty of Rarotonga, declaring the South Pacific a nuclear weapons–free zone. Note well the wrinkle here: nuclear weapons free, not nuclear-free zone. In other words, the treaty in no way bars the transit or even the stationing of nuclear-propelled vessels, though it does prohibit the presence of nuclear weapons in the region.[5]

Most of the world's states, including the Soviet Union, have signed the Protocols of Rarotonga, but not the United States, Britain, and France, which seem to fear the precedent that a nuclear weapons–free zone in even so remote an area as the South Pacific seems to set. The treaty of course derogates to a degree the "neither confirm nor deny" policy of the United States with respect to the emplacement of nuclear weapons on vessels or aircraft transiting or visiting the zone or countries in question. The Treaty of Rarotonga, however, leaves each signatory free to decide for itself whether to allow visits by U.S. or other vessels or aircraft without such disclosure. While New Zealand prohibits such visits under policies inaugurated by the Lange government, Australia, even under Bob Hawke's Labour government, does not.[6] Other South Pacific states have similarly not adopted a confrontational approach. In connection with the U.S. refusal to accept the Rarotonga protocols, it is interesting to observe that no such qualms attached to U.S. policy in the Western Hemisphere, where Washington long ago accepted the similar nuclear weapons–free zone prescriptions of the Treaty of Tatlelolco (1969).

Nature of U.S. Interests and Effects of the Maritime Strategy

A prudent, conservative reading of vital U.S. interests in the Pacific Basin region would judge them, particularly in the light of constrained U.S. resources and capabilities, to be almost entirely concentrated in the North and Central Pacific zones. It is important to ensure the defense of Korea, Okinawa, and Japan and its surrounding islands, as well as the key straits and approaches to those areas. Even more significant, the United States has vital interests and installations in the Aleutians, Alaska, Hawaii, and the island possessions in the Central Pacific Basin. At its extremity, the zone of relevant U.S. interests extends as far west and south as Taiwan and the Philippines. Consequently the United States should concentrate on these regions, which are also the most significant to the Soviets. With respect to the South Pacific and to Southeast Asia, U.S. officials should seek to reestablish something akin to the pre–World War II status quo: a region from which all great or superpowers are de facto excluded. (After all, neither British, French, nor U.S. or Dutch power in the Far Pacific was of any great significance before World War II.)

The United States fought World War II to remove excessive Japanese influence from the region. Thereafter, it established a presence that remained unchallenged until the recent Soviet arrival. It is important to prevent a full-blown U.S.-Soviet rivalry in this marginally important area so that the United States can again concentrate its increasingly constrained forces and capabilities on the regions where it has truly major interests and concerns.

Somewhat the same set of considerations that apply to the South and Southwest Pacific are relevant to the situation in the Indian Ocean, which should not be viewed as an area in which a primacy of U.S. interests exists or can be established. Primacy in the Indian Ocean should be exercised in the first instance by the littoral states, of which India is obviously a leading one, though the United States, for reasons sometimes hard to fathom but obviously relating to its obsessive anticommunism as well as to the situation in Afghanistan, assists and supports Pakistan to an extent that makes the establishment of a close relationship with India much more difficult. Yet in the longer term, especially with a stalemate likely between Iran and the Arab Persian Gulf states (principally Iraq and Saudi Arabia), India will probably hold the key to the future in the Indian Ocean.

The idea of a back-door entry into the Middle East is a nonstarter. It must be conceded, however, that pushed by irrational motives dealing largely with the Iran-contra affair, the Reagan administration has in fact forced open a back door by its risky concentration of naval power in the Persian Gulf. The sooner we are rid of this curious enterprise, in which we are serving only Japanese interests, the better. The impending Soviet withdrawal from Afghanistan also affords the United States an opportunity to shake off the Pakistan albatross. The latter looms as by far the most significant obstacle to a useful, albeit not an allied, relationship with an India able and willing to counterbalance Soviet power, as it is today willing to counterpoise Chinese power, in the Indian Ocean.

For that objective of U.S. policy to be achieved, the Indian Ocean, along with the South Pacific and South China Sea and Southeast Asia zones, will have to witness the withdrawal of the superpower military presence. Benign neglect instead of the current agitation and turmoil caused by the maritime strategy is the desirable goal, one that is in consonance with the constraints on U.S. economic and military power.

Since the early 1980s, the United States has pursued its aggressive confrontational maritime strategy, which seems to be designed to engage Soviet fleet elements (including antisubmarine warfare and air forces) wherever these are deployed, including specifically the southern Pacific and Indian oceanic zones, and thereby to draw Soviet forces and attention away from the central strategic front of superpower confrontation in Europe. This strategy is said to be both the rationale for and the product of former secretary of the navy John Lehman's 600-ship naval buildup, which concentrates powerful air carrier squads in every ocean and oceanic zone on the globe.[7]

How sound and to what avail has this strategy been, particularly in the southern Pacific and Indian Ocean zones? Other than merely confronting the Soviet navy, the strategy seems to have had little, if any, political objective. (It has, however, permitted the United States, whether for good or ill, to deploy massive naval-air contingents rapidly to the Persian Gulf for basically unclear and ambiguous objectives.) It has become apparent since the mid-1970s that the Soviet Union intends to match the United States in all aspects of military power in every major region and that it is systematically engaged in a great-power game of symbolic prestige and deployment, in which, like its rival, it will be second to none—though not necessarily first—anywhere in the world.

Under these circumstances, would not the proper political objective for the United States be to limit Soviet ambitions, and deployments, as well as its own? Is there any effective method, short of war, to keep the Soviets out of any zone other than, in effect, to buy or trade them out? to reach with them explicit agreements, which, in return for desired objectives, accomplish mutual withdrawals?

A possible strategy embodying this approach would be for the United States to attempt to couple a settlement of the vexing and still unresolved Indochina question with a favorable limitation of the Soviet navy's presence in the South Pacific and Indian Ocean zone and, even more specific, to limit the Soviet naval presence in the Central and East Pacific—the oceanic approaches to Hawaii and the U.S. West Coast—where the Soviet Navy has no business at all. Such a solution might be coupled with a mutual withdrawal of both superpowers from their current base facilities in Southeast Asia (Indochina and the Philippines). The possibility of such a settlement, along with some of the modalities and objectives that ought to be explored by the United States if it adopts this course, are discussed below.

In the absence of a settlement scheme, the maritime strategy, which has already considerably exacerbated the situation, is likely to lead to a growing number of dangerous showdowns and confrontations in secondary theaters and zones, areas in which U.S. staying power is basically limited and constrained. The maritime strategy has already had the effect of seriously exercising U.S. allies in the Pacific, which under that strategy are frequently called upon to play roles for which they are both ill suited and ill prepared.[8]

A Recommended New Strategy for the United States in the Southern Oceans Zone

The days of long and intimate U.S. association with the Philippines, marked by the notion of mutual defense and special economic ties, and by the presence of large U.S. military bases in the Philippines, are drawing to a close. A new situation can best be accommodated by an explicit agreement of the two superpowers for a mutual reduction of their presence in the South Pacific and Indian Ocean zone.

Under a new strategy, the United States would move to facilities and installations in Korea, Okinawa, and Japan those elements of the 13th Air Force, and its major communication facilities in the Philippines, that play a vital and effective role in the worldwide superpower confrontation. (The possibility that Taiwan might again become available should not be ruled out, though it is unlikely.) Similarly, major naval and marine units used primarily in the global strategic confrontation would move from Subic to existing facilities in Northeast Asia, backed as required by refurbished, strengthened, or new facilities in the western Pacific islands.

At the same time, the projection of U.S. power in the further South China Sea, the Southwest Pacific, and, above all, the Indian Ocean would be gradually reduced and eventually eliminated as part of a diplomatic strategy to reduce superpower tensions in these regions. The United States would in no sense abdicate its power position in Northeast Asia and the Central Pacific and Micronesia, but the Far South Pacific and Indian Ocean zones would increasingly be allowed to become regions of neutrality and reduced confrontation, under mutually agreed-upon, explicit terms. The United States would not abandon its facilities at Diego Garcia, but the signal would be clear that it would not seek to intervene in South Asia, the Persian Gulf, or the Near East by the back door. Such intervention in South Asia or the Persian Gulf would be futile in any case because of the increasing lack of U.S. capabilities given its preoccupation elsewhere (Central America, for example). As to the Near East, it is an area of such major intrinsic importance to both the United States and its NATO allies that a policy enabling entry from the Mediterranean and Southeast Europe is the only possible route of intervention.

The United States might at least support, if not partially design, a new grand strategy for the South Pacific–Southeast Asia–Indian Ocean region, not entailing bases in the Philippines. This could be done in association with some of its closer partners in the region and in possible consultation with Japan, and even with the PRC. What might be the general shape and some of the key elements of such a strategy?

1. The Philippines, as a member of the Association of Southeast Asian Nations (ASEAN), would look first to that body for its security now and into the twenty-first century. ASEAN, however, is not a military organization but only a loose association of countries in Southeast Asia with a basically similar outlook. The Philippines is the only one among them to have maintained a formal treaty of alliance with a superpower (although Thailand has frequently expressed a desire for a similar U.S. tie). It would be expected that the basic security orientation of ASEAN as well as its individual members would remain one of neutrality and reasonably genuine nonalignment. The United States would in due course inform the Philippines of its decision to abrogate the 1951 mutual security treaty, as well as to withdraw from the military bases. That action would leave the Philippines free for a foreign policy reorientation more fully compatible with ASEAN's long-standing (and thus far largely rhetorical) objective of establishing a ZOPFAN in Southeast Asia, which at least in theory excludes superpower military bases in the region.

2. As part of this process, the United States would expect the Philippines and the other members of ASEAN to explore with the members of the Indochina bloc, as well as in due course with the Soviet Union itself, the possibility of a Soviet withdrawal from naval and air bases at Danang and Cam Ranh Bay. The Soviet presence in these bases is at least in part a response to the presence and activities of U.S. forces at Subic and Clark. There is, however, no guarantee that the Soviets, undoubtedly engaged in a significant and worldwide naval buildup, will agree to withdraw from Indochina, even given the benefit of U.S. withdrawal from the Philippines. To increase the probability of a mutual withdrawal, the ASEAN powers might consider proposing an Indochina settlement that would essentially ratify Vietnamese hegemony—at the price of military withdrawal—in Cambodia, including recognition of a Heng Samrin regime, broadened, it is hoped, to include elements loyal to Prince Norodom Sihanouk. The present ASEAN policy of sponsoring a Cambodian government in exile and supporting guerrilla warfare inside Cambodia, largely by Khmer Rouge elements, has demonstrably failed to achieve its objective and is unlikely to be sustainable.

3. Worldwide recognition of a ZOPFAN in Southeast Asia would probably accompany the withdrawal of U.S. forces from the Philippines bases. This might be broadened to encompass a nuclear weapons–free zone. Under such a concept, ASEAN would ban the presence of Soviet, U.S., or other nuclear weapons throughout Southeast Asia, including (one would hope) Indochina. It would be difficult to see how the Indochinese communist states would be able to resist joining such a nuclear weapons–free zone; its proclamation might be a further incentive for the Soviets to join the United States in withdrawing from its bases in a region they have traditionally accorded low priority. Moreover, it is quite conceivable that Australia and New Zealand would be willing, if invited, to join what would then become the Southeast Asia–Southwest Pacific nuclear weapons–free zone. The United States and Australia would have to accept the consequences for their alliance from such a new situation; New Zealand's current defection from ANZUS invites them to do so in any case. Appropriate means of verification would have to be established to ensure respect of the nuclear weapons–free status of this zone by all nuclear powers.

4. In return for this complete departure from the prevailing status quo in Southeast Asia and the Southwest Pacific, entailing above all U.S. withdrawal from military bases previously considered vital in as strategic a country as the Philippines, the Soviet Union would be expected to make considerable concessions—in addition to withdrawing from its relatively small military presence in a traditionally low-priority area. Specifically, the United States would seek a negotiated agreement under which the Soviets— assuming changes in the status quo as projected in points in 1, 2, and 3—

would accede to limiting the Soviet Pacific fleet (except in Southeast and Northeast Asian waters) to those types of units that, in the view of both superpowers, are considered vital for the legitimate protection of Soviet strategic nuclear deterrent forces (specifically submarines and antisubmarine warfare vessels and aircraft). No other Soviet surface, underwater, or air units would be expected to prowl the eastern Pacific Ocean. Western Pacific zones such as Southeast Asia and Northeast Asia would remain, at least for a period, open to all units of the Soviet fleet.

5. The United States would in the same agreement expect a minimum reduction of one-third in the Soviet naval presence in the Indian Ocean. Its own naval presence there would be expected to decrease commensurately as well. The Indian Ocean never did assume the strategic importance that an overeager U.S. Navy sought for it in the 1960s and 1970s, when the United States was involved in Vietnam and potentially in the Horn of Africa, and sought back-door entry to the Middle East. Persian Gulf oil has almost totally lost its significance as a world fuel resource, except perhaps to Japan.[9] But Japan can secure Mideast oil just as well, if not better, under conditions of demilitarization as under circumstances of superpower confrontation in the Indian Ocean. Nor is Persian Gulf oil likely to regain its significance. The idea of back-door entry to the Middle East has proved futile and counterproductive and has exacerbated South Asian and Near Eastern tensions.

6. The proposals in points 4 and 5 might be rejected by the Soviets, especially if they were presented under conditions of tense superpower confrontation. Even with better superpower relations, the Soviets might still refuse to make concessions to obtain conditions they think would naturally arise if the United States were forced out of its Philippines bases. U.S. withdrawal from those bases, and the proclamation of a genuine ZOPFAN and possibly a nuclear-free zone in Southeast Asia and the Southwest Pacific, might be sufficient to bring about Soviet withdrawal or at least significant reduction from bases in Indochina—but not necessarily a reduction of fleets in the Pacific and Indian oceans. The proposals under points 4 and 5 would therefore have to be merely offers made under conditions of explicit negotiations. If the Soviets showed interest, they could expect a commensurate reduction of tensions in these regions; if they did not, the United States might in any case withdraw unilaterally from its Philippine bases, but without diminishing its pressure, vigilance, and presence in the Pacific and Indian Ocean regions, which could be ensured through the use of alternative facilities and basing arrangements.

7. Finally, it is hard to see how proposals for mutual U.S. and Soviet disarmament in the southern oceans could be objectionable to the PRC, provided it was assured of the continued presence of strong U.S. forces elsewhere in the region. The withdrawal of Soviet elements from Vietnam

might in itself benefit the PRC, while an effectively neutralized and possibly denuclearized Southeast Asia–Southwest Pacific should be acceptable to China so long as the United States maintains strong army, naval, and air forces and a major effective Soviet-containing presence in Northeast Asia, supported by strong elements of the U.S. Pacific Fleet based in Hawaii and points in between.

A strategy of mutual superpower disengagement from the southern oceans regions offers several important benefits. It would help convert that vast area into a zone of neutrality, thereby eliminating one arena in the cold war and reducing tensions between Washington and Moscow. That step would also improve relations between the United States and such important regional powers as New Zealand, the Philippines, and India, which have been strained by an intrusive U.S. military presence. Disengagement would reverse the expensive and dangerous strategic overextension symbolized by the maritime strategy—an issue of considerable relevance in an era of massive budget deficits and increasing constraints on military spending. Finally, disengagement would enable the United States to pay greater attention to its far more important security interests in the North Pacific and Northeast Asia.

Notes

1. Paul M. Kattenburg, "The Case for Ending the U.S.–Philippines Special Relationship," in Carl Landé (ed.) *Rebuilding a Nation: Philippine Challenges and American Policy* (Washington, D.C.: Washington Institute Press, 1987), pp. 547–60).

2. *Soviet Daily Press,* July 29, 1986, pp. 16, 18.

3. See K.A. Dunn and William O. Stoudenmaier, "Strategy for Survival," *Foreign Policy* 52 (Fall 1983): 22–42.

4. See, for example, Kenneth J. Conboy, "After Vladivostok: Gorbachev's Asian Inroads," Heritage Foundation Asian Studies Center Backgrounder No. 73, January 25, 1988; and Richard D. Fisher, Jr., "Blocking Soviet Gains in Asia with a Reinvigorated Reagan Doctrine," Heritage Foundation Asian Studies Backgrounder No. 76, March 25, 1988.

5. See Robyn Lim, "Nuclear Weapon Free Zones," Conference on Security and Arms Control in the Pacific, Australian National University Conference, August 1987.

6. For an analysis of the tension within ANZUS, see Ted Galen Carpenter, "Pursuing a Strategic Divorce: The U.S. and the ANZUS Alliance," Cato Institute Policy Analysis No. 67, February 27, 1986.

7. Dunn and Stoudenmaier, "Strategy."

8. See S. Simon, "The Maritime Strategy and America's Pacific Allies," Naval Postgraduate School Conference, August 1987.

9. Sheldon L. Richman, "Where Angels Fear to Tread: The United States and the Persian Gulf Conflict," Cato Institute Policy Analysis No. 90, September 9, 1987.

III
U.S. Security Commitments in the Third World

10
The Faulty Assumptions of U.S. Foreign Policy in the Third World

Peter J. Schraeder

T he United States, although once itself a revolutionary nation fighting against oppression and external control, consistently has failed to understand the growth of this phenomenon in the Third World. This misunderstanding has led to the formulation of ill-conceived U.S. foreign policies in the Third World, making the United States the enemy of social change and protector of the status quo. The purpose of this study is to analyze why the United States habitually has been on the wrong and losing side of social change in the Third World, especially since World War II. It examines the evolution of U.S. foreign policy toward revolutionary regimes, identifies the shortcomings and failures of that policy, and outlines an alternative strategy for the future.

Continuity and Change

A territorially and economically expansionistic United States in the early nineteenth century wanted to limit European influence in "our backyard"—hence the declaration of the Monroe Doctrine in 1823—because of fears that Central American revolutions would be "susceptible to outside influences."[1] As rising U.S. economic and political hegemony bore the fruits of the Monroe Doctrine by displacing substantial European interests in Central America, revolutions, and their accompanying economic and political instability, increasingly were viewed as injurious to U.S. interests. "The problem arose when Washington officials repeatedly had to choose which tactic best preserved [U.S.] power and profits: siding with the status quo for at least the short term, or taking a chance on radical change that might (or might not), lead to long term stability."[2] The choice was made clear in 1905 when the United States, through the Roosevelt Corollary to the Monroe Doctrine, assumed the role of hemispheric policeman to maintain order and stability. Historian Walter LaFeber explains how the Monroe Doctrine had been construed to provide the basis for an antirevolutionary and interventionist foreign policy in Central America:

Monroe and Adams had originally intended it [Monroe Doctrine] to protect Latin American revolutions from outside (that is, European) interference. Eighty years later the power balance had shifted to the United States, and the Doctrine itself shifted to mean that Latin Americans should now be controlled by outside (that is, North American) intervention if necessary. Roosevelt justified such intervention as only an exercise of "police" power, but that term actually allowed U.S. presidents to intervene according to any criteria they were imaginative enough to devise.[3]

The U.S. role of regional policeman became internationalized as it rose to superpower status at the end of World War II. Most important, U.S. foreign policy became an anticommunist crusade as competition increased with the Soviet Union, the other ascendant superpower to rise out of the ashes of the war. From this point forward, U.S. intervention in the Third World would be driven by hostile perceptions of the Soviet Union.

The Truman Doctrine, built on fears of communism dating back to the Wilson administration, provided the ideological basis for an anticommunist policy of intervention in the Third World. Casting the Greek civil war as a contest between Soviet-supplied communists and Western democratic forces of freedom, Truman, in an address before a joint session of Congress on March 12, 1947, called upon Americans "to support free peoples who are resisting attempted subjugation by armed minorities or by outside pressures."[4] The key thrust of the doctrine was to portray postwar instability as due to Soviet expansion and subversion, thereby legitimizing U.S. economic and military aid to threatened governments. The doctrine marked a watershed in U.S. foreign policy:

> For the first time in the postwar era, Americans massively intervened in another nation's civil war. Intervention was justified on the basis of anticommunism. In the future, Americans would intervene in similar wars for supposedly the same reason and with less happy results.[5]

Despite the global implications of the Truman Doctrine, its global applicability was still held in question. For example, George F. Kennan's famous "X" article, which provided the philosophical basis of what was to be referred to commonly as containment, was limited to the countries immediately bordering the Soviet Union, especially Western Europe. Kennan implied that the primary threat facing these bordering countries was their "psychological malaise," not the "Soviet military threat or the appeal of international Communism."[6] The correct U.S. response was therefore to engender political and economic as opposed to military components.

Kennan's limited view of containment and intervention was overshadowed by China's "fall" to communism in 1949 and the signing of the Sino-Soviet Treaty of Friendship and Cooperation in 1950, two events that led U.S.

policymakers to assume erroneously that a "monolithic" communist force was on the march in the Third World, especially Asia. This monolithic view of communism provided the basis for Paul Nitze's NSC-68 memorandum, which, in 1950, portrayed the Soviet Union "as indistinguishable from a world-wide Communist revolutionary movement, newly capable of initiating a war against the West and intent on world domination."[7] The policy prescription was stark: without an active U.S. military commitment to containment of communism on a global basis, weak Third World countries would succumb, one after another, like so many dominoes.

Nitze's view of monolithic communism being on the march seemingly would be confirmed by communist North Korea's invasion of South Korea shortly after NSC-68 was written. This historical event served as a catalyst, making NSC-68 the foundation for an active U.S. foreign policy of intervention in the Third World based on the twin themes of anticommunism and containment. Furthermore, these two themes would provide the basis of a cold war consensus that would last through four administrations and that would not be questioned until the United States became mired in a losing war in Vietnam.[8] President John F. Kennedy best captured the cold war consensus in his January 1961 inaugural address when he called upon Americans to "pay any price, bear any burden, meet any hardship, support any friend, oppose any foe" in the fight against communism.[9]

Despite changes in official perceptions of the Soviet Union and communism in the wake of U.S. defeat in Vietnam, the U.S. policy of intervention in the Third World remained rather consistent. For example, the Nixon and Ford administrations deviated from cold war internationalism by portraying the Soviet Union as a traditional superpower with which the United States could negotiate rather than as the head of a global communist threat. Yet, as it did during the 1950s and 1960s, U.S. policy toward Third World conflicts continued to be guided by the overarching importance attached to the East-West struggle and largely mirrored the accepted precepts of the cold war period: maintenance of the status quo, antipathy to revolutionary change, and active containment of the Soviet Union. The major change in the doctrine of containment, known as the Nixon Doctrine, was that regional Third World allies (such as Iran) would act as U.S. military proxies to maintain the regional status quo, and therefore U.S. interests, in the Third World.

The Carter administration offered the brightest hope for a positive Third World policy not driven by the ideological assumptions of the cold war period. Attempting to chart a bold new course in the Third World, President Carter, in a 1977 address at Notre Dame University, seemingly rejected the policies of containment and anticommunism:

> Being confident of our own future, we are now free of that inordinate fear of communism which once led us to embrace any dictator who joined us in

that fear. For too many years we have been willing to adopt the flawed and erroneous principles and tactics of our adversaries, sometimes abandoning our values for theirs. We have fought fire with fire, never thinking that fire is better quenched with water. This approach failed, with Vietnam the best example of its intellectual and moral poverty.[10]

Despite initial commitment to such a new course in the administration's first year, most noted by an active human rights policy, Carter returned to the comfort of cold war precepts as several events rocked his administration in its last two years: the fall of the shah of Iran, the hostage crisis, the Sandinista revolution, and the Soviet invasion of Afghanistan. As two policy analysts cogently argue:

> The most basic underlying assumptions that guided policy did not change. . . . Perhaps the most important continuity in vision was a widespread acceptance of the doctrine of containment—a commitment to prevent the "spread" not simply of Soviet power but of "communism." Revolutionary regimes of the left were still considered antithetical to US global interests, and the aim of US policy was still to minimise the chances of such outbreaks and "takeovers." . . . Few publicly questioned either the power of the United States to influence the character of Third World regimes or the necessity—indeed the global responsibility—to do so.[11]

The election of President Ronald Reagan in 1980 witnessed the complete embrace of the anticommunist cold war internationalism of the 1950s and 1960s and its concomitant tendency to view all Third World conflict and instability as the result of Soviet machinations. Transcending mere containment, the Reagan administration instead underscored the need to roll back recent communist advances in the Third World, most notably through U.S. paramilitary support of guerrilla forces fighting Soviet-supported Third World communist regimes. Popularly known as the Reagan Doctrine, it has been invoked to provide economic and military support to guerrillas fighting Soviet-backed regimes in Afghanistan, Angola, Cambodia, and Nicaragua.[12]

The enunciation of the Reagan Doctrine merely intensified a trend, which had begun in the nineteenth century, of greater U.S. intervention in the Third World: economic expansion during the twentieth century against external interests in Central America eventually prompted the United States to adopt a regional antirevolutionary foreign policy based on stability and the status quo. U.S. hegemony at the end of World War II, combined with the rise of the Soviet state as its greatest competitor in the Third World, facilitated the carry-over of an antirevolutionary, status quo foreign policy on a global basis and synthesized it with a virulent anticommunism. The resulting policy of containment ensured that all subsequent U.S. administrations (although with some variation) would be hostile to revolutionary change in the Third World, mistakenly formulating their respective Third World foreign policies through the restrictive framework of the East-West struggle. The inherent faults in following such a policy in the post–World War II period can be grouped under two themes: antagonism toward the Left and support of the Right.

Antagonism toward the Left

U.S. competition with the Soviet Union at the height of the cold war fostered a simplistic view of relationships with Third World elites. These elites were viewed as mere pawns to be won on the greater East-West chessboard, leading U.S. policymakers to ignore the strength of Third World nationalism and erroneously confuse it with communism. For example, Secretary of State John Foster Dulles depicted these elites as either pro-Soviet or pro-American, with nonaligned nations falling under the former category and ultimately being suspected of harboring procommunist tendencies. The net result was U.S. direct involvement in overthrowing several democratic nationalist regimes whose successors, in most cases, would come back to haunt the United States.

It is ironic that Iran, a nation that became the bête noire of both the Carter and Reagan administrations, has the dubious distinction of boasting the first nationalist regime to be overthrown by the United States in the post–World War II period. Premier Mohammed Mosaddeq came to power on May 1, 1951, and earned the disdain of the international community by nationalizing the British Anglo-Iranian Oil Company. Mosaddeq was head of the National Front, a nationalist coalition built around the oil issue. Although the U.S. State Department denounced him as leading the country on a path toward communism, his only real sin was attempting to gain control over his country's most important resource: oil. As is well known, the Eisenhower administration removed Mosaddeq in 1953 through a CIA-directed coup, restoring the pro-West shah Reza Pahlavi to power.

The irony of the coup is that although the United States gained a staunch ally in the short run, Washington would be faced in the long run with a virulently anti-American revolutionary regime. Most important, one can argue that the revolution's radical nature and fundamental anti-Americanism are due to the U.S. coup in 1953 and subsequent support of the shah over a period of twenty-five years. One cannot help but wonder how history would have been different if the United States had allowed a populist Iranian regime in 1953 run its course.

A second instructive case is the U.S. overthrow in 1954 of Guatemala's democratically elected and reform-minded Jacobo Arbenz Guzman. Arbenz, realizing that the key to success lie in land reform (a problem faced by all of Central America), sought to build on reforms initiated in the 1944 middle-class revolution by mobilizing disenfranchised groups into the political arena. He immediately ran into problems because the reform program included redistribution of 234,000 acres of unused land owned by United Fruit Company, the owners of which would vociferously protest these actions to the U.S. government. Arbenz also met with disfavor in Washington when he legalized the Guatemalan Communist party and brought a few of its leaders into the government. As in the Iran case, "U.S. policymakers came to perceive the Arbenz reforms as steps toward communism," a belief that led to a CIA paramilitary invasion by Guatemalan exiles that would overthrow Arbenz and install a military government led by Castillo Armas.[13]

Once again, U.S. intervention would destroy democratic social forces seeking reform, thereby setting in motion several processes that in the long-run would make political violence "a constant factor in Guatemalan life."[14] The next thirty-two years would find Guatemala ruled by a host of repressive military dictatorships, which would balk at any measure of social reform and thus fuel growing levels of guerrilla insurgency. Despite Guatemala's return to civilian rule in 1986, it remains to be seen if the military will relinquish any real degree of its power to the elected regime. One critic notes:

> Unless social reforms and a modicum of political democracy are genuinely implemented in Guatemala, the guerrillas, who have been defeated but not crushed, will again gather strength. By the end of the decade, Guatemala may no longer be a sideshow for U.S. policymakers.[15]

U.S. disfavor with (and misunderstanding of) the democratic left is most poignantly shown by the still largely concealed role of the United States in overthrowing the democratically elected socialist president of Chile, Salvador Allende Gossens in 1973. Secretary of State Henry Kissinger was reported to have stated: "I don't see why we need to stand by and watch a country go Communist due to the irresponsibility of its own people."[16] Kissinger's incredulous rationale for U.S. concern was that he had "yet to meet somebody who firmly believes that if Allende wins there is likely to be another free election in Chile."[17] Seymour Hersh rightly notes that this was a "ludicrous statement, in view both of Allende's graceful acceptance of defeat in the 1958 and 1964 elections and of Chile's long-standing commitment to democratic government."[18] Sadly, democratic elections would become a thing of the past after 1973 in Chile, not because of Allende's victory but rather because of his overthrow and replacement by the dictatorial General Augusto Pinochet.

The most ominous factor in these three cases is that the United States had assumed the right of overthrowing democratic regimes in the name of anticommunism and maintenance of U.S. interests in a given country. In the long run, the results have been sobering: Iran now boasts a radically anti-U.S. revolutionary regime, Guatemala has suffered a legacy of military dictatorships and guerrilla insurgencies, and Chile sports one of the most dictatorial regimes in the world. The crisis generated by U.S. involvement in Iran and the potential for future crises for U.S. foreign policy in both Chile and Guatemala suggest that perhaps the United States would have been better off siding with each country's democratic predecessors.[19]

It is important to note that success in overthrowing both the Mosaddeq and Arbenz regimes at relatively cheap cost and using covert means in the immediate postwar period undoubtedly gave subsequent U.S. administrations a false sense of power and ability to control the nature of other Third World regimes. One must also note that the United States was successful in both cases (and in Chile also) because the regimes represented fragile democratic coalitions with powerful enemies—most notably disenchanted militaries— that were all too happy to take control in exchange for U.S. economic and military support. As Washington was soon to learn, shaky democratic regimes are much easier to deal with than revolutionary movements based on nationalism.

U.S. intervention in Vietnam is perhaps the most tragic and written-about U.S. encounter with revolutionary nationalism. Nowhere has nationalism been more misunderstood and ignored. It is extremely difficult in retrospect to understand how the United States became involved in a land war with a people who had resisted Chinese and Cambodian attempts at control for centuries, maintained a guerrilla insurgency against occupying Japanese forces in World War II, and finally defeated French ambitions at restoring their colonial empire. U.S. intelligence agents reporting in 1945 to President Truman's secretary of state, James Byrnes, presciently noted that the Vietnamese were "determined to maintain their independence even at the cost of their lives [since] they have nothing to lose and all to gain."[20]

The irony of U.S. involvement in the Vietnam War is that the United States had covertly aided Vietminh leader Ho Chi Minh during World War II in his battle against the Japanese and that Ho had hoped the United States would guarantee Vietnam's independence at the end of the war.[21] The United States, rather than support Ho's quest for independence, would back the French return to Indochina, subsequently replacing the defeated forces of its ally with its own combat forces. The final result would be over 58,000 American soldiers killed and the first major U.S. defeat in the Third World.

The tragedy of Vietnam is twofold. First, it underscores the U.S. inability to recognize the legitimacy of popular revolutionary movements when they espouse leftist ideologies. As one foreign policy analyst has suggested, "It is now quite likely that early support for a still pro-American Ho Chi Minh rather than for his colonial masters might have created an ally instead of an enemy."[22] Although such a policy would most likely have ensured a communist Vietnam, it would also have meant a highly nationalist and independent Vietnam, seeking strong links with the United States and a less restrictive relationship with the Soviet Union than is currently the case. The second tragedy of Vietnam is that the first lesson still has not been learned.

The primary misconception driving U.S. foreign policy toward revolutionary regimes is that they, along with the Soviet Union, can "export" revolution to the Third World. According to this viewpoint, revolution is not caused primarily by regionally specific factors or internal contradictions of the nation in question (such as lack of land reform, starvation, nonexistent medical care) but rather is the result of communist aggression led by the Soviet Union. Typical of this approach is Reagan's characterization of revolutionary conflict: "Let us not delude ourselves. The Soviet Union underlies all the unrest that is going on. If they weren't involved in this game of dominoes, there wouldn't be any hot spots in the world."[23]

History simply does not support this proposition. Successful revolutionary movements at first fight with weapons acquired locally, usually from opposing forces; external arms do not arrive until the guerrillas have proved themselves on the battlefield.[24] For example, Fidel Castro received Soviet military support only after the revolution was won, and Ho Chi Minh initially armed his forces with Japanese and French arsenals captured during World War II. In fact, when Castro attempted to export revolution to Central America during the 1960s, he met with failure; the guerrilla forces were easily defeated due to their inability to attract a major following.[25] This point was driven home when Che Guevara, attempting to repeat the success of the 1958 Cuban revolution, led a band of guerrillas into eastern Bolivia in 1966. He was betrayed by the rural peasantry and summarily executed by the Bolivian armed forces.

The example of the Nicaraguan revolution is especially instructive. Although the Sandinista National Liberation Front (FSLN) received Cuban arms during the 1960s, this aid was discontinued after 1970, not beginning again until 1979 when the insurrection against Somoza already was well underway.[26] More significant is that Costa Rica, Venezuela, Panama, and Cuba coordinated arms deliveries to the Sandinistas, with the majority of arms during the final phases of the war coming from Venezuela and Panama.[27] This was hardly a communist conspiracy for revolution.

The Carter administration deviated from the dominant viewpoint that revolutions primarily are caused by external communist aggression, instead centering on the internal causes of upheaval and the need for structural reform to alleviate them. Despite this understanding, Carter's policy of resolving the internal conditions that breed insurgency failed because, like his predecessors, he favored excluding leftist groups from political participation. Genuine structural reform, and hence defusing of the guerrilla threat, "is highly unlikely as long as the left is automatically to be excluded from political participation."[28]

In the case of El Salvador, for example, a reform-minded junta took power in October 1979, aspiring to initiate structural changes that would defuse the country's growing guerrilla insurgency. The junta accepted leaders from the centrist opposition and was willing to carry out a dialogue with the radical left and include them in a future reconciliation government but had been stymied by rightist elements within the military.[29] The junta, politically willing to move against the rightist elements (a group whose power had to be broken before genuine structural reform could take place), hesitated for lack of Carter administration support: "Though Washington favored social reform, it balked at the October junta's willingness to bring the popular organizations into the government and to seek an accord with the guerrillas,"[30] inevitably leading to a continuing stalemate in El Salvador's guerrilla war.[31] When successor governments in the 1980s would attempt to initiate agrarian reform, one of the key problems fueling the guerrilla war, the net result would be failure: a still-powerful right would resist, and the left, still disenfranchised politically, would respond with increasing guerrilla attacks. Although favoring social reform, Carter's reliance on the cold war precept of limiting leftist participation ensured its doom. This trend has been exacerbated by Reagan's overwhelming commitment to a military solution of the conflict as opposed to a negotiated settlement.

A corollary to the export-for-revolution thesis is that a leftist revolutionary leader becomes a tool for international communism. The *Pentagon Papers*, for example, dismissed the possibility that Ho Chi Minh or Mao Zedong could be both nationalists and communists.[32] This point is extremely important: once policymakers deny the revolution any political or historical legitimacy, they then "presume a right of intervention to subdue it."[33] Although this view obviously has changed concerning the U.S. relationship with China in light of the enduring Sino-Soviet split, current U.S. thinking still views with suspicion Third World leaders seeking close relationships with the Soviet Union. Again this proposition is dubious at best. To be sure, Soviet allies such as Cuba follow the Soviet lead when it is viewed as complementary to their national interests. Common interests, however, should not be construed as the Soviets dictating orders: "The indigenous Revolutionary—Tito, Castro, Hoxa, or Ho—fiercely guards his independence. . . . His views are his own, for he has made his own revolution."[34] Furthermore, history is replete with examples of former so-called Soviet client states, including (but not limited to) China, Egypt, Ghana, Indonesia, Somalia, and Sudan, which have expelled the Soviets when the latter's presence becomes inimical to the foreign policy interests of the former. In Third World politics, self-interest and nationalism are thicker than ideology.

The faults and drawbacks of the U.S. inability to cope successfully with revolutionary nationalism are shown by the Reagan Doctrine and its support of so-called democratic freedom fighters in Nicaragua. To appreciate fully the Nicaraguan example, it is necessary to examine U.S. foreign policy toward Castro's Cuba, the first socialist revolutionary regime in Latin America.

Castro's success in overthrowing the popularly hated and U.S.-supported Batista regime in 1959, and subsequent stated desires to reform Cuba's economy along socialist lines, incurred the wrath of Washington. Rather than accept the validity of the Cuban revolution, the United States attempted to isolate Castro diplomatically, initiated a trade embargo (which continues to this day), authorized assassination attempts, and ultimately managed the ill-fated Bay of Pigs invasion of the island in 1961 by CIA-trained exiles.

The Bay of Pigs invasion, consciously designed by the CIA with the Guatemalan model in mind, met with utter disaster.[35] Unlike the weak democratic government confronted and overthrown in Guatemala, the United States had attacked a revolutionary regime enjoying almost total support among the general population and especially within the military. Rather than overthrow Castro, the attempted invasion merely strengthened his position on the island—the exact opposite of what the United States was trying to achieve. The explanation for this is simple: "When a regime has any large degree of popular support and legitimacy, a foreign state's force, pressure, and propaganda directed against the country may only cause the people to rally around their government."[36] More important, Castro, who was completely isolated by the United States, had no choice but to turn to the Soviet Union to ensure the longevity of his regime against potential future attacks by the United States. To be fair, it is undoubtedly true that Castro's sympathies lie with the Soviet Union's stance toward revolution and social change and that he held a deep mistrust for U.S. intentions concerning the Cuban revolution, even before the invasion. Yet Castro's famous "betrayal" speeches of April 16 and December 2, 1961, in which he declared his Marxist-Leninist beliefs and alliance with the Soviet Union, occurred after U.S. attempts to overthrow the revolution through the Bay of Pigs debacle.[37] One can argue that the U.S.-sponsored invasion substantiated Castro's fears and forced him into the willing embrace of the Soviet Union. Indeed, Soviet Premier Nikita Khrushchev ridiculed as "stupid" U.S. efforts "to drive Castro to the wall," nonetheless relishing the expected results: "Castro will have to gravitate to us like iron filings to a magnet."[38]

U.S. foreign policy in Nicaragua is repeating the mistakes made in Cuba during the last three decades. The Reagan administration has attempted to isolate Nicaragua diplomatically, has maintained a trade embargo, and is supporting a paramilitary group, the contras, in order to prevent another Soviet beachhead (tool for international communism thesis) in the Western Hemisphere (the first being Cuba). Although original justifications for supporting the contras wavered between interdicting arms being sent to Salvadoran guerrillas (export of revolution thesis) and forcing the Sandinistas to democratize their system of governance, the real aim, as in Cuba in 1961, seemingly has been the overthrow of the Sandinista regime: "At issue was not a particular Sandinista policy, but the Sandinistas themselves; the Sandinista cancer had to be extirpated lest it spread through Central America and into Mexico."[39]

Similar to the Cuban case, the Nicaraguan revolution enjoyed great popular support through the overthrow of Anastasio Somoza, one in a long line of hated and U.S.-supported dictators. Also, U.S. intervention into Nicaraguan affairs has enabled the Ortega government to silence its opponents more easily, concentrate power, and blame the United States for the increasingly evident failure of the economy. Most important is that U.S. attempts to isolate the Sandinista regime have unproductively radicalized the revolution, driving it even closer to the Soviet Union—the exact opposite of what the Reagan administration was attempting to achieve.

The primary problem with the Reagan approach is that it vastly underestimated the popular support of the Sandinista regime and the legitimacy of the 1979 revolution. The same mistake was made with Castro's Cuba, and nearly thirty years of confrontation with that regime has achieved little if any benefit for U.S. foreign policy. Rather than seeking to overthrow the Sandinista government, the United States should be wholeheartedly supporting the major tenets of the Arias peace plan. If the nations of the region are satisfied with allowing a socialist neighbor to coexist along their borders, albeit one that does not interfere in their domestic affairs, the United States should follow their wishes. Unfortunately, rather than muster its extensive influence in the region to ensure compliance with the proposal, the United States has aided its demise through continued intransigence and seeming insistence on achieving a military rather than a negotiated settlement.

Support of the Right

Antagonism to the left is only one-half of the U.S. foreign policy equation in the Third World. The complementary half includes support for anticommunist, pro-West elites and manifests itself in several different ways. The United States may provide military and economic aid to a pro-West faction during a civil crisis to ensure it ultimately takes power (for example, Mobutu and the Congo crisis in 1965), initiate a coup against a nationalist leader suspected of communist tendencies (such as Mosaddeq in 1953) and install an anticommunist stalwart in his place (for example, Shah Reza Pahlavi), or support the illegal seizure of a government by a U.S.-trained military officer (for example, Nicaragua's Anastasio Somoza Garcia in 1936).

What has warmed the ideological predilection of American elites and almost virtually guaranteed U.S. support are statements such as the following by Chilean dictator General Augusto Pinochet: "I am against communists and I will continue fighting until the end."[40]

The often disregarded long-term problem with this anticommunist strategy is that the regimes who have become the "bastions for democracy" and therefore staunch U.S. allies—the shah, Marcos, Batista, Mobutu, and Duvalier to name a few—are generally headed by traditional dictators lacking in popular support and primarily interested in personal aggrandizement. The United States therefore has created an inherently unstable link with the "dominant personality" as opposed to the "institutionalized government" of a Third World country.[41]

The case of Zaire illustrates the fragile nature of a regime installed and maintained by the United States. The Belgian Congo (Zaire) suffered extreme civil disorder upon independence on July 1, 1960, due to infighting among factions within the government and secessionist demands by several regional leaders. In response to increased instability, President Kennedy ordered the CIA to determine which Congolese faction would best serve U.S. interests. Covert military aid was extended beginning in October 1962 to the chosen candidate, a young colonel named Joseph Mobutu (currently Mobutu Sese Seko), who gradually would defeat his opponents and assume the leadership of Zaire by military coup in 1965. The short term undoubtedly seemed bright as Mobutu restored stability in Zaire, put the country on a capitalist pro-West path, and promised to be a staunch anticommunist ally in the Third World.

In the long run, however, Zairian society has regressed to the point that conditions for popular rebellion exist. The following statement by Thomas Callaghy, specialist on Zaire, details the unstable nature of the Mobutu regime:

> Its total foreign debt is now about $4.5 billion, economic growth has all but stopped, and the mass standard of living has fallen precipitously in recent years. Agricultural output is down dramatically; nutrition levels and literacy rates are falling dangerously; and social welfare services and the transportation network have seriously deteriorated. Unemployment and underemployment levels are dangerously high, inflation is rampant, and corruption permeates the political structure, particularly at the top. Mobutu and his political elite live grandly, while the vast majority struggle from day to day. Periodically, the regime grandiosely announces sweeping "policies" to deal with these problems, but they are never implemented in any serious way. For example, agriculture has been "priority of priorities" for years now, while rural decline continues. The regime's real substantive thrust is that of control and personal aggrandizement, despite its revolutionary rhetoric and Mobutu's attempt to wear Lumumba's mantle.[42]

The precarious nature of Mobutu's regime was highlighted by its inability to quell secessionist drives on its Shaba province in 1977 and 1978, having to rely on U.S.-airlifted Moroccan troops in 1977 and U.S.-airlifted French and Belgian troops in 1978. Callaghy warns that "Mobutu has made no real preparation for a succession and, if something were to happen to him, Zaire might well disintegrate again as it did during the early 1960s."[43] More to the point is a statement made by a Zairian intellectual: "We are suffering here, and it is because of the Americans. We cannot change the government because you support Mobutu for the copper. But the revolution will come, and we will kick you all out."[44]

The Zairian case is indicative of a problem that has plagued U.S. links with Third World dictatorships and ultimately has contributed to their revolutionary overthrow: the same dictators the United States has supported (and in several cases placed in power) because of their anticommunist, conservative beliefs are the same men who have shown a general disregard for social reform or broadly shared development policies targeted toward the majority of the population. Several of the following conditions intertwined to seal the fate of Marcos, the shah, Duvalier, Somoza, and many others: increasing income gaps between rich and poor; accumulation of vast wealth by the ruling family through personal control of major aspects of the economy; increasing mass poverty (from already low levels) in the rural areas and urban shantytowns; limited access to basic social services and lack of meaningful political participation for the majority of the population; and exclusion of the rising middle class from sharing in the political and economic benefits of the ruling class.[45]

The core of the problem is that the traditional dictator seeks legitimacy in the international arena—in the form of military and economic aid—rather than from the domestic environment. When the United States has been willing to fill this role, the dictator's need to foster popular domestic legitimacy through reform is sorely circumscribed. And as dissent against the regime grows, the tendency is toward greater repression rather than reform.

It is not difficult to understand why anti-American revolutions are almost inevitable against U.S.-supported dictatorships. In the case of Iran, for example, the United States installed a leader, the shah, lacking in popular support. As popular dissent against the regime grew, the shah, rather than open up the political system, increasingly relied on systematic repression through SAVAK, the highly feared secret police. Furthermore, lack of meaningful reform increased social inequalities within the urban areas (most notably Tehran) and raised expectations of the rural dwellers, the majority of whom were missed by the shah's great "white revolution."[46] To the vast majority of the population, the United States undoubtedly was looked upon as both the midwife and primary prop of the hated regime. When the end for the shah did come, it is not surprising that the revolution vented an accompanying anti-American rage. This case study is not unique but rather is indicative of a general trend (although with variation), including Cuba (1959), Ethiopia (1974), Vietnam (1975), and Nicaragua (1979).

What is difficult to understand is why the United States continues to associate itself with illegitimate dictatorships whose long-term viability is doubtful. The major reason is that the theme of anticommunism has been fused with the incremental nature of U.S. foreign policy relationships with Third World allies. Incrementalism, or a slowly increasing economic and military commitment to a Third World ally, is the result of a four-year U.S. presidential term favoring the continuance of existing foreign policy relationships. There usually is hesitancy in fundamentally decreasing ties with a "proved ally" of strategic importance, regardless of the inequities in its social structure or political illegitimacy, because of the fear that the regime will either turn to the Soviet Union or will be replaced by a more radical regime inimical to U.S. interests.[47] In short, the general maxim for U.S. relations with Third World allies has been: "If it ain't broke, why fix it!"

In the case of Mobutu, for example, U.S. administrations consistently have been willing to ignore the corrupt nature of his regime because of its strategic location in southern Africa, control over vast copper reserves, and role as a staunch bulwark against communism. President Nixon "was delighted to work with the anti-communist Mobutu."[48] Similarly, President Reagan assured Mobutu of strong U.S. support, making issues of corruption and reform secondary to Zaire's role in the containment of international communism.[49] Even President Carter, despite original intentions of pursuing a vigorous human rights stance in Zaire, ended up supporting Mobutu. Lack of a "viable alternative" to Mobutu amid fears that pressure "would be accompanied by chaos" ensured that human rights took a backseat to national security interests.[50]

President Carter's human rights program, which would question the utility of identifying the United States with inherently unstable dictatorships, had the potential of deviating from the incrementalist norm. Although promotion of human rights was the guiding theme of Carter's involvement in successfully achieving the transition to majority rule in Zimbabwe, its application generally was reserved for countries, such as Guatemala, not considered strategically significant to the United States. When the pursuit of human rights clashed with perceived national security interests, especially in proved allies of strategic importance (examples are Iran, the Philippines, South Korea, and Zaire), the former took a backseat to the latter.[51] Similarly, when events in a country targeted for a vigorous human rights campaign reached a crisis stage in which the traditional ally was threatened by hostile leftist forces, the cold war reflex to support the dictator won out:

As instability gave way to insurrection in Nicaragua, the Carter Administration was caught in Hobson's choice of standing by its commitment to human rights or subordinating humanitarian concerns to the traditional ones of national security. . . . The result was a paralysis of policy during the critical months of 1978, and an eventual decision to salvage Somoza long after that became an impossibility.[52]

Carter's human rights campaign, already compromised by numerous exceptions for national security reasons, increasingly was pushed to the background as the issues of containment and anticommunism took on even greater importance in the last two years of the administration.

The Philippines today presents a poignant example of everything that is wrong with the incrementalist nature of U.S. foreign policy. Five successive U.S. administrations from President Johnson to President Reagan (1966–1986) disregarded Ferdinand Marcos's corruption and systematic destruction of Filipino democracy because of his staunch anticommunism and ownership of bases perceived as integral to U.S. global defense. Richard Kessler, specialist on the Philippines, notes:

As long as the communist insurgency was under control and the Filipino people were not rioting, U.S. policy did not change. . . . [Marcos] understood that the United States remained concerned primarily about the bases and that consequently no U.S. policymaker would look into the underlying structure of his rule.[53]

In fact, the United States intervened in promoting the departure of Marcos only after it had become clear that he had lost his ability to maintain power.[54] Luckily for the Reagan administration, the replacement regime was not a radical fundamentalist regime like that of Khomeini but rather was led by the moderate, pro-U.S. Corazon Aquino.

Yet despite optimism in Aquino's democratic revolution, the regime is extremely fragile and unstable. The U.S.-supported Marcos systematically had looted the economy and destroyed its democratic framework over a period of twenty years such that 70 percent of the population lived in poverty in 1986 (as compared to 28 percent in 1965, the year before Marcos first came to power), a communist-led insurgency grew from 11 people in 1968 to an armed force of 20,000 in 1985 (active in all seventy-four provinces), and politicization of the armed forces has led to numerous coup attempts and continuing mutinies throughout the country since Aquino took power.[55] Despite Aquino's best intentions of restoring democracy, the country has been left a legacy of instability that will be extremely difficult to overcome.

The most damning aspect of the current crisis in the Philippines is that it was avoidable. Kessler convincingly argues that the United States had several opportunities between 1966 and 1986 to force Marcos from power or to distance the U.S. from his excesses . . . [which] would not have required actions that might be viewed as American manipulation of Philippine politics. On the contrary, such actions would have been viewed as American support for the will of the Filipino people.[56]

Most notably, the United States could have displayed strong disapproval when the possibility of marshal law and subsequent suspension of the constitution was broached in 1972 and then carried out in the same year (suspension of the constitution, which limited a leader to two terms, was necessary for Marcos to stay in power). Marcos was afraid of the U.S. reaction, and strong U.S. disapproval could have succeeded in deterring him.[57] Unfortunately, both before and after the declaration of marshal law, Marcos received tacit U.S. support.

In short, U.S. disregard for Marcos's dismantling of democracy in the Philippines to protect short-term interests of easy access to strategic bases clearly has been detrimental to U.S. interests in the long run, and conditions there are likely to worsen rather than improve. Indeed, the popular press has noted that the Philippines has become increasingly nationalistic and anti-American, and, even worse, U.S. soldiers for the first time are being sought and killed by communist guerrillas.[58]

Endless Enemies or Future Friends?

The twin themes of antagonism to the left and support of the right have served as the foundation for a faulty U.S. foreign policy in the Third World. In the words of one writer, it has made the United States and the Third World "endless enemies."[59] How should U.S. foreign policy be changed so as to shed its image as the enemy of social change and protector of the status quo, instead providing the basis for a long-term relationship in which the United States becomes the standard-bearer for positive social change in the form of democracy and broadly shared development? In short, how can these "endless enemies" become "future friends"?

The United States must first discard the ill-conceived notion that Third World countries are merely pawns in the greater East-West struggle and that the primary source of conflict in these countries is external Soviet interference. Viewing social change through East-West glasses ensures a reactive policy constrained by the ideological blinders of anticommunism. The United States must instead analyze the regional or internal causes of a particular conflict. In this fashion, the conflict becomes important in its own right and lends itself to resolution based on internal structural changes. When the United States has followed such a prescription, as in Zimbabwe (formerly Rhodesia), the results have been gratifying.

In the case of Zimbabwe, the United States and Great Britain cooperated in pressuring the white minority regime of Ian Smith to accept universal suffrage and rapid transition to black majority rule even though this virtually ensured a regime dominated by the Patriotic Front (PF), a coalition of two guerrilla groups led by avowed Marxists and supplied by the Soviet Union and China. This case is significant for three reasons: (1) a more ideological approach would have eschewed supporting the PF because of its obvious communist links and outspoken sympathy of its leaders for Marxism; (2) the United States recognized the legitimacy of the guerrilla struggle and that its resolution depended on internal political and economic reforms; and (3) the United States recognized the positive role to be played by the radical left in the reform equation. Indeed, despite the Marxist rhetoric of Zimbabwe's prime minister, Robert Mugabe, he has clearly followed a pragmatic policy of socioeconomic reform and maintenance of extensive links with the West, underscoring that ideology should not be the yardstick by which the United States determines enemies or allies in the Third World. Most important, British-American willingness to involve the left in meaningful political participation where it previously has been denied a role demonstrated that it can be the key to alleviating long-term guerrilla insurgency.[60]

What do these three lessons mean for future U.S. involvement with guerrilla insurgencies? In the case of El Salvador, for example, it would require recognition by the United States that the revolution is driven by lack of social reform and not by the Soviet-Cuban bloc and that therefore the guerrilla struggle of the FDR-FMLN is caused by legitimate, unfulfilled popular needs. Although reliance on massive military aid may be able to suppress the rebels in the short run (as is currently the case under the Reagan administration), in the long run, it merely strengthens those forces opposed to reform, virtually ensuring the reemergence of guerrilla struggle (witness Guatemala's recurrent guerrilla wars). The proper U.S. approach should be to emphasize its belief in the negotiated resolution of the conflict between the Salvadoran government and the FDR-FLMN, based on national reconciliation and socioeconomic reform.

Similar to the need to recognize the legitimacy of guerrilla struggle as an outgrowth of unfulfilled popular needs, U.S. foreign policy also must learn to deal constructively with revolutionary regimes when they do achieve power. Again, the key to this policy is that opposing ideologies do not in and of themselves preclude a mutually beneficial relationship (note growing U.S. ties with Marxist Mozambique, extensive oil trade with Marxist Angola, and a fruitful relationship with China). Yet often the relationship between the United States and the revolutionary regime is at first strained. In the case of Nicaragua, the Sandinista leadership was suspicious of U.S. attitudes toward the revolution, primarily due to past U.S. support for Somoza and previous intervention in Latin America, while the United States feared that the Sandinistas were going to become the center for Soviet-Cuban destabilization efforts in Central America. Fears should not become the basis for foreign policy; when they do, they create a self-fulfilling prophecy.

The Carter administration broke with the traditional U.S. approach of generating hostility toward revolutionary regimes by attempting to build a constructive relationship with the Sandinistas in 1979. Hoping "to avoid repeating the errors of 1959–1960, when U.S. hostility drove the Cuban revolution to the left and into the arms of the Soviet Union," Carter's primary objective was to provide incentives to the Sandinistas to maintain the pluralist nature of the revolution.[61] U.S. efforts were rewarded. As Carter left the presidency, "U.S.-Nicaraguan relations were normal, if not friendly, and the radicalization of the revolution which Carter had sought to avert had not yet happened."[62] The election of the Reagan administration and its hostile attitude toward the Sandinista regime hastened a degeneration of the relationship, especially after it became apparent in 1981 that Washington was funding the contras through CIA efforts in Honduras. As one policy analyst noted, the Reagan administration was not interested in compromise, embarking instead "on its Nicaraguan policy with the firm belief that the Sandinistas must be overthrown or, at least, theirs must become a revolution of misery, a frightful object lesson to the people of the region."[63] Yet although Washington's paramilitary war has exhibited the ability to disrupt Nicaragua's economic and political system, as surely it did in Cuba and North Vietnam, it is inadequate if the goal is overthrowing the Sandinistas or forcing them to accept U.S. demands to dismantle their system of governance. The Reagan administration, just as U.S. policymakers had done in Cuba in 1961, has failed to recognize the continued popular support of the Nicaraguan revolution.

U.S. inability to dictate militarily to the Sandinistas is indicative of a theme that should be a guiding factor in U.S. foreign policy: the increasing nonutility of (para)military intervention in achieving long-term goals in the Third World. Yet as two authors have lamented:

> Vietnam's "lesson"—that intervention against revolutionary nationalism in the Third World is at least futile and unacceptably costly, and at most, immoral, inhumane, and arrogant—has been lost in the higher circles of government. Instead, the war seems to have taught that the use of force abroad must be better managed, that the key issues concern public relations and command and control rather than political goals and values.[64]

It seems that despite the defeat of counterinsurgency in Vietnam and the failure of the paramilitary war in Cuba in 1961, the Reagan administration continues to make the same mistakes by seeking similar solutions in El

Salvador and Nicaragua, respectively, as well as in numerous other areas of the Third World.

This does not mean, however, that the United States must adopt a strict policy of nonintervention in the Third World. In the case of Afghanistan, for example, several circumstances intersect to make military aid to the *mujahedin* guerrillas a worthwhile cause. According to accepted precepts of international law, the Soviet Union illegally has invaded and occupied the country, the Afghanis are almost unanimous in desiring Soviet withdrawal, and the guerrillas enjoy overwhelming regional and international support. In contrast, U.S. aid for the contras in Nicaragua has been declared illegal under international law, the majority of Nicaraguans oppose U.S. intervention, and U.S. actions generally run counter to both regional and international opinion, even among traditional U.S. allies.[65] Yet as one policy analyst has warned, U.S. military aid to the *mujahedin* should be limited to achieving the withdrawal of foreign occupation forces and should be accompanied by negotiations to achieve these objectives:

> But the arms we supply, and our contact with Afghans, must be governed by the knowledge that when the issue of Soviet occupation is resolved, other, local issues will continue to divide the Afghans, both within the country and in relations with their neighbors. We must not be lured into a continuing dispute that would ally us against new and so far undreamed-of enemies.[66]

The purpose of U.S. support should not be to bleed the Soviets but rather should be based on achieving a negotiated settlement that recognizes Afghanistan's right to self-determination as well as placating Soviet fears of a hostile nation on its frontier.

The discussion thus far has centered on how the United States must restructure its relationship with the revolutionary left. The complementary component of this policy is the necessity to decrease U.S. economic and military aid links with authoritarian Third World allies. Rather than providing aid to authoritarian regimes that pass an anticommunist litmus test and rely on repression to maintain social order, U.S. aid programs must be revised to reflect more positive, long-term goals for U.S. foreign policy.

The restructuring of U.S. aid programs should follow relatively straightforward, yet stringent, guidelines.[67] Economic aid should be provided only to nations respectful of the human rights of their people and committed to broadly shared development targeted toward the majority of the population. A regime committed to these two principles increases its domestic support and represents a positive, long-term investment for the United States. Military aid should be much more restrictive in nature. It should be limited to regimes based on some form of popular consent (not necessarily a multiparty, democratic system) that are confronting a legitimate military threat. The theme of popular consent is extremely important. If this attribute is missing, U.S. military support becomes the basis for internal repression and control, again working counter to long-term U.S. interests in the Third World.

The first step in such a program would entail the cutting of all aid to authoritarian clients whose domestic politics match none of the guidelines, as in Zaire. Experience should have taught U.S. policymakers that Zaire's highly corrupt political and economic system, coupled with the obvious U.S. role as primary supporter of the regime, provides the recipe for potential disaster. Rationales for continued support of Mobutu, such as President Carter's fears that lack of an alternative will ensure chaos, although potentially true, also create a self-fulfilling prophecy. Mobutu has no incentive to reform as long as the United States and other Western donors continue to underwrite Zaire's economy, thus almost ensuring a further deterioration of the Zairian economy and the broadening of the base for popular rebellion. The propitious time for the United States to act is now rather than when a guerrilla insurgency is almost on the verge of victory and a crisis situation has developed (the route usually taken by the United States) or when Mobutu dies and there is no replacement. By cutting aid now, Mobutu will be forced to make the choice to reform. If he is unable or unwilling, perhaps another group of leaders, better able to do the job, will take power. Most important, it is the United States, by acting now, that sets the agenda for a future relationship with Zaire through a positive long-term vision based on human rights and broadly shared development.[68]

Withdrawal of special relationships previously held with authoritarian Third World countries does not mean the United States should adopt an isolationist foreign policy. Rather, it indicates that it will commit its valuable resources only to nations sharing an interest in promoting and maintaining societies built on popular consent and broadly shared development. In this sense, the United States should cultivate close relationships with regimes carrying out these programs, assisting financially or technically as needed.

Inevitably the United States will find itself closely involved with an ally whose democratic institutions and processes will be subverted by a leader or faction desirous of assuming personal control and power, such as when President Marcos stole the 1969 Philippines elections or declared marshal law in 1972 to maintain himself in power (counter to the country's constitutional system). In cases like this, the United States should utilize its economic and military influence (gradually curtailing both types of aid, beginning with military) with the country in question to foster a return to democratic practices. This type of action would not have been regarded negatively by the Filipino people but rather as support for the will of the people themselves.[69]

The important point of the Philippines case study is that five U.S. administrations refused to pursue this type of policy because of strategic concerns over U.S. base rights in the Philippines. In fact, it was this type of "strategic exception" that contributed to the failure of Carter's human rights policies. Even if one accepts the U.S. strategic need for bases in the Philippines or elsewhere in the world, long-term interests logically demand that the United States not turn a blind eye while democracy is destroyed in order to maintain these security interests. As the United States learned the hard way in Iran, Ethiopia, Nicaragua, and in other nations of so-called strategic concern, past or present, disregard for the repressive nature of the regimes lacking popular support is a sure-fire way to lose these strategic interests in the long run, as well as foster the creation of a hostile anti-U.S. regime.

Finally, the United States inevitably finds itself confronted with authoritarian governments that systematically abuse the rights of their peoples but are not reliant on the United States for either military or economic aid. Because the United States cannot and should not be the guardian of all the countries of the world, it should maintain no more and no less than proper relations with these governments. In extreme cases, the United States may join other nations in adopting multilateral sanctions to change the nature of a particular regime. But sanctions should be pursued only when certain legitimizing factors intersect: the nation in question grossly violates the norms of international human rights, and the action is supported by the vast majority of the target nation's population and also overwhelmingly regionally and within the international system. One case study that fits these requirements is South Africa. The key to this type of policy is that the United States should act within a multilateral framework in coordination with other nations, and not merely according to its own ideological whims, as too often has been the case in the past (for example, Chile from 1970 to 1973).

In summary, past U.S. foreign policy in the Third World, built upon the twin themes of antagonism to the left and support of the right, has been both counterproductive and detrimental to long-term U.S. interests. Rather than pursuing negative status quo policies of anticommunism and counter-insurgency, the United States should instead become the standard-bearer for positive social change in the form of democracy and broadly shared development. The guiding principle of such a policy would be diplomatic negotiation rather than the increasingly outmoded tool of military force. Officials must resist falling prey to short-term exigencies at the expense of long-term U.S. interests.

Notes

1. Walter LaFeber, *Inevitable Revolutions: The United States and Central America* (New York: W.W. Norton, 1983), p. 15.

2. Ibid.

3. Ibid., p. 38.

4. Quoted in Ronald J. Stupak, *American Foreign Policy: Assumptions, Processes and Projections* (New York: Harper & Row, 1976), p. 188.

5. Walter LaFeber, *America, Russia and the Cold War: 1945–1980* (New York: John Wiley, 1980), p. 58.

6. Richard A. Melanson, *Writing History and Making Policy: The Cold War, Vietnam, and Revisionism* (Lanham, Md.: University Press of America, 1983), p. 13.

7. Ibid., p. 15.

8. See Jerel A. Rosati and John Creed, "Perceptual Dissensus: National Elite Perspectives on American Foreign Policy" (paper presented at the Tenth Annual Scientific Meeting of the International Society of Political Psychology, San Francisco, July 4–7, 1987).

9. Stupak, *American Foreign Policy*, p. 217.

10. Quoted in Jerel A. Rosati, *The Carter Administration's Quest for Global Community: Beliefs and Their Impact on Behavior* (Columbia, S.C.: University of South Carolina Press, 1987), p. 42.

11. Morris J. Blachman and Kenneth Sharpe, "De-Democratising American Foreign Policy: Dismantling the Post-Vietnam Formula," *Third World Quarterly* 8, no. 4 (1986): 1271–1308.

12. For a critical overview of the Reagan Doctrine, see Ted G. Carpenter, "U.S. Aid to Anti-Communist Rebels: The 'Reagan Doctrine' and Its Pitfalls," Cato Institute Policy Analysis no. 74, June 24, 1986.

13. Robert Trudeau and Lars Shoultz, "Guatemala," in Morris J. Blachman, William M. Leogrande, and Kenneth Sharpe, eds., *Confronting Revolution: Security through Diplomacy in Central America* (New York: Pantheon Books, 1986), p. 28.

14. Richard Millett, "Guatemala's Painful Progress," *Current History* 85, no. 515 (December 1986): 413.

15. Piero Gleijeses, "The Reagan Doctrine and Central America," *Current History* 85, no. 515 (December 1986): 437.

16. Quoted in Seymour Hersh, *The Price of Power: Kissinger in the Nixon White House* (New York: Summit Books, 1983), p. 265.

17. Quoted in ibid., p. 278.

18. Ibid.

19. For an analysis of impending crises in both countries, see Pamela Constable and Arturo Valenzuela, "Is Chile Next?" *Foreign Policy* 63 (Summer 1986): 58–75; and Gleijeses, "Reagan Doctrine," pp. 401–37.

20. Stanley Karnow, *Vietnam: A History* (New York: Viking Press, 1983), p. 147.

21. Ibid., p. 147.

22. Louis René Beres, "The End of American Foreign Policy," *Third World Quarterly* 8, no. 4 (1986): 1262.

23. Quoted in Arthur Schlesinger, Jr., "Foreign Policy and the American Character," *Foreign Affairs* 62, no. 1 (Fall 1983): 5.

24. Richard J. Barnet, *Intervention and Revolution: America's Confrontation with*

Insurgency Movements around the World (New York: World Publishing Company, 1968), p. 56.

25. For a brief analysis, see Andrew Wheatcroft, *The World Atlas of Revolutions* (New York: Simon & Schuster, 1983), pp. 150–63.

26. William M. Leogrande, "The United States and the Nicaraguan Revolution," in Thomas Walker, ed., *Nicaragua in Revolution* (New York: Praeger, 1982), p. 233.

27. Ibid.

28. Morris J. Blachman et al., "The Failure of the Hegemonic Strategic Vision," in Blachman, Leogrande, and Sharpe, eds., *Confronting Revolution*, p. 335. Although the Kennedy administration also centered on the internal causes of revolutionary upheaval (placing more emphasis on external communist subversion than in the first two years of the Carter administration), it also centered on excluding leftist groups from participation.

29. William M. Leogrande et al., "Grappling with Central America: From Carter to Reagan," in Blachman, Leogrande, and Sharpe, eds., *Confronting Revolution*, p. 304.

30. Ibid.

31. Gleijeses, "Reagan Doctrine," p. 436.

32. Melvin Gurtov and Ray Maghroori, *Roots of Failure: United States Foreign Policy in the Third World* (Westport, Conn.: Greenwood Press, 1984), p. 173.

33. Ibid.

34. Barnet, *Intervention and Revolution*, p. 56.

35. Peter Wyden, *Bay of Pigs* (New York: Simon & Schuster, 1979), p. 20.

36. Barry Rubin, *Modern Dictators, Third World Coup Makers, Strongmen, and Populist Tyrants* (New York: McGraw-Hill, 1987), p. 315.

37. Melvin Gurtov, *The United States against the Third World: Antinationalism and Intervention* (New York: Praeger, 1974), p. 109.

38. Quoted in Ted G. Carpenter, "The United States and Third World Dictatorships: A Case for Benign Detachment," Cato Institute Policy Analysis no. 58, August 15, 1985, p. 7.

39. Gleijeses, "Reagan Doctrine," p. 403.

40. Constable and Valenzuela, "Is Chile Next?" p. 69.

41. Henry F. Jackson, *From the Congo to Soweto: U.S. Foreign Policy toward Africa since 1960* (New York: Quill, 1984), p. 42.

42. Thomas Callaghy, "Republic of Zaire," in George E. Delury, ed., *World Encyclopedia of Political Systems and Parties* (New York: Facts on File Publications, 1987), 2:1305.

43. Ibid., p. 1306.

44. Quoted in René LeMarchand, "Zaire: The Unmanageable Client State," in René LeMarchand, ed., *American Policy in Southern Africa* (Lanham, Md.: University Press of America, 1981), p. 157.

45. For an excellent discussion of these factors, see Rubin, *Modern Dictators*, esp. pp. 76–108.

46. Ervand Abrahamian, *Iran between Two Revolutions* (Princeton: Princeton University Press, 1982), pp. 426–49.

47. For an examination of incrementalism as it applies to the U.S.-Somalia

relationship, see Peter J. Schraeder and Jerel A. Rosati, "Policy Dilemmas in the Horn of Africa: Contradictions in the U.S.-Somalia Relationship," forthcoming.

48. Madeleine Kalb, *The Congo Cables: The Cold War in Africa from Eisenhower to Kennedy* (New York: Macmillan, 1982), p. 48.

49. David A. Dickson, *United States Foreign Policy towards Sub-Saharan Africa: Change, Continuity and Constraint* (Lanham, Md.: University Press of America, 1985), p. 135.

50. Jackson, *From the Congo to Soweto*, p. 48; Dickson, *United States Foreign Policy*, p. 138.

51. Michael T. Klare and Cynthia Arnson (with Delia Miller and Daniel Volman), *Supplying Repression: U.S. Support for Authoritarian Regimes Abroad* (Washington, D.C.: Institute for Policy Studies, 1981), p. 15.

52. Leogrande, "The United States," p. 64.

53. Richard J. Kessler, "Marcos and the Americans," *Foreign Policy* 63 (Summer 1986): 46.

54. Beres, "End of American Foreign Policy," p. 1253.

55. Kessler, "Marcos and the Americans," pp. 41–42; Kessler, *US Policy toward the Philippines after Marcos* (Muscatine, Iowa: Stanley Foundation, 1986), p. 11.

56. Kessler, "Marcos and the Americans," p. 49.

57. Ibid., p. 50.

58. See Seth Mydans, "Two U.S. Airmen Slain at Philippine Base," *New York Times*, October 29, 1987, p. 3. A similar case of incrementalism and crisis that in the long run has contributed to rising anti-Americanism is South Korea. See Selig S. Harrison, "Dateline South Korea: A Divided Seoul," *Foreign Policy* 67 (Summer 1987): 154–75; Tim Shorrock, "The Struggle for Democracy in South Korea and the Rise of Anti-Americanism," *Third World Quarterly* 8, no. 4 (October 1986): 1195–1218.

59. Jonathan Kwitny, *Endless Enemies: The Making of an Unfriendly World* (New York: Congdon & Weed, 1984).

60. Leogrande et al., "Grappling."

61. Leogrande, "The United States," p. 72.

62. Ibid., p. 76. This is not to say, however, that this success would have continued had Carter won a second term. Indeed, the Sandinistas may have pursued a conflictual policy regardless of that pursued by the United States.

63. Gleijeses, "Reagan Doctrine," pp. 404–5.

64. Gurtov and Maghoori, *Roots of Failure*, p. 166.

65. For the European position on the Reagan Doctrine, see Evan Luard, "Western Europe and the Reagan Doctrine," *International Affairs* 63, no. 4 (Autumn 1987): 563–74.

66. Kwitny, *Endless Enemies*, p. 404.

67. The following guidelines for a preferred U.S. aid policy are drawn from Blachman, Leogrande, and Sharpe, *Confronting Revolution*, p. 353.

68. The Zairian case study is not unique but rather is indicative of U.S. relations with numerous Third World allies. For a similar argument favoring a cutoff of U.S. aid links to Somalia, see Schraeder and Rosati, "Policy Dilemmas in the Horn."

69. Kessler, "Marcos and the Americans," p. 49.

11
The Reagan Doctrine: Why a Good Offense Is Not the Best Defense

David Isenberg

One of the best-known warnings about the perils of entangling foreign commitments came in an address by Secretary of State John Quincy Adams on July 4, 1821. Responding to proposals that the United States assist republican movements in Latin America and elsewhere, Adams cautioned his adventurous countrymen that

> [America] goes not abroad, in search of monsters to destroy. She is the well-wisher to the freedom and independence of all. She is the champion and vindicator only of her own. . . . She well knows that by once enlisting under other banners than her own, were they even the banners of foreign independence, she would involve herself beyond the power of extrication, in all the wars of interest and intrigue, of individual avarice, envy, and ambition, which assume the colors and usurp the standard of freedom.

It is risky, of course, to speculate about what historical figures would think and say about present-day situations. Nevertheless, it does not seem farfetched to assume that if John Quincy Adams could be brought forward in time and told that the current foreign policy of the United States is to intervene in conflicts throughout the Third World in order to support anti-Soviet "democratic revolutions," he would be aghast. Yet that is the rationale of the so-called Reagan Doctrine.

The Reagan Doctrine is a rigid, simplistic, and ill-considered response to a geopolitical system in flux. It views conflicts in the Third World as part of a global game of Monopoly in which the superpower with the most developing countries in its sphere is the winner. Furthermore, it puts the security and prestige of the United States at stake by mandating U.S. involvement in areas of the world where U.S. interests are not vital. Finally, it emphasizes military aid to insurgencies and ignores other options available to the Untied States, such as moral, economic, and political pressure.

The Reagan Doctrine has ignited controversy since it was first formally articulated in President Reagan's State of the Union message of February 6, 1985. One reason is that no decisions are more important to the United States than when, how, and against whom it should wage war. Even more contentious and difficult an issue than the role of overt war making is that of covert or paramilitary operations because the pertinent decisions are completely shielded from the scrutiny of the American people and most U.S. officials. And though the Reagan Doctrine does not call for deploying U.S. troops in overseas conflicts, it definitely entails a type of war, albeit limited.

The genesis of the Reagan Doctrine can be traced to Reagan's first administration, when several elements of the president's foreign policy had in common the goal of prevailing in military and political competitions with the Soviet Union. A 1982 *New York Times* news analysis stated that "as Administration officials explain the theory of prevailing, it means pushing Russian influence back inside the borders of the Soviet Union with the combined pressure of a military buildup along with diplomatic, economic and propaganda measures."[1] A 1983 *Washington Post* editorial noted an offhand comment by the president that the U.S. position toward guerrillas should be based on "what kind of a government they are opposing."[2] In January 1983 the president signed a decision directive—a classified executive order—that permitted the National Security Council to coordinate interagency "political action strategies" in order to counter moves by the Soviet Union and its surrogates.[3]

Still, none of those elements had been codified in an explicit doctrine. It took the events that preceded the U.S. intervention in Grenada in the fall of 1983 to alert the Reagan administration to an opportunity to roll back communist influence. Technically, as Stephen Rosenfeld of the *Washington Post* observed,

> There was no anti-communist insurgency on Grenada for the United States to support. Nevertheless, the President counted substantial gains from his invasion. He had used force under an anticommunist banner and won plaudits in the political and diplomatic arenas, no small matter for an Administration eager to show that it was no Gulliver tied down by liberal Lilliputians. More importantly, for the first time, communism—if you apply the label to the elements deposed in Grenada—had been shown to be reversible.[4]

Underlying those political and military initiatives was the assumption, still prevalent in the administration, that contrary to a tenet of the Carter presidency, there had not been an inevitable decline in the ability of the United States to influence, even control, the evolution of international relations.

Although the administration has never clearly articulated the goals of the Reagan Doctrine, that has not prevented it from equipping and training U.S. military, paramilitary, and intelligence forces for a far greater use of low-intensity conflict operations, of which the doctrine is an important subset. Under President Reagan, the CIA's covert operations have more than tripled. Although not all of them are intended to support anticommunist insurgencies, there are far more covert operations with that purpose than there were in the prior administration.[5] Five of the most well-publicized and well-documented are the ones in Afghanistan, Nicaragua, Angola, Cambodia, and Ethiopia.

The Reagan Doctrine's increased emphasis on covert operations was seen as a mandate for increasing military capabilities, both outside and inside the intelligence realm. As part of the Department of Defense reorganization legislation passed in 1986, Congress established an assistant secretary of defense for special operations and low-intensity conflict, along with a four-star special operations command, which controls all special operations forces stationed in the United States except naval special warfare groups.

One of the difficulties in implementing the Reagan Doctrine is that there is not much agreement on precisely what the doctrine is. To some policymakers and journalists, it seems to be a restatement of the old sports cliché that "the best defense is a good offense." To others it is reminiscent of the rollback doctrine espoused by John Foster Dulles. To still others it is merely a call for the selective counterpressure advocated by George Kennan in his classic definition of limited containment. Consequently the administration's policy toward anticommunist insurgencies "has been a mishmash of ad hoc decisions, or nondecisions, as to who gets aid, with no apparent consistency or strategy."[6]

Much of the confusion seems to stem from the term *doctrine* itself. As conservative intelligence analyst Angelo Codevilla observed,

> The very word "doctrine" over these Presidential statements has conveyed the image of a determined Administration policy aimed at the objective of driving the Soviets and their surrogates out of Afghanistan, Angola and Nicaragua. Yet, the test of policy in a democracy lies less in the declaratory statements of the head-of-state (irrespective of his sincerity) and more in the substantial decisions and actions taken by the government. Particularly in the [Reagan] Administration, with its strong emphasis on the "cabinet approach," foreign policy is the "resultant," in the geometric sense, of the policy preferences of the major "baronies" involved in the policymaking process: the State Department, the Defense Department, the Central Intelligence Agency, and their respective allies in the National Security Council and the U.S. Congress.[7]

It is fair to say that those agencies have their own institutional biases and agendas when it comes to implementing an administration policy. Some have been more enthusiastic about applying the Reagan Doctrine than others. For example, the CIA has used the doctrine as a mandate to reinvigorate and greatly expand its paramilitary and covert operations.[8] On the other hand, the State Department has been at bitter odds with the Defense Department over the latter's interest in assisting RENAMO, the resistance movement in Mozambique.

Despite the multiplicity of interpretations to date, the doctrine does have its supporters. Charles Krauthammer, generally credited with coining the term *Reagan Doctrine* in 1985, wrote more recently:

> It [the Reagan Doctrine] says that recent Soviet acquisitions at the periphery of empire—Angola, Afghanistan, Nicaragua—are not permanent. They are open to challenge. And we support the challenge. The Reagan Doctrine declares overt U.S. support for the anti-communist resistance movements. By declaring Soviet gains reversible, it saves selective containment from being a policy of gradual, but inexorable, retreat. It thus reestablishes an equilibrium—a dynamic equilibrium—in the strategic equation between the United States and the U.S.S.R. Moreover, by not requiring global resistance at every point, but allowing the United States to choose its terrain, it restores initiative to the American side.[9]

That view highlights a major premise of the Reagan Doctrine: that because U.S. foreign policy had been far too reactive and had failed to forestall Moscow's incursions, once the Soviets had gained a foothold, they were able to keep it. Secretary of State George Shultz epitomized that view:

> In the nineteenth century we supported Simon Bolivar, Polish patriots and others seeking freedom—reciprocating, in a way, the aid given to us in our own revolution by other nations, like France. If we turned our backs on this tradition, we would be conceding the Soviet notion that communist revolutions are irreversible while everything else is up for grabs; we would be, in effect, enacting the Brezhnev doctrine into American law. So long as communist dictatorships feel free to aid and abet insurgencies in the name of "socialist internationalism," why must the democracies—the target of this threat—be inhibited from defending their own interests and the cause of democracy itself?[10]

Such assessments give the Soviets more credit than they deserve. Far from making inexorable advances in recent years, they have suffered serious setbacks. A 1986 study by the Center for Defense Information found the following:

> The pro-Soviet bloc of nations' share of world power is 20 percent, as opposed to 70 percent for the pro-West and China camp.

> From 1958 to 1980, only once (1973–1974) did more than one year go by without a nation's falling out of the Soviet-influenced category.

> After World War II the Soviets had significant influence in 9 percent of

the world's nations. They peaked at 15 percent in the late 1950s and have since dropped to 11 percent. Of the 164 countries in the world, the Soviets now have significant influence in 18.[11]

When one considers that the number of independent nations in the world has increased greatly since World War II, from about 70 in 1945 to about 164 today, and that nearly all the new countries were formerly colonies of Western powers, the magnitude of the Soviets' failure to exercise significant influence in anticolonial regimes seems even more striking. Indeed, if the pattern of Soviet influence reflects the operation of the domino theory—the fate of one nation affects the fate of another in a continuous chain reaction—it is taking a most convoluted form.

In an attempt to gain public approval for the Reagan Doctrine, its adherents have cast it as a commitment to support democracy everywhere. In his State of the Union message of February 4, 1986, President Reagan said,

> To those imprisoned in regimes held captive, to those beaten for daring to fight for freedom and democracy, for their right to worship, to speak, to live, and to prosper in the family of free nations, we say to you tonight: You are not alone, freedom fighters. America will support with moral and material assistance your right not just to fight and die for freedom but to fight and win freedom—to win freedom in Afghanistan, in Angola, in Cambodia, and in Nicaragua.[12]

Without belaboring the obvious, people are struggling and dying for freedom in many countries, both communist-dominated and noncommunist, that the administration does not feel impelled to support. The massacre of Haitians as they attempted to vote in late 1987 is but one example. That contradiction has never been resolved. As Rosenfeld observed, the Reagan Doctrine's

> original rationale—that freedom is a universal right—is open and unlimiting; if freedom is a universal right, it must be wrong not to try and seat it everywhere, even in the Soviet homeland, no matter what the cost. The actual implementation of the Reagan Doctrine, however, has been confined to a relatively few places. . . . The gap between the doctrine's universal aspirations and its particular applications is a source of frustration to its more ardent advocates; to others it is cause for relief.[13]

The administration's bold rhetoric notwithstanding, the Reagan Doctrine has been implemented selectively, which undermines the claim that it is intended to promote democracy and freedom everywhere. Roger Hansen, a professor at the Johns Hopkins School of Advanced International Studies, noted,

> If the ideology in the doctrine is discounted as public relations packaging for a realpolitik effort to weaken the Soviet position in the Third World— or more ambitiously to "bleed the Soviets to death" in their peripheral empire—then the Reagan Doctrine can be argued to represent a more coherent policy in support of a strategic effort at containment. And that policy is simply one of supporting, with the appropriate degree of "realist" prudence, anti-communist insurrections in the Third World. If and when neoconservatives support this realist interpretation of the Reagan Doctrine they necessarily reject the sine qua non of their entire foreign-policy perspective: global containment built upon realist foundations will lead to American isolationism; only ideological foundations can successfully sustain the strategy.[14]

Certainly few supporters of the Reagan Doctrine have suggested trying to liberate East European nations from their communist governments. Indeed, the United States refrained from giving more than rhetorical support to the Solidarity movement in Poland when it was being suppressed by the Jaruzelski regime, and for good reason: such an action would not have gone unchallenged.

A policy of supporting anti-Marxist insurgents in the Third World also creates more subtle but still potentially unpleasant consequences for U.S. policymakers. Richard Betts, a senior fellow of the Brookings Institution, has been one of the few observers to address those consequences. In an op-ed article in the *New York Times,* he wrote:

> If the American-backed insurgents are beaten, Moscow will gain. If, on the other hand, the guerrillas thrive, the Marxist regimes under attack will have an increasing incentive to take more decisive action against their sanctuaries. . . . Increasingly on the defensive, Moscow may just hunker down. But as the Reaganites themselves have pointed out, it is hardly safe to assume that the Russians have no intention of using their awesome military power. Might the Kremlin decide to "go to the source" of one of those third world problems? Could we afford either to stand aloof or to be dragged in?[15]

That is an important point because one of the virtues attributed to the Reagan Doctrine is that it would not involve U.S. troops. Yet because of U.S. support for the contras, the Sandinista army crossed the border to attack Honduran base facilities. Washington then felt compelled to dispatch U.S. military personnel stationed in the region to help ferry Honduran troops to the scene, increasing the risk that the U.S. troops would come under fire.

Aiding anti-Marxist guerrilla movements ties the United States to their fortunes. If such a movement should face defeat, Washington policymakers would be forced to choose between allowing it to fail, which would not be an easy course once Americans' sympathies had been engaged and U.S. prestige was at stake, or expanding U.S. involvement in the conflict. That dilemma might be resolved in favor of direct U.S. military intervention—a concern that has not been eased by the administration's argument that the collapse of the contras might necessitate such intervention in Nicaragua.

The ineffectiveness of some of the guerrilla insurgencies makes the situation especially gloomy. Again consider Nicaragua, whose insurgents have received the most attention from the United States. Colonel Rod Paschall, director of the U.S. Army Military History Institute, noted,

> There is no indication that the insurgents have established any measure of population support in the countryside of Nicaragua. Nor is there evidence of an effective urban underground working against the Sandinistas. Insurgent leaders have recently expressed a desire for aircraft to handle their resupply problems: an indication that local support from the peasantry is lacking. . . . The prospect for the Nicaraguan insurgents to win on the force of their own arms is not a bright one.[16]

Although the contras have received some support from the civilian population, especially in the northern provinces, Colonel Paschall was correct in concluding that they cannot defeat the Sandinistas solely by means of their own military resources. The contras' willingness to negotiate with the Sandinistas in accordance with the Arias peace plan is an acknowledgment of that fact.

Although the Reagan Doctrine has been likened to the failed rollback-cum-liberation policy of the 1950s, it has a different target, as George Liska, a political science professor at Johns Hopkins University, explained:

> This time the net is cast out wider: the theatre is no longer limited to Eastern Europe but encompasses the Third World at large. The means, too, have been enlarged, from propaganda only in the 1950s to propaganda plus military assistance and "humanitarian aid" in the 1980s. At the same time the ambition has dwindled: regaining Angola for democracy does not rate with liberating Poland from communism.[17]

A habitual mistake of Reagan Doctrine supporters is to equate opposition to specific communist regimes with opposition to communism per se. That is simplistic. Wars may start as a result of dissatisfaction over inequitable economic divisions, religious or ideological differences, political jealousies, or ethnic animosities. In many parts of the world, including southern Asia, Latin America, Africa, and the Middle East, violent intrastate conflict in which a nongovernmental body attempts to overthrow and replace an established government is a common, if not normal, vehicle of political change. Such internal wars have proliferated in the wake of decolonization, modernization, Westernization, and economic development. During periods of rapid societal change, many governments are unable to control the tensions that simmer beneath the surface of political life, and they erupt into revolutionary violence.

The latest crop of insurgencies is hardly a new phenomenon. Samuel Huntington pointed out that between 1961 and 1968, 114 of the world's 121 major political units endured significant violent conflicts. And in 1966 Robert McNamara claimed that of the 164 internationally significant outbreaks of violence during the previous eight years, only 15 were military conflicts between two states.[18]

Many advocates of the Reagan Doctrine argue that it demonstrates U.S. resolve and restores the credibility that they claim the nation lost during the Vietnam War and its aftermath. Because of Washington's preoccupation with the nuclear threat and its tendency to view almost every international incident in a bipolar context, every conflict involving the Soviet Union assumes universal significance, which makes establishing credibility a never-ending task.

In classical realist thinking, interests are the starting point in the definition of foreign policy goals. Interests determine whether commitments should be made—and in the absence of such commitments, U.S. credibility is not at stake. Thus, commitments are based on particular interests and acquire concrete meaning only in particular situations. But in the cold war thinking in which the Reagan Doctrine is rooted, prior commitments are not a necessary condition for the creation of challenges to U.S. credibility by the Soviet Union; rather, such challenges automatically arise from the role of the United States as bloc leader. Concern with credibility itself defines U.S. interests and plays the largest role in determining which commitments the nation undertakes and what priority it gives to carrying them out; the specific situation is less influential. That role tends to impose ill-defined commitments on the United States. Robert Johnson, a professor of international relations at Colgate University, noted,

> The substitution of credibility for interests as a definition of U.S. stakes has unfortunate results because it provides no guidance to policymakers as to the appropriate level of U.S. concern and effort. It is an indefinitely expansible rationale, which tends to be stretched to cover whatever action policy-makers consider necessary in order to avoid "losing" at a particular moment. . . . We must be concerned with U.S. credibility, but it should not be a substitute for defining U.S. interests.[19]

Supporters of the Reagan Doctrine have often argued that the United States should aid various insurgencies because they are fighting for freedom and democracy—a standard that not many of the groups currently receiving aid could fulfill. As foreign policy analyst Ted Galen Carpenter noted,

> Just as the revolutionary environments are diverse, so too are the ideological orientations of the various insurgent movements. . . . In reality, ideological coloration varies considerably from country to country and even among competing rebel factions within individual countries.[20]

There is little reason to assume that if the resistance movements in Afghanistan, Cambodia, Angola, Mozambique, and Nicaragua came to power, the new governments would be based on a free enterprise system and respect for individual rights. Even U.S. officials charged with executing the Reagan Doctrine have admitted that careful discrimination is needed. For example, Richard Armitage, assistant secretary of defense for international security affairs, wrote,

> Obviously, every resistance group will not be perfect, and not every group that professes anti-communism deserves our support. The resistance of one tyrant to another's tyranny is not a sufficient claim on U.S. assistance, for we do not believe it is correct or useful to overthrow one tyranny in favor of another.[21]

In addition, many of the insurgent groups are so wracked by infighting over command and control that they are far less effective than one would expect. Most notable in that regard are the contras. The bitter fights between the Democratic Revolutionary Alliance (ARDE), an early Nicaraguan resistance group led by Eden Pastora, and the Nicaraguan Democratic Forces (FDN) are now the province of historians, as Pastora lost his bid to combat the Sandinistas yet remain free of CIA control. The leadership of the United Nicaraguan Opposition (UNO), the political umbrella organization that was supposed to unite all the contra forces, recently disintegrated; Adolfo Calero and Arturo Cruz, respectively UNO's most prominent conservative and liberal, resigned from their posts.

Moreover, the goals of aiding resistance movements in communist-ruled countries differ from country to country. In some cases, Washington's goal is to help counter external aggression. In others, it is to overthrow an indigenous regime, which can be a more difficult task. According to Congressman Stephen Solarz (D–New York),

> In Afghanistan and Cambodia, the aim is to induce two countries to withdraw their troops from their neighbors and, if possible, to convince the Soviet and Vietnamese occupiers that their security interests can be protected

in other ways. In Angola and Nicaragua, the task is much more ambitious: to get sovereign governments to relinquish power in the face of foreign pressure. The Soviet Union and Vietnam might someday find it in their interests to leave Afghanistan and Cambodia. But if Nicaragua's Sandinistas and the Angolan leaders decide to give up power, it will not be the result of some combination of pressure and negotiations. They will have to be driven physically from office. Consequently, military pressure to facilitate a settlement makes sense in Afghanistan and Cambodia but not in Angola and Nicaragua.[22]

Without broad public support for the policy of giving covert support to anticommunist insurgents, Congress is unlikely to continue approving military aid appropriations for that purpose. But according to recent polls, public support for the Reagan Doctrine is exceedingly weak. A survey sponsored by the Chicago Council on Foreign Relations indicated that

> two-thirds of the public favors giving no aid or economic aid only to rebel groups fighting communist-supported governments in places like Afghanistan and Angola. Only 24 percent of the public favors both military and economic aid. . . . Forty-two percent of the public is opposed to any aid. The public's concern that such actions will involve the country militarily in places like Central America has led to a distinct lack of enthusiasm for the Reagan Doctrine.[23]

The Iran-contra affair can be viewed as a response to that lack of support. As the House and Senate investigating committees noted,

> The common ingredients of the Iran and Contra policies were secrecy, deception, and disdain for the law. A small group of senior officials believed that they alone knew what was right. They viewed knowledge of their actions by others in the Government as a threat to their objectives. They told neither the Secretary of State, the Congress nor the American people of their actions.[24]

Furthermore, giving assistance to insurgents can come into conflict with other policy goals. For example, the Reagan administration has been sending Stinger antiaircraft missiles to Afghan rebel groups, and members of Congress fear that the weapons could fall into the hands of Iran or Middle Eastern terrorists linked to Tehran and end up being used to shoot down civilian airliners.[25]

A journalist reported that "in one incident two guerrilla commanders allegedly sold up to 16 Stingers to Iran for the equivalent of $1 million."[26] There have also been charges that both the Afghan rebels and the contras have engaged in narcotics trafficking in order to fund their operations. In 1985 officials of the FBI, the U.S. Drug Enforcement Administration, and

U.S. Customs were reported to have "reliable" evidence that the contras were involved in guarding and refueling cocaine-laden planes at remote airstrips in northern Costa Rica and transporting drugs to a stash house in San José for shipment to the United States. Colombian drug traffickers were said to be paying the contras $50,000 a load for such assistance.[27]

Although lip-service is often paid to the idea that U.S. aid for anticommunist insurgents should be openly proposed and allocated, the mode that has been preferred by far is covert funding. That practice creates serious lapses in oversight and accountability; it is extremely hard to ensure that funds are used for the purposes for which they were appropriated. The U.S. General Accounting Office (GAO) has confirmed allegations that millions of dollars in covert military aid earmarked for the Afghan insurgents failed to reach them.[28] More well known are the reports that large amounts of the U.S. aid allocated to the contras never reached their intended recipients. In late 1986 the GAO concluded that the procedures used by the State Department's Nicaraguan Humanitarian Assistance Office were not sufficient to ensure that the funds had been used as mandated by law.[29] In early 1987 the rebel commanders fighting in southern Nicaragua formally broke with the largest contra group, the FDN, because they had failed to receive any of the $100 million in new U.S. aid.[30]

On the other hand, the covert operations themselves are often anything but secret or clandestine. With accounts of them regularly splashed across the front pages of *Time, Newsweek,* and major newspapers, the particulars of such operations are known all over the world. That exposure most assuredly deprives the executive branch of the opportunity to invoke the old plausible deniability defense when an operation fails. The Soviets know which anticommunist groups are being supported by the United States. Moreover, not only are U.S. allies put in a difficult position when activities that blatantly violate the norms of international law are widely publicized, but such activities foment anti-U.S. attitudes among the citizens of other nations.

There is cause for concern that the Reagan Doctrine will lead to an erosion of the international legal norm that prohibits sovereign states from intervening in each other's affairs except in self-defense. U.S. involvement in Nicaragua, Angola, Ethiopia, and Mozambique is especially problematic because those governments are widely recognized as legitimate in the international community. The Reagan Doctrine could be construed as licensing other nations to embrace interventionist policies, which would deprive the United States of a moral and legal basis for opposing their actions.

More important, the doctrine's emphasis on covert operations has emboldened U.S. officials to violate both international and national laws, as the investigation of the Iran-contra affair revealed. The administration undertook a number of actions that violated either the spirit or the letter of the law, including mining Nicaraguan harbors, building military facilities in Honduras with "exercise" funds, certifying that the contras had made human rights improvements when that was not the case, ignoring violations of the Neutrality Act by those funding and planning paramilitary operations against the Sandinistas, allowing them to bypass the House and Senate Select Committees on Intelligence when planning such operations, ignoring the jurisdiction of the World Court, and violating the Boland amendment's prohibition against giving military aid to the contras, the War Powers Resolution, and the charter of the Organization of American States, to name a few.[31]

One of the most widely publicized illegalities was the CIA's authorship of a manual, *Psychological Operations in Guerrilla Warfare*, reported in October 1984. The manual urged "selective use of violence" to "neutralize" Nicaraguan officials—a clear violation of executive order 12333, which prohibits direct or indirect U.S. participation in assassinations.[32] Not as well publicized but even more alarming was the 1982 violation of a provision of the same executive order that prohibits covert operations "intended to influence U.S. political processes, public opinion, policies or media." Former contra leader Edgar Chamorro later revealed that the CIA had paid FDN officials to visit the United States to drum up support for their cause and had directed their lobbying efforts.[33] The CIA went to great lengths to improve the FDN delegation's lobbying skills; it even staged mock press conferences. Chamorro wrote,

> The advisers were really concerned about a particular question they knew we would have to answer: whether we had met with, or been organized by, people from the outside. Again, we were instructed to say that we had not met with anyone else, and it was particularly important that we deny having met with any U.S. government officials.[34]

Critics of the Reagan Doctrine have noted that the increased use of covert operations is undermining the ability of Congress to oversee U.S. foreign policy and that such benefits of open debate as the reduction of errors in decision making and policy implementation are thus being lost. Congressman Lee Hamilton, chairman of the House Select Committee on Intelligence, made an important distinction when he argued that while covert operations can be a useful tool in carrying out an agreed-upon policy, they should not be used as a means of circumventing a national policy debate.[35]

Because the original purpose of the Reagan Doctrine was in large part to provide a justification for continuing to aid the contras, it is ironic that the Nicaraguan operation represents the most flagrant misapplication of the doctrine. Whereas the resistance groups in such countries as Afghanistan and Cambodia are fighting armies of occupation and puppet governments that lack international recognition, the contras are not. As Congressman Solarz noted,

> Their goal is the overthrow of a government that, for good or ill, is recognized by and has diplomatic relations with most of the countries of the world, including the United States. In essence, the contras and the Sandinistas are locked in a civil war, a contest among Nicaraguans for the future of their country. . . . I have also opposed aid to the contras because I worry about the implications of such support for our broader foreign policy. There are many governments around the world whose internal arrangements we abhor, and who are engaged in efforts to destabilize their neighbors. Should the United States therefore support opposition movements against those regimes? That seems to be a formula for widespread interventionism, which would be unacceptable to the American people and opposed by our friends around the world.[36]

The very zeal with which the administration has pursued its campaign against the Sandinistas has made that campaign more vulnerable to defeat. Washington's extensive involvement with the contras and their outside assistance network, the U.S. military buildup in Honduras, and the investment of U.S. prestige in those efforts have invalidated the argument that the application of the Reagan Doctrine carries a low risk. Robert Matthew of the North American Congress on Latin America noted, "A foreign policy informed primarily by moral idealism is a slippery slope. One either plants the flag of victory at the top or tumbles to ignominious defeat. The consequence of casting the Nicaraguan conflict in universal terms is having to confront intolerable loss in the absence of victory."[37]

Covert activities, when conducted at the insistence of a strong executive branch in defiance of public opinion, can involve excessive secrecy, inadequate oversight, and ultimately scandal, as was the case with the Iranian arms sale and the diversion of funds to the contras. The exploits of former National Security Council staffer Lieutenant Colonel Oliver North now seem the stuff of which comic operas are made: soliciting funds from Brunei, Saudi Arabia, Singapore, Israel, and South Korea, maintaining Swiss bank accounts, organizing private resupply efforts. But North's efforts to skirt or break the law made difficult operations impossible and exacted a very high political price. The Tower commission stressed that point when it concluded,

> If these activities were illegal, obviously they should not have been conducted. If there was any doubt on the matter, systematic legal advice should have been obtained. The political cost to the President of illegal action by the NSC staff was particularly high, both because the NSC staff

is the personal staff of the President and because of the history of serious conflict with the Congress over the issue of Contra support.[38]

Even conservative supporters of the Reagan Doctrine have admitted that the scandal has dealt it a stunning blow. Senator Gordon Humphrey (R–New Hampshire) said, "Unless the administration regains its self-confidence, I would expect to see growing timidity about applying the Reagan Doctrine."[39] Indeed, former president Nixon expressed uncertainty about when the Reagan Doctrine should be applied even prior to the scandal. In *No More Vietnams*, Nixon wrote, "It is tempting to boldly proclaim that we will help anyone anywhere who fights against a repressive Communist regime, but we must recognize the limits of what we can do. . . . The test should be whether there is some reasonable chance for success."[40]

In a sense, the Reagan Doctrine is not so much a reflection of a desire to roll back Soviet influence in the Third World as a manifestation of the renewed nationalism that has characterized the United States in the 1980s, which in turn is a by-product of the process of "redeeming" a generation that experienced defeat in a war and contrition over a war. In that respect, the doctrine is consistent with the historic role of the United States as a crusader for democracy.

Still, as Robert Tucker put it, "a prudent crusader is nonetheless a crusader."[41] Even if it was implemented cautiously, the Reagan Doctrine would have the United States attempt to extend freedom to other nations in a manner difficult to reconcile with conventional notions of international order. That is because it reflects the administration's interpretation, strongly colored by conservative ideology, of recent history. Former secretary of defense James Schlesinger observed,

> The setbacks that the United States experienced in the 1970s were attributed in no way to the limits of American power, but simply to the lack of will. The solution was equally simple: American strength and American will. Be determined. Overcome all obstacles. A cult of toughness became the norm. There was a widespread failure to understand the real restraints on American power and the American public's deep-seated ambivalence about the use of force, including the disguised use of force.[42]

Moreover, as Tucker observed, "In the new formulation, only legitimate governments have the right to demand nonintervention from others. Legitimacy is compounded of two elements: consent of the governed and respect for inalienable rights. Only governments established on such foundation are legitimate."[43]

Yet adherents of the Reagan Doctrine do not feel impelled to overturn all governments that are not legitimate. It is only leftist regimes that they deem fitting targets of intervention. The problem with that approach is that the United States is not necessarily threatened by the existence of such regimes. As became apparent when both Yugoslavia and China defected from the Soviet camp, nationalism can impel even communist governments to follow anti-Soviet policies. It is only the foreign policies of other countries, not their domestic political systems, with which the United States must be concerned.

This is not to say that the United States should always refuse to support insurgencies, anticommunist or otherwise. Rather, it should decide which resistance movements to support on a case-by-case and country-by-country basis, inquiring whether providing such aid will advance U.S. interests.

The support for the Reagan Doctrine stems from the assumption that the failure of the United States to intervene in Third World conflicts will always result in Soviet gains. As Christopher Layne wrote in *Foreign Policy*, "This is the price Americans pay for regarding the world as both politically and ideologically bipolar. This perspective rules out the existence of marginal areas and depicts international politics as a zero-sum game in which a single setback will inevitably have repercussions elsewhere."[44]

The Reagan Doctrine necessitates an all-or-nothing approach and a failure to distinguish vital from secondary national interests. It does not require the United States to weigh the ends and means of its policy or to define its goals in the Third World realistically. As such, the doctrine is not only an unwise policy prescription but a spendthrift one, and it should be rejected.

Notes

1. William R. Bode, "The Reagan Doctrine," *Strategic Review* (Winter 1986): 21.

2. Ibid., p. 22.

3. David Brock, "Reagan Doctrine's Darkest Days," *Insight*, March 16, 1987, p. 10.

4. Stephen S. Rosenfeld, "The Guns of July," *Foreign Affairs* 64, no. 4 (Spring 1986): 700–701.

5. Stephen D. Goose, *Low Intensity Conflict and Covert Operations* (Washington, D.C.: Center for Defense Information, 1986).

6. David B. Ottaway and Joanne Omang, "U.S. Course Uncharted on Aid to Insurgencies," *Washington Post*, May 27, 1985, p. 1.

7. Angelo Codevilla, "The Reagan Doctrine—(As Yet) Declaratory Policy," *Strategic Review* (Summer 1986): 18.

8. See Patrick E. Tyler and David B. Ottaway, "Casey Enforces 'Reagan Doctrine' with Reinvigorated Covert Action," *Washington Post*, March 9, 1986, p. A1.

9. Charles Krauthammer, "The Day Harry Truman Remade the World," *Washington Post*, March 12, 1987, p. A19.

10. George P. Shultz, "New Realities and New Ways of Thinking," *Foreign Affairs* 63, no. 4 (Spring 1985): 713.

11. Stephen D. Goose, "Soviet Geopolitical Momentum: Myth or Menace? Trends of Soviet Influence around the World from 1945 to 1986," *Defense Monitor* (Center for Defense Information) 15, no. 5 (1986).

12. Paul M. Weyrich, in "Are We Moving toward a New Foreign Policy Consensus?" *National Interest* 4, no. 4 (Summer 1986): 11.

13. Rosenfeld, "Guns of July," p. 702.

14. Roger D. Hansen, "The Reagan Doctrine and Global Containment: Revival or Recessional?" *SAIS Review* (Winter–Spring 1987): 56.

15. Richard K. Betts, "If the U.S. Backs Rebels," *New York Times*, May 30, 1985, p. A23.

16. Rod Paschall, "Marxist Counterinsurgencies," *Parameters* 16, no. 2 (Summer 1986): 14.

17. George Liska, "The Reagan Doctrine: Monroe and Dulles Reincarnate?" *SAIS Review* (Summer–Fall 1986): 83.

18. John Garnett, "The Role of Military Power," in *Contemporary Strategy*, 2d ed., ed. John Baylis et al. (New York: Holmes & Meier, 1987), 1:87.

19. Robert H. Johnson, "Exaggerating America's Stakes in Third World Conflicts," *International Security* (Winter 1985–1986): 44.

20. Ted Galen Carpenter, "U.S. Aid to Anti-Communist Rebels: The 'Reagan Doctrine' and Its Pitfalls," Cato Institute Policy Analysis no. 74, June 24, 1986, pp. 11–12.

21. Richard L. Armitage, "Tackling the Thorny Questions on Insurgencies," *Defense/85* (October 1985): 17.

22. Stephen J. Solarz, "When to Intervene," *Foreign Policy* (Summer 1986): 30–31.

23. John E. Reilly, "America's State of Mind," *Foreign Policy* (Spring 1987): 52.

24. *Report of the Congressional Committees Investigating the Iran-Contra Affair, with Supplemental, Minority, and Additional Views*, 100th Cong., 1st sess., 1987, S. Rpt. 100–216, H. Rpt. 100–433.

25. David B. Ottaway, "Afghanistan Rebels Due More Arms," *Washington Post*, April 5, 1987, pp. A1, 19.

26. Edward Girardet, "Afghan Resistance Stung by Charges of Arms Trafficking to Iran," *Christian Science Monitor*, November 5, 1987, p. 9. See also Molly Moore and David B. Ottaway, "Iran Said to Obtain U.S.-Made Stingers," *Washington Post*, October 10, 1987, p. A1.

27. Peter Kornbluh, *The Price of Intervention: Reagan's War against the Sandinistas* (Washington, D.C.: Institute for Policy Studies, 1987), p. 202. See also Leslie Cockburn, *Out of Control: The Story of the Reagan Administration's Secret War in Nicaragua, the Illegal Arms Pipeline, and the Contra Drug Connection* (Boston: Atlantic Monthly Press, 1987).

28. Elaine Sciolino, "Afghan War: Was Aid Stolen?" *New York Times*, March 24, 1987, p. A14.

29. *Central America: Problems in Controlling Funds for the Nicaraguan Democratic Resistance*, NSIAD-87-35 (Washington, D.C.: General Accounting Office, 1986), p. 1.

30. William Branigan, "Divisions Detract from Contra Advances," *Washington Post*, January 29, 1987, p. A29.

31. For an analysis of possible or probable U.S. violations of thirty national and international laws, see *U.S. Policy in Central America: Against the Law* (Washington, D.C.: Arms Control and Foreign Policy Caucus, 1984).

32. Susan Benda, "Violations of Law in the Covert War against Nicaragua," *First Principles* (Center for National Security Studies) 12, no. 2 (April 1987): 7.

33. Edgar Chamorro, *Packaging the Contras: A Case of CIA Disinformation* (New York: Institute for Media Analysis, 1987), p. 10.

34. Ibid., pp. 10–11.

35. Lee Hamilton, "Angola: Open Talk, Covert Aid," *Washington Post*, June 12, 1986, p. A25.

36. Testimony of Congressman Stephen J. Solarz before the Subcommittee on Foreign Operations of the Senate Committee on Appropriations, 99th Congress, 1st sess. May 8, 1985, pp. 9, 11.

37. Robert Matthews, "Sowing Dragon's Teeth: The U.S. War against Nicaragua," *NACLA Report on the Americas* (July–August 1986): 18.

38. *Report of the President's Special Review Board* (Washington, D.C.: Government Printing Office, 1987), p. IV-6.

39. David B. Ottaway, "Stunning Blow to a Doctrine," *Washington Post*, February 15, 1987, p. A32.

40. Richard Nixon, *No More Vietnams* (New York: Arbor House, 1985), p. 219.

41. Robert W. Tucker, "Exemplar or Crusader? Reflections on America's Role," *National Interest* (Fall 1986): 68.

42. James Schlesinger, "Reykjavik and Revelations: A Turn of the Tide?" *Foreign Affairs: America and the World 1986* 65, no. 3 (1987): 438.

43. Tucker, "Exemplar or Crusader?" p. 67.

44. Christopher Layne, "The Real Conservative Agenda," *Foreign Policy* (Winter 1985–1986): 88.

12

Neither with Us Nor against Us: Revisiting an "Immoral and Shortsighted Conception"

Terry L. Deibel

T he adjectives in the chapter subtitle are those of John Foster Dulles, spoken in June 1956 at what might be considered the height of the cold war. Although the twin crises over Suez and Hungary would soon demonstrate the limits of Western solidarity, the secretary of state had just finished building a global alliance system designed to contain a seemingly monolithic communist bloc. That system's treaties with forty-two nations had in Dulles's view abolished the "obsolete" principle of neutrality, which "pretends that a nation can best gain safety for itself by being indifferent to the fate of others."[1] In the logic of a bipolar world, Dulles clearly felt, those not with us were against us.

Although much has changed in the thirty years since the secretary spoke, his dismissal of a neutral posture in the superpower contest as not only bad policy but bad morality seems accepted by virtually all sides of the policy debate in the United States. Particularly in the United States of Ronald Reagan, where macho bipolarism had until recently received a new lease on life after the pusillanimity of the Carter years, even to suggest exploration of the value of genuine nonalignment seems bizarre, if not outrageous. Neutralism is, after all, the apparent opposite of containment, which seems to demand that all possible forces of the free world be marshaled against those of totalitarian communism.

Given such conventional wisdom, the arguments that follow may require a few preliminary justifications and explanations. First, I do not propose to discuss neutralism as a substitute for containment and the commitments that support it. Those arrangements have been successful bulwarks of U.S. security since their construction more than thirty years ago. But any careful student of security commitments in the Third World cannot fail to be impressed with the difficulty and tendentiousness of the old cold war paradigm of alliance and deterrence, as Earl Ravenal has called it,[2] in this

The views expressed in this chapter are solely those of its author and should not be attributed to the Department of Defense or any other agency of the U.S. government.

postcolonial, post-Vietnam, and post-Watergate era, whatever its past advantages and successes. It is in fact largely because of those problems that neutralism warrants a fresh look.[3]

Second, there is simply no question that a reflexive negativism regarding genuine nonalignment is unjustified. In fact, even while Dulles was denouncing it, Eisenhower was defending it, and for reasons (elaborated below) that any good military man can appreciate. Not allowing a place for neutralism of some sort in U.S. foreign policy has all kinds of unfortunate consequences, even for a successful containment policy. Indeed, a good case can be made that containment can work *better* if room is made for genuinely nonaligned states in a less highly polarized international environment.

Third, there are modern reasons why reconsidering the role of neutralism in U.S. foreign policy may be useful. One is the new sophistication of Mikhail Gorbachev's regime. Whatever the real changes in Soviet actions may prove to be, Gorbachev has at the very least transformed the style of Soviet diplomacy from a public relations disaster into an asset of considerable proportions, one that will demand a far more flexible and adept U.S. response.[4] Another reason for a fresh look at neutralism is the continuing, if not growing, resistance of Third World states to identification with the United States, driven mainly by the negative effects that visible U.S. ties can have on internal political stability and by fears (should war occur) of becoming a nuclear target by association.[5] As Hans Morgenthau put it more than twenty-five years ago, "Having recognized that political non-commitment is the only policy many of the new nations can afford to pursue, we must find a positive relationship to them."[6]

But by far the most compelling reason for a reassessment of the role of neutralism lies not overseas but at home, in the current power position of the United States. Although Ronald Reagan came to office determined to reverse the relative decline in U.S. power during the 1960s and 1970s, his presidency has been characterized by massive federal budget deficits, the loss of markets for farming and manufacturing overseas, and the emergence of the United States as the world's largest debtor nation. Not only does this deterioration of position in the world economy directly reduce the nation's power abroad; it also has led to severe funding constraints for the instruments of foreign and national security policy—foreign aid, security assistance, diplomatic representation, and military forces—that are needed to counteract that relative decline. And there is every indication that these constraints will grow as decision makers try to dig the country out of the debt accumulated during the 1980s.

Genuine nonalignment is important in this context because a polarized world is an expensive world for U.S. foreign policy. Enemies have to be opposed; allies have to be supported. Today, the U.S. share of gross world product is about half what it was when Dulles was building his alliance system. If the United States cannot afford to oppose a hundred-odd enemies in the Third World, neither can it afford to support a hundred allies there. The only logical solution is to look for some way of avoiding either.

Any reconsideration of neutralism and nonalignment from the perspective of U.S. foreign policy poses questions in three areas. First, can we define an authentic neutralism, a stance of genuine nonalignment, that would fit with and reinforce containment? Second, if so, would it be something the United States wants to encourage? That is, would its advantages outweigh its risks and costs? Third, if such a policy recommends itself, what practical policy steps would be needed to implement it?

Contemporary Neutralism

Defining neutralism for the purposes of this inquiry is anything but a simple task, for it and related terms have been tossed about for several hundred years, acquiring complex layers of meaning and connotation along the way. Ponder, for example, the following list: *neutrality, neutralization, neutralism, impartiality, equidistance, nonalignment, disengagement, detachment*. All have something to do with the policy to be explored here, but none is exactly right, and each has at least some connotations that a sensible U.S. policy would wish to avoid.

Much can be learned about the evolution of thought on this subject by noting that the 1935 *Encyclopaedia of the Social Sciences* carried definitions of "neutrality" and "neutralization" by international lawyers Philip Jessup and George Grafton Wilson, whereas its 1964 successor, the *International Encyclopedia of the Social Sciences*, included instead a piece on "neutralism and nonalignment" by a political scientist, Myron Weiner.[7] Attention has shifted, in other words, from neutrality as a legal concept to neutralism as a political posture, and a lot has happened along the way.

The earlier term, *neutrality*, is a rather specialized one denoting the legal position of a state that elects to stay out of a shooting war. Beginning modestly in the fifteenth and sixteenth centuries, the international law of neutrality came into full use in the eighteenth and especially the nineteenth century as a device to restrict the spread of armed conflict.[8] Though never fully agreed on, these laws gradually delineated the rights and duties of belligerents and neutrals, those fighting and those hoping not to fight. The general idea was that warring parties should allow states wishing to remain at peace to pursue trade and other activities as long as these did not materially affect the outcome of the conflict. Theoretically any state could remain neutral as long as it fulfilled its duties under the law. In reality, neutrality was precariously maintained (if at all) against the challenges of belligerents that thought neutrals' activities were hindering their war effort or helping their enemies.

Indeed, even a vigorous attempt to be neutral in law would not necessarily make a nation impartial in fact. Although the neutral state was, as the term's roots imply, *ne uter* ("not either") in the sense of joining with either side in the conflict, completely evenhanded neutral conduct still often tended to have rather one-sided effects. For example, because one belligerent usually had a more powerful navy or a more autarchic economy than the other, the flow of neutral trade usually tended to compensate for the weaker party's disadvantages and hence to favor it over its stronger opponent. This is why Woodrow Wilson found it almost impossible to maintain U.S. legal neutrality while retaining the political impartiality he felt was needed for his attempts to mediate an end to World War I.[9] Nor did the much-disputed law on the subject always seem to demand evenhanded or detached conduct. Well into the eighteenth century the word *friend* was used interchangeably with *neutral*, while Grotius argued that a neutral state need not refrain from giving aid to belligerents as long as it did so equally.[10] More recently, George Grafton Wilson contended that "neutralized" states—those maintaining a legal or traditional status of perpetual neutrality during periods of peace and successive wars—could legally make alliances for their own defense.[11]

This distinction between formal neutrality and political disengagement, as well as the broader point that staying in the middle is for the purpose of staying out of conflicts, are important to an understanding of the post–World War II meaning of *neutralism*. The core of neutralism as a foreign policy, practiced mainly by new nations in the Third World, lies in dissociation or detachment—not from hot wars but from the cold war.[12] Having moved from the legal to the political realm, however, neutralism tends to get more complicated, for it is one thing to allow a state some political partiality when the goal is military detachment but a far more difficult trick to combine a degree of political involvement with overall political disengagement. The Nonaligned Movement (NAM) is itself a commentary on the problem. Few of its members can be considered equidistant from the two superpowers, and in many cases (such as Cuba or Pakistan) their detachment from the bipolar struggle is most incomplete. Indeed, the only modern condition essential to a state policy of nonalignment seems to be abstention from formal military alliances.

The motives behind contemporary neutralism seem to be two, and from them flow much of the character of neutralist policy. The first is fear of war, especially thermonuclear war, giving rise to what Morgenthau called "escapist" neutralism.[13] Apparently rejecting the idea that war occurs as a conscious act of state policy, neutralists talk as though the very tension of the cold war—incorporating sharp ideological differences and feeding on misunderstanding and distrust—might well lead to a hot war, which in the atomic age would be catastrophic for bystanders and belligerents alike.[14] Avoiding this danger is seen as far more important than helping one side or the other "win" the cold war, since many neutralists see little moral difference in the two antagonists' conduct of their "hostilities" and refuse to make a choice between the fundamental values of the two contesting societies.[15]

Neutralists wish, then, not only to avoid being a nuclear target by association but also to help defuse tensions and promote mutual understanding by mediating between East and West, promoting nuclear-free areas, or at the very minimum refusing to be drawn into the conflict as "cold belligerents." Their neutralism can be seen as a strategy of deterrence via noncommitment,[16] or, in the earlier terminology, as a kind of "preventive neutrality": feeling that they cannot stay out of any future general war, they seek to do what they can to prevent it taking place.[17]

The second motive behind the popularity of neutralism among new nations lies in their quest for full national independence and sovereignty.[18] Nationalism alone seems almost to preclude any other stance for nations that were colonies only a short time ago and remain weak in both power projection capacities and internal political stability. These states naturally feel that to join either superpower would be to accept virtual satellite status, whereas from a position outside the major alliance systems they can play the superpowers against each other, threatening to join the rival bloc if not properly treated by either one and accepting aid from each with as few strings as possible.[19] Internally, such a stand of independence versus a subordinate position pays big dividends to leaders espousing it, helping to legitimize their rule by making it clear that the government is representing only the state's own national interests and not those of any outside power. At the same time, this kind of strong nationalistic and self-reliant posture can reduce the chance of dangerous schisms within the ruling elite between conservatives, who might favor close relations with the former colonial power, and radicals, who often desire links to the socialist camp.[20]

For reasons of independence and self-interest, then, as well as for the security of the weak in a world dominated by the strong, neutralism connotes a certain detachment or disengagement from the superpower struggle. But it is important to note the limits of such abstention, the way in which partiality—or at least an acute lack of equidistance—intrudes on neutralism as it did on neutrality. Although disarmament has been imposed on some neutralized states,[21] most neutrals are anxious to buy the weaponry they consider necessary to keep their local rivals at bay, and they often enter into long-term supply relationships with the superpowers (like India's with the Soviet Union and Egypt's with the United States). Modern neutrals also reject the automotive connotation of the word *neutral*, the suggestion that their foreign policy is mechanically disengaged and going nowhere.[22] They intend to be active internationally and often take foreign policy positions that clearly favor or criticize one side or the other in the cold war. Of course, neutralism also does not specify anything about internal systems of government or economic and cultural orientation. India, for example, is Western economically and politically but Eastern militarily, while Yugoslavia is certainly a communist polity but quite genuinely nonaligned in its foreign and security policy.[23]

All of these connections and characteristics have implications for a state's perceived impartiality or equidistance from the two superpowers. Although one might argue that in a genuinely neutralist or nonaligned policy all of the factors that make for commitment should be absent, the reality of international politics simply does not conform with this view.[24] Indeed, one writer in the 1960s argued that a country with foreign military bases on its soil could still be considered neutralist.[25] Even the litmus test of abstention from alliances is little help in a world where security commitments are becoming less and less formal, shedding the treaties and trip wire forces that gave them shape in Dulles's time and taking the form of facilities access agreements, joint planning and exercising, and informal promises of support.[26] Gradually it becomes less and less obvious where neutralism ends and alignment begins.

Supporting a Policy of Genuine Nonalignment

So far this discussion has focused on neutralism from the perspective of the countries that practice it. What would or could a policy supporting genuine nonalignment look like from the perspective of a superpower, specifically the United States? And what would be its advantages and disadvantages in the context of a broader strategy of containment?

Any effort to discuss such a policy must deal straight off with the fact that neutralism has taken on an anti-Western character in the postcolonial era. Quite obviously, the United States has little interest in encouraging nonalignment of the kind practiced by Cuba, Nicaragua, Ethiopia, and other states that misappropriate the term to cover a policy clearly aligned with the Soviet bloc.[27] But the more genuine neutralism practiced by literally dozens of states in Africa and Asia has also often been anti-Western and anti-American, as well as associated with one-party authoritarianism and socialist (if not Marxist) economic regimes.

It is important to keep in mind that the anti-Western nature of these policies has been by and large the result of the historical accident that imperialism was for these countries a distinctly Western phenomenon. In that context, being a nationalist, a champion of one's own state's independence and sovereignty, meant being anti-Western. And the appeal of Marxist socialism as a model for internal political and economic organization sprang from similar pragmatic roots: it provided a justification for the centralized state control thought necessary for economic development and national cohesion.[28]

U.S. policymakers should recognize that both of these historical reasons for the anti-Americanism often found in neutralism are far less powerful today than they have been in the past and that their influence can be expected to diminish still more rapidly in the future. We are now, after all, nearing the end of the third postcolonial decade. As the memory of Western colonialism fades, the second generation of new state leaders will begin to appreciate that the world's largest remaining empire is socialist and not Western in origin, and that the recent decrease in the West's capabilities and stomach for colonial adventures has been accompanied by an increase in the power projection capabilities and activities of the East. The continuing failure of socialist models of economic development and the success of the market-based newly industrializing countries (NICs) will have similar effects; indeed, it is already causing substantial changes in economic policies in many nonaligned countries, and the most dramatic changes are occurring in those original but now discredited socialist economic models, Gorbachev's Russia and Deng's China.

It should be increasingly possible, in other words, for the United States to welcome genuine neutralism, real nonalignment, without worrying that those who are not with us will indeed turn out to be against us. This is not to say that neutrals will support the United States in the U.N. General Assembly or that they will refrain from either criticizing U.S. policy or adopting important policies of their own that may run counter to U.S. interests. On the contrary: U.S. policymakers must expect that these states will act in accordance with their own national interests and that in many cases their interests will be different from those of the United States. A policy supporting neutralism would accept the likelihood of such differences and deal with them through the ordinary processes of diplomacy.

It would also accept that sovereign states have the right to determine their own form of internal governance and generally that the projection of American values has a limited role in U.S. foreign policy. A hundred years ago an accepted maxim of international law prohibited interference by one sovereign state in the internal affairs of another. That rule became increasingly difficult to maintain as modern means of communication, transportation, and power projection have shrunk the globe and brought us intimate knowledge of internal conditions in other countries as well as greater means to interfere in them. At the same time, the Wilsonian idea that autocratic regimes are inherently aggressive—and its modern variant that communist regimes are inherently expansionist—has made it difficult for policymakers possessing the means of intervention to ignore internal changes that seem to presage ill for U.S. security. The Nixon-Kissinger foreign policy was the last in recent times to argue that U.S. policy ought to be linked to states' external behavior and not to their internal polities or policies.[29] The Carter human rights policy and Reagan's active support for democratic government and free enterprise economies seem to be based on the opposite premise.

A proneutralist policy would strongly question whether the United States is better off in a world of massive, government-sponsored intervention by states in each others' internal affairs and especially whether the requirements of security demand that it undertake such intervention. Granted, an all-democratic world would be a world safe for democracy. But did the United States, even when its relative power was greatest, have the capacity or the will to create such a world? A United States making room for neutralism in its foreign policy would instead define its security requirements for most other countries in rather limited and wholly external terms, that is, in terms affecting only their behavior outside their borders. Significantly, those requirements would all fall within the confines of genuine nonalignment, of disengagement from the East-West struggle: simply put, that there be no alignment with the Soviet Union and, especially, that neutral countries not join military alliances with the Soviet Union, not allow their territory to be used as bases for Soviet power projection (as Cuba did in 1962), and not physically export the implements of revolution.

Policy Advantages

Few countries could challenge such a policy as being against their interests. Indeed, it would be fundamentally supportive of the sovereign independence so important to relatively new and weak nations. As such, it would be a morally powerful position for the leader of the free world coalition. It is not the United States, after all, that insists that the world be made over in its image or that the forces of history inevitably must determine that result. The policy proposed here would be consciously pluralist, designed to make the world safe for diversity. Like traditional legal neutrality, it would allow states their internal freedom as well as freedom in their foreign policy, as long as (to put it in the earlier language) their actions did not materially affect the outcome of the cold war. Such a policy would strengthen rather than weaken the moral force of U.S. containment policy by demonstrating American values and suggesting that those who support the United States do so of their own free will.

There are other advantages to this kind of pluralist U.S. policy. A major one is that it would reduce tensions and therefore the dangers of war associated with a tight bipolar system and do so independent of the changing climate of direct U.S.-Soviet relations on which at least the fear, if not the reality, of war depends. There is little question that a containment policy that rigidly divides the world into friends and enemies promotes bipolarity, and bipolarity is clearly a correlate of war.

Indeed, perhaps the most difficult to understand of Dulles's attitudes was the equanimity with which he accepted and encouraged containment's world-splitting tendencies. Dulles seemed to see bipolarity as a virtue, but it is important to note that his famous denunciation of neutrality came in the context of a life devoted to collective security of the kind embodied in the U.N. Charter.[30] Given the U.N.'s inability to act due to the cold war, the secretary of state believed that collective security could be assumed by the alliances he had done so much to create.[31]

Unfortunately Dulles confused collective security with collective deterrence and defense. The former can work only within an association of states freely committed to it, an association prepared to deal with one of its own members that uses violence in contravention of pledges already agreed to. In reality as well as in theory, a collective security arrangement (like the U.N.) cannot deal with states outside its membership, whereas a collective defense organization (like NATO) is designed explicitly for that purpose and cannot deal with disputes between its members (like Greece and Turkey). Contrary to Dulles's view, then, collective security is the antithesis of a world divided into opposing alliances, which for the very reason of that division is more and not less war prone.

Thus, whatever the necessity for collective deterrence and defense, they are an imperfect solution with substantial disadvantages. The desirability of muting the bipolar division of the world was recognized in the Nixon-Kissinger vision of a pentagonal world order, and the relative decline of both the Soviet and U.S. power positions, together with the U.S. recognition of China and the latter's equidistant policy, has brought us much closer to that possibility than in the early 1970s. Along with a lessening of tension, a pluralistic U.S. policy would at a very minimum provide the United States with greater diplomatic flexibility and more freedom of action. But the major advantage of a policy leaving room for genuine nonalignment is its suitability to the very different relative power position of the United States in the post-Vietnam era.

The utility of neutralism in peacetime for a nation engaged in cold war is similar in this sense to that of neutrality for a belligerent in wartime. Britain from 1775 to 1779 did not challenge France in spite of the aid Whitehall knew the French were giving to the American Revolution, nor did the Allies in World War II attack Spain in spite of Franco's help to the Axis. Their tolerance for neutrality was based on the fact that turning these neutrals into belligerents would have cost more than letting them continue their mischief as neutrals. As John Gaddis puts it, one of the elementary laws of strategy is to limit one's enemies to as few as possible.[32] If such logic is sound economy of force under the exigencies of war, how much more does it recommend itself in the less dangerous circumstances of peace?

Given the relative power of the United States in the 1980s and 1990s, the same reasoning applies with almost equal force to relationships with allies. As was so often the case, President Eisenhower had a more balanced view of the issue than did his secretary of state. In 1960 he told a group of African leaders that the United States did "not urge—indeed, we do not desire—that you should belong to one camp or the other."[33] He made the reasons clear in a letter written in 1956:

> It is a very grave error to ask some of these nations to announce themselves as being on our side. . . . Such a statement on the part of a weak nation like Burma, or even India, would at once make them our all-out ally and we would have the impossible task of helping them arm for defense.
>
> Moreover, if a country would declare itself our military ally, then any attack made upon it by Communist groups would be viewed in most areas of the world as a more or less logical consequence. . . . The reaction . . . would be, "Well, they asked for it."
>
> On the other hand, if the Soviets attacked an avowed neutral, world opinion would be outraged.[34]

Here was an intrinsically sensible approach—and this at a time when the United States was far more able to support far-flung allies than today.

But what of the downside of a pluralist policy? Is it possible to combine a toleration, even admiration, for neutrals with the commitments needed for successful containment? Would U.S. allies be lured away by the attractiveness of a U.S.-sanctioned nonalignment, or would encouragement be given to those who use neutralism as a cover for anti-Western, antiallied policies? And what would happen to such a policy in a less than benign international environment? Does it, in fact, require a certain level of cooperation from neutrals or even the Soviet Union or a certain structure to the international distribution of power?

However counterintuitive it may seem at first glance, careful consideration of the arguments advanced above will show that U.S. support for genuine neutralism is not only compatible with a strong containment policy but increasingly required by it. From the American point of view, such a policy would help ensure the concentration of limited resources on critical alliances rather than spreading them so thin that those commitments essential to containment cannot be supported effectively. The Soviet Union, at least under Gorbachev, should not object to the resulting reduction of global competition and tension, even if the policy fosters the kind of genuine self-reliance that is most effective in deterring Moscow's adventurism. And from the neutrals' viewpoint, a containment policy welcoming neutralism should counteract both of the major motivations for dissociation from the United States, recognizing as it does their desire for independence and autonomy while reducing the level of international tension and with it the apparent danger of nuclear war. Nor could neutrals sensibly object to the continuation of a vigorous containment policy alongside U.S. support for their own nonalignment. Indeed, just as the preservation of neutrality in a hot war requires a balance of power among advantaged and disadvantaged belligerents, so neutralism in the cold war is possible only so long as the power of the Soviet Union is held in check.[35] In other words, just as containment increasingly needs neutralism, so neutralism has always been impossible without containment.

Does this mean that a containment policy making room for genuine nonalignment needs cooperation from neutrals or the Soviet bloc? It would be foolish to deny that some international conditions would make such a policy easier to pursue than others. Although support for real self-reliance and independence provides a good argument against neutral threats to join the other bloc, it will certainly help if Third World governments refrain from attempting to play one superpower off against the other. Also, a world of détente is doubtless more congenial to a less alliance-prone world, and vice-versa; the same can be said about a more balanced global political system, one including several great powers rather than two overwhelmingly powerful states.

But the fact that many of these conditions seem at present to be possible or even likely neither changes the need for policies to encourage them nor denies that a pluralistic policy could function in a world less congenial than we may now hope for. Above all, it seems quite unlikely that critical U.S. allies would terminate their relationships in ways detrimental to U.S. security just because the United States champions the cause of genuine nonalignment. These states have powerful reasons of their own for association with the United States, none of which would be altered through a more open containment policy.

Policy Implementation

Implementing such a policy would not call for radical or disruptive shifts in U.S. statecraft, a fact of considerable importance since major changes every eight or four (or even two) years are extremely costly in financial and political terms. No allies would be jettisoned, no great security risks incurred, and U.S. credibility need not be called into question.

The initial phase of a pluralist policy could be declaratory in nature, making clear to the world that the United States no longer considered genuine neutralism obsolete, immoral, or shortsighted but that, in accordance with its pluralistic traditions and its long-standing support of self-determination, it recognized the right of each nation to choose its own form of internal governance so long as it lived in peace with its neighbors and remained genuinely nonaligned.[36] However, it would probably be better not to announce a new policy publicly but simply to accept the utility of real nonalignment and make progressively clear by our actions that we understand and support it.

Gradually the specifics of U.S. diplomacy in a variety of regional and country contexts would come into conformity with this new appreciation of international diversity. In Central America, for example, the United States would cease demanding internal changes in Nicaragua's government as the price for a regional settlement and shift the focus of its diplomacy to Managua's external behavior and the denial of its territory to Soviet forces.[37] Application of the Reagan Doctrine would have to be confined to those cases where external aggression and not civil war was the primary concern.[38] And the United States would no longer use the harder tools of its foreign and security policy—covert action, security assistance, or outright military action—in dramatic attempts to influence internal developments on a global scale.

This does not mean that Americans would refrain from supporting similar societies or from discouraging antidemocratic and socialist experiments. Rather, the question is one of priorities and of the means used to support them. The basic desideratum has never been stated better than by John Quincy Adams, in 1821, when the problem was to prevent President Monroe from acting on popular enthusiasm for direct intervention in the Greek civil war:

> Wherever the standard of freedom and Independence has been or shall be unfurled, there will [America's] heart, her benedictions and her prayers be. But she goes not abroad, in search of monsters to destroy. She is the well-wisher to the freedom and independence of all. She is the champion and vindicator only of her own.

Following this logic, the United States would certainly not give economic aid to societies organized on economic principles that guarantee its uselessness, and it would make the case quite strongly that politically open societies are more productive and likely to provide better government for their citizens than closed ones. But it would not use its military or economic power to destabilize countries simply because of their internal character or because the peaceful foreign policies they pursue on their own are contrary to U.S. interests. It would give whatever assistance it could to nations with foreign and internal politics coincident with its own, and U.S. trade and investment would naturally flow to them. But in a fiscally constrained environment, its major tools of economic and security support would necessarily have to be reserved for allies, states whose allegiance is needed for reasons of vital interest.

At bottom, what is being proposed here is a greater tolerance for what Morgenthau called "all kinds and degrees of political non-commitment" as well as of political alignment.[39] Today it is impossible to place all states into simple categories of aligned or nonaligned, committed or uncommitted. Rather there are degrees of commitment or alignment, as well as degrees of neutralism and nonalignment. In an increasingly diverse and diffuse world order, each has its uses for and should have its place in U.S. foreign policy. Hans Morgenthau had a good sense of what was needed twenty-five years ago:

> The uncommitted nations may well incline toward one or the other side in their moral preferences, political sympathies, economic interests, and even limited military support. The reconciliation of these different shades of neutralism with the interests of the United States, without compelling the neutralists to enter into an explicit commitment, will put [American] statesmanship . . . to its supreme test.[40]

Notes

1. John Foster Dulles, "The Cost of Peace," *Department of State Bulletin*, June 18, 1956, pp. 999–1000.

2. Earl C. Ravenal, "Containment, Non-Intervention, and Strategic Disengagement," in Terry L. Deibel and John Lewis Gaddis, eds., *Containing the Soviet Union* (Washington, D.C.: Pergamon-Brassey's, 1987), p. 184.

3. I have described these at length elsewhere. See, for example, "Hidden Commitments," *Foreign Policy* 67 (Summer 1987): 46–63.

4. In addition to their new arms control proposals, changing substantive positions in Soviet diplomacy include the decision to pay all debts to the U.N. system (including those for peacekeeping), agreeing to withdraw their troops from Afghanistan, settlement with the Chinese on the thalweg for border delimitation, and at least partial cooperation on the U.N. Iran cease-fire resolution.

5. The recent difficulties in the ANZUS treaty with New Zealand prove that this liability is felt not only by Third World states.

6. Hans J. Morgenthau, *The Restoration of American Politics* (Chicago: University of Chicago Press, 1962), p. 339.

7. Edwin R.A. Seligman and Alvin Johnson, eds., *Encyclopaedia of the Social Sciences* (New York: Macmillan, 1935), 11:360–67; David L. Sills, ed., *International Encyclopedia of the Social Sciences* (New York: Macmillan, 1964), 11:166–72.

8. See, for example, Peter Lyon, *Neutralism* (Leicester, U.K.: Leicester University Press, 1963), p. 18.

9. Arthur Link, *Wilson the Diplomatist* (Chicago: Quadrangle Paperbacks, 1963), chap. 2.

10. Jessup, "Neutrality," *Encyclopaedia* pp. 360, 361.

11. Such a claim would not be accepted today. Austria, for example, explicitly renounces joining military alliances or allowing foreign bases on its territory. George Grafton Wilson, "Neutralization," *Encyclopaedia* p. 365.

12. See, e.g., Weiner, "Neutralism and Nonalignment," *International Encyclopedia* p. 166; Lyon, *Neutralism*, pp. 16, 20; Marek Thee, "Towards a New Conceptualization of Neutrality: A Strategy for Conflict Resolution in Asia," Occasional Paper no. 9, Center for the Study of Armament and Disarmament (Los Angeles: California State University, 1982), p. 6.

13. Morgenthau, *Restoration*, p. 335.

14. Lyon, *Neutralism*, p. 63.

15. Ibid., pp. 67–68.

16. Weiner, "Neutralism," p. 167.

17. Lyon, *Neutralism*, pp. 62–72.

18. Ibid., p. 72.

19. Morgenthau, *Restoration*, pp. 335–38.

20. Weiner, "Neutralism," pp. 168–69.

21. For example, Austria. But armed neutrality of the kind practiced by Switzerland and Sweden is the normal situation, the idea being that a credible self-defense is a necessary condition for the practical maintenance of neutrality. Thee, "Towards a New Conceptualization," pp. 13–15.

22. Weiner, "Neutralism," p. 166.

23. Thee, "Towards a New Conceptualization," p. 12.

24. For an examination of these factors and how they operate to produce commitment, see my *Commitment in American Foreign Policy: A Theoretical Examination for the Post-Vietnam Era*, National Security Affairs Monograph Series 80-4 (Washington, D.C.: National Defense University Press, April 1980), pp. 13–25.

25. Lyon, *Neutralism*, p. 111.

26. See Deibel, "Hidden Commitments."

27. Morgenthau calls this "pseudo neutralism." *Restoration*, p. 337.

28. Lyon, *Neutralism*, pp. 76–82.

29. Of course, Kissinger and Nixon violated their own principles more than once, particularly with regard to the Allende regime in Chile.

30. See Townsend Hoopes, *The Devil and John Foster Dulles*, (London: Andre Deutsche, 1974).

31. Dulles, "Cost of Peace," p. 999.

32. John Lewis Gaddis, "The Evolution of Containment," in Terry L. Deibel and John Gaddis, eds., *Containment: Concept and Policy* (Washington, D.C.: NDU Press, 1986), 1:8.

33. Morgenthau, *Restoration*, p. 335.

34. Cited by John Lewis Gaddis, *Strategies of Containment* (New York: Oxford University Press, 1982), p. 154.

35. Morgenthau, *Restoration*, p. 341.

36. See, in particular, the conditions spelled out on p. 200.

37. These conditions, by the way, are in my view sufficient for a modus vivendi with the Sandinista regime. It seems to me quite unlikely that that regime will negotiate its way out of power and equally unlikely that the American people will support its removal by force. Any realistic policy with a reasonable hope of success must recognize those two facts and design an approach where the ends are compatible with the available means. While we do not know whether the Sandinistas would settle on these terms, it seems quite possible if the United States uses all the levers at its command (including the contras) to support such a negotiating position and makes clear that any violation of a resulting treaty would be met with immediate and overwhelming force.

38. This is one of the criteria proposed for the Reagan Doctrine by Congressman Stephen J. Solarz in "When to Intervene," *Foreign Policy* 63 (Summer 1986); but see my letter and Solarz's reply in *Foreign Policy* 65 (Winter 1986–1987).

39. Morgenthau, *Restoration*, p. 340.

40. Ibid.

13

Benign Realism: A New U.S. Security Strategy in the Third World

Ted Galen Carpenter

T he policy of the United States toward the nations of Asia, Africa, and Latin America (loosely termed the developing world or Third World) has met with repeated disappointment.[1] The initial expectation of U.S. leaders that most of the nations emerging from the wreckage of the European colonial empires would emulate Western political and economic values failed to materialize. Instead decolonization produced an assortment of dictatorships.

Even Washington's more pragmatic objective of enlisting Third World states in the struggle to contain Soviet expansionism was not wholly successful. Important regional powers, such as India, opted for nonalignment (often with a pro-Soviet bias), provoking U.S. annoyance and recriminations. There was, to be sure, a proliferation of multilateral and bilateral agreements, especially in the late 1940s and the "pactomania" era of the 1950s. The 1947 Rio Treaty explicitly linked U.S. security to that of its hemispheric neighbors and set the pattern for the creation of NATO, SEATO, and other regional security pacts. Important bilateral mutual security treaties were also concluded with such nations as South Korea, Nationalist China, and Pakistan. Most of those commitments remain in effect.

Such formal multilateral and bilateral agreements, while significant, do not indicate the full extent of U.S. global obligations. Informal but entirely real security relationships—Israel being the most notable example—have emerged since the dawn of the cold war. Finally, various implicit commitments have arisen from the promulgation of presidential doctrines. This pattern was established early in the cold war with the enunciation of the Truman Doctrine in March 1947. President Truman pledged the United States to assist friendly governments facing either external aggression or challenges from "armed minorities." Although the catalyst for that presidential statement was Moscow's pressure on Greece and Turkey (and it is evident in retrospect that Truman and his advisers were most concerned to thwart Soviet expansion in Europe), the Truman Doctrine's rhetorical scope was universal. Consequently it became the basis for undertaking political and military commitments throughout the Third World.

Two other presidential doctrines, though more geographically limited, also served to deepen U.S. involvement in Third World affairs. The Eisenhower Doctrine in 1957 committed the United States to protect the territorial integrity and political independence of Middle East nations from communist aggression. The Carter Doctrine subsequently envisaged a similar guardianship of the status quo in Southwest Asia and the Persian Gulf region.

The multilateral and bilateral treaties, informal guarantees, and presidential doctrines have created a security network of global proportions. Aside from obligations to defend the NATO signatories and Japan, the United States has committed itself to defend more than forty nations, most of them in the Third World. This effort to line up client states—and Soviet efforts to do the same—has made the Third World a major cold war arena.

Washington's acquisition of clients has been, at best, a mixed blessing. U.S. leaders frequently have found themselves acting as sponsors for ruthless autocrats, including the shah of Iran, Nicaragua's Anastasio Somoza, the Philippines' Ferdinand Marcos, and Zaire's Mobutu Sese Seko. Providing billions of dollars in economic and military aid as tangible expressions of support for authoritarian clients has earned the enmity of long-suffering populations. Moreover, as U.S. policymakers have discovered repeatedly, "friendly" autocrats can fall from power with astonishing swiftness, leaving serious power vacuums and, all too often, virulently anti-U.S. successor governments.[2] The overthrow of the shah and the collapse of the Somoza dictatorship are only the two most dramatic examples.

Attempts to prop up crumbling autocracies can prove even more deadly. The United States expended an enormous amount of blood and treasure to preserve pro-U.S. regimes in South Korea and South Vietnam. The latter effort was a fiasco, but even the former produced more than 30,000 dead U.S. soldiers and generated bitter domestic divisions. It is highly unlikely that the American people would care to repeat either experience.

The generally unsatisfactory U.S. record in the Third World is attributable to a woeful confusion of objectives. U.S. leaders have simultaneously pursued strategic, economic, and ideological goals without establishing a hierarchy of concerns. Instead they have defined all three goals as matters vital to national security, requiring extensive political and military commitments to allies and clients. Even worse, this approach has no discernible geographic limitations.[3] The assumption that the United States has crucial interests everywhere and must be prepared to defend them serves as the foundation for interventionism on a global scale, creating unnecessary dangers and the potential for self-inflicted defeats.

U.S. policymakers have failed to understand that only strategic considerations are typically vital to the maintenance of national security. External economic factors rarely impinge on security in drastic fashion, and ideological factors almost never do so. Of course, strategic, economic, and ideological developments do not operate in hermetic compartments; some interaction and overlap are inevitable. Nonetheless, they are relatively distinct goals, and effective methods for implementing one may prove ineffective at achieving the others. Moreover, some tactics, including many that the United States has adopted during the cold war, are counterproductive in all three realms.

Economic rationales for supporting Third World clients while opposing left-wing regimes and insurgent movements embody both narrow and broad policy goals. The former include maintaining access to vital raw materials and keeping overseas markets open to U.S. products and investments; the latter encompass the desire to promote an international economic system based on the principles of capitalism and open trade. Both are worthy objectives, but they are—or at least should be—subordinate to strategic interests. Moreover, it is highly questionable whether extensive political and military ties with client states help achieve them.

Defenders of the current policy insist that any other course would result in a proliferation of Marxist regimes, causing the United States and other Western nations to become beleaguered capitalist islands in a collectivist economic sea. It is not possible, they argue, for the United States, with its economy based on free enterprise, to endure in a world dominated by state-run Marxist systems.

That argument has several serious flaws. First, it embraces the fallacy that countries controlled by right-wing governments are automatically receptive to U.S. economic policies, while nations dominated by left-wing regimes are consistently hostile. Second, it overstates U.S. dependence on foreign supplies of certain resources and reaches the alarmist conclusion that this alleged dependency seriously jeopardizes the republic's security and well-being. Finally, it ignores the danger that sponsoring unpopular political clients might actually undermine the promotion of Western economic values.

Although it is true that right-wing governments are somewhat more receptive than their left-wing counterparts to U.S. trade and investment initiatives, the assumption that rightist governments routinely support U.S. economic objectives is erroneous. Washington encountered ample evidence of that fact in the 1970s when two of its closest Middle East clients—Iran and Saudi Arabia—helped engineer the massive oil price hikes of the Organization of Petroleum Exporting Countries (OPEC). Neither nation was willing to eschew financial gain because of gratitude for U.S. political and military support. A similar episode occurred in 1980 when the Carter administration imposed a grain embargo on the Soviet Union for its invasion of Afghanistan. Argentina's military junta, a regime the United States had utilized to combat leftist insurgencies in Latin America, promptly seized the opportunity to increase its grain sales to the Soviet Union.[4]

Just as right-wing regimes are not automatic economic allies, left-wing governments are not necessarily commercial adversaries. When the United States has not blocked trade with leftist countries, it has often flourished. Today, the United States enjoys extensive commerce with Angola, Yugoslavia, and China, and all three nations seem quite receptive to Western trade and investment overtures.

It is theoretically possible that a hostile state dominating the global market in some vital commodity might attempt to blackmail the United States or other Western nations. The U.S. naval buildup in the Persian Gulf is motivated at least in part by a determination to forestall such a possibility with respect to oil supplies. But that danger is remote for two reasons. First, as various scholars have shown, the entire concept of the West's resource dependency is overblown.[5] Second, even in those rare instances in which a dependence exists, the supplying country could engage in extortion only if it was willing to suffer the economic consequences of withholding a lucrative export from the world market. Such self-destructive behavior is improbable since governments of whatever ideological orientation typically operate according to the principle of economic self-interest.

Economic realities usually transcend political differences. Most Third World nations benefit from extensive commercial ties with the industrialized West, especially the United States, often the principal market for their exports and a vital source of developmental capital. That status gives the United States subtle but extremely significant leverage in influencing the policies of these states.[6] Sponsoring political and military clients is not a prerequisite to secure national economic goals.

A proliferation of left-wing regimes undoubtedly undermines the larger objective of a world composed of like-minded capitalist nations. But supporting authoritarian, albeit supposedly pro-Western, regimes does nothing to further that objective. Indeed, such patronage is highly counterproductive because it closely identifies the United States with the policies of corrupt, repressive governments. When aroused populations overthrow such regimes, there is a virtual reflex action to repudiate everything American, including capitalist economics. The United States scarcely promotes the appeal of free enterprise when it helps link that system to kleptocrats such as Marcos and Mobutu in the minds of Third World peoples.

The ideological rationale for Washington's system of client states is also deficient. Americans have long viewed their country as a beacon on the hill, guiding humanity to a better future. An important component of that sense of mission is the desire to see other nations emulate its democratic political system. There is also a more pragmatic objective based on the assumption that a proliferation of democratic states would make the world a safer place. According to that thesis, democracies rarely wage war against other democracies and virtually never engage in blatant acts of aggression.[7] The thesis maintains further that democratic regimes are unlikely to ally themselves with a totalitarian power such as the Soviet Union, thereby reducing its geopolitical influence.

Although those assumptions have some validity and possess considerable appeal, there is nonetheless a serious danger of confusing ideological and security aims. Democracies are less prone to launch wars against other democracies, but such conduct is not unthinkable. (Even under democratic governments, Greece and Turkey have nearly come to blows on several occasions over Cyprus and disputed islands in the Aegean Sea.) Similarly, to contend that democratic governments are incapable of engaging in acts of aggression oversimplifies reality. The concept of aggression itself is subjective and ambiguous, but it is apparent that democratic countries have at least arguably been aggressors on several occasions. Examples include Israel during the Six Day War in 1967, India in its 1971 conflict with Pakistan, and the United States in the Spanish-American and Vietnam wars.

The belief that democratic governments will automatically be pro-American and anti-Soviet is equally spurious, as India's intimate political and military association with the Soviet Union demonstrates. India's economic interests (lucrative Soviet aid and trade packages) and security concerns (a disputed border with China and the presence of a hostile U.S. client, Pakistan, on another border) have combined to override any ideological qualms New Delhi might have concerning the Soviet Union. Even in a predominantly democratic world, U.S. leaders would be making a serious error where they to assume that similar situations might not entice other democracies into the Soviet camp.

Aside from such faulty assumptions, U.S. policymakers have made critical tactical blunders in their attempts to create a more ideologically congenial world. The most significant error is the belief that there is an underlying affinity between traditional authoritarian regimes and Western democracies. Former U.S. ambassador to the United Nations Jeane Kirkpatrick has developed that thesis at some length, emphasizing a qualitative distinction between traditional autocracies and totalitarian systems of the revolutionary left. She has contended that the former are "less repressive" than the latter, are "more susceptible to liberalization," and are "more compatible with U.S. interests."[8]

Kirkpatrick is generally right in arguing that totalitarian dictatorships are worse than authoritarian ones, but the difference is not sufficient to justify moral and tangible U.S. support for autocratic clients. Her assumption that in its role as sponsor, the United States can encourage liberalization and help such regimes evolve into more democratic systems also overstates the probability of political evolution. In reality, such transformations are rare; many of Kirkpatrick's own examples—Spain, Greece, and Brazil—involve the restoration of democratic systems that authoritarian elements had previously overthrown.[9]

Beyond that problem, Kirkpatrick and those who embrace her thesis ignore the detrimental impact caused by U.S. sponsorship of friendly autocrats. Military and economic aid to such clients makes the United States an accomplice in numerous acts of repression. That approach is doubly unwise: not only does it earn the hatred of brutalized populations, but it also helps corrupt tyrants suppress democratic opponents, who are usually more open in their opposition and therefore easier targets. The weakening or elimination of democratic forces enables undemocratic elements eventually to dominate antigovernment coalitions. Graphic examples of that process occurred in Nicaragua and Iran, paving the way for virulently repressive successor regimes. Even when such results do not occur, an autocratic legacy severely damages a nation's political culture, as we have witnessed in the Philippines, thus weakening prospects for long-term democracy.

The United States hardly promotes democratic values by its paradoxical support for traditional autocracies. This important realization apparently has dawned belatedly on the Reagan administration, as evidence by its eleventh-hour abandonment of Marcos and the withdrawal of support from Duvalier in Haiti and Noriega in Panama. It is a lesson that needs to be applied more consistently.

Although the administration may have finally recognized that aiding authoritarian dictators does not advance the cause of democracy in the Third World, it has adopted another strategy that is nearly as ill advised. The Reagan Doctrine of providing aid to insurgents seeking to overthrow left-wing regimes in such countries as Nicaragua, Afghanistan, and Angola is touted as support for "freedom fighters." Proponents of the doctrine justify assistance as a means to roll back the Soviet empire and bring liberty to Third World nations.[10]

The Reagan Doctrine has numerous defects.[11] It blithely assumes that all revolutionary leftist regimes are Soviet puppets, an assertion that might come as a surprise to the leaders of Yugoslavia and China. It vastly overestimates the democratic orientation of various insurgent movements, as demonstrated by Reagan's description of the Nicaraguan rebels as the "moral equal" of America's own founding fathers. In reality, those movements, though ideologically diverse, have a pronounced tendency toward authoritarianism.[12]

Finally, advocates of the Reagan Doctrine routinely confuse security and ideological justifications for their policy, oscillating wildly from one to the other. Even in the absence of ideological factors, it is possible to advocate aid to the Nicaraguan insurgents on security grounds, given Central America's proximity to the United States. But the same cannot be said for rebel movements in Angola or Afghanistan, much less those in Mozambique,

Ethiopia, and Cambodia, where ambitious proponents of the Reagan Doctrine want to push forward.[13] In those nations, the doctrine must stand or fall on the basis of its potential to further the cause of democracy in the Third World. There is little evidence that Washington's adoption of imitative Leninist subversion techniques by sponsoring ideologically murky insurgencies is an effective strategy to achieve that result. Quite the contrary, such clumsy meddling threatens to involve the United States in a host of complex political and military entanglements while rekindling Third World fears about U.S. imperialism.

The argument that the United States should support Third World dependents for economic or ideological reasons has little merit. Even the belief that such assistance can be justified on the basis of strategic self-interest depends on important subsidiary assumptions. The concept of strategic objectives or interests is inherently complex, but it implies a close relationship to security issues.[14] Unfortunately proponents of interventionism typically define security interests in an expansive manner. They habitually assume that the global alliance system of the United States is a seamless web and insist that an adverse political change anywhere represents a significant geostrategic advance for the Soviet Union and a corresponding defeat for the United States.[15]

This assumption impels Washington to support pliant regimes throughout the Third World. U.S. officials regard certain countries as forward staging areas for the projection of U.S. military power. A succession of administrations continued to support the Marcos dictatorship, for example, in order to preserve U.S. access to the military installations at Subic Bay and Clark Field.[16] The loss of those bases, U.S. leaders argued, would seriously complicate the defense of other Far Eastern allies. Pakistan serves a similar function today with regard to South Asia. Not only do U.S. officials view Pakistan as a bulwark against Soviet expansionism, but they have used it as a conduit to provide military aid to rebels fighting the Red Army in neighboring Afghanistan. In exchange, the United States provided the authoritarian government of President Muhammad Zia ul-Haq with billions in economic and military aid.[17]

A more sophisticated interventionist rationale views specific client states as keystones or forces for stability in their respective regions. That belief figured prominently in Washington's long-standing support for the shah of Iran. Jimmy Carter epitomized the U.S. attitude in his 1977 New Year's Eve toast to the shah when he stated that "Iran, because of the great leadership of the Shah, is an island of stability in one of the more troubled areas of the world."[18] Since the shah's abrupt departure a little more than a year after Carter's optimistic pronouncement, the United States has accorded the Saudi Arabian monarchy the status as the principal stabilizing power in the region. Fear for the safety of its Saudi client (as well as smaller client states) was one crucial factor leading the Reagan administration to expand the U.S. naval presence in the Persian Gulf during 1987.[19]

Washington continues to view other nations as regional keystone powers warranting its support. The cozy relationship with the Mobutu dictatorship results from the perception that Zaire serves such a function in sub-Sahara Africa. Egypt plays a similar role in the Middle East, and the regime of Hosni Mubarak has profited handsomely from the largesse of its U.S. sponsor.

One should question whether the United States has vital strategic interests in areas thousands of miles from its shores. Yet Washington's cold war policy assumes that the mere presence of distant Third World clients increases its own security. It is difficult to sustain such a proposition even from the standpoint of strategic denial—the belief that the existence of a pro-Western regime at least keeps a country out of the Soviet camp. From the standpoint of any positive contributions such clients might make, the notion becomes even more dubious. A plethora of small, militarily insignificant nations, frequently governed by unstable and unpopular regimes, would not significantly augment U.S. strength in a showdown with the Soviet Union.

In fact, it is more plausible to view these attempts to preserve an assortment of Third World clients as weakening U.S. security. These efforts drain U.S. financial resources. At least $65 billion of the 1987 military budget paid for operations in the Persian Gulf, Southwest Asia, and other Third World regions.[20] Moreover, the United States spent an additional $14 billion on various military and economic assistance programs. Formal and informal commitments to client states also stretch U.S. military forces dangerously thin. Pentagon officials try to minimize that problem through a variety of gimmicks, including assigning dual missions—defense responsibilities in more than one region—to certain units. This solution is little more than a mirage, for it ignores the possibility of simultaneous conflicts.[21] It is not a credible doctrine to either allies or adversaries since not even the most creative military strategists have yet found a way to deploy the same unit in two places at the same time. Such gimmickry, however, is ample testimony to U.S. strategic overcommitment.

Worst of all is the danger that a vulnerable Third World client will provide an arena for ill-advised U.S. military intervention. Vietnam demonstrated that such a danger is not merely theoretical. The recent U.S. naval buildup in the Persian Gulf holds the potential for disaster; it has entangled the United States in a multitude of intractable religious and political quarrels in an exceptionally volatile region some 8,000 miles from the American homeland.

The strategic drawbacks of the current U.S. Third World policy underscore the need to forge a narrower and more realistic definition of vital U.S. security interests. Too often, policymakers have ignored both the domestic and international constraints on a global interventionist strategy. Domestically, the republic's political system, with its separation of powers, checks and balances, and democratic accountability, is ill suited for the practice of amoral geopolitics, much less the pursuit of imperium. Moreover, since the Vietnam War, the American public has consistently been wary of U.S. military intervention in the Third World.[22]

International constraints on U.S. policy are equally daunting. Third World nations are notoriously sensitive to actions that hint of Western imperialism. (Until recent years, they have been less wary of Soviet imperialistic exploits.) U.S. conduct will inevitably be scrutinized by a skeptical, if not hostile, audience—especially given Washington's record of intervention. Any interference in the affairs of Third World nations, whether in the form of economic embargoes, covert CIA actions, or direct projections of military power, promptly inflames anti-American sentiment. That same pervasive nationalism ensures intense and protracted resistance to interventionist measures, as U.S. leaders discovered during the Vietnam conflict.

Nor can the United States count on consistent support from Western allies. To the contrary, the European nations and Japan usually distance themselves from U.S. meddling in the Third World. At best, they see such conduct as a dangerous distraction for their superpower protector, siphoning scarce military resources from the defense of their respective regions. Beyond that concern, they conclude that supporting U.S. interventionism would often undermine their own economic and political interests in the Third World.

Those domestic and international constraints should lead U.S. policymakers to adopt a security strategy that minimizes the risk of political and military entanglements. Such a strategy must be able to attract and sustain adequate domestic support, must be consistent with fundamental American political values, and must be sufficiently limited and well defined to have a high probability of success. Finally, the relationship of the policy objective to core U.S. security requirements must be exceedingly clear not only to discourage probes by adversaries but also to minimize any adverse reaction to U.S. defense measures among Third World and Western states.

Such criteria are quite demanding, and they all suggest that interventionist initiatives should be undertaken sparingly. That option should be reserved for cases involving an obvious and immediate threat to the security of the American people. There are times when it may be necessary for the United States to provide military aid to a strategically essential client, impose economic sanctions on a recalcitrant power, or even inject U.S. forces into combat situations.[23] But such measures must become the exception, rather than the rule, of U.S. conduct toward the Third World.

It is especially important to avoid the confusion of economic, ideological, and strategic objectives. Too often U.S. leaders equate economic or ideological challenges with dire security threats.[24] That tendency leads to ill-conceived, costly, and unnecessary interventionist episodes.

U.S. policy toward Nicaragua is a textbook example of confusing ideological and security considerations. The Reagan administration has concluded that the continued presence of a radical leftist regime in Managua is unacceptable. One can make a cogent argument for that position. Few people would deny that the Caribbean Basin is important to the security of the United States. The existence of one Soviet client, Cuba, already creates the potential for a significant security threat; the emergence of a second client raises obvious concerns. But the focus of U.S. apprehension should be on the nature and magnitude of the Sandinista government's ties to Moscow. The use of Nicaraguan territory by Soviet military units or the installation of offensive weapon systems would be clearly intolerable, but even less egregious steps such as massive military aid programs or the conversion of Nicaragua into a base for major subversion efforts might warrant a decisive U.S. response.[25]

Washington would be justified in insisting, not suggesting, that Nicaragua maintain a discreet political and military distance from the Soviet bloc. At the same time, it is unwarranted to assume, as the Reagan administration apparently does, that a radical leftist government such as Nicaragua's will automatically be a Soviet surrogate. Two of Moscow's most implacable adversaries, Yugoslavia and China, are ruled by Leninist dictatorships. U.S. policy toward Nicaragua should therefore contain two components. First, it should avoid actions such as trade embargoes that leave Nicaragua little alternative but to develop stronger links to the Soviet bloc. Second, it should exhibit a determination to eliminate the Sandinista regime if, in spite of U.S. restraint, Nicaragua becomes a Soviet outpost. Adopting that dual approach would maximize domestic support for the policy and diminish international opposition, since the United States would be predicating hostile action on an identifiable threat to U.S. security interests.

The Reagan administration, however, has focused on the Sandinista government's ideological sins and insisted that it institute internal democratic reforms. Washington has also adopted counterproductive trade sanctions and provided support for an armed insurgency—steps virtually guaranteed to compel Managua to seek Soviet assistance. There is nothing wrong with the United States' desire to promote democratic principles and civil liberties in Nicaragua or anywhere else. But is is essential to avoid confusing that goal with the more crucial objective of protecting vital U.S. security interests. Democratic values might be desirable, but from the standpoint of U.S. security, it is not necessary for Nicaragua to be democratic; it is only necessary for that country to refrain from being a Soviet surrogate.

A promiscuously interventionist foreign policy results from a confusion of economic and ideological aims with strategic security interests. Even worse, it weakens prospects for achieving any of those objectives. That is most apparent in the ill-advised U.S. support of repressive Third World clients, but it also characterizes other aspects of U.S. foreign policy. Conversely, a broadly noninterventionist approach to Third World affairs would enable policymakers to distinguish among economic, ideological, and strategic goals and make it considerably easier to develop coherent strategies in all three realms.

The United States can promote its economic objectives in the Third World most effectively by practicing, not just preaching, the virtues of free trade. The size and dominance of the U.S. economy make it an unparalleled and often irreplaceable market for the exports of Third World nations. Vigorous commerce combined with the need for U.S. investment capital can forge economic links that developing countries will be most reluctant to sever. The United States can also generate considerable influence merely through the example of its own economic system. As the world's leading economy, the United States is a candidate for emulation by Third World nations seeking the keys to growth and prosperity, particularly in the aftermath of disillusioning experiences with disastrously counterproductive collectivist nostrums.

The ability of the United States to influence ideological developments in the Third World is more limited but nonetheless significant. There are political factions that sincerely embrace the principles of limited government and individual rights embodied in the American Revolution. Although the emergence of democracy remains a distant goal in many Third World societies and depends on favorable internal developments, the United States can offer encouragement and subtle forms of support to prodemocratic factions.

In promoting Western ideological values, U.S. leaders should be guided by a fundamental principle of the medical profession: "First, do no harm." The United States should at least not undercut indigenous democratic forces by sponsoring authoritarian dictators. All too often Washington's political support and aid programs have propped up such tyrants far beyond the time they could have clung to power through their own resources. It would have been far more difficult for the likes of Marcos, Duvalier, and Sudan's Ja'far Numayri to have withstood mounting domestic opposition without substantial U.S. military and economic aid packages.

The potential impact of the democratic example of the United States is vitiated by U.S. practices in the Third World. A pervasive stench of hypocrisy exists when the world's leading democracy embraces an assortment of petty dictators. Washington's present strategy enables the Soviet Union to pose as the champion of Third World independence. Without the cover afforded by clumsy U.S. machinations, the Soviet Union's grasping imperialism would soon stand exposed, and Moscow, not Washington, might well become the principal target of nationalistic wrath throughout Asia, Africa, and Latin America. The widespread anger over the Soviet Union's invasion of Afghanistan suggests the potential for similar responses on other issues.

Most important, a generally noninterventionist approach to Third World affairs would strengthen rather than endanger the republic's strategic interests. Noninterventionism would especially reduce the risk of U.S. military involvement in complex quarrels generally irrelevant to U.S. security. The United States has little to gain and much to lose by becoming a participant in brushfire conflicts or by injecting itself into internecine political struggles. Yet both Washington's traditional support for authoritarian clients and the newer Reagan Doctrine involve the danger of such undesirable entanglements.

There will undoubtedly be occasions when the United States must utilize economic or military power in the Third World to protect its strategic interests. But such a response should be largely confined to a legitimate security zone in the Western Hemisphere. Adverse developments in Asia and Africa, however unpleasant or annoying, rarely impinge on vital U.S. security interests. The nation's geographic position still affords a daunting obstacle to any projection of hostile conventional military force from outside the hemisphere. The Soviet nuclear threat exists largely independent of geographic factors; Moscow's acquisition of military clients in most portions of the Third World does not materially alter the nuclear equation.

On those occasions when the United States perceives serious security problems in the Third World, it should assess each threat on a case-by-case basis and deal with it unilaterally. Formal mechanisms such as the mutual security treaties with Pakistan and South Korea or multilateral agreements such as the Rio Pact and the mercifully defunct SEATO are precisely the sort of arrangements the republic must avoid. They afford too many opportunities for irresponsible clients with their own political agendas to involve the United States in their quarrels. Pakistan's frequent clashes with India, for example, have created needless crises for the United States and poisoned Indo-U.S. relations.

The avoidance of formal commitments should apply even to the Western Hemisphere. U.S. participation in a Central American regional defense association, for instance, would tie U.S. policy to the goals or whims of small, politically unstable dependents.[26] Since the United States should intervene only in response to significant threats to its vital security interests, it must be able to determine, unilaterally, which threats breach that crucial threshold.

Compartmentalizing economic, ideological, and strategic objectives and defining U.S. security interests in a more rigorous, restrained manner offers the United States an effective alternative to its current policy in the Third

World. That approach avoids the pitfalls of either surly isolationism or promiscuous interventionism. It is a strategy of benign realism, an effort to deal with Third World nations as diverse entities, not merely as pawns in the cold war confrontation with the Soviet Union. Benign realism would not ignore economic and ideological goals or sacrifice them on the altar of an amoral realpolitik, but it would subordinate them; interventionist initiatives would be undertaken only to meet serious security threats. A security-based strategy would recognize that American dollars are too scarce and American lives too previous to be risked for any lesser purpose.

Notes

1. In a strict sense, Latin America is not part of the Third World since that term is usually confined to nonaligned nations of Asia and Africa that achieved their independence after World War II. Most Latin American countries, however, share Third World political and economic problems, and they are frequently caught in the cross fire between the two superpowers. For those reasons, I have included Latin America in the discussion of U.S. security strategy toward the Third World.

2. For discussions of that process, see Jonathan Kwitny, *Endless Enemies: The Making of an Unfriendly World* (New York: Congdon and Weed, 1984); T.D. Allman, *Unmanifest Destiny* (Garden City, N.Y.: Dial Press, 1984); and Walter LaFeber, *Inevitable Revolutions* (New York: W.W. Norton, 1984).

3. Trenchant critiques of that lack of geographic selectivity include Donald E. Nuechterlein, *America Overcommitted: United States National Interests in the 1980s* (Lexington, Ky.: University Press of Kentucky, 1985); and Alan Tonelson, "The Real National Interest," *Foreign Policy* (Winter 1985–86): 49–72.

4. Ted Galen Carpenter, "The United States and Third World Dictatorships: A Case for Benign Detachment," Cato Institute Policy Analysis no. 58, August 15, 1985, p. 12; Aldo Cesar Vacs, *Discreet Partners: Argentina and the USSR since 1917* (Pittsburgh: University of Pittsburgh Press, 1984).

5. Michael Shafer, "Mineral Myths," *Foreign Policy* (Summer 1982): 154–71; Sheldon Richman, "Where Angels Fear to Tread: The United States and the Persian Gulf Conflict," Cato Institute Policy Analysis no. 90, September 9, 1987.

6. Richard Feinberg, *The Intemperate Zone: The Third World Challenge to U.S. Foreign Policy* (New York: W.W. Norton, 1983).

7. R.J. Rummel, "The Freedom Factor," *Reason* (July 1983): 32–38.

8. Jeane Kirkpatrick, *Dictatorships and Double Standards* (New York: Simon and Schuster, 1982), pp. 44, 49.

9. Carpenter, "United States and Third World Dictatorships," p. 15.

10. George P. Shultz, "New Realities and New Ways of Thinking," *Foreign Affairs* (Spring 1985): 705–21.

11. Critical assessments of the Reagan Doctrine include Stephen S. Rosenfeld, "The Guns of July," *Foreign Affairs* (Spring 1986): 698–714; Robert Johnson, "Rollback Revisited—A Reagan Doctrine for Insurgent Wars?" *Policy Focus*

(Washington, D.C.: Overseas Development Council, 1986); Christopher Layne, "The Real Conservative Agenda," *Foreign Policy* (Winter 1985–1986): 73–93; and Christopher Layne, "The Overreaching Reagan Doctrine," *Wall Street Journal*, April 15, 1987.

12. Ted Galen Carpenter, "U.S. Aid to Anti-Communist Rebels: The 'Reagan Doctrine' and Its Pitfalls," Cato Institute Policy Analysis no. 74, June 24, 1986, pp. 11–20.

13. Layne, "Real Conservative Agenda," pp. 82–83, 92.

14. Primary strategic interests include the need to create conditions that minimize the danger of either military attack or military blackmail by an adversary. Those interests must then be balanced against such important factors as the costs of various defense arrangements and the desirability of avoiding a domestic garrison state.

15. The tendency of U.S. policymakers to exaggerate the significance of Third World conflicts and the magnitude of Soviet geopolitical gains is discussed in Nuechterlein, *America Overcommitted;* Tonelson, "Real National Interest"; Melvyn P. Leffler, "From the Truman Doctrine to the Carter Doctrine: Lessons and Dilemmas of the Cold War," *Diplomatic History* (Fall 1983): 245–66; Robert Johnson, "Exaggerating America's Stakes in Third World Conflicts," *International Security* (Winter 1985–1986): 32–68; and Stephen D. Goose, "Soviet Geopolitical Momentum: Myth or Menace?" *Defense Monitor* 15, no. 5 (1986).

16. Raymond Bonner, *Waltzing with a Dictator: The Marcoses and the Making of American Foreign Policy* (New York: Times Books, 1987), pp. 207–20.

17. Selig Harrison, "Cut a Regional Deal," *Foreign Policy* (Spring 1986): 126–47.

18. *Public Papers of the Presidents of the United States: Jimmy Carter, 1977* (Washington, D.C.: Government Printing Office, 1978), p. 2221.

19. Richman, "Where Angels Fear to Tread."

20. Earl C. Ravenal, "An Alternative to Containment," Cato Institute Policy Analysis no. 94, November 23, 1987, p. 9.

21. Ibid., pp. 4–6.

22. Discussions of domestic constraints and the problems interventionists have encountered in attempting to overcome them include Layne, "Real Conservative Agenda"; Paul M. Weyrich, "A Conservative's Lament: After Iran, We Need to Change Our System and Grand Strategy," *Washington Post*, March 8, 1987; Kenneth E. Sharpe, "The Real Cause of Irangate," *Foreign Policy* (Fall 1987): 19–41; Kenneth E. Sharpe, "The Post-Vietnam Formula under Siege: The Imperial Presidency and Central America," *Political Science Quarterly* (Winter 1987–1988): 549–69; Eliot A. Cohen, "Constraints on America's Conduct of Small Wars," *International Security* (Fall 1984): 151–81; and Ravenal, "An Alternative," pp. 15–17, 21.

23. I specifically exclude covert measures by the Central Intelligence Agency as a legitimate option. If a security threat is sufficient to warrant U.S. action, the response should be direct, open, and accompanied by candid explanations. Covert activity inevitably breeds suspicion about U.S. motives throughout the Third World, and it is often undertaken when domestic support for a policy is lacking.

24. The habitual tendency of U.S. officials to confuse ideological and security interests in discussed in Layne, "Real Conservative Agenda"; Tonelson, "Real

National Interest"; and Terry L. Deibel, "Hidden Commitments," *Foreign Policy* (Summer 1987): 46–63.

25. A concise discussion of the rationale for a security-based strategy toward Nicaragua is included in Alan Tonelson, "An Alternative to the 'Contra' War," *New Republic*, October 5, 1987, pp. 20–24.

26. See, for example, Daniel James, *Central America and Mexico* (Washington, D.C.: Washington Institute, 1987), pp. 7–13.

IV
Containment and Its Alternatives

14

Two Cheers for Containment: Probable Allied Responses to U.S. Isolationism

Stephen M. Walt

S ince World War II, U.S. grand strategy has focused on two main objectives. The first goal is to deter a war with the Soviet Union. In the nuclear age, the importance of that goal is hardly debatable. The second goal is maintaining the political division of industrial Eurasia. The rationale for this is equally straightforward: if Western Europe were dominated by a single power, its capabilities would pose a serious long-term threat to U.S. security.[1] This motive underlay U.S. intervention in both world wars and the establishment of current alliances with Western Europe and Japan. By deploying U.S. troops as a visible sign of this commitment, the ability to achieve both goals has been significantly enhanced.

Does this strategy still make sense? According to a number of recent analyses, the answer is no. Drawing upon a variety of arguments, these "neoisolationists" call for the United States to abandon its traditional overseas commitments in favor of new arrangements. Some argue that the focus on Europe is no longer relevant and that the United States should redirect its military efforts away from Eurasia and toward the Third World or the Pacific Basin. Others acknowledge that Europe is still a vital region but assert that the United States can safely withdraw because allies there are capable of defending themselves. Virtually all believe that U.S. overseas commitments are a major cause of its economic problems. With a few exceptions, they all seek a major reduction in the U.S. military presence abroad. Some view a return to isolationism as the ideal option.[2]

There is a grain of truth in each of their claims, but the overall case is unconvincing. Accordingly, I argue here that a return to isolationism is neither necessary nor desirable. Instead, the strategy of limited containment proposed by George Kennan, Walter Lippmann, and Hans Morgenthau remains the best choice. This strategy calls for the United States to prevent the Soviet Union from gaining control of certain key centers of industrial

I would like to thank Joshua Epstein, Aaron Friedberg, Charles Glaser, Helene Madonick, and Stephen Van Evera for their comments on earlier drafts of this essay.

power. Although the relative decline of U.S. power requires adjustments in strategy (indeed, what is needed is a return to this more limited vision), moderate reforms would be better than radical surgery.

I base this conclusion on four main arguments. First, advocates of isolationism overlook the enduring importance of traditional geopolitical interests and underestimate the contribution that U.S. allies make to its security. Thus they would abandon important allies precisely when these states have become most valuable. Second, although allies would do more to defend themselves if the United States did less, it is unlikely that they would do enough to compensate for a complete U.S. withdrawal. Third, a U.S. withdrawal would increase the danger of war—regardless of how U.S. allies responded—without guaranteeing that the United States would be unaffected by it. Finally, containment is not the real cause of the economic problems of the United States, and isolationism is not the best answer. That the United States must adjust to its relative decline is obvious, but a gradual retrenchment is better than a headlong retreat. Implementing containment properly can correct present difficulties while protecting vital interests.

U.S. Interests and the Balance of World Power

What role do U.S. allies play in the present balance of power? Contrary to the usual pessimism, the U.S. international position is basically sound. In particular, the United States and its allies surpass the Soviet alliance network on most critical indexes of national power. They surpass the Soviet alliance network by nearly three to one in GNP, by over two to one in population, and by at least 20 percent in annual defense spending. Both alliances have about the same number of men under arms.[3]

This favorable imbalance of power is no accident. As a consequence of its geographic proximity, expansionist ideology, and considerable military power, the Soviet Union poses a far greater threat to the industrialized world than the United States does. As a result, the nations of industrial Eurasia are strongly inclined to ally with the United States. Thus the Western Alliance includes virtually all of the world's strategically significant states, while the Soviet Union's main allies combine serious internal problems with widespread regional unpopularity. Where the United States enjoys close ties with West Germany, France, Great Britain, Japan, and China, the Soviet Union enjoys the "opportunity" to prop up states like Cuba, Angola, Ethiopia, South Yemen, and Vietnam.[4] Much of Eastern Europe is an economic liability as well, and its loyalty to Moscow is questionable.[5] By comparison, NATO is a model of strength and cohesion.

Why the Western Alliance Is Still Important

In short, the global balance of power greatly favors the United States. Even more important, however, is the major role that U.S. allies play in producing this favorable situation. Although each alliance's combined share of global economic capacity has changed relatively little since 1950, the relative U.S. percentage has declined steadily while that of its allies has increased. For example, the United States produced 39 percent of gross world product in 1950, with Western Europe and Japan contributing 17 percent. By 1980, the U.S. share had dropped to 21.5 percent, and its allies' share had grown to more than 30 percent. In terms of military spending, the U.S. share of the global total declined from 51 percent in 1960 to 26 percent in 1983, while that of Europe and Japan had grown to nearly 15 percent. The trend is reflected in other categories as well, such as the number of men under arms. In 1952, the United States mustered more than twice the number of troops provided by France, Great Britain, Japan, and West Germany combined. By 1958, the ratio had fallen to 1.56 to 1 and to 1.38 to 1 by 1972. When the rest of NATO is included as well, the present U.S. share drops below 50 percent of the NATO total.[6]

Among other things, these trends mean that the geopolitical case for a U.S. commitment to Eurasia is stronger today than it was immediately after World War II. At the beginning of the cold war, the loss of Western Europe would have been serious but not insurmountable; after all, Western Europe was just beginning its postwar recovery and would have added little to Soviet military potential. Although the allies' subsequent recovery means that they are better able to defend themselves today, it also means that their security is more important to the United States. The loss of Western Europe would increase Soviet war-making capabilities far more now than it would have several decades ago. Thus while the Western Alliance retains an impressive lead over its principal adversary, the United States is increasingly dependent upon allied contributions to achieve this favorable result. Those who would abandon these arrangements should consider how the world would look were these same assets either absent from the equation or arrayed against the United States. The prospect is not comforting: Soviet hegemony in Eurasia would provide them with an advantage of more than 2.5 to 1 over the United States in population and gross national product, to say nothing of direct military assets. Put differently, as the ability of the United States to defend Europe unilaterally has decreased, U.S. interest in contributing to a reliable defense has grown.[7]

Why the Third World Is Still Irrelevant

This analysis suggests that maintaining the political division of industrial Eurasia remains the primary geopolitical interest of the United States. By the same logic, the case for a greater U.S. commitment in the Third World is extremely weak.[8] With the partial exception of oil from the Persian Gulf, U.S. interests in the Third World are minor at best. The entire Third World produces less than 20 percent of gross world product, scattered over more than 100 countries. Africa has a combined GNP that is less than that of Great Britain alone, and Latin America has a combined GNP that is smaller than that of West Germany. Because modern military power rests primarily on industrial might, the strategic importance of the Third World is small.[9]

Nor does the United States have important economic interests there. Trade is only 14 percent of U.S. GNP, and nearly 75 percent of all U.S. trade is with allies in Western Europe, Canada, and Japan. U.S. trade with the Third World is modest, and most of it is with Latin America. The same is true for overseas investment; most U.S. investments are in other developed countries. Thus the United States has little reason to worry about economic interests in the developing world.[10]

Alarmists often point to alleged U.S. dependence on raw materials from the Third World, especially so-called strategic minerals like chrome and cobalt. Such fears are wildly exaggerated. The magnitude of a state's mineral imports does not determine its dependence on others; what is important is the cost of replacing these commodities or doing without them. Although the United States imports all or most of its annual consumption of minerals such as chrome, it does so because that is cheap, not because that is the only alternative. A lengthy embargo is a remote possibility—why would a poor Third World country cut off its only source of revenue?—and the United States can rely upon alternative suppliers, plentiful stockpiles, and a variety of substitutes if supplies were ever interrupted. In short, the danger of a resource war is minuscule.[11]

The belief that the United States must increase its military presence in the Third World rests on misconceptions as well. Despite abundant evidence to the contrary, some policymakers still argue that the United States must act in the Third World in order to preserve U.S. credibility elsewhere. President Reagan has stated, "If we cannot win in Central America, our credibility will collapse and our alliances will crumble."[12] The president's reasoning is dubious; U.S. allies unanimously oppose this waste of resources. In any event, the belief that a failure to intervene in the Third World will lead major allies to defect is not supported by either logic or evidence.[13]

The U.S. stake is reduced further by the durable power of Third World nationalism. Because hostility to foreign control is intense, neither superpower has been able to dominate the Third World. Thus there is little danger of a Soviet empire in Asia or Africa, and the United States does not need to establish an empire of its own. We can be equally sanguine about Soviet geopolitical momentum. Contrary to right-wing mythology, Soviet influence in the developing world has, if anything, declined since the 1950s.[14] Even if it had increased, the stakes in the Third World are too small to affect the global balance significantly.

Clearly the fundamental interests of the United States have not changed. Preserving the political division of Eurasia is still the most important objective. Because Soviet military power lies in close proximity to these regions, alliances with Europe and Japan and a continued rapprochement with China should remain the backbone of U.S. foreign policy. Its success thus far suggests that the United States should not abandon this strategy lightly. By contrast, U.S. strategic interests in the Third World are slight. Those who would withdraw from NATO in order to increase U.S. capabilities in the Third World have got it exactly backward; they would weaken the U.S. position in the places that matter in order to stand guard in the places that do not.[15]

Is NATO Obsolete?

It can be argued that the past successes of the United States have made traditional commitments unnecessary. For most neoisolationists, the economic and military revival of Western Europe and Japan means that U.S. forces there are no longer necessary. To convince Western Europe to provide more for its own defense, they call on the United States to withdraw its personnel (a step Irving Kristol has referred to as "shock treatment"), thereby stimulating these allies to do more and freeing resources within the U.S. economy.[16] In short, rather than give allies a free ride, the United States should start free riding on them.

This prescription rests on several assumptions. First, it assumes that U.S. allies do not contribute their fair share to Western defense efforts. Second, these writers assume that these allies will do more only if the United States withdraws, thereby forcing them to balance the Soviet Union on their own. Third, they assume that the European effort to maintain the balance would be completely effective, thereby preserving a robust deterrent. And if deterrence did fail, some suggest that the United States could simply stay out of the war.[17] Let us consider each of these assumptions.

Do U.S. Allies Free Ride? (and If So, Why?)

At first glance, the distribution of burdens within the Western Alliance appears extremely skewed. Although Western Europe's combined GNP now exceeds that of the United States, the United States still contributes over 50 percent of NATO's annual defense expenditures. Europe's share of the total has grown steadily, but it is still smaller than the U.S. contribution. The situation is even worse in the case of Japan; although some estimates credit it with the world's second largest GNP, Japan ranks only tenth in annual defense spending and spends 1 to 2 percent of its GNP on defense. Thus the accusation that the United States is bearing an unfair burden is partly true, and the U.S. interest in obtaining a more equitable distribution of effort is obvious.

Before concluding that withdrawal is the best way to accomplish that, however, several mitigating factors should be noted. First, prior to the Reagan administration's ill-founded orgy of defense spending, U.S. allies' share of the burden had been increasing steadily. From 1969 to 1979, for example, Western Europe's share of NATO's combined defense expenditures increased from 22.7 percent to almost 42 percent.[18] Second, focusing solely on military spending ignores a host of important allied contributions, including the territory upon which most NATO forces are stationed, their provision of host nation support for U.S. troops, and the economic aid they supply to NATO members like Turkey. In addition, U.S. defense costs are increased by the all-volunteer force, while most of its allies rely upon conscription.[19] Thus the true level of free riding is usually overstated.

Even more important, the disproportionate burden borne by the United States may be due less to free riding than to differing perceptions of the threat. Because U.S. allies do not believe that the Soviet Union is as dangerous as the United States does, they do not spend as much to oppose it. Similarly, because they do not share the U.S. fear of leftist forces in the developing world, they do not spend much trying to oppose or overthrow such regimes. Thus the United States spends more not because its allies are lazy or decadent but because U.S. policymakers (and taxpayers) have adopted more extreme goals. In short, if excessive military spending has damaged the U.S. economy, the wound is partly self-inflicted.[20]

Accordingly, rather than abandoning the Alliance in a fit of pique, a better response to the burden-sharing problem would be to work for greater consensus within the Alliance on the true extent of the threat faced. If the U.S. assessment is correct—implying that allies should do more—then the United States should back it up with careful analysis and persuasive argumentation. But if the allied view of the threat is more accurate (and I believe it is), then the United States could safely do less provided that Europe maintains its present effort. In either case, the defense burden within NATO would be distributed more equitably.

Will Its Allies Balance If the U.S. Withdraws?

A central strand in the isolationist argument is the belief that U.S. allies will balance rather than bandwagon following a U.S. withdrawal.[21] In particular, they argue that Europe and Japan would respond by greatly increasing their own defense efforts if the United States were absent. Thus the danger of

Finlandization is exaggerated, and the United States can safely withdraw its forces.[22]

Once again, there is an element of truth to this assertion. Balancing is the dominant tendency in international politics, and U.S. policymakers have greatly exaggerated the danger of bandwagoning in the past. This means that the United States does not have to fight in the Third World in order to reassure its allies in Europe. It also suggests that these allies will do more if the United States does less; indeed, that is precisely what has occurred in the past.

Some neoisolationists, however, take this insight to an illogical extreme. Reducing the U.S. commitment might encourage allies to spend more, but liquidating it entirely might not. Although balancing is more common than bandwagoning, the latter does occur in certain circumstances. For example, weak or vulnerable states may be tempted to bandwagon when threatened by a superior power if they are too small to stand alone and if they are unable to attract adequate allied support. In the 1930s, for example, the failure of Britain and France to take adequate measures to defend their allies encouraged states like Belgium, Poland, and Hungary to accommodate Nazi Germany rather than balance against it. More recently, President Zia ul-Haq of Pakistan refused to take a firm stand against the Soviet occupation of Afghanistan until he was assured of adequate U.S. backing.[23] Thus we cannot discount the possibility of bandwagoning entirely, particularly if the United States were to withdraw completely. Britain, France, and Germany would probably balance, but the rest of NATO might not.

A further reservation should also be noted. Although balancing is more common than bandwagoning, there is nothing automatic or instantaneous about this process. Withdrawal might force U.S. allies to rethink their own security policies, but we cannot be sure about the decisions they will make or how quickly these decisions would be reached. Even if balancing did occur, it would probably take time before these countries achieved the domestic consensus necessary for a serious effort. This problem would be especially serious in Japan, because the past forty years have left Japan deeply divided on national security issues.[24] And if the major European powers chose not to increase their defense efforts, the United States might be far worse off than it is today.[25]

Who Will They Balance? (and How Well?)

These insights suggest the real question. The issue is not whether Europe and Japan would do more following a U.S. withdrawal; it is whether they would do enough. There are clearly grounds for concern. Together with West Germany, the United States provides the best-trained and best-equipped troops in NATO. Moreover, the United States supplies roughly 20 percent of NATO's combat aircraft, and they are among NATO's most capable planes. To compensate for the loss of U.S. support, Europe would have to mobilize at least 500,000 more troops along with the associated military hardware.[26] Given present demographic trends in Europe—resulting in the declining number of eligible conscripts—that is an extremely unlikely event. (This is a problem for the Warsaw Pact as well, but it is neither as serious nor as difficult to overcome politically.)[27] It is worth noting that those who call for a U.S. withdrawal have yet to provide a detailed analysis of what an independent European force would look like, what it would cost, and how effectively it could fight or deter.[28] In this respect, the proposal that the United States withdraw within five years—as Melvyn Krauss and Christopher Layne have suggested—reveals a worrisome disregard for basic military realities. If Europe tried to replace the U.S. presence that quickly, the resulting economic dislocations would defeat the effort, just as the Reagan administration's hasty and ill-planned defense buildup may have wasted much of the money that was spent.[29]

These concerns are reinforced by several other considerations. First, even if the allies balanced after a U.S. withdrawal, they might do so in ways the United States would eventually regret. Such a step would almost certainly lead Britain and France to increase their nuclear capabilities, and it would encourage West Germany to acquire a nuclear force. Given the destabilizing effects of this development, withdrawal is not an option to embrace quickly. Although an independent German deterrent would eliminate concerns about the credibility of the U.S. nuclear guarantee, the obvious risks should not be overlooked.[30]

Second, although some authors believe that a U.S. withdrawal would ease intra-alliance tensions, the opposite result is far more likely.[31] Historically, alliances among equal partners have been more contentious than those in which one state occupied the leading role. NATO is no exception. The loss of U.S. leadership would mean less unity within NATO and a less effective defense. Similarly, in the absence of mutual security cooperation, the tendency for economic rivalries to spill over into the realm of security would reemerge. And once the United States withdrew, its ability to link economic concessions to its security commitments would vanish entirely, which means that resolving contentious economic conflicts would be far more difficult. As the bitter economic rivalries of the 1930s suggest, U.S. isolationism is not a recipe for greater cooperation among the industrial powers.

Third, even if the United States were gone, the logic of collective action would still apply. Because security is a collective good, weaker powers are always tempted to let stronger powers provide it for them.[32] This tendency would continue; the weaker powers in Europe would lean heavily on France, Germany, and Great Britain. History suggests these three might not do enough themselves. In the 1930s, for example, Britain and France tried to pass the burden of opposing Hitler onto each other, which severely weakened their efforts to contain Germany.[33] This problem is less serious for the Warsaw Pact because the Soviet Union provides virtually all of its military power. Thus even if Western Europe commands greater latent resources than the Warsaw Pact and even if these states all balanced following a U.S. withdrawal, NATO would be weaker than it is with the United States involved.

Most important, the global presence of the United States helps safeguard its allies from one another. As a result, they can concentrate on balancing the Soviet Union because they do not need to worry about balancing each other. Although the Soviet Union would probably remain the principal threat (especially in the short term), rivalries within Europe would be more frequent and more intense once the United States withdrew.[34] This may appear farfetched after forty years of tranquillity but not if we remember the four centuries of conflict that preceded them. This problem could be even greater in the Far East, where a precipitous U.S. withdrawal would trigger renewed regional tensions.[35] Thus U.S. allies might balance if the United States withdrew, but they might do so in unexpected ways—against one another or in collaboration with the Soviet Union. After all, states balance against threats, not against power alone, and countries in close proximity usually worry more about each other than about more powerful states farther away.[36] For example, if the United States abandoned its commitments in the Far East, the possibility of a Soviet-Japanese rapprochement directed at China could not be excluded. For the United States, the marriage of Soviet resources with Japanese technology and capital would not be a reassuring prospect.

In short, although balancing is more common than bandwagoning, this tendency does not mean the United States would be better off leaving the defense of Eurasia to others. The neoisolationists are correct to discount the danger of Finlandization, but their confidence that Europe and Japan would fully compensate for a U.S. demobilization is too optimistic. Nor is this a possibility we can safely ignore because the United States retains an interest in helping preserve its allies' independence and in preventing a major war. As a result, we must consider a further question: how would a U.S. withdrawal affect deterrence?

Isolationism and Deterrence

Advocates of isolationism argue that this strategy will not increase the likelihood of war or that the United States could stay out of the war if it occurred. Both arguments are dubious.

Most of these writers assume that deterrence would be preserved by increased defense efforts on the part of U.S. allies. But even if one assumes that Europe and Japan increased their defense efforts enormously—and the more likely scenario is that they would do more but not enough—the robustness of deterrence would still decline. As John Mearsheimer has shown, deterrence is most likely to fail when a potential aggressor believes it can win a short and relatively cheap war. By contrast, if it is convinced that war would mean a protracted and bloody struggle, deterrence is likely to hold.[37]

How would a U.S. withdrawal affect this calculation? Although a war in Europe is unlikely, the probability would increase if the Soviet leadership believed that they could wage war in Europe without the United States' becoming involved. With the United States firmly committed, the Soviets face a coalition with vastly greater latent capabilities. But if the United States has withdrawn, it would be much easier for the Soviets to convince themselves that a blitzkrieg might succeed and that all opposition would cease once they reached the English Channel. Students of history will recognize that this is precisely the type of deterrence failure that produced World Wars I and II. Because Britain did not make its commitment to France clear in 1914, Germany's leaders persuaded themselves that Britain would not fight. Because Hitler doubted the Allied commitment to Poland in 1939, he chose to risk war despite British and French warnings. And had Germany's leaders known that they would eventually face the power of the United States, both of these wars might have been avoided entirely. The U.S. commitment to Europe helps prevent a similar miscalculation today because U.S. troops provide a potent reminder that the Soviet Union cannot attack Europe without facing the United States as well.[38]

It is equally unwise to assume that the United States could easily stay out of a major war on the Eurasian landmass. Despite a tradition of isolationism and very modest military assets, the United States was drawn into three of the last four European wars. The reasons for its involvement in these conflicts—preventing a Eurasian hegemony and maintaining freedom of the seas—could be equally relevant in the future. Although the United States might remain neutral, it would be foolish to count on this possibility. The better approach is to prevent such a war in the first place. A strategy of containment focused on industrial Eurasia accomplishes precisely that.

In short, by weakening deterrence in a region that remains a vital U.S. interest, an isolationist strategy would increase both the danger of war and the resulting danger of more extensive U.S. involvement. Stephen Van Evera recently noted, "History warns that the U.S. gets into great European wars by staying out of Europe—not by being in."[39] Because withdrawing neither reduces the odds of war nor guarantees U.S. neutrality, the United States is more likely to avoid war by maintaining its present commitments.

Is Containment Really the Problem?

We should also question whether U.S. overseas commitments are as onerous as the neoisolationists maintain. Advocates of withdrawal often suggest that these costs cannot be sustained and that efforts to do so will destroy the economic well-being of the United States and its basic national values. Thus Earl Ravenal has argued that the costs of containment "will wreck our economy and warp our society," and David Calleo implies that present military commitments have produced a "fiscal nightmare."[40] In this view, the dangers of withdrawal are less worrisome than the economic apocalypse envisioned if the United States does not cut back.

This is a puzzling assertion. To begin, it is contradictory: we are told that helping defend our allies is prohibitively expensive, yet we are also told our allies can defend themselves rather easily.[41] Although these analysts correctly reject the litany of pessimism that has been used to justify the U.S. defense buildup, they ignore the crucial role that U.S. forces play in creating the present balance in Europe. Contrary to the deceptive and meaningless counts often used to compare NATO and Warsaw Pact capabilities, more sophisticated assessments of the balance reveal that NATO's wartime prospects are quite good, provided that U.S. forces are included. So long as the United States remains a full partner, deterrence will remain robust. Thus an effective defense of Europe does not require extraordinary sacrifices, even if one omits the imposing deterrent effects of nuclear weapons.

It is equally odd to argue that the United States lacks the wherewithal to contribute its fair share to defend vital U.S. interests. The United States alone controls more industrial power than the entire Warsaw Pact; with a proper strategy and with adequate allied support, mounting an effective and credible defense should be well within its means. Thus the claim that overseas commitments will lead to an economic disaster is exaggerated at best. Quite the reverse is true: the fact that the United States has many powerful allies enables it to spend a smaller percentage of its national income on defense than the Soviet Union does.

To be sure, excessive defense spending can hurt the U.S. economy, although how much depends upon specific macroeconomic circumstances. Those who blame the relative decline of the U.S. economy on its overseas alliances, however, make several fundamental errors. First, they overlook the other factors that have hurt U.S. productivity, including a low rate of personal savings, the costs of assimilating a diverse array of ethnic groups, the advantages of late industrialization enjoyed by Japan and the export-oriented economies of East Asia, and the lack of a coherent industrial policy.[42] Some of these ills might be corrected by spending less on defense but not all of them.

Second, and much more important, it is not containment itself that is the problem, even when it involves a large overseas military presence. Stationing troops abroad is cheaper than keeping them at home and buying the lift capacity to move them; furthermore, U.S. allies pay a large share of the basing costs in Europe. Instead, problems emerge when the United States pursues goals that have nothing to do with containment or when it seeks military capabilities in excess of its needs. When these errors are paired with fanciful fiscal policies like Reaganomics, it is hardly surprising that the U.S. economy suffers.

Unfortunately, this has been a common occurrence. Instead of confining its efforts to the key centers of industrial power, the United States has repeatedly pursued an array of additional objectives around the globe.[43] At the same time, it has been reluctant to pay the full price of its ambitions. As David Calleo has shown, the combination of the Vietnam War and the Great Society helped trigger worldwide inflation, an effect exacerbated by President Johnson's refusal to raise taxes.[44] Richard Nixon's decision to increase his reelection chances by stimulating the economy in 1970–1971 made the problem worse. Similarly, current U.S. budget and trade deficits are due on large part to Reaganomics and an excessive defense buildup.[45] None of these policies was required by containment; indeed, the Reagan administration's defense programs are a major departure from this strategy.[46] The result is both ironic and unfortunate; an administration that sought to restore U.S. primacy has so mismanaged economic and defense policies as to make isolationism seem attractive.

In short, because excessive defense spending can be a drain on the U.S. economy, we should seek ways to reduce it. The radical surgery proposed by neoisolationists, however, is neither necessary nor wise. If a reduction in defense expenditures is in order, we should design our military forces to implement containment properly rather than spend money on unnecessary capabilities or on the defense of marginal areas. If overseas commitments must be trimmed, then we should abandon peripheral interests first and vital ones last. What commitments and capabilities would such a strategy imply, and what effects would it have?

Maintaining Containment: U.S. Grand Strategy from an Alliance Perspective

A revised U.S. strategy should emphasize two features. First, it should focus the U.S. defense effort on vital interests: industrial Eurasia and Persian Gulf oil. Second, it should emphasize defensive measures rather than offensive ones because defense is easier in the contemporary era and because a defensive posture is not as threatening to allies or adversaries.

Under this approach, the United States would continue to focus its primary attention on preventing Soviet expansion on the Eurasian landmass. This goal is best accomplished by maintaining its present alliances with Western Europe and Japan, together with a selective group of states in the developing world. At the same time, the United States must correct the economic imbalances produced by the irresponsible extravagances of the Reagan administration. Specifically, the U.S. budget deficit must be substantially reduced (if not eliminated). Achieving this goal will require significant reductions in U.S. defense spending.[47] To facilitate this end, the United States should seek a more equitable division of labor within the Alliance itself. This task is especially important in the case of Japan; the world's second or third largest economy should not depend so heavily upon U.S. protection. How can these various goals be achieved?

Interests and Commitments

If a reduction in U.S. commitments is in order, the Third World is the place to start. With the exception of the Persian Gulf, the United States has few, if any, significant economic or strategic interests in the developing world. And its economic interests do not require that it control these regions militarily.[48]

Accordingly, the knee-jerk opposition of the United States to leftist forces in the Third World should be abandoned. Marxist ideology rarely binds states to Moscow, as the examples of Mao, Tito, Togliatti, Mugabe, Berlinguer, Carillo, and Pol Pot all demonstrate. All too often, U.S. hostility serves primarily to keep these regimes allied with the Soviet Union. Examples like Mozambique, China, and Angola suggest that such regimes are unlikely to stay there once the United States adopts a more conciliatory stance. As George Kennan's original formulation of containment prescribed, the United States should concentrate on weaning leftist regimes away from Moscow rather than reinforcing their allegiance through misplaced belligerence.

Among other things, this means that the United States should abandon the Reagan Doctrine and reduce its power projection capabilities in the Third World. Such a step would enable it to reduce the navy from fifteen carrier battle groups to no more than ten and to demobilize at least one marine division and its associated sea and airlift assets. These reductions would save more than $75 billion over the next ten years.[49] Furthermore, once all the costs are included, abandoning the Reagan Doctrine might save an additional $10 billion per year.[50] In short, · by reducing military commitments in the Third world, significant savings can be realized without jeopardizing its basic interests.

In the same vein, the United States should rethink its security arrangements with a number of its Third world clients. Although some of these allies provide valuable facilities, most are more of a liability than an asset. Military aid to Zaire, Somalia, the Sudan, and most of Central America, for example, does little to strengthen U.S. security. Because most of the Third World is of marginal strategic importance, cutting unnecessary military aid makes sense here as well.[51]

To be sure, there will be a number of exceptions to this general prescription. Because the Soviet empire expands by conquest (and not through proxy forces, foreign aid, or ideological solidarity), direct Soviet expansion should still be opposed. This is the appropriate response even when the stakes are minimal (as they are in Afghanistan) because it is in the U.S. interest to encourage the Soviet Union to abandon the aggressive use of force. Thus arms shipments to the Afghan rebels should continue until arrangements for a Soviet withdrawal are completed. Other special cases include Israel (for strategic, moral, and political reasons) and several Persian Gulf states, although the latter generally pay their own way. The Rapid Deployment Force (RDF) should remain intact, but it should be designed and sized strictly for the Persian Gulf mission.

Missions and Capabilities

Now the question is whether the United States can defend its interests effectively while spending less. Answering this question properly requires going beyond the misleading "beancounts" that the Defense Department often uses to persuade that the nation is still too weak.[52] What do more sophisticated analyses reveal?

Beginning with Europe, the best assessments suggest that the conventional balance is far better than NATO's critics contend. The widespread belief that NATO cannot mount a robust conventional defense is odd—to say the least—given that NATO spends roughly 20 percent more than the Warsaw Pact every year and has about the same number of men under arms. Moreover, roughly 15 percent of Soviet forces are directed at China, which makes NATO's task even easier. In the words of Kenneth Waltz, "If we are militarily weaker than they are, we must be doing something very wrong."[53]

In fact, the situation is reassuring. The static comparisons that are often invoked to show Warsaw Pact superiority (in division, tanks, aircraft, artillery tubes, and so forth) are essentially meaningless because they ignore the areas in which NATO is superior (aircraft quality, naval forces, logistics, command and control, and training). Such comparisons also omit the natural advantages to the defender, the low readiness of Soviet reserve divisions, the importance of so-called force-to-space ratios (that is, the number of men needed to defend a given area irrespective of the size of the attacking force), the lower reliability of Warsaw Pact equipment, and the dubious loyalty of Eastern European armies. When these factors are taken into account,

NATO's ability to mount an effective conventional defense (assuming that the United States is involved) looks reasonably bright.[54]

This does not mean that victory is assured, of course. To improve the odds, NATO should spend less to increase its offensive capabilities—such as deep-strike aircraft for so-called Follow-On Force Attacks (FOFA)—and spend more on capabilities designed to thwart a Soviet armored breakthrough. Greater effort should also be devoted to improving NATO's conventional sustainability and to acquiring additional defensive assets. For example, close support aircraft like the A-10 are a better choice than high-priced items like the F-15 or Tornado because the mission performed by the latter is both more difficult and less important. Greater attention to terrain preparation would help slow a Pact advance and improve exchange ratios as well. Properly implemented, measures like these would also permit reductions in NATO's force structure. Moreover, efforts to reduce waste through joint procurement and production agreements would give NATO more real defense capability per dollar. Such reforms are not exciting—merely useful and cost-effective.

Much the same situation applies to the Persian Gulf. The widespread belief that NATO cannot mount an effective defense of Persian Gulf oil rests largely upon ignorance. The Iranians would probably mount an impressive resistance to any invasion, as Iraq has learned to its regret, and a Soviet attack would also face enormous geographical and logistical obstacles. A Soviet invasion force would have to travel more than 800 miles of primitive mountain roads filled with numerous choke points. Soviet forces in the region lack the logistical support and air cover needed for such a campaign, which eliminates the possibility of surprise and leaves them vulnerable to defensive interdiction. Because the oil fields are in the south, far from the Soviet border, and because a Soviet invasion would reverse Iran's current antipathy to the United States, the prospects for mounting a successful defense are excellent without expanding the RDF.[55]

NATO is in good shape to deal with its most important contingencies. Where, then, should reductions be made? The most obvious target is the U.S. Navy. Under its so-called Maritime Strategy, the Reagan administration justified a major buildup of U.S. naval forces by claiming it would enable us to conduct offensive naval operations against the Soviet homeland in the event of war. Unfortunately, one element of the strategy is potentially destabilizing (Soviet ballistic missile submarines are a major target), and the rest of the strategy is unfeasible and unnecessary. Even a 600-ship navy (with 15 aircraft carriers) is far too small to do much damage to the Soviet landmass. Moreover, anything it might accomplish is probably easier to do with other weapons. (And because the carriers would have to operate within range of Soviet land-based aircraft, this strategy could give new meaning to the term *sunk costs*.) In short, the maritime strategy manages to be both destabilizing and ineffective at the same time, a remarkable if dubious achievement.[56]

This does not mean that the navy is unimportant. By ensuring that the sea-lines of communication to Europe and the Far East would remain open, the navy makes an important contribution to deterrence. But NATO's naval forces were already capable of performing this mission before the U.S. buildup, which means that the money spent to expand the navy was essentially wasted. It is especially ironic that an administration that seemed most worried about Soviet superiority in tanks and artillery devoted its main efforts to areas in which the United States was already far ahead (aircraft carriers, among others). by diverting funds away from the army and air force and toward the navy (the least important yet most heavily funded service), the Reagan administration has managed to undermine the U.S. economic position and weaken deterrence simultaneously.[57]

The navy is also useful for Third World intervention, but the United States already has more than enough sea power for this unimportant mission. Eliminating unnecessary naval forces—at least five carrier battle groups, the refitted battleships, and a variety of miscellaneous assets—could by itself reduce U.S. defense expenditures by as much as 5 percent over the next ten years.

U.S. strategic nuclear forces can be significantly reduced as well. In the nuclear age, the most important task is preserving a robust second-strike capability, a goal rather easy to achieve. According to one recent estimate, 100 one-megaton airbursts would kill between forty-five and seventy-seven million Soviet citizens.[58] Most estimates agree that the United States would have at least 4,000 strategic warheads and 1,000 EMT left after a successful Soviet first strike. The same is true in reverse: although Soviet forces are more vulnerable than those of the United States, they would still have over 500 EMT left after a U.S. first strike.[59] So long as each side's own second-strike capability is maintained, both are deterred. *Nuclear superiority* is thus a largely meaningless term, and efforts to achieve it are wasteful at best and destabilizing at worst.[60]

Defying this logic, both superpowers devote considerable effort and expense to acquiring additional counterforce capabilities. The effort has been utterly futile; both superpowers have far more survivable warheads now than they did twenty years ago. Because an escape from mutual assured destruction is probably impossible, the United States should abandon its counterforce programs while maintaining a robust retaliatory capability. Procurement of the Midgetman, MX, and Trident D-5 missiles and the B-1B and Stealth bombers can be canceled, along with the costly schemes for land-mobile missiles and the like. The present submarine force should be maintained, along with the Minuteman IIIs, the MX missiles already deployed, and a growing number of air-launched cruise missiles (eventually incorporating

Stealth technology.) This force would save billions over the next ten years without undermining deterrence in the slightest.

For the same reasons, the United States should cancel the SDI. The available evidence suggests that it will not work, and we would not want it even if it did.[61] Despite its name, SDI is an offensive weapon that threatens the Soviet Union's second-strike capability. Assuming it did work, deploying it would create an especially unstable world. (With defenses in place, both sides would be forced to search frantically for a way to overcome them, driven by the understandable fear that the other side might achieve a breakthrough first and gain a first-strike capability overnight.) A modest research program should continue as a hedge against uncertainty, but plans for testing and deployment should be abandoned. SDI may have some value as a bargaining chip for arms control, but it is time to cash it in. A savings of $20 billion or more over the next five years could be achieved.

Implications

What effects would these reforms produce? Obviously they would save a great deal of money. According to Joshua M. Epstein, reductions less extensive than those proposed here would save approximately $50 billion in budget authority over the next two years.[62] If maintained for five years, these cuts would reduce the U.S. budget deficit substantially, even in the absence of other measures.[63] With additional reductions in domestic programs and a modest tax increase, U.S. budgetary difficulties would be largely eliminated.

Even more important, the strategy outlined here would correct the perception that Europe was free riding on the United States. If the United States returned to a more appropriate defense budget, the share of GNP devoted to defense would be roughly equal to that of its principal European allies, particularly when their other contributions are included. In effect, the United States would be adopting a European approach to a grand strategy, which focuses on the main threat (the Soviet Union) and downplays the Third World and the futile quest for nuclear superiority.

This strategy would reduce U.S. burdens significantly while preserving deterrence in critical regions. Because the U.S. contribution would decline (but not disappear), the allied share of NATO expenditures would continue to grow. Because they could still count on the U.S. commitment, however, regional rivalries would be defused, and any tendency toward defeatism would be minimized. The United States would remain the largest member of the Alliance and could still exert a leading role. This approach is far less risky than the radical surgery advocated by others, and minimizing risk is worth the expense.

What about Japan? Encouraging Japan to bear its fair share of the costs of containment is important, but it must be done in ways that preserve Japanese-U.S. amity and do not ignite regional rivalries in the Far East. These objectives can be met by reducing U.S. forces gradually, concentrating reductions on naval and air assets. The goal is not to eliminate the U.S. presence but to shift the burden for sea and air control to Japan and other regional U.S. allies. This cannot be done precipitously, but the process should begin soon.

Japan can and should make other contributions. Given that it cannot make a direct military contribution to protecting oil supplies in the gulf, helping defray these costs through direct payments is certainly in order. Japan should be encouraged to increase its financial aid to less developed countries, either through international institutions like the World Bank or through bilateral grants. Japanese support for regional associations like ASEAN (whose members currently receive security assistance from the United States) would also be desirable. The Japanese have moved in this direction already (for example, they are Pakistan's largest source of foreign aid and provide substantial sums to the Philippines as well), but they should be encouraged to do even more. In this respect, diplomacy is more likely to succeed than shock treatment. Efforts to coerce Japan into a dramatic defense buildup are more likely to galvanize Japanese resistance.[64]

Thus the real issue is what combination of carrots and sticks will preserve Alliance cohesion while fostering a greater allied contribution. A precipitous U.S. withdrawal will provoke resentment and would be correctly interpreted as yet another attempt by the United States to pass the cost of its fiscal follies onto its allies. A substantial but careful retrenchment is more likely to galvanize allies into doing more and in ways that the United States would not subsequently regret. Having repeatedly requested that the United States get its fiscal house in order, allies can hardly complain if the United States at last takes steps to do so—assuming, of course, that it does not abandon them in the process.

Conclusion

After four decades, the changing patterns of world power dictate a number of adjustments in U.S. grand strategy. Its present commitments are probably excessive, and we must therefore determine where and how to reduce them. By calling for a rigorous reassessment, the neoisolationists have made a valuable contribution to this process. Unfortunately, the solution they propose is too extreme. Where reform is needed, they call for dissolution. Where adjustments should be made, they call for radical surgery. Yet if their confident predictions are wrong—and the weight of the evidence is against them—their prescription could have catastrophic results. Most important, the solution they propose is not necessary. Amputation will cure a skinned knee, but less extreme treatments are usually preferable.

By returning U.S. grand strategy to the essentials of containment—and in particular, by reversing the Reagan administration's disastrous excesses—we can correct our present insolvency without jeopardizing our vital interests. Containment has worked remarkably well thus far, and the recipe that has brought forty years of peace should not be casually discarded. Although amendments are in order, this basic strategy remains the best choice.

Notes

1. For the classic works expounding this view, see George Kennan, *Realities of American Foreign Policy* (Princeton, N.J.: Princeton University Press, 1954); Walter Lippmann, *The Cold War: A Study of U.S. Foreign Policy* (New York: Harper & Bros., 1948); and Hans J. Morgenthau, *A New Foreign Policy for the United States* (New York: Praeger, 1969). For a summary and analysis, see John Lewis Gaddis, *Strategies of Containment* (New York: Oxford University Press, 1982), chap. 2.

2. Although there are important differences among them, representative examples of the neoisolationist position can be found in: David Calleo, *Beyond American Hegemony: The Future of the Western Alliance* (New York: Basic Books, 1987); Christopher Layne, "Atlanticism without NATO," *Foreign Policy* 67 (Summer 1987): 22–45, and "Ending the Alliance," *Journal of Contemporary Studies* 6 (1983): 5–31; James Chace, "Ike Was Right," *Atlantic Monthly* (July–August 1987): 39–41, and "A New Grand Strategy," *Foreign Policy* 70 (Spring 1988): 3–25; Earl C. Ravenal, "Europe without America: The Erosion of NATO," *Foreign Affairs* 63 (Summer 1985): 1020–35, and "NATO: The Tides of Discontent," Policy Papers in International Affairs 23 (Berkeley: Institute for International Studies, 1985); Melvyn Krauss, *How NATO Weakens the West* (New York: Simon & Schuster, 1986); and Irving Kristol, "What's Wrong with NATO?" *New York Times Magazine*, September 25, 1983, pp. 64–71. Other analysts call for a redeployment of U.S. military assets (away from Europe and toward the Pacific or the Third World) without advocating a reduction in U.S. capabilities or expenditures. See, for example, Jeffrey Record, "Beyond NATO: New Military Directions for the United States," in *U.S. Strategy at the Crossroads: Two Views*, ed. Jeffrey Record and Robert J. Hanks (Cambridge, Mass.: Institute for Foreign Policy Analysis, 1982); and Zbigniew Brzezinski, *Game Plan: How to Win the U.S.-Soviet Contest* (Boston: Little, Brown, 1986).

3. See Stephen M. Walt, *The Origins of Alliances* (Ithaca: Cornell University Press, 1987), pp. 274–76, and "Alliance Formation and the Balance of World Power," *International Security* 9 (Spring 1985): 3–43.

4. Among the ten countries with the largest annual defense expenditures, only Poland is closely allied with the Soviet Union. Seven of the remaining eight are aligned with the United States. See U.S. Arms Control and Disarmament Agency (ACDA), *World Military Expenditures and Arms Transfers, 1985* (Washington, D.C.: Government Printing Office, 1985), p. 5.

5. See Valerie Bunce, "The Empire Strikes Back: The Evolution of the Soviet Bloc from a Soviet Asset to a Soviet Liability," *International Organization* 39 (Winter 1985): 1–46.

6. Some of this shift is due to U.S. demobilization at the end of the Korean War, but the steady increase in Japanese, French, and especially West German military strength was equally significant. See *The Military Balance, 1973–74* (London: International Institute for Strategic Studies, 1974), p. 79; and ACDA, *World Military Expenditures, 1985*.

7. It can be argued that the invention of nuclear weapons and the emergence of high-tech industries have made a focus on industrial power largely irrelevant. By this logic, reliance upon nuclear deterrence and U.S. geographic isolation would permit a return to the pre–World War II strategy of isolationism. Even if a Eurasian hegemony did emerge, this argument goes, it would not pose a significant threat to a nuclear-armed and geographically distant United States. Although this argument is not without merit, I question the conclusion for three reasons. First, although the United States can maintain a robust nuclear deterrent rather easily today, the prospect of a lengthy strategic arms race with a Eurasian hegemony possessing over twice the U.S. GNP could be daunting, particularly if such an empire were able to exploit the technical capacities of Western Europe and Japan. Second, a Eurasian hegemony would also enjoy the other benefits (such as economic influence and cultural impact) that dominant great powers have always enjoyed. Thus the U.S. ability to shape international events would be reduced significantly in such a world. Eurasia would be difficult to conquer and exploit even in the absence of a U.S. commitment, but present U.S. strategy provides an affordable insurance policy against this remote but serious contingency. Finally, because the U.S. commitment to Europe helps deter any war there and because the most plausible route to a nuclear war is through the escalation of a conventional conflict, the U.S. commitment also helps minimize the danger of nuclear war.

8. A recent blue-ribbon study of long-range security requirements for the United States places great emphasis on the need to improve U.S. military capabilities in the Third World. After pointing out that "nearly all the armed conflicts of the past forty years have occurred in . . . the Third World," the panel suggests that "the United States will need to be better prepared to deal with conflict in the Third World." Unfortunately, the authors of the report offer no evidence or even an extended discussion regarding why events in the Third World should be considered vital to U.S. military or economic interests. The strategic and economic importance of the Third World is assumed; the policy conclusion follows predictably from the initial (unsupported and dubious) premise. In general, this report should be viewed as an example of political advocacy, not as a serious effort to analyze security problems objectively or systematically. See Fred C. Iklé and Albert Wohlstetter, *Discriminate Deterrence: Report of the Commission on Integrated Long-Term Strategy* (Washington, D.C.: Government Printing Office, 1988), esp. pp. 13–22.

9. The analysis in the previous two paragraphs is based on Stephen Van Evera, "Why Europe Should Remain the Focus of American Grand Strategy: A Geopolitical Assessment," in *U.S. Policy toward Eastern Europe, Western Europe, and the Soviet Union,* Hearing before the Subcommittee on European Affairs, Committee on Foreign

Relations, U.S. Senate, 99th Cong., 1st sess., October 3, 1985, pp. 51–76; and Barry R. Posen and Stephen Van Evera, "Departure from Containment: Reagan Administration Defense Policy," in *Eagle Resurgent,* ed. Kenneth A. Oye, Donald Rothchild, and Robert Lieber (Boston: Little, Brown, 1987), pp. 75–114.

10. Trade with Latin America is about 15 percent of total U.S. trade, trade with Africa only 5 percent, and trade with East Asia (minus Japan) only 15 percent. Despite OPEC, the Near East is responsible for a mere 8 percent. See *World Almanac and Book of Facts 1985* (New York: Newspaper Enterprise Association, 1984).

11. The available supply of most strategic minerals is highly elastic to changes in price. Estimates of "proved world reserves," for example, are based on the current price; if it goes up, the quantity of reserves increases because marginal sources can be exploited at a profit. An embargo would immediately trigger a price increase, thereby making it economically feasible to reopen mining facilities that are currently unprofitable. Thus a resource war might have some mild economic consequences but little more than that. On this basic issue, see Kenneth N. Waltz, "The Myth of National Interdependence," in *The International Corporation,* ed. Charles Kindleberger (Cambridge, Mass.: MIT Press, 1970), pp. 205–23, and *Theory of International Politics* (Reading, Mass.: Addison-Wesley, 1979), chap. 7. On strategic minerals, see Michael Shafer, "Mineral Myths," *Foreign Policy* 47 (Summer 1982): 154–81, and Stephen D. Krasner, "Oil Is the Exception," *Foreign Policy* 14 (Spring 1974): 68–83.

12. See "Speech to a Joint Session of Congress on Central America," *New York Times,* April 28, 1983, p. A12.

13. See Jerome Slater, "Dominoes in Central America: Will They Fall? Does It matter?" *International Security* 12 (Winter 1986–1987): 105–34, and Walt, *Origins of Alliances,* chap. 5.

14. See David T. Johnson and Stephen D. Goose, "Soviet Geopolitical Momentum: Myth or Menace? Trends in Soviet Influence around the World from 1945 to 1986," *Defense Monitor* 15 (1986).

15. Examples of this basic misconception are Record, "Beyond NATO"; Layne, "Atlanticism without NATO"; Chace, "A New Grand Strategy"; and Brzezinski, *Game Plan.*

16. See Kristol, "What's Wrong with NATO," p. 71.

17. See Ravenal, "Europe without America," pp. 1031–33.

18. See Robert J. Art, "Fixing Transatlantic Bridges," *Foreign Policy* 46 (Spring 1982): 70.

19. If European manpower were priced according to U.S. pay scales, their annual defense expenditures would increase by roughly 22 percent. This does not tell us which manpower system is more efficient or effective, but it does help explain why European expenditures are less than those of the United States. See Ruth Sivard, *World Military and Social Expenditures 1981* (Leesburg, Va.: World Priorities, 1981), p. 37.

20. On this point, see Posen and Van Evera, "Departure from Containment."

21. On the concepts of balancing and bandwagoning, see Walt, *Origins of Alliances,* chaps. 2, 5; "Alliance Formation and the Balance of World Power"; Waltz, *Theory of International Politics,* pp. 126–27. For additional discussion and evidence,

see Stephen M. Walt, "Testing Theories of Alliance Formation: The Case of Southwest Asia," *International Organization* 42 (Spring 1988).

22. See Calleo, *Beyond American Hegemony;* Layne, "Atlanticism without NATO"; Chace, "A New Grand Strategy," pp. 12–13; Brzezinski, *Game Plan*, p. 204; and Krauss, *How NATO Weakens the West*, p. 37.

23. In 1979, Zia dismissed a U.S. offer of $400 million in economic and military aid as "peanuts." His reluctance to confront the Soviet Union was indicted by his statement that "one cannot live in the sea and create enmity with whales." When more extensive allied backing became available, however, Zia quickly switched to firm support for the Afghan resistance. Thus decisions to balance are much more likely when powerful allies are available to help.

24. See Mike M. Mochizuki, "Japan's Search for Strategy," *International Security* 8 (Winter 1983–1984): 152–79.

25. Indeed, because preventing Soviet expansion is so important to the United States, the real surprise is not that allies free ride. Rather, it is that they contribute as much as they do.

26. This is a conservative estimate. The United States currently deploys over 300,000 army and air force personnel in Europe. In the event of war, designated reinforcements would increase the total by more than 200,000 combat troops and supporting personnel. These figures omit U.S. naval forces, which suggests that the figure of 500,000, if anything, understates the numbers that Europe would need to mobilize to replace the U.S. contribution. See *The Military Balance, 1987–88* (London: International Institute for Strategic Studies, 1987), pp. 24–25.

27. For example, the number of West German males between the ages of 17 and 30 will decline by more than 30 percent in the next decade. Similar trends apply to France and Britain as well. See *The Military Balance, 1983–84* (London: International Institute for Strategic Studies, 1983), pp. 145–47.

28. One recent attempt is Calleo, *Beyond American Hegemony*, chap. 9. Calleo argues that Europe can easily match the Warsaw Pact by greater reliance upon reserves, but even he does not provide an adequate description of the force he envisions or its effectiveness against the Warsaw Pact.

29. On this point, see Richard Stubbing, "The Defense Program: Buildup or Binge?" *Foreign Affairs* 63 (Spring 1985): 848–72.

30. The case for German acquisition is presented in David Garnham, "Extending Deterrence with German Nuclear Weapons," *International Security* 10 (Summer 1985): 96–110. For a critique, see Ivo Daalder and Jay Kosminsky, "Extending Deterrence with . . . WHAT?" *International Security* 10 (Spring 1986): 201–5.

31. Authors claiming that a reduced U.S. role would increase allied cohesion include Layne, "Atlanticism without NATO;" and Eliot A. Cohen, "The Long-Term Crisis of the Alliance," *Foreign Affairs* 61 (Winter 1982–1983): 325–43.

32. The classic analyses of the collective goods problem are: Mancur Olson, *The Logic of Collective Action: Public Goods and the Theory of Groups*, (Cambridge: Harvard University Press, 1965), and Mancur Olson and Richard Zeckhauser, "An Economic Theory of Alliances," *Review of Economics and Statistics* 48 (1966): 266–79.

33. See Barry R. Posen, *The Sources of Military Doctrine: France, Britain, and Germany between the World Wars* (Ithaca: Cornell University Press, 1984).

34. See Joseph Joffe, "Europe's American Pacifier," *Foreign Policy* 54 (Spring 1984): 64–82.

35. This point is nicely made in Henry A. Kissinger, "The Rearming of Japan—and the Rest of Asia," *Washington Post*, January 29, 1987, p. A25.

36. See Walt, *Origins of Alliances*, pp. 158–65, 263–65.

37. See John J. Mearsheimer, *Conventional Deterrence* (Ithaca: Cornell University Press, 1983).

38. Moscow's sensitivity on this point seems clear, given that it carefully probed the probable U.S. reaction to a preemptive Soviet attack on China in the late 1960s. See Henry A. Kissinger, *White House Years* (Boston: Little, Brown, 1979), pp. 183–87.

39. See Van Evera, "Why Europe Should Remain the Focus of American Strategy."

40. See Earl Ravenal, "The Case for a Withdrawal of Our Forces," *New York Times Magazine*, March 6, 1983, p. 75; Calleo, *Beyond American Hegemony*, p. 165 and passim. Calleo argues that "five divisions [committed to Europe] that are the product of a sustainable military budget are greatly superior to ten that are the product of a fiscal nightmare." The clear implication is that the current U.S. commitment has created this "nightmare." But as I argue below, the commitment to NATO—and in particular, the five divisions that Calleo would remove—is but a small part of the problem.

41. See Calleo, *Beyond American Hegemony*, chap. 9; Chace, "A New Grand Strategy," pp. 12–13.

42. For a good discussion of this issue, see Robert Gilpin, *War and Change in World Politics* (Princeton: Princeton University Press, 1981), pp. 159–68.

43. For evidence on this point, see Richard J. Barnet, *Intervention and Revolution: America's Confrontation with Insurgent Movements around the World* (New York: Meridian, 1968); Barry M. Blechman and Stephen S. Kaplan, *Force without War: U.S. Armed Forces as a Political Instrument* (Washington, D.C.: Brookings Institution, 1978); and Melvin Gurtov, *The United States against the Third World* (New York: Praeger, 1974).

44. See Calleo, *Beyond American Hegemony*, and "Inflation and American Power," *Foreign Affairs* 59 (Spring 1981): 781–812.

45. For a powerful critique of Reagan's economic strategy, focusing upon its debilitating effects on U.S. competitiveness in the world economy, see Robert Gilpin, *The Political Economy of International Relations* (Princeton, N.J.: Princeton University Press, 1987), pp. 345–52, 362.

46. See Posen and Van Evera, "Departure from Containment."

47. Reducing defense spending is only one of the necessary steps. For a variety of other suggestions, see Robert Gilpin, "American Policy in the Post-Reagan Era," *Daedalus* 116 (Summer 1987): 33–67, and Peter G. Petersen, "The Morning After," *Atlantic* 260 (October 1987): 43–69.

48. For persuasive analysis of the low U.S. interest in the Third World, see: Robert Johnson, "Exaggerating America's Stakes in Third World Conflicts," *International Security* 10 (Winter 1985–1986): 32–68; Richard Feinberg, *The Intemperate Zone: The Third World Challenge to U.S. Foreign Policy* (New York: Norton,

1983); and Richard Feinberg and Kenneth A. Oye, "After the Fall: U.S. Policy toward Radical Regimes," *World Policy Journal* 1 (Fall 1983): 201–15. The case of Latin America is examined in Lars Schoultz, *National Security and U.S. Interests in Latin America* (Princeton: Princeton University Press, 1986), and Slater, "Dominoes in Central America."

49. The ten-year cost of a carrier battle group is roughly $25 billion. I am indebted to Joshua M. Epstein for sharing his calculation of these costs with me, though he is, of course, not responsible for my use of his figures.

50. In addition to the direct cost of supporting insurgent forces, the Reagan Doctrine has also forced the United States to increase its own military operations (for example, in Central America) and to provide increased economic and military aid to Pakistan, Honduras, and other neighboring countries. See Robert H. Johnson, "Rollback Revisited—A Reagan Doctrine for Insurgent Wars?" in *Policy Focus* (Washington, D.C.: Overseas Development Council, 1986), p. 9.

51. On these points, see Terry L. Deibel, "Hidden Commitments," *Foreign Policy* 67 (Summer 1987): 46–63.

52. The public debate on defense issues consists largely of propaganda, most of it produced by the Pentagon. For a summary of the various methods used to distort analysis, see Posen and Van Evera, "Departure from Containment"; Les Aspin, "Games the Pentagon Plays," *Foreign Policy* 11 (1973); and Michael Salman, Kevin Sullivan, and Stephen Van Evera, "Analysis or Propaganda: Measuring American Strategic Nuclear Capability: 1969–1988," in *Nuclear Arguments*, ed. Steven E. Miller and Lynn Eden (Ithaca: Cornell University Press, forthcoming). For historical background on this problem, see Stephen M. Walt, "The Search for a Science of Strategy: A Review Essay," *International Security* 12 (Summer 1987): 140–65.

53. See Kenneth N. Waltz, "Faltering Giant," *Inquiry*, February 23, 1981, p. 27.

54. Using a variety of systematic approaches, the following works offer optimistic appraisals of the current conventional balance in Europe: Barry R. Posen, "Measuring the European Conventional Balance: Coping with Complexity in Threat Assessment," *International Security* 9 (Winter 1984–1985): 47–88, and "Is NATO Decisively Outnumbered?" *International Security* 12 (Spring 1988): 186–202; Joshua M. Epstein, *The 1988 Defense Budget* (Washington, D.C.: Brookings Institution, 1987), and "Dynamic Analysis and the Conventional Balance in Europe," *International Security* 12 (Spring 1988): 154–65; John J. Mearsheimer, "Why the Soviets Can't Win Quickly in Central Europe," *International Security* 7 (Summer 1982): 3–39, and "Numbers, Strategy, and the European Balance," *International Security* 12 (Spring 1988): 174–85; William W. Kaufmann, "Nonnuclear Deterrence," in *Alliance Security: NATO and the No-First-Use Question*, ed. John Steinbruner and Leon V. Sigal (Washington, D.C.: Brookings Institution, 1983), pp. 43–90; and William P. Mako, *U.S. Ground Forces and the Defense of Central Europe* (Washington, D.C.: Brookings Institution, 1983). More pessimistic assessments may be found in Kim R. Holmes, "Measuring the Conventional Balance in Europe," *International Security* 12 (Spring 1988): 166–73; Andrew Hamilton, "Redressing the Conventional Balance: NATO's Reserve Military Manpower," *International Security* 10 (Summer 1985): 111–

36; and, of course, the publication *Soviet Military Power* (Washington, D.C.: U.S. Department of Defense, annual publication).

55. The best analysis of the Persian Gulf case is Joshua M. Epstein, *Strategy and Force Planning: The Case of the Persian Gulf* (Washington, D.C.: Brookings Institution, 1986). See also Keith Dunn, "Constraints on the USSR in Southwest Asia: A Military Analysis," *Orbis* 25 (Fall 1981): 607–31.

56. See Epstein, *1988 Defense Budget*, pp. 45–55, and "Horizontal Escalation: Sour Notes on a Recurring Theme," *International Security* 8 (1983–1984): 19–31; William W. Kaufmann, *A Thoroughly Efficient Navy* (Washington, D.C.: Brookings Institution, 1987).

57. On these points, see John J. Mearsheimer, "A Strategic Misstep: The Maritime Strategy and Deterrence in Europe," *International Security* 11 (Fall 1986): 3–57.

58. See Barbara G. Levi, Frank N. van Hippel, and William H. Daugherty, "Civilian Casualties from 'Limited' Nuclear Attacks on the USSR," *International Security* 12 (Winter 1987–1988): 168–89.

59. See Epstein, *1988 Defense Budget*, pp. 21–27; Salman, Sullivan, and Van Evera, "Analysis or Propaganda."

60. The best recent presentation of this view is Robert Jervis, *The Illogic of American Nuclear Strategy* (Ithaca: Cornell University Press, 1984).

61. For studies challenging the feasibility of SDI, see American Physical Society Study Group, *Science and Technology of Directed-Energy Weapons* (Woodbury, N.Y.: American Physical Society, 1987); Kurt Gottfried, "The Physicists Size Up SDI," *Arms Control Today* 17 (July–August 1987): 28–32; John Tirman, *Empty Promise: The Growing Case against Star Wars* (New York: Vintage Books, 1986); and Sidney Drell, David Holloway, and Philip Farley, "Preserving the ABM Treaty: A Critique of the Reagan Strategic Defense Initiative," *International Security* 9 (Fall 1984): 51–91. For analyses suggesting that SDI would be undesirable even if it were possible, see Charles Glaser, "Why Even Good Defenses May Be Bad," *International Security* 9 (Fall 1984): 92–123, and "Do We Want the Missile Defenses We Can Build?" *International Security* 10 (Summer 1985): 25–57.

62. See Epstein, *1988 Defense Budget*, p. 56.

63. The deficit now stands at about 3.6 percent of GNP, which means that reducing the defense budget from more than 6 percent of GNP to under 5 percent would reduce the deficit by almost a third.

64. See Mike M. Mochizuki, "The United States and Japan: Conflict and Cooperation under Mr. Reagan," in Oye et al, *Eagle Resurgent?*

15
The Pitfalls of Containment

Alan Tonelson

No one can approach the task of critiquing containment without considerable trepidation. Of course, the past forty years have been filled with criticisms of different varieties of containment and of the means chosen to implement containment. But relatively few challenges have been raised to the principal ideas behind containment as it has been practiced throughout the postwar era—the view that a fundamental goal of U.S. foreign policy should be opposing Soviet expansionism wherever it takes place, as well as its corollary: that the United States has vital interests in the security of every part of a world that represents a seamless security web.

Indeed, critiquing these core ideas of containment is tantamount to critiquing not simply the only broad foreign policy strategy that the United States has known in the lifetimes of most living souls but the very nature of international affairs as they have evolved since 1945. One might as well, it seems, carp about reality itself. It is no accident that the memoirs of one of containment's chief architects are titled *Present at the Creation*.

Thus to challenge containment fundamentally would seem to require a soaring flight of imagination. It puts the onus on the critic—especially on the critic sympathetic to the idea of strategic independence—to imagine alternate realities and strategic postures at least arguably better than the ones shaped by containment.

Nevertheless, despite the title of Acheson's memoirs, containment was borne of an act not of God but of humans. Containment came not from the mountaintop but Foggy Bottom. It has been the product of imperfect creatures with imperfect knowledge. More specifically, containment has been a human response to specific, inherently transient circumstances, not a manifestation of eternal truths. Historian Lloyd C. Gardner has written that "to see the Cold War as a struggle between two scorpions in a bottle reduces history to a cast of witless characters."[1] The same holds for containment.

Thus, even if containment was, if not the only possible way to meet the United States' international wants and needs during the late 1940s, nevertheless a defensible, justifiable way to do so, the question still remains: Is containment a defensible, justifiable way to meet the United States' international wants and needs today?

In my view, the ineffective record of U.S. foreign policy for the past twenty-five years indicates that the answer is "no." If containment as the animating idea of this foreign policy merits much of the credit for its early postwar successes, surely it deserves an equal amount of the blame for its more recent failures. And these are much less a matter of defeat in Vietnam, or humiliation at the hands of Persian Gulf oil kingdoms or Shiite Muslim radicals, or confusion and impotence in the face of potential security challenges in its own Caribbean backyard, than of a long-running imbalance between available foreign policy resources and objectives. This gap is weakening the critical foundations of U.S. security: its economic vitality, its economic sovereignty, its technological prowess, and the health of its democracy. Staggering trade and budget deficits, the recent stock market turbulence, and the Iran-contra scandals are only the latest and most dramatic signals that the economic and political system of the United States can no longer bear the costs of a foreign policy based on containment.

The strand running through this indictment is the charge that far from protecting the most important U.S. interests, containment has encouraged their neglect. Worse, containment, as conceived four decades ago and practiced faithfully since then, could have only led to these results. The strategy is irremediable. There exists no improved, say, more selective, version of containment that policymakers can turn to, for two principal reasons.

First, the containment strategy is not based primarily on a plausible definition of U.S. interests. Indeed, it is based primarily on no specific definition of U.S. interests whatever—that is, on no finite set of specific, intrinsically important foreign policy objectives, be they needs or wants. Instead it flows largely from an analysis of the international system that the United States operates in, and particularly of the threats that the nation faces. The assumption is that correctly identifying the principal trends and threats present in the system will illuminate the best possible policy responses.

Second, containment has always been far more than a cut-and-dried response to the foreign policy challenges of 1947, 1967, 1987, or any other year. It has also been a characteristically American response to these challenges. Containment's implementors have not been machines that perceived problems with perfect accuracy and objectivity and that then devised the simplest, most logical, or most efficient solutions possible. They have been individuals who are the products of a specific society, and as such they have been imbued with the psychological, moral, cultural, and intellectual heritage of that society. More specifically, containment is a reflection—in many ways the quintessential expression—of three ideas about international relations and the nature of the international system that have influenced U.S. foreign policy since the founding of the republic.

Threats and Interests

A nation's foreign policy can ultimately navigate by one of two conceptual lodestars. The first is securing or protecting a specific set of foreign policy assets, however they are threatened. These assets receive emphasis because of their perceived intrinsic importance to a country's fortunes. The second lodestar is countering and ultimately neutralizing powers whose very existence as well as activities are perceived to be threatening. The nation choosing this strategy may respond to the moves of the power viewed as a menace even if these moves do not threaten assets of intrinsic importance. All governments— from Western-style democracies to communist dictatorships to theocracies— face this conceptual choice. The two lodestars often cannot be kept completely separate, and a wise foreign policy must inevitably be influenced by both to varying extents. But eventually one will prove dominant.

The architects of containment saddled the United States with a threat-based strategy. This is not to say that since the late 1940s, U.S. officials have never thought in terms of protecting intrinsically important assets. George Kennan, for example, frequently urged the United States to focus on Japan and Western Europe because of their industrial and military potential. In fact, this focus has led historian John Lewis Gaddis to argue that Kennan's original version of containment was interest based and that preoccupation with threats came only with the adoption of NSC-68 in 1950.[2]

Yet Kennan's writings during this period, including the landmark 1947 article in *Foreign Affairs* that first outlined the containment strategy, refer too frequently to the need to halt Soviet expansionism wherever it occurred to characterize NSC-68 as a sharp break in U.S. strategy. Sometimes Kennan's language was unambiguously universalist. Other times he sought to describe certain kinds of Soviet challenges that did not warrant U.S. responses, but his criteria held little promise of producing restraint or selectivity in practice.[3] Moreover, one would be hard pressed to show that before or after the X article, U.S. leaders have spent nearly as much time and energy debating different sets of U.S. interests as the nature of the threat to these interests. And serious debate on the latter topic has been rare enough.

The choice of threat-based over interest-based analysis has been a serious mistake. All else being equal, interest-based thinking provides a sounder grounding for foreign policy because it accords more closely with fundamental maxims of strategy. An interest-based policy flows from relatively knowable considerations. Although defining one's own needs and wants is hardly simple, it is still inherently much easier than assaying someone else's. When dealing with other countries and cultures, the problem is compounded. And it is rendered that much more difficult in the case of the Soviet Union, which is not only alien but highly secretive. As Kennan acknowledged in the *Foreign Affairs* article, titled, "The Sources of Soviet Conduct," "There can be few tasks of psychological analysis more difficult than to try to trace the interaction of [ideology and circumstances] in the determination of official Soviet conduct."[4] And, ironically, James Forrestal, whose determination to find the key to Soviet motivations was matched only by Kennan's, once confessed that "I doubted if even the Russians themselves" knew what their actual objectives were.[5]

In addition, the focus on threats rather than interests has tended to lead to an excessive focus on an adversary's intentions as opposed to capabilities, as threat-obsessed policymakers find themselves constantly wondering where and how the adversary will strike next. But analyzing adversaries' intentions involves dealing not only with relative unknowables but with intangibles as well—with mind reading as opposed to bean counting. The record of analysts in this field, in fact, has been less than impressive. In 1972, for example, Kennan ventured that Soviet power had mellowed considerably since 1947, when "The Sources of Soviet Conduct" was published.[6] Yet less than three years later came the burst of Soviet adventurism in the Third World that helped to scuttle détente. Just as important, the focus on intentions, and especially on Soviet motives, assumes that in international affairs, one can distinguish fairly easily between offensive and defensive actions. History, however, contains many instances of empires, including the Russian empire, expanding for avowedly defensive reasons.

Concentrating on intentions also makes it very difficult to control the costs of foreign policy. It is hard enough to estimate the costs of defending another country or region against a military threat or of strengthening it through foreign military or economic aid, but in theory it can be done. Yet how can one estimate the costs of forcing a breakup or a mellowing of Soviet power? And since subversion is a relatively cheap method of aggression, containment actually helped the Soviets overcome their overall resource disadvantage in relation to the United States.

As a result, containment also gives the Soviets the capability to force the United States into a dangerously overextended posture. And strategic overextension in turn has weakened the domestic economic base that is the ultimate source of U.S. strength and prosperity. Although U.S. leaders throughout the era of containment have been keenly aware of the limited resources available to implement containment, its logic has forced them time and time again to violate maxims of sound economic policymaking and jeopardize domestic economic health to preserve an overly ambitious foreign policy.

The pattern was set by the authors of NSC-68, who recommended closing the gap between the nation's available resources and foreign commitments by simply stimulating economic growth through demand management techniques.[7] Such Keynesian policies spurred noninflationary growth as long as U.S. domestic social spending remained modest. In the early 1960s, however, the Kennedy administration's attempt not only to replicate the Truman military spending policies but also to expand the welfare state significantly initiated an addiction to inflation and deficit spending that the United States has still not kicked. At the same time, the foreign military deployments, foreign aid programs, and private direct investment abroad that reflected U.S. international predominance also contributed to sizable balance of payments deficits. Rather than adopt fiscally sounder policies, which would have inevitably entailed some reduction in the U.S. world role but also created a firmer foundation for long-term economic strength, U.S. leaders chose to sustain their overextended position through political pressures on allies to hold onto dollars despite their declining value.[8]

In addition, throughout the post–World War II period, the enormous U.S. defense establishment has siphoned off valuable funds and talent from research and development on civilian goods and surely hampered the long-term competitiveness of civilian industry. Finally, both monetary and security considerations led the United States to acquiesce in blatant protectionism by Japan and members of the European Economic Community long after their postwar recoveries were complete. Restrictive allied trade practices clearly contributed to the decline of many key domestic industries.

Another strategic problem presented by a threat-based policy is its surrender of initiative to the adversary. Walter Lippmann first noticed this in 1947 in a series of columns for the *New York Herald Tribune* that marked the first comprehensive public critique of Kennan's "X" article.[9] Lippmann observed that Kennan's proposal to apply counterforce wherever Soviet expansionism reared its head would permit Moscow to dictate the place and often the terms of each individual confrontation. Just as important, such a policy would give the Kremlin control over the breadth of engagement around the world.

Which Threat?

Finally, a threat-based foreign policy raises the knotty question of which threat one is responding to. Most lists drawn up by U.S. postwar makers of foreign policy have included outright Soviet invasion of another country, but after this obvious choice, the going gets tricky. What, for example, about subversion—something that Washington is still struggling to identify and define, as the endless controversy over Nicaraguan arms shipments to the Salvadoran rebels has demonstrated. What about Soviet intervention in a conflict at the request of another country—a phenomenon whose nature and implications for the United States are not clarified by calling it adventurism. What about purely internal, albeit violent, developments abroad that result in setbacks for the United States, such as civil wars and revolutions? Even worse, what about peaceful, purely internal events abroad with equally adverse consequences, such as elections that bring communists or other anti-American groups to power?

Nothing has been more responsible for the confusion of post–World War II U.S. foreign policy—and particularly the confusion of the post-Vietnam period—than the difficulty of determining "Which threat?" It is directly responsible for the rhetorical contortions and contradictory actions that have repeatedly undermined U.S. foreign policy's domestic support and created grave doubts abroad the judgment and reliability of the United States.

Lacking a firm conception of national interest with which to organize definitions of the threat, U.S. foreign policy has been chasing a will-o'-the-wisp for much of the past four decades. Was the threat communism itself? Since Yugoslavia bolted from the Soviet bloc, it has been clear that nothing about a nation's domestic ideology need cause problems for the United States. The current relationship with China illustrates this point even more strikingly. Was the threat the expansion of Soviet power and influence? If so, how can the latter be reliably identified or measured? And wouldn't the requirements of prudence force Washington to assume that every left-wing political movement at large in the world was an actual or potential Soviet ally and to oppose their attaining power? Moreover, what of anti- or non-Soviet movements whose triumph could create problems for the United States?

In the interests of creating a stable world out of wartime chaos, President Truman portrayed his 1947 call for big infusions of U.S. economic aid to Greece and Turkey as an attempt to prevent violent changes in the international status quo. He argued that the imposition of totalitarian regimes anywhere in the world would jeopardize U.S. security.[10] Yet neither Truman nor any of his aides ever explained why this should be so. Moreover, Truman himself retreated from this standard only two years later when a violent change in the status quo occurred in the world's most populous country, the PRC. The president and his party paid for their universalist rhetoric as the public understandably judged them according to universalist standards. And still the problem remained of responding to peaceful changes in the status quo adverse to the United States. Clearly communist electoral victories in France or Italy in the late 1940s would have endangered the United States more than a North Korean conquest of South Korea in 1950.

The failure to recognize national interest, not threats, as the best foundation for U.S. foreign policy has had American leaders turning rhetorical cartwheels and even descending into unvarnished absurdity as they sought to justify their foreign policy actions and inaction. For example, shortly after he urged the Truman administration to present its Greek-Turkish aid request in apocalyptic terms, Senate majority leader Arthur Vandenberg introduced legislation granting the United Nations a veto over the Truman Doctrine.[11] Granted, U.S. influence then in the world organization made such a veto extremely unlikely; still, Vandenberg's measure hardly buttressed the case that the fate of Western civilization hinged on blunting communist advances in the Aegean.

Korea provided even worse examples of top-level foreign policy confusion. Before the communist attack of June 1950, not only Dean Acheson but General Douglas MacArthur had in public statements all but explicitly placed Korea outside the U.S. defense perimeter in the Far East.[12] Indeed, in the autumn of 1947, the Joint Chiefs of Staff reported to Truman that the United States had little strategic interest in maintaining its occupation units on the peninsula, and earlier that summer, General Albert C. Wedemeyer argued that if war broke out in the Far East, U.S. units in Korea would represent a military liability.[13] Yet the North Korean invasion plunged the United States into a full-fledged conventional conflict that lasted three years, costing more than 33,000 dead and $54 billion.

All the same, in the middle of the war, while debating the British on the merits of opening cease-fire negotiations, Acheson suggested that getting thrown out of Korea militarily was preferable to the United States to starting talks during a period of relative military weakness. Explained Acheson cryptically, "We would have made our point."[14]

U.S. policy during the Vietnam War continued this tradition. What was the United States battling? Soviet expansionism? Chinese imperialism? North Vietnamese aggression? Aggression itself? Dictatorship? Communism? During the Kennedy-Johnson years, all of the above were given as answers at various times, though logically these goals were not necessarily identical. In his renowned speech at the Johns Hopkins University in April 1965, when he proposed a billion-dollar economic development scheme for communist as well as noncommunist Southeast Asia, Lyndon Johnson declared, "The rulers in Hanoi are urged on by Peking. . . . The contest in Vietnam is part of a wider pattern of aggressive purposes."[15] In his memoirs, Johnson even spoke of resisting the designs of a "Djakarta-Hanoi-Peking-Pyongyang axis."[16] Yet in February 1966, the president described the nation's purpose as "simply put, to prevent the forceful conquest of South Viet-Nam by North Viet-Nam."[17]

This emphasis on stopping aggression was one sign of U.S. leaders' concern with an inherently problematic set of dangers that may be called process-oriented threats. Citing these threats suggested that the United States was at least as concerned with how unfavorable outcomes came about in Southeast Asia as with the outcomes themselves. Thus Dean Rusk told the Senate Foreign Relations Committee during its highly publicized Vietnam hearings in 1965 that "if the war in South Vietnam were . . . merely an indigenous revolt, then the United States would not have its own combat troops in South Vietnam." What occasioned direct U.S. military intervention, according to Rusk, was "the effort of North Vietnam to impose its will by force."[18]

This rationale for military intervention implied that the United States would acquiesce in a peaceful communist triumph in Vietnam (for example, through the ballot box)—a message that Rusk surely did not wish to convey at the time. Yet at the outset of the Kennedy administration, White House adviser Walt W. Rostow told a Soviet journalist that the United States was indeed willing to accept peacefully elected communist governments. "What we find objectionable, and a threat to the peace," he explained, "is when a system is imposed by a small militant group by subversion, infiltration, and all the rest."[19] Neither Rusk nor Rostow ever explained how this position could be squared with the official insistence that the cold war was an ideological as well as a strategic struggle. Nor did they explain why the strategic risks posed by a peaceful communist triumph anywhere in the world would be more tolerable than those of a forcible communist triumph.

The confusion intensified during the Nixon-Ford administrations. As revealed throughout the memoirs of Richard Nixon and Henry Kissinger, the reality of impending U.S. military withdrawal from Southeast Asia forced U.S. officials from one unconvincing rationale for prolonging the agony to the next—and often back. With no durable notion of the threat—not to mention of U.S. interests—American leaders variously spoke of the need to maintain a noncommunist South Vietnam, to ensure that South Vietnam could determine its own fate, to give South Vietnam a fair chance to determine its own fate, and, finally, to withdraw in such a way as to preserve American honor—a goal that critics charged masked a cynical attempt to ensure a "decent interval" between the U.S. pullout and Saigon's collapse, in order to preserve U.S. credibility.[20] In fact, the last imperative was probably the most powerful all along. As early as 1965, national security adviser McGeorge Bundy suggested that the main threat U.S. policymakers faced in Vietnam was "the charge that we did not do all we could."[21]

Nor has official confusion cleared up in the post-Vietnam era. U.S. descriptions of threats have only become more byzantine—especially the less significant the threatened region or country. Asked to explain Washington's concern with Soviet-Cuban intervention in the Angolan civil war during the mid-1970s, Kissinger explained that the United States could not "remain indifferent while an outside power embarks upon an interventionist policy— so distant from its homeland and so removed from Russian interests."[22] Of course, these criteria might have legitimized Soviet intervention in Afghanistan four years later.

During its early years, the Reagan administration justified its blanket hostility to left-leaning Third World regimes by pointing to the so-called Kirkpatrick thesis. Here, the former U.N. ambassador argued that Third World dictatorships fell neatly into two categories: leftist totalitarian and rightist authoritarian. Even more convenient, the former were not only more abhorrent morally and less susceptible to reform than the latter, they were held to be invariably hostile to the United States as well. Kirkpatrick's dichotomy was scrapped in the face of rather disingenuous congressional and naive public calls for an evenhanded U.S. human rights policy. But had it survived, it would surely have foundered on the fact that few Third World regimes are well organized enough to satisfy any classification scheme.[23]

Kirkpatrick's thesis is only one example of a distinctive post-Vietnam variant on threat-based foreign policy—what may be called analysis-based foreign policy. In other words, many U.S. foreign policy thinkers in and out of government have recently sought to anchor U.S. foreign policy not to a notion of interests or even of specific threats but in analyses of the international scene stressing the behavior of specific states or groups of states, the dynamics of the current international system, and allegedly predominant trends and currents in world history. No wise foreign policy can neglect these factors, but these analyses alone lead to no definitive policy conclusions because they say nothing specific about the nature of U.S. interests.

The liberal mainstream of the Democratic party and its academic advisers have produced most of the analysis-based foreign policy thinking so far. For example, they have promoted the view that takeovers of Third World countries by radical forces can usually be accepted by the United States because these movements are generally homegrown, not Soviet creations, and primarily nationalistic, not communistic. Often the liberals add that economics will always force new radical governments to seek good relations with the West. But the liberals fail to acknowledge that even homegrown radical regimes can deal serious blows to the United States—witness the Iranian theocracy. They consistently underestimate the role that political ideology and religion can play in the revolutionary process, particularly in the all-important short run. Confident liberals also evade the question of how Washington should respond to takeovers by out-and-out Soviet clients. One suspects that most of these liberals would still shy away from military intervention.[24]

Indeed, two other analysis-based arguments seem to have been developed by liberals to deal with this problem, at least obliquely. The first contends that the world has entered a revolutionary new phase of international politics in the last twenty years—call it the age of interdependence—in which the utility of military force has declined steeply and that of economic and diplomatic power has risen correspondingly. The second is the dogma of multilateralism and its corollary, regionalism. These hold that the United

States should not intervene in foreign conflicts if its allies do not like the idea or if local countries signal disapproval. (No one any longer seriously argues that Washington should wait for U.N. approval before springing into action.) In other words, other countries generally know best, because of greater overall diplomatic experience and expertise, simple proximity, or reasons not explicitly stated.

The age-of-interdependence argument, however, seems to be belied by the continued insistence of most other nations on arming themselves to the teeth. Military might may be on the wane, but the word has clearly not spread far beyond the liberal think tanks. And even if the interdependence thinkers are right, what should the United States do until the word does spread? Sit back and confidently await the inevitable collapse of foreign military ventures? And even if the New Agers would have us react vigorously—and most would, since their definitions of U.S. vital interests are usually just as universal as that of the "militarists"—what if their preferred diplomatic and economic tools do not work either? Does the United States simply accept defeat stoically? Is a setback easier to bear because it reflects "the right side of history"?

Similar questions arise concerning multilateralism and regionalism. As many neoconservatives have charged, too often these positions have served as covers for inaction and defeatism. The multilateralists and regionalists refuse to acknowledge that U.S. interests do not always overlap with those of the allies—much less with those of nonaligned Third World states located near trouble spots.

The countries of Central America, for example, have one overriding objective: to prevent the United States from throwing its weight around the hemisphere too overtly and thus polarizing and destroying their fragile internal political balances.[25] They can hardly be blamed for their concerns, but their situations hardly create confidence that these countries will move swiftly and vigorously to respond to violations of a Central American peace plan. The regionalists in particular also fail to explain what sound principle of statecraft argues for giving a veto over U.S. national security policy to regimes that—in most of the Third World—are pathetically weak, hopelessly corrupt, abominably brutal, or some combination of these. Finally, what do the multilateralists and regionalists advise when the allies or local states are split on the question of intervention? How do we decide whom to listen to?

At the same time, noninterventionists have not been completely innocent of the sin of analysis-based thinking either. Many of today's most cogently reasoned calls for severing or reducing U.S. security ties with various allies depend on a series of predictions about other countries' behavior that "cannot be proved. And . . . cannot be disproved," to use Kennan's forty-year old phrasing.[26]

These noninterventionists may be called the new pluralists. To oversimplify a bit, they argue that the bipolar international system that emerged after World War II was unnatural and could not last. Power had to diffuse, they contend, and many point out that much economic power has already diffused. The major obstacle to Western Europe and Japan, in particular, doing more to defend themselves is the absolute security guarantee they still enjoy. Take it away, say the new pluralists, and these allies will, however reluctantly, become self-reliant once again. History, they contend, shows that nations balance, not bandwagon, in the face of imposing military threats.[27]

The problem is that no one knows for sure. What if the new pluralists are wrong? What if history does not repeat itself? What if Western Europe and Japan permit themselves to become Finlandized? For all of their cogent criticisms of current alliance arrangements, the new pluralists are unlikely to convince mainstream opinion to make the case that the minuses of U.S. alliance commitments today so outweigh the pluses that the United States would be better off even if the Atlanticists' worst fears came to pass. Although they have performed a valuable service in reminding Americans that alliances are not free, the new pluralists need to examine the costs and benefits of U.S. alliances much more closely and comprehensively than they have to date.

Containment's Nonrational Side

One of the greatest obstacles to finding a basis for U.S. foreign policy other than containment is the insistence of its advocates that circumstances since 1945 have permitted no alternative. As Eugene V. Rostow, a leading maker of U.S. foreign policy throughout the postwar era, stated as recently as December 1987, "There are no alternative strategies for the future. We must pursue, reform, and improve the strategy of collective security we have been trying to build for the last forty years, or perish."[28] But containment was hardly a value-free response to these circumstances. Much more research will be needed to determine just how influential "rational" and "nonrational" considerations have been, but an essential first step is to recognize that a nonrational side has existed.

Three clusters of characteristically American beliefs and values regarding the international system and foreign relations stand out as nonrational sources of containment. Since each has shaped U.S. diplomacy since the days of the founding fathers, it is no surprise that they have shaped containment as well. The first cluster proceeds from the notion that the world in which U.S. foreign policy must operate is something that is unfinished structurally and destined for systemic change. Since the eighteenth century, the conviction that neither individual foreign countries and territories nor the international system itself has yet reached its final form, and that they may well reach this form in the policy-relevant future, has led Americans to view international affairs as a teleological phenomenon. And the notion of progress so central to the entire post-Enlightenment Western intellectual tradition has produced the idea that the end toward which international affairs are moving is a happy one: a world free of power politics and conflict and free as well of the need to conduct foreign policy in the first place.

The unfinished-world belief has also induced Americans to distinguish sharply between peoples—which are seen as permanent players on the world stage—and governments—which are seen as all too transient. Hence the long-standing American views that (1) a state's domestic character largely determines its foreign policy behavior; (2) war is unnatural (attributable primarily to the existence of nondemocratic governments); and (3) establishing a pacific world environment of popularly governed countries must be a principal U.S. foreign policy goal, not simply an American aspiration.

Containment has embodied many of these convictions. Most important, containment was a teleological concept from the beginning. As is widely known, in the "X" article Kennan portrayed containment as a policy that could promote the breakup or mellowing of Soviet power. Indeed, Kennan tantalizingly suggested that either of these aims could be substantially accomplished through frustrating Soviet expansionism for between ten and fifteen years. In addition, Kennan's original *Foreign Affairs* analysis was based squarely on the proposition that the Soviet Union's internal makeup was the decisive determinant of its external behavior. Transform the system, and the reasons for U.S.-Soviet conflict would vanish.

More broadly, one cannot study the memoirs of containment's other architects without being struck by their certainty that they would and could create a new world out of the ashes of war. Even leaders who privately snickered at the idea of purging armed conflict from international relations contributed to the raising of popular expectations by repeatedly mouthing idealistic words in public. Moreover, consider the energy they devoted to setting up the Bretton Woods system, as well as the frequency with which they spoke of creating and preserving world order. Clearly these both reflected a belief that if conflict and economic nationalism could not be eliminated, at least they could be controlled and managed on a worldwide basis.

The second cluster of beliefs revolves around the practice that U.S. foreign policy has inherited from England of searching for standards of foreign policy behavior not necessarily linked to national interest. The geographic isolation and relative security of England and the United States has always afforded their leaders more latitude in the international arena than their continental and European counterparts enjoyed. Often freed from the philosophically cut-and-dried imperative to obey necessity in foreign affairs, English and American statesmen have been able to search for other lodestars to guide their diplomacy.

Kennan, of course, opposed basing U.S. foreign policy on general principles and advocated a particularistic approach. But his failure to sustain an interest-based rationale for containment left the field open for a futile but quintessential American search for non-interest-related standards that continues today.

The moralism of U.S. foreign policy is one widely noted product of this search for standards; as international relations theorist Arnold Wolfers has observed, a belief that human existence often permits choice has always been associated with efforts to construct systems of ethics.[29]

This moralism has not only fostered traits such as naiveté and self-righteousness in U.S. foreign policy. It has encouraged Americans to view the rest of the world as an undifferentiated whole—a signal characteristic of every strategy of containment. Since the mainstream of Western philosophy teaches that morality is not divisible and that moral precepts cannot be selectively applied without fatally weakening them, Americans have naturally tended to see the world that these precepts are supposed to govern as indivisible as well. Consequently Americans do not naturally differentiate among states or regions in their conduct of foreign affairs. The sole exceptions have been the Western Hemisphere and the Far East. The special attention devoted to these regions has reflected no strategically coherent sense of U.S. foreign policy priorities but a belief that these lands and their allegedly decadent, non-Western cultures lay outside the state system. Therefore the United States could play active roles in their affairs without dirtying its hands participating in power politics.

Another underappreciated by-product of moralism relevant to containment is what may be called psychologism—the practice of investing states with human traits. Attributing state behavior to the kinds of emotional-psychological drives that determine human behavior, such as greed and aggression, Americans have developed little appreciation of the irreconcilable security dilemmas forced on most countries by an anarchic world system. Therefore they have developed little appreciation of impersonal national interests as a major factor in state behavior at all. As a result, U.S. foreign policy has focused more on system-wide purges or control of these undesirable traits than on assessing how their own specific interests relate to those of other states or regions.

At the base of containment is the psychologistic notion—generated understandably by the tragic events of the 1930s and 1940s—that the primary threat to peace and freedom in the world comes from the so-called aggressor nations—ruthless, ambitious states motivated mainly by greed and power lust. U.S. foreign policy rhetoric since the 1930s has continually emphasized these points, referring to imperial Japan, fascist Italy, Nazi Germany, and later the Soviet Union and the PRC as "predators," "gangsters," or "international outlaws" that threatened countries that were "peace loving" and "law abiding." Kennan's description of the Soviet Union clearly fits this pattern, and his prescription of counterforce for blocking Soviet expansionism comes rather close to turning foreign policy into a matter of crime and punishment, although by the mid-1950s, Kennan was stressing the need for diplomatic solutions to the cold war, especially in Europe.

The third cluster of ideas is less distinctively American than the first two. It is based on the view that sharp distinctions cannot and should not be drawn between the international and domestic arenas. Its most important ramification is the insistence that the ideas of nation on the one hand and a larger world mission on the other are inseparable. Indeed, the sine qua non of nationhood is seen as a conscious effort to play a part as a nation in the epic of human history. Just as important, this international activism is justified less in economic or security terms than for its allegedly beneficial effects on the American character and the health of American democracy. The key point is not the content of the self-perceived mission of the United States in world affairs but the view that the United States must seek its destiny in the international sphere.

The post–World War II record of U.S. foreign policy—speeches, proclamations, memoirs, scholarly studies, journalistic accounts—repeatedly shows that containment, and internationalism itself, springs in large part from an elemental belief that playing an active world role is something that the United States should do for its own sake. Some have argued for activism because it is in some unexplained sense "proper" for a country as powerful as the United States. As Truman stated in his radio address to the delegates who had just signed the U.N. Charter in San Francisco in 1945, "It is . . . the duty of . . . powerful nations to assume the responsibility toward a world of peace."[30] Others have described foreign policy as a test of national character. But all have insisted that domestic development by itself is a narrow, parochial, and unworthy objective for the United States.

Nothing so became the "X" article, for example, as its conclusion, a twentieth-century call to manifest destiny that deserves to be quoted at length:

> The issue of Soviet-American relations is in essence a test of the overall worth of the United States as a nation among nations. To avoid destruction, the United States need only measure up to its own best traditions and prove itself worthy of preservation as a great nation.
>
> Surely there was never a fairer test of national quality than this. In the light of these circumstances, the thoughtful observer of Russian-American relations will find no cause for complaint in the Kremlin's challenge to American society. He will rather experience a certain gratitude to a

Providence which, by providing the American people with this implacable challenge, has made their entire security as a nation dependent on their pulling themselves together and accepting the responsibilities of moral and political leadership that history plainly intended them to bear.[31]

After the Truman Doctrine speech of March 12, 1947, a *New York Herald Tribune* editorialist was somewhat more down to earth: "What the President was saying was that if the American system is to survive, it must prove its value—just as the totalitarian system has been trying to prove its own value—as an article of export." George Marshall and Dean Acheson, for their part, spoke contemptuously of those who would turn their backs on this test of national worth. "Now that an immediate peril is not plainly visible," said Marshall in a February 1947 speech at Princeton University, "there is a natural tendency to relax and return to business as usual, politics as usual, pleasure as usual."[32]

Reacting at a press conference to Herbert Hoover's Fortress America speech of December 1950, Acheson said that the lessons of the 1930s had led Americans to reject "any policy of sitting quivering in a storm cellar, waiting for whatever fate others may wish to prepare for us."[33] To be sure, Acheson assailed on strategic grounds as well Hoover's recommendation to concentrate U.S. resources on hemispheric defense. But his language strongly suggests that he was at least equally upset with what he considered the cowardly nature of the proposal.

Foreign Policy after Containment

If there can indeed be foreign policy without, or after, containment, what would such a foreign policy look like? Any discussion of defining U.S. interests more precisely must begin with this fundamental premise: beyond core security considerations such as maintaining military security and political independence, in a strong, secure democracy, the task of defining interests is an inherently subjective exercise. Americans must decide on a set of interests through the political process and reconcile their needs and wants in the world with the amount of resources they are willing to spend on behalf of these objectives.

Thus one primal fear expressed by containment's proponents need not come to pass. Thinking about interests as opposed to threats or general doctrines does not make isolationism inevitable. Indeed, in theory, an interest-based foreign policy could be quite ambitious. Yet the mood of the electorate today indicates that Americans favor balancing resources and commitments by reducing the latter rather than by increasing the former.

A sound noncontainment foreign policy could be based on the following strategic principles.

First, the fundamental purpose of U.S. foreign policy is to sustain and, where feasible, to increase U.S. military strength and economic vitality and to preserve its economic and social freedoms. Struggling with the Soviet Union for international predominance or advancing the cause of freedom worldwide are only possible means to these ends, not ends in and of themselves.

Second, U.S. calculations of foreign policy costs and benefits will emphasize tangible measures of economic and military strength, not symbolic considerations.

Third, in these calculations, the United States will assign greater weight to the security imperatives of preserving political freedom of action and achieving greater economic self-sufficiency and place less emphasis on achieving a more efficient use of global resources. Efficiency-oriented policies have too often weakened the U.S. economy and U.S. security.

Since the mid-1930s, U.S. foreign economic policy has assumed that an expanding international economic pie serves U.S. interests on net, and it has sought to stimulate this growth by dismantling international barriers to trade and capital movements. Yet in a world of chronically insecure and therefore fiercely competitive nation-states, efficiency cannot be the only goal of foreign economic policy. Nations rightly also strive to preserve their economic sovereignty and to control their own economic destiny. And where possible, they seek to use economics as a weapon in their struggle for security, either by hoarding or protecting their own strategically or economically valuable resources and industries or by denying such strategic assets to adversaries.[34]

The results of the single-minded preoccupation of the United States with efficiency are all around us: dangerous national dependence on foreign sources of strategically important commodities and goods such as oil and advanced computer chips; an astonishingly passive acceptance of the decline of critical industries as the inevitable consequence of changing international patterns of comparative advantage; lax technology transfer policies; and actual encouragement of a growing national addiction to foreign capital. The policy imperative is not to abandon efficiency and rush down a mercantilistic, autarkic path. Instead, it is to strike a much better balance between efficiency and security concerns—all the more necessary if the United States wants to maintain the economic base to function as the free world's military and economic leader.

Fourth, U.S. actions in the international arena will flow first from analyzing relatively knowable factors, primarily its own international requirements and preferences, instead of relatively unknowable factors such as ultimately unprovable theories about adversary motives or about emerging trends in world affairs.

A policy that accords with these principles and with the public mood would significantly reduce the scale and costs of U.S. world involvement over the long run. Politically and militarily, the policy would feature a tighter focus on North America (including Mexico), Western Europe, and Japan, plus new measures to redistribute the burden of Western defense where necessary.

As important as Western Europe and Japan are, they are not worth the indefinitely continued weakening of the U.S. economy—the certain result of endless trade and budget deficits made inevitable by the continued massive subsidization of allied defense. Western Europe would be pressured to increase its military spending first by an announcement that U.S. NATO-related spending will be frozen at current levels and that perceived shortfalls in Western conventional military postures will henceforth be made up by allied governments. If the allies meet the shortfall, the United States would maintain its conventional contributions and retain the option of increasing them if and when economic conditions permit.

If allied governments did not make up the shortfall within a specified period, the United States would begin to phase out the great bulk of its ground troops over a specified period, leaving only a token conventional force. Large numbers of U.S. servicemen should not be assigned to carry out military missions to which Washington is unable and allied governments are unwilling to allocate adequate resources. Battlefield nuclear weapons would be withdrawn as well. In addition, in an effort to make the most cost-effective contribution to the security of this still important region, the United States might offer to increase its conventional air power in Western Europe. The United States would not formally withdraw its nuclear umbrella from Western Europe. But a smaller U.S. trip wire would clearly reduce the pressures on a U.S. president to risk nuclear holocaust to save U.S. soldiers facing Soviet attack. At the same time, such a force would symbolize at relatively low cost continuing U.S. solidarity with NATO-Europe. And the United States would retain the option of nuclear retaliation, thus preserving a degree of what McGeorge Bundy has called "existential deterrence."

This policy would transform NATO from the grudgingly accepted U.S. protectorate that it is today to a genuine alliance: a group of equals each contributing what it wishes to counter a commonly perceived threat. Such a posture would also return NATO to the original expectations of its founders on both sides of the Atlantic. The end result would be a much-reduced U.S. military presence in Western Europe (for inflation alone will turn a spending freeze into a force-cutting mechanism), but the pointedly finite level of commitment would be appropriate and strategically sensible in regard to allies demonstrably unwilling to mount an adequate conventional defense.

U.S. options are necessarily more limited regarding Japan, which represents an increasingly more valuable strategic prize. Washington should freeze spending on Japan-related forces and tie future increases—even to keep up with inflation—to the removal of Japanese trade barriers, tariff and nontariff. And instead of pressuring Japan to increase the share of its GNP devoted to defense, the United States should press Tokyo to finance a portion of those U.S. military deployments directly affecting Japanese security, notably in the Persian Gulf, and to contribute more economic assistance to strategically important Asian countries.

Whatever economic benefits the United States loses as a result of diminished hegemony over Western Europe and Japan could be more than compensated for by improved economic performance due to the greater availability of funds for domestic investment. Rebuilding domestic economic strength is also a more reliable path to prosperity than extorting favors and special treatment from increasingly resentful allies.

Regarding oil and the Persian Gulf, the aim of the United States in the long run should be to reduce the importance of the gulf. The United States should greatly diversify its sources of energy by aiding in the construction of more Middle East oil pipelines to replace gulf shipping lanes; encouraging further diversification of worldwide crude oil production, especially in the relatively unexplored Third World, stimulating increased domestic oil production and greater conservation (including some form of oil import fee or gasoline tax and the elimination of incentives for oil companies to expand reserves by "drilling on Wall Street" rather than exploring ecologically); and restoring federal support for renewable energy sources that has been cut by the Reagan administration. Until these policies begin to take effect, significant resources will have to be spent preserving the flow of oil through the gulf.

Economically, the new U.S. foreign policy would make a much greater effort to tally the near-term, concrete costs of U.S. trade and monetary policies and to maximize the benefits through greater receptivity to departures from international regimes. For example, through increasing numbers of bilateral trade agreements with countries prepared to conform with U.S. standards on government subsidies, market access, fair labor practices, and other indexes of fair trade, the United States would develop a trade policy that more accurately reflects the diversity of its trading partners and trade relationships. The United States would also feel freer to establish explicit political and military quid pro quos in exchange for access to its market. The present GATT (General Agreement on Tariffs and Trade) system, by contrast, leads Washington to apply uniform practices and standards to free market and socialistic, openly mercantilistic and free trading states alike.

Regarding the Third World, the new interest-based foreign policy would feature much less active support for human rights; a much more standoffish attitude toward Soviet activity (which should be of little or no concern unless it affects regions of genuine importance to the United States); and a foreign aid program that reemphasizes bilateral channels where feasible as well as explicit political, economic, and military quid pro quos with aid recipients.

But at the moment, with containment still so solidly entrenched in the official mind, it is less important to push any particular non-containment-based U.S. foreign policy than to urge Americans to begin thinking about interests. The fundamentally new U.S. foreign policy that is needed will not be adopted lock, stock, and barrel from a journal article or a conference paper. It will instead emerge gradually from the push and pull of the political process. In addressing foreign policy problems, policy analysts will not be able to impose their own answers on the body politic. But they can prompt Americans to ask the kinds of questions that can lead to sound and durable conclusions.

Notes

1. Lloyd C. Gardner, *Architects of Illusion: Men and Ideas in American Foreign Policy, 1941–1949* (Chicago: Quadrangle Books, 1970), p. xi.

2. John Lewis Gaddis, *Strategies of Containment: A Critical Appraisal of Postwar American National Security Policy* (New York: Oxford University Press, 1982), p. 95.

3. Ibid., pp. 27, 28, 30; Gardner, *Architects of Illusion*, p. 293.

4. George F. Kennan, *American Foreign Policy, 1900–1950* (New York: Mentor Books, 1951), p. 89.

5. *The Forrestal Diaries*, ed. Walter Millis with the collaboration of E.S. Duffield (New York: Viking, 1981), p. 72.

6. " 'X' Plus 25: Interview with George F. Kennan," *Foreign Policy* 7 (Summer 1972): 13.

7. Gaddis, *Strategies of Containment*, pp. 93–94.

8. David P. Calleo, *The Imperious Economy* (Cambridge: Harvard University Press, 1982), pp. 10–14.

9. See Walter Lippmann, "The Cold War," *Foreign Affairs* 65 (Spring 1987): 869–84.

10. Joseph Marion Jones, *The Fifteen Weeks* (New York: Harcourt, Brace & World, 1955), p. 272.

11. Ibid., p. 184.

12. Dean Acheson, *Present at the Creation: My Years in the State Department* (New York: W.W. Norton, 1969), p. 357.

13. Harry S. Truman, *Memoirs, Vol. 2: Years of Trial and Hope* (Garden City, N.Y.: Doubleday, 1956), 325, 346.

14. Ibid., p. 407.

15. *The Vietnam Reader*, rev. ed., ed. Marcus G. Raskin and Bernard B. Fall (New York: Vintage Books, 1967), p. 345.

16. Leslie H. Gelb and Richard K. Betts, *The Irony of Vietnam: The System Worked* (Washington, D.C.: Brookings Institution, 1979), p. 107.

17. Ibid., p. 188.

18. *The Vietnam Hearings,* intro. J. William Fulbright (New York: Vintage Books, 1966), pp. 4, 238.

19. Gaddis, *Strategies of Containment,* p. 210.

20. Arnold R. Isaacs, *Without Honor: Defeat in Vietnam and Cambodia* (New York: Vintage Books, 1984), p. 490.

21. Gaddis, *Strategies of Containment,* p. 267.

22. Lynn E. Davis, "Containment and the National Security Policy-making Process," in *Containment: Concept and Policy,* ed. Terry L. Deibel and John Lewis Gaddis (Washington, D.C.: National Defense University Press, 1986), 1:121.

23. See Alan Tonelson, "Human Rights: The Bias We Need," *Foreign Policy* 49 (Winter 1982–1983): 52–74.

24. See Alan Tonelson, "The Real National Interest," *Foreign Policy* 61 (Winter 1985–1986): 49–72.

25. See Tom Farer, "Contadora's Hidden Agenda," *Foreign Policy* 59 (Summer 1985): 59–72.

26. Kennan, *American Foreign Policy,* p. 104.

27. See David P. Calleo, *Beyond American Hegemony: The Future of the Western Alliance* (New York: Basic Books, 1987); Christopher Layne, "The Real Conservative Agenda," *Foreign Policy* 61 (Winter 1985–1986): 73–93.

28. Eugene V. Rostow, "A Breakfast for Napoleon: There Is No Alternative Strategy" (paper prepared for discussion at a Cato Institute conference, "Collective Security or Strategic Independence? Alternative Strategies for the Future." Washington, D.C., December 2–3, 1987), p. 2.

29. *The Anglo-American Tradition in Foreign Relations,* ed. Arnold Wolfers and Lawrence B. Martin (New Haven: Yale University Press, 1956), p. xxi.

30. Truman, *Memoirs,* 2:291.

31. Kennan, *American Foreign Policy,* p. 106.

32. Jones, *The Fifteen Weeks,* pp. 103, 172.

33. Acheson, *Present at the Creation,* p. 490.

34. David P. Calleo and Benjamin M. Rowland, *America and the World Political Economy: Atlantic Dreams and National Realities* (Bloomington: Indiana University Press, 1973), pp. 128, 138–39.

16
The Requisites of Containment

Earl C. Ravenal

Since the beginning of the cold war, U.S. national strategy has been devoted to the containment of the Soviet Union and Soviet-inspired communism. In that time, the "paradigm" of this national strategy has consisted of two basic elements: deterrence and forward defense or alliance—both devoted to containing communist power and influence. Deterrence is roughly equated with strategic nuclear forces; the United States seeks to maintain at least a balance of strategic nuclear arms with the Soviet Union and to provide a nuclear umbrella over its allies and various other countries. Forward defense or alliance involves U.S. protection, mostly by means of general-purpose forces, of allies and other countries that occupy strategic positions or have sympathetic social and political values.

It has often been said that containment has stood the test of time. Yet compared to what? Containment must be arrayed against its costs, the expectations held of it, and the projected costs and expectations of alternative doctrines of national strategy. Indeed, containment has been subjected to critiques from both sides: that its costs and risks are excessive, and that its accomplishments have been meager and a more ambitious strategy is in order.

The problem with the strategy of containment has been the continuing high costs associated with the requisite military preparations and the occasional egregious costs of heightened crises and regional wars; and the risk, under certain circumstances, of being plunged into nuclear war. The costs can be attributed mostly to the generation of conventional forces, primarily for the defense of Europe; the risks can be attributed to reliance on the earlier use of nuclear weapons, also particularly in a confrontation arising from a conventional war in Europe. To some extent, cost can be transmuted into additional risk, and risk can be transformed into mere cost. (That is what is meant by lowering or raising the nuclear threshold.) But the choice itself arises from the policy of containment of the Soviet Union.

So containment must be judged by its requisites, and by the capacity—political, social, and economic—of the system to sustain those requisites. Indeed, the debate about the requisites of containment is the main game in town. Though one misses an explicit, full addressal of the issue and consideration of the alternatives, containment underlies, and is implicit in, all the surrogate debates conducted on various topical points of policy (including those on the future of NATO). But the requisites of the grand strategy of containment are tangible; it must be—and is being—paid for. And the only tangible alternative to containment (that is, an alternative that makes a real and significant difference) is the position of disengagement. Therefore, unless containment is confronted more or less directly, and unless disengagement is considered as a viable policy alternative, national security debates will be unreal—symbolic, at best—certainly transitory in their results; policy "solutions" will be incomplete and precarious; and the costs (in all dimensions of cost, including not only fiscal and economic, but also social, political, and constitutional) borne by American society will be persistent and disabling.

The Price of Defense

Perhaps the present U.S. national strategy could be tolerated, if it could be demonstrated that its cost could be trimmed without impairing the ability to implement the strategy, and if the nation found itself in comfortable fiscal circumstances. But neither is the case. Powerful critics have asserted, with considerable empirical support in the quantification of global and regional power balances, that even what the Reagan administration requested for defense, let alone what Congress finally granted the administration, was grossly insufficient to execute the tasks of containing Soviet communism around the world. Leonard Sullivan, Jr.'s estimate for projecting a confident conventional defense against Soviet arms is as follows:

> Expanding our conventional forces by 20% over the next 10 years to offset the numerically, qualitatively, and geographically expanding threat requires that defense outlays rise . . . to 9½ of the GNP [and that defense authorizations rise to 10%].[1]

That 10 percent, applied to the probable 1988 GNP of $4.77 trillion, would mean a defense budget authorization of $477 billion.

If anything, the United States is spending too little, not too much, to implement the policy of containment.[2] Another way of displaying this fact is to note the continuing shift of strategic concern to the Persian Gulf at the relative expense of Europe. This process, begun in what could be called the second Carter administration (after the fall of the shah of Iran in January 1979), can be measured in terms of the number of U.S. land divisions, tactical air wings, and naval carrier battle groups primarily allocated to the gulf (for 1989, $5\frac{2}{3}$ land divisions and an equivalent portion of tactical air and surface navy, out of a total of 21 land divisions, army and marine). Explicit acquisition of this "new" area of strategic responsibility would not be troublesome, were it not also for the administration's assumption of multiple simultaneous deployments. In his fiscal year 1986 posture statement, Secretary of Defense Caspar Weinberger stated:

> Our forward-defense strategy dictates that we be able to conduct concurrent deployments to widely separated areas of the globe. Our present goal is to achieve the capability to deploy forces to a remote theater such as Southwest Asia, while maintaining an acceptable capability to reinforce NATO and key areas of Northeast Asia.[3]

The intention to deploy forces simultaneously raises the issue of double counting. A close reading of the force allocation embodied in the secretary's statement indicates that, to some extent, the Pentagon intends a double assignment of certain units—characteristically for the Persian Gulf and also for Europe or East Asia and the western Pacific. This not only violates the First Law of Thermodynamics but raises the question of the strategic overextension of general-purpose forces. In more general terms, it suggests an imbalance of commitments and resources.

This problem did not originate with the Reagan administration. It has characterized U.S. force planning since the two-and-a-half war doctrine of the Kennedy administration and even the one-and-a-half war doctrine of the Nixon administration—and before either of those the Eisenhower administration. But the Reagan administration has somewhat exacerbated the contradiction with its implication of a wider strategic scope of simultaneous responses to Soviet aggressions and with its more tangible implementation of the commitment to defend the Persian Gulf and Southwest Asia, without significantly increasing the force structure or overall military manpower. Of course, there is no law against creating such gaps and contradictions; and they can be maintained, often for some time, since these states of affairs are not always tested sharply or conclusively by events. But ultimately, events— or the foreshadowing of events by analysis—will challenge these relationships; and something will have to give.

The urgent question, then, is whether the United States can afford even its present scope of containment, let alone the more rigorous, demanding, and consistent version of the Reagan administration's strategy proposed by its still more hawkish critics. How can the United States pay for it and in what ways? For surely it must be paid for. What the United States faces, at the end of the Reagan administration, is a crisis of solvency, in several pertinent sense of the word: not merely fiscal solvency but also a gross misalignment between the country's strategic objectives in the world and its manifest willingness to pay for them.

It will not do for proponents of vigorous containment to impugn the patriotism of those who see the situation itself arguing for significant retrenchment, or to dismiss the fiscal problem by reciting the abstract proposition that the economy could support even higher defense spending— for example, by sharply raising taxes. The fact that there are options does not make them more desirable or politically feasible. All of the fiscal options (taxes, inflation, more government borrowing) are not simply unpalatable, but destructive. Resources (and support) are not automatically granted; to be available to the state, they must be mobilized from society, which is the base and context of the state. Even if the government could balance its books by exacting more resources in the form of taxes (and possibly also conscription at low military wages) to support a large defense establishment and extensive foreign commitments, that would be just the end of one problem and the beginning of another. Solvency means that the external and internal stances of the country comport with each other. An extensive, engaged foreign policy and a large, active military posture require big, intrusive, demanding government. If, as Americans were promised by the Reagan administration, they were to have a more reserved, less extensive government, then they must have a more detached, disengaged foreign policy. The dilemma has been especially cruel for the conservative president who said in his first inaugural address that "government is the problem."

The Problem of Analysis

The broad challenge to contemporary U.S. foreign policy is how to perpetuate containment of the Soviet Union in an era of multiple constraints, both international and domestic. Some of these constraints are limits, and thus are more or less unalterable. Others are trade-offs—that is, the price Americans have to pay to achieve certain objectives of their state and society by containing the Soviet Union. They must consider whether society is really committed to pay that price—not just rhetorically, but objectively—that is, not just in the verbalizations of a crust of elites, but in the supportive actions of all of society, taken as a policymaking system. The question of the perpetuation of containment will not be determined by its abstract desirability, or even by its "necessity," but rather by whether containment is viable strategically and consonant with domestic values. Among those values are economic solvency and the quality of society, including accustomed freedoms and the unique political system that Americans undertake to defend in the first place.

That is a profound and complex question. Yet, in typical critiques of containment, the goal of containing the Soviet Union is assumed; it is taken as indispensable, not challengeable in itself. True, various constraints— budgetary, demographic, resource, popular support—are often enumerated.

But such exercises generally move abruptly, negligently, and optimistically to a proposed series of mild correctives. Questions relating to the sufficiency of the proposed moves are begged, simply in the way the moves are described. Often, as a centerpiece of these proposals, certain force multipliers or other gimmicks are suggested, such as dual missioning of forces—that is, treating as expeditionary forces, available for broader regional assignments, the units the United States keeps in Europe and Northeast Asia. Such superficial analyses and wishful prescriptions usually ignore the obvious dilemma: that global flexibility can be achieved only by robbing the primary areas of some measure of protection.

Such proposals fail because of their underlying methodology, a way of thinking that characterizes much of the current debate on containment itself. In a nutshell, containment may be a nice idea, but foreign policy is not made of attractive ideas peddled with competitive virtuosity and zeal. Certainly a policy such as containment is not self-executing; there are the essential questions of what may be needed to implement the policy, whether those things will be forthcoming, and at what price. Only in the context of these questions can Americans understand the scope of choices—even understand what it means to choose. Most policy writing, whether official or critical, consists of lists of things that "must" be done. Rarely is it based on an assessment of costs, limits, and feasibility, or a comparison of alternatives. Rarely does it invoke numbers or even imply quantities of things that must be exacted or expended. Gaps are bridged, if at all, by pure verbalisms, exhortations of will, or the mere advocacy of shifts in our orientation.

But policy, particularly foreign policy, is not a set of items that must be obtained, preserved, or remedied in the world, without reference to situation or contingent cost. It is certainly not the official expression of objectives of state. Rather, policy is an entire system's probable responses to future contingent challenges over a range of issues and geographical areas. Many of the elements that form these responses will not be determined by national authorities. Some policy determinants consist of institutional, military, and resource dispositions that make it more likely that the country will respond in a certain way. Other determinants include situations at the time of future decisions or actions, also to varying degrees beyond control, though not totally beyond prediction. That is why the description of a proposed foreign policy must begin by tracing the constraints of the international and domestic systems. These are the starting points in the partially predictive process that indicates what foreign policy orientation "ought to" be.

This kind of real-world analysis must be applied to containment as the emblematic U.S. foreign policy of the past four decades. An old expression inquires whether the game is worth the candle. In our critique of containment, we should ask: (1) What is the game? (2) What is the requisite candle? (3) Can we afford the candle? And (4) is there another game in town?

Universality and the Mirage of Selective Containment

We start with the name of the game: the concept of containment. At the outset, we encounter an essential dispute: Was containment originally intended to be universal in its application? More interestingly, is containment by its very nature—or rather by the nature of the threat it is designed to meet—universal?

A literal reading of George Kennan's original text (though he seems to have done his best, for almost all of the period that his doctrine of containment has been extant, to obscure and alter, and even to oppose, this interpretation) indicates that containment was to be universal.[4] (It was also—again contrary to Kennan's current interpretation—to be forceful, and only temporary because it embodied the hope of reforming Soviet conduct.) Indeed the "original" George Kennan made containment's universality the centerpiece of his analysis of Soviet conduct in 1947, in his celebrated image of the Soviet threat:

> Its political action is a fluid stream which moves constantly, wherever it is permitted to move, toward a given goal. Its main concern is to make sure that it has filled every nook and cranny available to it in the basin of world power.

Further, Kennan prescribed

> a long-term, patient but firm and vigilant application of counter-force at a series of constantly shifting geographical and political points, corresponding to the shifts and maneuvers of Soviet policy . . . a policy of firm containment, designed to confront the Russians with unalterable counter-force at every point where they show signs of encroaching upon the interests of a peaceful and stable world.[5]

Kennan now claims that he has been grossly misinterpreted; that he always intended to emphasize geographical selectivity (that is, Europe and its approaches from the east, the south, and the sea), and to confine the U.S. response primarily to economic means—a retrospective exegesis, or prosthesis, that leaves his earlier disciples dismayed and his earlier critics incredulous.[6] Given Kennan's characterization of the Soviet threat, one wonders how a geographically and functionally limited U.S. response could have been sufficient. That is particularly so if the purpose of containment was not to make a token defense but to present Soviet leaders with such a prospect of frustration that the motives and dynamic of their society would be profoundly altered. Hydraulic metaphors, no less than their subject, should flow in all directions. If the threat is of such a character that there is a case for containing it at all, then containment must be universal. Selectively containing that kind of threat is like trying to hold water in a two-dimensional vessel.

Nevertheless, selectivity is the most prevalent kind of argument purporting to mitigate the need for extensive armament and deployments in the implementation of containment. It can take two forms: selectivity of commitment (the objectives of U.S. policy and strategy) and selectivity of means (the military forces and weapons).

Selectivity of commitment is proposed as a way of bringing obligations and costs into line (and also as a way of minimizing the occasions for war). The argument for selectivity fixes on places and defensive objects that make a difference according to some criterion. Virtually all proponents of selectivity would still contain adversaries in some sense; but they are selective in that they strive for some principle of limitation and impute to their more extreme opponents the scheme of universality.

Most proposals of selective intervention—as diverse as those of Kennan, Robert W. Tucker, Stanley Hoffmann, and Ernst B. Haas—are subject to the same problems.[7] All lead back to, or are operationally indistinguishable from, the more comprehensive versions of containment. This is true in several respects:

1. They support virtually all the same objects of U.S. defense—objects, as it turns out, that comprise the major portion of present and projected U.S. defense expenditures.[8]

2. They would implicitly support, in addition to the supposedly necessary prime objects, a host of minor, intrinsically dispensable objects "for the sake of" the major objectives.

3. When—and if—these proposals are costed out, they may turn out to be even more expensive than the supposedly universal schemes they would supplant. This is because, in emphasizing certain situations as vital, they tend to add these to all the others, which they are wary of discontinuing.

4. Finally, the logic of threat and response, coupled with the diagnosis of the nature or source of the threat, leads these supposedly limitationist arguments back to an espousal of any act or response that would constitute effective containment. Selectivity becomes universality, though the authors of these proposals sometimes disown or disfigure their intellectual offspring.

George Kennan starts by seeking a principle that limits U.S. political and military intervention and ends by asserting and implying a scope of instances that is tantamount to virtually universal involvement. Ironically, Kennan has been rewarded for this policy thrust with accusations of "isolationism."[9] In *The Cloud of Danger* Kennan advocates "the reduction of external commitments to the indispensable minimum . . . the preservation of the political independence and military security of Western Europe, of Japan, and—with the single reservation that it should not involve the dispatch and commitment of American armed forces—of Israel." (No doubt Kennan would now also include the Persian Gulf and Southwest Asia.[10] Evidence for this surmise is in Kennan's article on the op-ed page of the *New York Times* in the immediate aftermath of the Soviet invasion of Afghanistan in late December 1979, in which, after calling for "mature statesmanship," he hastened to reassure: "These words are not meant to express opposition to a prompt and effective strengthening of our military capabilities relevant to the Middle East. . . . [As for the] big stick . . . who could object?") True, Kennan would like to abandon "several obsolescent and nonessential positions: notably those at Panama, in the Philippines, and in Korea."[11] But he cannot deny the extent to which the primary commitments depend, physically and psychologically, on those "nonessential" positions.

In fact, one should not be unduly impressed by modifying and mollifying adjectives such as "limited," "selective," or "moderate." One must look for the operative clauses, almost as if the policy argument were a legal or diplomatic document. Most proposals of selectivity are not even intrinsically limitationist, because they retain much the same major objectives, the same logic, and the same pretexts for intervention as the proposals of the more extensive hawks. The imperative of containment overrides the qualifications.

The problem is generic to selective versions of containment. Containment, of its essence, must remain contingently open-ended—indeed, triggered by contingencies determined by the adversary. The circumstances of Soviet aggressive or expansive behavior are not subject to American definition and delimitation. Implicit in the definition of the "Soviet threat" is that the Soviets exercise the initiative. Therefore, once committed to containment, how can the United States keep it limited?

The problems of selectivity are seen even more clearly in the essay of Ernst B. Haas. Haas's plan "scales down and redefines some American world order values, recognizing that we cannot, without risking our own ruin, continue the attempt to mold the world in our image." It also aims at a "delinking of issues." Haas even permits himself to be skeptical of the existence of "a 'Soviet threat,' " or, for that matter, a "free world." But the main problem with Haas's prescription of "selective engagement" is the absence of any numbers—defense budget or military manpower projections.

Confronted with the question, "Where should we be ready to fight?" Haas recites the familiar litany: "Western Europe, Japan, South Korea, and the Pacific." To this, he adds "regimes so close to the United States as to afford the adversary an opportunity for offensive action . . . Canada and Mexico . . . Cuba." This is already quite a list. And Haas appends two nonstrategic criteria: "the military defense of all democratic countries against Soviet threats, provided these countries wish to be defended . . . [and] threats by allies of the Soviet Union against Third World countries with a democratic tradition." There is yet another, economic, objective: "key commodities that are essential for the economic welfare of the democratic countries."[12]

These proposed objects of U.S. protection are not in themselves absurd. The point is that, in the name of selectivity, they add up to a good part of the world—all the United States is now committed to defend, and perhaps more. My calculation is that the areas and objectives that Haas mentions are already costing the United States about $221 billion out of the $224 billion allocated to general-purpose forces in the 1989 defense budget. Verbal criteria, such as selective engagement, whatever else they might signal, do not save Americans much or absolve the United States from the risk of confrontation and escalation.

In the end, selective containment is not the only alternative to universal containment. Rather, it is just a middle position between universal intervention and consistent nonintervention (the uninvited guest at this contentious banquet). Limitationists think their middle positions must be more realistic because the extreme positions are unacceptable or unmentionable. But, contrary to its pretense of unique realism, this middle position, because of its contradictions and its operational correspondence with more extensive containment, is almost fictional. It is an artifact of the debate, not a real policy of state. The extremes of universal containment and consistent disengagement may be unpalatable, but that is just the point. The choice of extreme positions approximates the present predicament of the United States. In the face of this real and poignant choice, the formula of "selective" intervention or "moderate" containment is more an incantation than a proposal.

Defining the Containment Problem Away

Selectivity in its various forms is not the only false approach invented to avoid the burdens and risks of containment. Several positions of the liberal center and liberal left either deny the need to contain or attempt to subsume the containment paradigm in a new and presumably more acceptable framework.

Some of these arguments deny the empirical premise—the "threat"—

and attempt to explain away a succession of Soviet moves, both regional intrusions and arms buildups. There are three variants: (1) "we are still ahead"; (2) "their moves are not what you think they are"; and (3) "their moves are somehow our fault, reactions to our own provocations." All are the familiar stuff of the former revisionists of the cold war. These arguments have an increasingly hollow ring. They may be useful correctives, but over the past decade, they have had to become more imaginative, even more fanciful. For some reason, whether compensatory or aggressive, the Soviets have mounted a major political and military challenge to the West; at least they have done a collection of things that equate to such a challenge in the knowledge that they would be so interpreted. In distinction from such arguments, which would deny the problem in order to justify doing less, a realistic analysis would admit the seriousness of U.S. inaction in order to measure its consequences against those of doing what is sufficient to confront the problem directly.

Another attempt to solve the problem of the situation of the United States is to displace it, finding a surrogate goal that is more congenial or putatively more amenable to solution than the unilateral pursuit of security. The classic solution is to posit "world order norms," conditions of the international system that should be sought instead of the narrower and presumably more contentious security interests of the United States. An elaborate expression of this thesis is Stanley Hoffmann's book, which embodies in its title the choice he sees as meaningful and critical: *Primacy or World Order.*[13] As Hoffmann puts it:

> We should strive for the advent of an international system that goes beyond the past forms of moderation characteristic of balance-of-power eras. The resort to force and the accumulation of weapons will have to be drastically curtailed by a combination of balances of force and cooperative schemes for arms control and the settlement of disputes. Interdependence will have to be made bearable and beneficial both by collective management and by the reduction of excesses of mutual dependence or of the dependence bred by inequality—so that the actors will be provided with greater autonomy and with a greater sense of security.

In prescribing the pursuit of world order goals, Hoffmann seems under the sway of the image he has invented to describe world politics: the chessboards. This image suggests that statesmen can, at will, play on this or that board (strategic, political, economic) to the exclusion of other boards, where they can leave the game dormant; or that they can default on one board and move to another, with no time limit on their moves. But the functions of world politics are more like overlays than separate boards. In every national move, statesmen operate on several levels simultaneously.

They trace on one and, without willing it, also on the others. Even if there are chessboards, it is not entirely up to the players to determine which board to play on or when to switch from one to another. They play when summoned by challenges, and it is the requisite of security that usually defines the challenge, and other players who determine the occasion.

In any case, the kind of world order we would recognize as congenial or livable would include a vast component of U.S. primacy. World order is not self-enforcing, and no one can hope for overarching impartial mechanisms or wish for the dominance of another great power. So in the critical cases it would even be hard to distinguish world order from effective U.S. primacy. More important for prescribing U.S. security policy, it would be hard to distinguish the amount of power needed for the more direct and comprehensible tasks of self-protection from the amount—presumably Hoffmann would say the lesser amount—sufficient to establish world order. Indeed, it might take a concentration and persistence of U.S. power far in excess of the more modest requirements of U.S. security to enforce world order. That effort would often be misspent, and might also be frustrated. A simple will to move the international system toward a more cooperative, managed basis would likely meet the residual suspicion of major U.S. antagonists in the world, or the competition of ambitious, rising regional contestants, or the hostility of a myriad of other, less powerful but dissatisfied nations that do not relish the intrusive U.S. distribution of the things of the world, however constructive Americans may think it is.

The Question of Means

If the objects of containment cannot be selectively limited, and the containment problem itself cannot be defined or subsumed out of existence, perhaps some relief from the burdens of extensive containment can be found in the means through which the policy would be executed. One approach is to assert that military means are interchangeable with nonmilitary means and that the substitution is a matter of choice or preference. But this proposition is not much more than a placebo. To propose nonmilitary means, or any other kind of means, one must have in mind certain interests that might be served or protected by them. Of course, everyone hopes that, in a crisis of conflicting interests, diplomacy, economic inducements, and sympathetic ties will help resolve the problem. But it is fair to ask: What if those nonmilitary instruments do not work? Or if they work only because military instruments lurk in the background—that is, if they depend for their efficacy on the threat of force? Simply to ignore this problem is to be thrown back on a nonpolicy: hoping that nothing happens.

The argument for nonmilitary means amounts to a displacement—

actually a transcendence—of the security problem. One version is represented in the current writings of George F. Kennan. It is his hope to "demilitarize" the foreign policy of the United States, and the Soviet Union, too, relying on other means to achieve the ends of security—or to arrive at another kind of security. In this case, Kennan, who pleads so humanely for the right outcomes, relies on a diagnosis that is ultimately false and arrives at prescriptions that are misleading and distracting. Kennan's attitude toward the current Soviet challenge and the predicament of the United States is expressed poignantly in an article called "Cease This Madness"—an impassioned appeal directed to the leadership of both the United States and the Soviet Union.[14] Laying about him evenhandedly with imputations of blame—equating, for example, the Soviets' depriving their youth of liberty with our society's granting them too much liberty—he proceeds to impugn the "madness" that underlies the "dreadful militarization of the entire East-West relationship." He avers: "For the maintenance of armed forces on a scale that envisages the total destruction of an entire people there is no rational justification."

There is no question that Kennan is describing a real peril to humanity, but his remarks only underscore the tragic predicament of both nations: the perverse but still recognizable rationality of arms competition. What one could call, ruefully, strategic interdependence is not madness in the ordinary sense of the word. Kennan's frequent charge of "militarization" and his rather vague advice—"thrust [these] destructive powers . . . from you"—in the end simply reflect his long-standing impatience in the presence of military factors, an impatience born of the disdain of the diplomatist to do his homework in the military stuff of the strategic nuclear age. What remedy follows from this dual ascription of cause: madness and militarization? Simply, that "the decision-makers of the two superpowers . . . should . . . take their military establishments in hand and insist that these become the servants, not the masters and determinants, of political action"—as if the military created the foreign policies of either state.

A variant of the argument for nonmilitary means is the well-worn thesis of the disutility of military force. This is another attempt to avoid the price, and even the calculus, of U.S. national objectives. The argument plays upon an equivocation: that U.S. military power, in relation to that of others, is in decline, and that military power in general is less usable, less translatable into political advantages.

It is probably true that the pure application of military force is declining in its effect on situations, that it is increasingly cost-ineffective, and that its means are becoming more widely diffused among multiple centers of political and strategic initiative. But military force is still integral to the structure of international relations. Indeed, the debate that underlies assessments of the efficacy of military force is over the extent to which the structure of the international system is determined by strategic or nonstrategic factors, resting in turn on the distribution and exploitation of military or nonmilitary resources and advantages.[15] And, of course, military power, if asymmetrically possessed in a particular situation, can be decisive.

As for nonmilitary means, one can cite a variety of instruments to influence other parties, through incentives as well as threats.[16] Everyone favors nonmilitary instruments where they are appropriate. But to defend, decisively and confidently, a nation's security, one needs force, at least residual force. If the object is to minimize the use of military force, the task is to devise a system and a foreign policy that do not occasion violent intervention. Nonmilitary means might have to be taken into the calculus, but they do not excuse us from the calculation.

An associated confusion arises when we ask whether our political leaders could enhance U.S. power in the world by mobilizing national will. It had become a fashion to deplore the supposed absence of presidential leadership— at least until the Reagan restoration of 1981, in which the United States was dealt the semblance of presidential leadership in spades. The absence of this commodity was deplored precisely because it was felt that will was not only the necessary but a sufficient condition for restoring U.S. influence in important international situations.

Pundit-journalists, professorial strategists, and even many national security bureaucrats talk almost obsessively about will. Foreign challenges and probes are seen as tests of U.S. resolve; Vietnam was a "trauma" that impaired the capability to respond to threats; the United States is paralyzed by a "failure of nerve." But this terminology itself is a tissue of anthropomorphisms and reifications. We are not talking about will in some primal personal sense; the responses referred to are not subjective psychological phenomena. We are talking about the operation of a complex political and social system—not even an organism except in a partially useful but mostly misleading metaphor. "Will" represents a construct—that is, a complex resultant or relationship, which includes as one interactive component the ability of a president to generate and sustain the support of the rest of the political system for some specific purpose. What we are really describing, then, is the structure of a problem and the structure of the system that deals with the problem.

Policy, far from being a matter of pure choice, an object of will, is more determined by constraints, both external and internal. (Thus, if there was a trauma that was occasioned by the Vietnam War, it has to be analyzed in terms of the altered operation of the U.S. political system. The most important fact "about" Vietnam is what it revealed about the constrained operation of the U.S. system and the constrained ability of the nation to coerce the conduct of others in the international system.) Above all, what is not appreciated, even by those who consider themselves makers of foreign policy, is that you do not "make" foreign policy as you make boats or houses or gadgets or soup. The question is not even "who" makes policy, but "what" makes policy.

To determine the responses of the U.S. system, then, we cannot look to factors of will, predilection, or even intention. Rather, we are thrown back on the analysis of the strategic orientation that is conditioned by our preparations and built into our institutions, and our capabilities and constraints. Those factors constitute, respectively, the logic and the logistics of national action. They are both what makes certain responses seem "necessary" and what causes other responses to be impossible.

An Alternative to Containment

The entailments and disabilities of the policy of containment suggest consideration of a major, coherent alternative. Such a policy would be one of strategic disengagement and nonintervention. In such a program both of the cardinal elements of the present U.S. strategic paradigm would change. Instead of deterrence and alliance, the United States would pursue war avoidance and self-reliance. U.S. security would depend more on abstention from regional conflicts and, in the strategic nuclear dimension, on finite essential deterrence.

These are not rhetorical terms. Although an extensive statement of their meaning and their implications for U.S. forces is not possible here,[17] suffice it to say that the U.S. military program would be designed to defend the most restricted perimeter required to protect core values: the political integrity of the United States and the safety of its citizens and their domestic property. That is a much smaller perimeter than the one the United States is now committed to defend. It would defend against military threats directed against the homeland. That is not, in the first instance, an overtly geographical criterion, and deliberately not. The United States should not be fixated on drawing lines in the sand, though this is the simplest and most comprehensible exercise. Rather, we should be concerned to characterize correctly the nature and import of other countries' actions and appreciate the characteristics of foreign events that cause us to consider them "threats." Functional criteria may be less definitive than geographical ones, but they are more important. In a program of nonintervention, the United States would defend against an umbra of direct threats to those values that are so basic that they are part of the definition of state and society. Because those values are inalienable, their defense must be credible. It would also defend against a penumbra of challenges that are indirectly threatening but are relevant because of their weight, momentum, direction, and ineluctability. We would be looking for a new set of criteria—decision rules—that condition and bound responses to future events that could be considered challenges. This is an intensive, rather than extensive, definition.

The concomitant is that the United States would encourage other nations to become self-reliant, to hedge. In fact, other countries that are foresighted already discount U.S. protection in a wide range of possible cases, despite formal U.S. obligations to come to their assistance. This does not imply that all these countries face imminent threats, simply that some are impressed more by the reality of U.S. circumstances than by U.S. reassurances and have drawn the appropriate conclusions.

War avoidance invokes primarily, though not exclusively, the strategic nuclear component of the counterparadigm. The United States will always need a strategy that discourages direct nuclear attacks on the homeland or intolerable coercion of national political choices by nuclear threats. But today, given the parity between the nuclear arsenals of the two superpowers, U.S. safety depends on maintaining a condition that is called crisis stability, wherein both sides have a strong incentive to avoid striking first with their nuclear weapons.

A design for nuclear stability would go like this: Since an enemy's first strike must logically be a damage-limiting attack against nuclear forces, the United States should eliminate its land-based systems as they become even theoretically vulnerable to a Soviet preemptive strike. These systems are inevitably vulnerable, despite the efforts of a succession of administrations to put them in multiple or closely spaced shelters (as with the MX) or to acquire a redundant and dispersed force (as with the prospective Midgetman single-warhead missiles). Instead, the nation should move to a dyad of strategic nuclear forces: submarines, and bombers armed with medium-range air-launched cruise missiles. Then in its targeting doctrine, to discourage further a Soviet first strike, the United States should not aim at Soviet missiles. (Nor does it make any strategic or moral sense to aim at Soviet cities.) Rather, it should develop a list of some 3,000 military targets, such as naval and air bases, concentrations of conventional forces, military logistical complexes, and arms industries that are relatively far from large civilian population centers.

Finally, since nuclear war is most likely to occur through escalation by the United States in the midst of conventional war—probably in Europe or possibly in the Middle East—Americans must confront their attitude toward the first use of nuclear weapons. I believe the United States should impose upon itself an unconditional doctrine of no first use of nuclear weapons.

The two elements of war avoidance and self-reliance constitute a new paradigm. They amount to a principled policy of nonintervention that is consistent enough to merit the status of a major alternative. We would no longer consider peace to be seamless and indivisible. There might well be continuing troubles in the world, including cases where a Soviet-sponsored faction perpetrates a forcible revision of the local military balance. If the United States were to intervene, it might win a few rounds (witness the obvious example of Grenada in November 1983). But the list of feasible interventions is far shorter than the list of desirable ones, and even shorter than the list of "necessary" ones.

But we must respond to the expected, and frequent, charge that a noninterventionist foreign policy would lay the world open to Soviet expansion or revolutionary violence. In the last analysis, a true noninterventionist position does not depend on trust in Soviet intentions. There are critics, mostly on the political left, who would reduce defense expenditures and have the United States withdraw from its foreign positions because they see the "Soviet threat" as trivial or nonexistent. But a consistent noninterventionist position takes Soviet power seriously. It simply accepts the possibility of the United States suffering some foreign losses in order to preserve the integrity of its own economy, society, and political system.

Yet there are reasons to doubt the unvarnished projection of a Soviet political-military windfall. They depend on a more sophisticated calculus of the motives—the propensity to intervene—of a potential aggressor, on an unavoidably complex analysis of the course and future of the international system, and on a somewhat speculative projection of the status of Western Europe without the United States.

Just how the Soviet Union would react to a noninterventionist U.S. foreign policy is difficult to determine. However, a potential aggressor will not simply consider the odds of victory or defeat, but must weigh whether potential gains, minus the costs of achieving them, exceed what could be achieved without attacking. That is a very different—and a much more discouraging—calculus.

Beyond that, a serious proposal of nonintervention must make some assumptions about the world—that is, the global political-military balance, specifically between the United States and the Soviet Union; the situation in important regions of the world; and, particularly, the fate of Western Europe.

The case for nonintervention is made largely in terms of the evolving international system, offering increasing challenges and temptations but also imposing greater costs and risks for less ample and less secure gains, arrayed against the constraints of the domestic system—social, economic, political— which are themselves becoming tighter and more troublesome. This leads to a consideration of the characteristics of the emerging international system, in which, more than upon which, U.S. foreign policy will have to operate. At issue is the changing shape of the international system.

The world—the international system—is not just an inert environment for the making of foreign policy, or so much malleable clay or putty for the designers of an active and manipulative foreign policy. The structure or design of the international system, it is true, is in some senses a proper object of foreign policy. But it is also, in important ways, a determinant of foreign policy. More precisely, the world is to be taken more as a set of parameters, or givens, than dependent variables. The external environment and its evolutionary possibilities constitute a framework within which each nation must choose. The parametric characteristics of the international system are to some extent alterable by individual nations, more or less according to their power. And, to be sure, the United States, now and in the foreseeable future, will, preeminently among the individual nations, have the ability to set and modify those parameters through its own choices and actions. But these characteristics and possibilities of the international system are parameters precisely in that it requires a further expense or effort to alter or widen them, and that effort might be less efficient than a policy of operating within the parameters.

The world that we will confront as we move beyond the turn of the millennium will evolve further from the world that we have experienced during the past four decades. We can identify six critical conditions:

1. The high probability of troubles, such as embargoes, expropriations, coups, revolutions, externally supported subversions, thrusts by impatient irredentist states, and calculated problems of defense perimeters.

2. Increasing interdependence. But this has a different implication from the one that proponents of interdependence would recognize. Interdependence is a set of functional linkages of nations: resources, access routes, economic activities and organizations, populations, and the physical environment. These areas harbor problems that could be aggravated to the point where they become threats to the security of nations, demanding, but not suggesting, solutions.

3. The probable absence of an ultimate adjustment mechanism, in the form of a supranational institution that can authoritatively police the system, dispensing justice and granting relief, especially in those extreme cases that threaten to unhinge the system.

4. Unilateral interventions rather than collaborative world order.

5. Perhaps the most important condition: the unmanageable diffusion of power, beyond some ideal geometry of powerful but "responsible" states. Instead, this process is likely to proceed to a kaleidoscopic interaction of multiple political entities. By all measures of power—military (nuclear or conventional, actual or potential), economic (total wealth or commercial weight), or political (the thrust to autonomy and achievement)—there may be fifteen or twenty salient states, not necessarily equal and not necessarily armed with nuclear weapons, but potent to the point of enjoying the possibility of independent action. The diffusion of power will have several aspects. One is that limits will

become evident in existing unions, and cracks will appear in existing military alliances. Another aspect of diffusion is the impracticality of military power, whether nuclear, conventional, or subconventional. (That is not, however, to assert either the absolute or the relative disutility of military force.)

6. The incoherence of domestic support, not just in the United States but to a certain extent in all, and not just when political systems are free from external pressure, but precisely when they most need steady support. The lack of public support might not prevent intervention, but it might critically inhibit its prosecution.

The net result of these tendencies is that general unalignment, as a pattern or type of international system, is likely to succeed the present multipolar balance of power, just as the balance of power succeeded the earlier regime of bipolar confrontation. This would be a world of circumscribed regional powers. Although absolute disparities, technological and military, might increase, in terms of usable power there might be more of a convergence of the present superpowers, great powers, and middle powers, including some accomplished or would-be regional hegemones.

In the face of this, in most general terms, the policy choice for the United States is whether to attempt to control its environment or to adjust to its environment. The indicated prescriptive conclusion is that, although challenges and opportunities will arise, it will be increasingly unnecessary and undesirable for the United States to intervene in regional situations. It will be unnecessary because the very presence of either a regional hegemone or a partial hegemone or a perpetually conflicted situation will be an obstruction to the other superpower, or to any other external power. There would be less to worry about in our own abstention. It will be increasingly undesirable for the United States to intervene in regional situations because these situations will be messy and interminable. They will tend to be profitless, because intervention will be expensive and results, even if achieved, transient.

For the United States, the most important region is Europe. What would be the probable status of Europe without U.S. protection? I would envisage a Europe that is independent politically and diplomatically and autonomous strategically, that acts in greater military concert, though not political unity or strategic unanimity. Actually Europe could go quite far toward defending itself without help from the United States. It need not be Finlandized, either in whole or in part. If the United States were to withdraw, the principal European countries would probably increase their defense spending gradually, perhaps to 5 or 6 percent of their GNP. The countries of Western Europe, even if not formally united in a new military alliance, have the economic, demographic, and military resources, and the advantage of natural and man-made barriers, to defeat or crucially penalize a Soviet attack.[18]

The alternative of strategic disengagement and nonintervention is objective, substantive, and consequential. This judgment is reinforced by a comparison of costs. The United States can make large cuts in its defense budget if—but only if—it severely limits its foreign policy objectives. It could defend its essential security and central values with a much smaller force structure than it now has. Such a force structure would provide the following general-purpose forces: eight land divisions (six army and two Marine Corps), twenty tactical air wing equivalents (eleven air force, four Marine Corp, and five navy), and six carrier battle groups. With the addition of a dyad of nuclear forces, submarines and cruise missile–armed bombers, this would mean manpower of 1,125,000 (330,000 army, 300,000 air force, 360,000 navy, and 135,000 Marine Corps). The total defense budget at the end of the decade of adjustment would be about $150 billion in 1989 dollars. In contrast, the Reagan administration originally requested, for 1989, twenty-one land divisions and forty-four tactical air wing equivalents, with fourteen carrier battle groups; this force requires 2,138,000 men and a budget authorization of $291 billion.

These differences will multiply considerably unless the United States changes its course. The U.S. defense budget will be about $451 billion by 1998, and cumulative defense spending during that decade will be over $3.6 trillion. Under a noninterventionist policy, the 1998 defense budget would be 53 percent less, and the cumulative cost over a decade would be about $2.5 trillion.[19]

Conclusion: The Shape of the Debate

The case for nonintervention is not a pure prescription of a state of affairs that is inherently and universally attractive. It is prescription mingled with prediction. Nonintervention is proposed as an adjustment to the world as it is shaping up and to the constraints of the polity, society, and economy. The national orientation of the United States should not depend entirely on whether some objective, such as containment, is worthy of its commitment. Worthy causes are not free. There is a price to be paid, and that price has been growing higher. The multidimensional costs of containment (the specific acts and the general stance of perpetual preparedness) should be weighed against the consequences of not containing and not preparing to contain. Part of the prediction is that the United States, taken as a decision-making system, will not pay those costs.

The consistent pursuit of nonintervention by a nation will entail a fundamental change in its foreign policy and national strategy. It would have to test its foreign and military policies against the harder questions about national security. This means distinguishing sharply between the interests of allies and dependents and the interests of itself. We would also have to learn to differentiate interests from security. This is not to deny that our interests (defined in terms of the objective goals of actual individuals and organizations) are real, and mostly legitimate. It is rather to challenge the automatic notion that the United States must prepare to defend its panoply of interests by the use or threat of force, overt or covert, wholesale or piecemeal, through proxies or by itself.[20]

And it is to challenge the notion that milieu goals—the shape and character of the international system, balance in general or with a particular antagonist, and even the more abstract concept of order in the system—should be assimilated into the schedule of objects that the United States must pursue and, by implication, defend. Sometimes, in the typical inflated and debased political rhetoric of our times, these more abstract and generic milieu goals are disguised as more immediate, even vital, security interests. But "vital" should be reserved for those truly supreme interests that derive so strictly from our identity as a nation that they could not credibly be alienated, even by an official expression.

When put up against these more stringent criteria, most interests are alienable, in the sense that we can choose not to defend them against all kinds of threats. The United States can draw back to a line that has two interacting and mutually reinforcing characteristics: credibility and feasibility—a line that it must hold, as part of the definition of its sovereignty, and that it can hold, as a defensive perimeter and a strategic force concept that can be maintained with advantage and within constraints over the long haul.

Such a national strategy would not, admittedly, maximize gross U.S. "interests" in the world. But it would be designed to optimize the net interests of American society in the world, in terms of the value of these interests measured against the costs (and costs disguised as risks) of defending them. Ultimately, we may have to settle for less than we would like—even for less than we think we need.

Notes

1. "The FY Defense Debate: Defeat by Default," *Armed Forces Journal International* (May 1983).

2. This is an entirely different argument from that of the critics of containment who ridicule its passive stance and its failure to bring about the originally advertised downfall or evolution of the Soviet government. The latter point of view is sometimes labeled containment-plus. It is the program of, for example, most of the authors gathered in Aaron Wildavsky, ed., *Beyond Containment: Alternative American Policies toward the Soviet Union* (San Francisco: ICS Press, 1983).

Wildavsky himself denigrates existing U.S. policy as "minimal containment," "piecemeal resistance," and "defensive." He proposes to bring about nothing less than "political pluralization" within the Soviet Union—indeed, as a necessary condition for avoiding the eventual Soviet move to "subjugate" the United States. Yet—typically of such advocates—Wildavsky purports to eschew "physical force," instead begging the essential question by postulating the sufficiency of mere "political warfare"—a sort of Radio Free Europe writ large, a lot of noise at ramparts more substantial than the walls of Jericho. For instance, Wildavsky would "unmask" through "publicity" Soviet privilege and corruption, by "broadcasting . . . consumer information" to Soviet citizens.

The most that can be said for this sophisticated troublemaking is that it is cheap—except that Wildavsky and other such militant hawks would add it to, not substitute it for, everything else the United States is doing in the tangible defensive dimension.

3. *Annual Report*, FY 86, Secretary of Defense (Washington, D.C.: U.S. Government Printing Office, 1985), p. 39.

4. "The Sources of Soviet Conduct," *Foreign Affairs* (July 1947). Evidence of Kennan's mitigating interpretation is presented in John Lewis Gaddis, *Strategies of Containment* (New York: Oxford University Press, 1982).

5. Kennan, "Sources."

6. See " 'X' Plus 25: Interview with George F. Kennan," *Foreign Policy* (Summer 1972): 14ff, referring to Kennan, *Memoirs, passim*. My interpretation of Kennan's original intent is reinforced by a letter he wrote the next year, in which he said: "It is the Russians, not we, who cannot afford a world half slave and half free. The contrasts implicit in such a world are intolerable to the fictions on which their power rests. *The final establishment of communist principles can only be universal*. It assumes a Stygian darkness. If one ray of light of individual dignity or inquiry is permitted, the effort must ultimately fail." Unmailed letter to Walter Lippmann, April 6, 1948, quoted by Eduard Mark, "Mr. 'X' Is Inconsistent and Wrong," in Martin F. Herz, ed., *Decline of the West: George Kennan and His Critics* (Washington, D.C.: Ethics and Public Policy Center, 1978), p. 160.

7. George F. Kennan, *The Cloud of Danger* (Boston: Little, Brown/Atlantic Monthly Press, 1977); Robert W. Tucker, "The Purposes of American Power," *Foreign Affairs* (Winter 1980–1981); Stanley Hoffmann, "The New Orthodoxy," *New York Review of Books*, April 16, 1981, and "Foreign Policy: What's to Be Done?" *New York Review of Books*, April 30, 1981; Ernst B. Haas, "On Hedging Our Bets: Selective Engagement with the Soviet Union," in Wildavsky, ed., *Beyond Containment*.

8. The three main theaters, which virtually all proponents of supposed selectivity of U.S. commitment, intervention, and deployment would retain—Europe/NATO, the Middle East including the eastern Mediterranean and the Persian Gulf/Southwest Asia, and East Asia/Western Pacific—take $209 billion of the $224 billion for general-purpose forces, out of the $291 billion initially requested budget authority for fiscal year 1989. Thus, the peripheral regions, some part of which most proponents of selectivity might dispense with, take only about 5 percent of the defense budget. There may be good and even sufficient reasons for not intervening in such peripheral

areas, but they are not budgetary. In this respect, at least, selective containment is hardly less demanding than supposed global containment.

9. As Kennan's critic, Edward N. Luttwak, puts it: "There is no such freedom in determining whether X should be protected at all. The strategic goals of foreign policy are not to be decided by exercises in definition; they are defined for us by the very nature of our country, and by the circumstances of world politics." "The Strange Case of George F. Kennan," *Commentary* (November 1977).

10. "George F. Kennan, On Washington's Reactions to the Afghan Crisis: Was This Really Mature Statesmanship?" *New York Times,* February 1, 1980.

11. Kennan, *Cloud of Danger*, p. 230.

12. Haas, "On Hedging."

13. Stanley Hoffmann, *Primacy or World Order: American Foreign Policy since the Cold War* (New York: McGraw-Hill, 1978).

14. George Kennan, "Cease This Madness," *Atlantic* (January 1981).

15. This is a debate conducted by, among others, Seyom Brown, "The Changing Essence of Power," *Foreign Affairs* (January 1973), and *New Forces in World Politics* (Washington, D.C.: Brookings, 1974); and by Robert W. Tucker, "A New International Order?" *Commentary* (February 1975), and *The Inequality of Nations* (New York: Basic Books, 1977).

16. A striking inventory of such nonforcible—or at least nonviolent—means is presented in Richard W. Fogg, "Creative, Peaceful Approaches for Dealing with Conflict," *Journal of Conflict Resolution* (June 1985).

17. But see Earl C. Ravenal, *Defining Defense: The 1985 Military Budget* (Washington, D.C.: Cato Institute, 1984).

18. See the more ample treatment of this point in Earl C. Ravenal, *NATO: The Tides of Discontent* (Berkeley: University of California, Institute of International Studies, 1985).

19. These figures, based on official Pentagon estimates, assume 4 percent inflation plus 1 percent real annual increases. My alternative assumes 4 percent inflation only, with my prescribed cuts taken over a ten-year period.

20. As in the case of the Persian Gulf, some national interests cost more to defend than they are worth. See the analysis in Earl C. Ravenal, "Defending Persian Gulf Oil," *Intervention* (Fall 1984), and "The Strategic Cost of Oil," testimony before the Subcommittee on the Panama Canal and the Outer Continental Shelf, Committee on Merchant Marine and Fisheries, U.S. House of Representatives, 98th Congress, 2nd sess. June 27, 1984.

Index

About the Contributors

Doug Bandow is a senior fellow at the Cato Institute and a nationally syndicated columnist for the Copley New Service. In 1981–1982 he served as a special assistant to the president, studying manpower and strategic military requirements for the Office of Policy Development. He is also a former editor of *Inquiry* magazine. He is a regular contributor to such newspapers as the *New York Times*, the *Los Angeles Times*, the *Wall Street Journal*, and the *Washington Post*. Bandow holds a J.D. from Stanford University.

Terry L. Deibel is a professor of national security policy and associate dean of faculty at the National War College. Previously he was an assistant professor of international affairs at the Georgetown University School of Foreign Service. He has also been a policy analyst at the International Programs Division of the Office of Management and Budget and at the State Department's Bureau of Politico-Military Affairs. In addition, Deibel has been an international affairs fellow at the Council on Foreign Relations, a senior staff member at the Center for Strategic and International Studies, and a resident associate at the Carnegie Endowment for International Peace. He is the author of *Presidents, Public Opinion and Power: The Nixon, Carter and Reagan Years* and other works.

Stephen D. Goose is a legislative assistant for foreign policy issues for Congressman Robert Mrazek (D–New York). Previously he was a senior research analyst at the Center for Defense Information. Goose has written for a number of publications, including *Bulletin of Atomic Scientists, Pacific Defense Reporter*, the *New York Times*, the *Chicago Tribune*, and the *Los Angeles Herald Examiner*. He is a frequent guest on local and national television and radio programs. Goose holds an M.A. from the Johns Hopkins School of Advanced International Studies.

A. James Gregor is a professor of political science at the University of California at Berkeley. He is also an adjunct lecturer at the Foreign Service Institute of the State Department and a visiting lecturer at the National War College. He is the author of fourteen books, including *Arming the Dragon: U.S. Security Ties with the People's Republic of China* and *The Philippine Bases: U.S. Security at Risk*. He is also the author of articles for dozens of scholarly journals. He is the recipient of many academic awards and honors, including a Guggenheim Fellowship. Gregor holds a Ph.D. from Columbia University.

David Isenberg is a research associate with the Project on Military Procurement. Previously he served as a research fellow with Business Executives for National Security, and he has worked for the Center for Defense Information and the North American Congress on Latin America. A recipient of degrees from the University of Oregon and American University, Isenberg has written articles on defense and foreign policy topics for a variety of publications.

Paul M. Kattenburg is Distinguished Professor emeritus at the University of South Carolina, where he previously was the Charles L. Jacobson Professor of Public Affairs. He is a former U.S. foreign service officer and has held posts in Saigon, Bonn, and Manila. From 1969 to 1973 he served as coordinator of political studies at the Foreign Service Institute of the State Department. He is the author of a number of journal articles, as well as the book *The Vietnam Trauma in American Foreign Policy, 1945–75*. Kattenburg holds a Ph.D. in international relations from Yale University.

Melvyn Krauss is a professor of economics at New York University and a senior fellow at the Hoover Institution. He has written widely for scholarly journals and is a regular contributor to such publications as the *New York Times* and the *Wall Street Journal*. Krauss is also the author of a number of books, including *How NATO Weakens the West, Development without Aid*, and *The New Protectionism*. He has taught at colleges and universities in the United States and Canada and throughout Western Europe.

Christopher Layne is a foreign policy scholar at the Cato Institute. A widely published expert on foreign policy issues, he has written for such scholarly publications as *Foreign Policy, Journal of Contemporary Studies*, and *New York University Journal of International Law and Politics*. He is a frequent contributor to such newspapers and magazines as the *Los Angeles Times*, the *Wall Street Journal*, the *Chicago Tribune*, and the *New Republic*. Layne has held teaching positions at the University of California at Berkeley, Whittier College Law School, and California State University of Bakersfield. He holds a Ph.D. in political science from the University of California at Berkeley, a diploma in historical studies from the University of Cambridge, an LL.M. in international law from the University of Virginia Law School, and a J.D. from the University of Southern California Law Center.

Edward A. Olsen is a professor of national security affairs and Asian studies at the Naval Postgraduate School. Previously he served as the Japan-Korea specialist at the Department of State, Bureau of Intelligence, Office of East Asian and Pacific Affairs. Olsen is the author of four books, a contributor to several edited volumes, and the author of more than one hundred articles on Asian affairs and U.S.-Asian relations. He holds degrees from the University of California at Los Angeles and at Berkeley and American University.

Earl C. Ravenal is Distinguished Research Professor of International Affairs at the Georgetown University School of Foreign Service and a senior fellow at the Cato Institute. He is one of the nation's most prominent foreign policy experts and the author of a number of books, including *NATO: The Tides of Discontent, Never Again: Learning from America's Foreign Policy Failures,* and *Defining Defense: The 1985 Military Budget.* He has written over one hundred and fifty articles for such publications as *Foreign Policy, Foreign Affairs,* the *Atlantic,* the *New Republic,* and the *New York Times Magazine.* From 1967 to 1969 Ravenal was director of the Asian Division of the Office of the Secretary of Defense. He has been a fellow of the Woodrow Wilson International Center for Scholars and the Washington Center for Foreign Policy Research. He has lectured or taught at more than fifty American and foreign universities and academies. He holds a Ph.D. from the Johns Hopkins University School of Advanced International Studies, as well as other degrees from the University of Cambridge and Harvard University.

Eugene V. Rostow is Distinguished Visiting Research Professor of Law and Diplomacy at National Defense University. He is also a professor emeritus and a senior research scholar at Yale University, whose faculty he has been on since 1938. From 1981 to 1983 he served as director of the Arms Control and Disarmament Agency. He has also been under secretary of state for political affairs and dean of the Yale Law School and has held visiting professorships at the University of Cambridge, Oxford University, and the University of Chicago. He has written a number of books and many articles for scholarly and popular publications. He holds an LL.B. from Yale and was awarded an LL.D. from Cambridge in 1962 for the quality of his scholarly work. In addition, he holds a number of honorary doctorates.

Peter J. Schraeder is the John West Doctoral Fellow at the University of South Carolina. He has previously served as a research fellow in Djibouti for the State Department, and he has taught and conducted research at Somali National University in Mogadishu and at the University of South Carolina. Schraeder has written articles for several African studies journals, including *Journal of Modern African Studies, Northeast African Studies,* and *Horn of Africa.* He is currently at work on two books, *Djibouti* and *Intervention* *in the 1980s: United States Foreign Policy in the Third World,* of which he is editor. He holds an M.A. in international studies from the University of South Carolina, where he is a Ph.D. candidate.

Alan Tonelson is a research fellow at the Twentieth Century Fund, for which he is writing a book on redefining U.S. foreign policy interests. Previously he was an associate editor of *Foreign Policy,* the *Wilson Quarterly,* and the *Interdependent.* He is a member of the Council on Foreign Relations and has lectured on U.S. foreign policy at the Johns Hopkins University School of Advanced International Studies and at the White Burkett Miller Center for Public Affairs at the University of Virginia. He is a frequent contributor to many publications, including *Foreign Policy,* the *Atlantic,* the *New York Times,* the *Washington Post,* and the *New Republic.* He is a summa cum laude graduate of Princeton University.

Stephen M. Walt is an assistant professor of politics and international affairs at Princeton University. He has previously been a resident associate at the Carnegie Endowment for International Peace, a research fellow at the Harvard University Center for Science and International Affairs, and a guest scholar at the Brookings Institution. He is the author of *Origins of Alliances,* as well as numerous articles on international politics and national security. Walt has been awarded fellowships by Harvard University and the Institute for the Study of World Politics and is the recipient of a MacArthur Fellowship in International Security. He holds a Ph.D. from the University of California at Berkeley.

Aaron Wildavsky is a professor of political science and public policy at the University of California at Berkeley and is a past president of the American Political Science Association. He is the author of numerous scholarly and popular works, including *The New Politics of the Budgetary Process,* and is also the editor of *Beyond Containment.* Wildavsky's latest book is *Searching for Safety,* recently published by the Social Philosophy and Policy Center.

About the Editor

Ted Galen Carpenter is director of foreign policy studies at the Cato Institute. Previously he was a research associate for the Ideas and Action Project at the University of Texas, directed by former national security adviser Walt W. Rostow. An expert on defense and foreign policy issues, Carpenter is the author of more than thirty articles. In addition to various scholarly journals, his work has appeared in such publications as the *New York Times*, the *Wall Street Journal*, the *Chicago Tribune, Reason, Harper's*, and the *Nation*. Carpenter holds a Ph.D. in U.S. diplomatic history from the University of Texas.